Oncourse: The Remix

Plotting Your Academic
And Life Success Through Purposeful Critical Thinking

Hambric | Downing

D1500478

CENGAGE
Learning

Australia • Brazil • Japan • Korea • Mexico • Singapore • Spain • United Kingdom • United States

CENGAGE
Learning·

Oncourse: The Remix: Plotting Your Academic And Life Success Through Purposeful Critical Thinking,

On Course: Strategies for Creating Success in College and in Life, 7th Edition
Skip Downing

© 2014 Cengage Learning. All rights reserved.

Senior Project Development Manager:
Linda deStefano

Market Development Manager:
Heather Kramer

Senior Production/
Manufacturing Manager:
Donna M. Brown

Production Editorial Manager:
Kim Fry

Sr. Rights Acquisition Account Manager:
Todd Osborne

For product information and technology assistance, contact us at
Cengage Learning Customer & Sales Support, 1-800-354-9706

For permission to use material from this text or product,
submit all requests online at **cengage.com/permissions**
Further permissions questions can be emailed to
permissionrequest@cengage.com

This book contains select works from existing Cengage Learning resources and was produced by Cengage Learning Custom Solutions for collegiate use. As such, those adopting and/or contributing to this work are responsible for editorial content accuracy, continuity and completeness.

Compilation © 2013 Cengage Learning

ISBN-13: 978-1-285-87717-4

ISBN-10: 1-285-87717-9

Cengage Learning
5191 Natorp Boulevard
Mason, Ohio 45040
USA

Cengage Learning is a leading provider of customized learning solutions with office locations around the globe, including Singapore, the United Kingdom, Australia, Mexico, Brazil, and Japan. Locate your local office at:
international.cengage.com/region.
Cengage Learning products are represented in Canada by Nelson Education, Ltd.
For your lifelong learning solutions, visit **www.cengage.com /custom.**
Visit our corporate website at **www.cengage.com.**

Printed in the United States of America

Table of Contents

Preface   xv

Acknowledgments   xxv

Travel with Me   xxvii

Chapter 0   Course Orientation & Critical Thinking   1

Chapter 1   Getting On Course to Your Success   1

Chapter 2   Accepting Personal Responsibility   39

Chapter 3   Discovering Self-Motivation   75

Chapter 4   Mastering Self-Management   111

Chapter 5   Employing Interdependence   149

Chapter 6   Gaining Self-Awareness   181

Chapter 7   Adopting Lifelong Learning   215

Chapter 8   Developing Emotional Intelligence   253

Chapter 9   Staying On Course to Your Success   289

Bibliography   299

Index   303

To Carol, my compass

Contents

Look for the **Wise Choices in College** feature to help you learn the **essential study skills** necessary to succeed in college—reading, note-taking, studying, memorizing, test taking, and writing.

Preface   xv

Acknowledgments   xxv

Travel with Me   xxvii

1 Getting On Course to Your Success   1

Taking the First Step   2
What Is Success?   2
The Power of Choice   3
Write a Great Life   4
Assess Yourself   5
Forks in the Road   10
A Few Words of Encouragement   10
Journal Entry 1   12

One Student's Story Jalayna Onaga   13

Understanding the Culture of Higher Education   13
Culture Shock   15
The Culture of Higher Education   15
Choices and Culture   18
Journal Entry 2   19

Becoming an Active Learner   21
How the Human Brain Learns   21
Three Principles of Deep and Lasting Learning   22
The CORE Learning System   25
Journal Entry 3   27

One Student's Story **Kase Cormier**   28

On Course Principles [AT WORK]   29

▶ **BELIEVING IN YOURSELF** Develop Self-Acceptance   31

Self-Esteem and Core Beliefs   31

Know and Accept Yourself   32

Journal Entry ④   33

[Wise Choices in College] College Customs   34

---

2 Accepting Personal Responsibility   39

[CASE STUDY IN CRITICAL THINKING] The Late Paper   40

Adopting a Creator Mindset   41

Victim and Creator Mindsets   42

Responsibility and Culture   43

Responsibility and Choice   44

Journal Entry ⑤   46

One Student's Story **Brian Moore**   47

Mastering Creator Language   47

Self-Talk   48

The Language of Responsibility   51

Journal Entry ⑥   53

One Student's Story **Alexsandr Kanevskiy**   54

Making Wise Decisions   55

The Wise Choice Process   55

Journal Entry ⑦   59

One Student's Story **Freddie Davila**   60

Personal Responsibility [AT WORK]   61

▶ **BELIEVING IN YOURSELF** Change Your Inner Conversation   63

The Curse of Stinkin' Thinkin'   63

Disputing Irrational Beliefs   65

Stereotype Threat   66

Journal Entry ⑧   67

One Student's Story **Dominic Grasseth**   68

Wise Choices in College Reading   69
Reading: The Big Picture   69
Before Reading   70
While Reading   71
After Reading   73

3   Discovering Self-Motivation   75

CASE STUDY IN CRITICAL THINKING Popson's Dilemma   76

Creating Inner Motivation   77
A Formula for Motivation   78
Value of College Outcomes   80
Value of College Experiences   81
Journal Entry 9   83

One Student's Story Chee Meng Vang   83

Designing a Compelling Life Plan   84
Roles and Goals   85
How to Set a Goal   86
Discover Your Dreams   87
Your Life Plan   88
Journal Entry 10   89

Committing to Your Goals and Dreams   90
Commitment Creates Method   91
Visualize Your Ideal Future   92
How to Visualize   93
Journal Entry 11   93

One Students' Story James Terrell   94

Self-Motivation AT WORK   95

▶ **BELIEVING IN YOURSELF** Write a Personal Affirmation   98
Claiming Your Desired Personal Qualities   99
Living Your Affirmation   100
Journal Entry 12   101

One Student's Story Donna Ludwick   102

Wise Choices in College Taking Notes   103
Taking Notes: The Big Picture   103
Before Taking Notes   104
While Taking Notes   105
After Taking Notes   109

4 Mastering Self-Management   111

CASE STUDY IN CRITICAL THINKING The Procrastinators   112

Acting on Purpose   113
Harness the Power of Quadrant II   113
What to Do in Quadrants I and II   115
Journal Entry 13   116

One Student's Story Jason Pozsgay   117

Creating a Leak-Proof Self-Management System   118
Time and Culture   118
Monthly Calendar   119
Next Actions List   120
Tracking Form   121
Waiting-For List   121
Project Folder   121
The Rewards of Effective Self-Management   122
Journal Entry 14   123

One Student's Story Allysa LePage   127

Developing Self-Discipline   127
Staying Focused   128
Being Persistent   129
Journal Entry 15   131

One Student's Story Holt Boggs   132

Self-Management **AT WORK**   134

➤ **BELIEVING IN YOURSELF** Develop Self-Confidence   136
Create a Success Identity   136
Celebrate Your Successes and Talents   137
Visualize Purposeful Actions   137
Journal Entry 16   139

One Students' Story Ashley Freeman   140

Wise Choices in College Organizing Study Materials   141
Organizing Study Materials: The Big Picture   141
Before Organizing Study Materials   141
While Organizing Study Materials   142
After Organizing Study Materials   146

5 Employing Interdependence 149

CASE STUDY IN CRITICAL THINKING Professor Rogers' Trial 150

Creating a Support System 151
Seek Help from Your Instructors 152
Get Help from College Resources 152
Create a Project Team 153
Start a Study Group 153
Journal Entry 17 156

One Student's Story Jason Matthew Loden 157

Strengthening Relationships with Active Listening 157
How to Listen Actively 158
Use Active Listening in Your College Classes 159
Journal Entry 18 160

Respecting Cultural Differences 161
Showing Respect 162
Journal Entry 19 166

Interdependence AT WORK 167

BELIEVING IN YOURSELF Be Assertive 169
Leveling 169
Making Requests 171
Saying "No" 171
Journal Entry 20 172

One Student's Story Amy Acton 174

Wise Choices in College Rehearsing and Memorizing Study Materials 175
Rehearsing and Memorizing Study Materials: The Big Picture 175
Before Rehearsing and Memorizing Study Materials 176
While Rehearsing and Memorizing Study Materials 176
After Rehearsing and Memorizing Study Materials 179

6 Gaining Self-Awareness 181

CASE STUDY IN CRITICAL THINKING Strange Choices 182

Recognizing when You Are Off Course 183
The Mystery of Self-Sabotage 183
Unconscious Forces 184
Journal Entry 21 185

One Student's Story Sarah Richmond   186

Identifying Your Scripts   186

Anatomy of a Script   187

How We Wrote Our Scripts   188

Self-Defeating Habit Patterns   190

Journal Entry 22   191

One Student's Story James Floriolli   192

Rewriting Your Outdated Scripts   192

The Impact of Outdated Beliefs   193

Doing the Rewrite   194

Journal Entry 23   194

One Student's Story Annette Valle   198

Self-Awareness (AT WORK)   199

▶— BELIEVING IN YOURSELF Write Your Own Rules   201

Three Success Rules   202

Journal Entry 24   203

One Student's Story Brandeé Huigens   204

Wise Choices in College   Taking Tests   205

Taking Tests: The Big Picture   205

Before Taking Tests   205

While Taking Tests   206

After Taking Tests   212

7 Adopting Lifelong Learning   215

CASE STUDY IN CRITICAL THINKING A Fish Story   216

Developing a Learning Orientation to Life   217

Growth Mindsets and Fixed Mindsets   218

How to Develop a Growth Mindset   220

Journal Entry 25   222

One Student's Story Jessie Maggard   223

Discovering Your Preferred Ways of Learning   224

Self-Assessment: How I Prefer to Learn   224

Journal Entry 26   230

One Student's Story Melissa Thompson   230

Employing Critical Thinking   231

Constructing Logical Arguments   232
Asking Probing Questions   232
Applying Critical Thinking   233
Journal Entry 27   235

Lifelong Learning (AT WORK)   236

➤ **BELIEVING IN YOURSELF** Develop Self-Respect   239
Live with Integrity   239
Keep Commitments   241
Journal Entry 28   243

Wise Choices in College   Writing   244
Writing the Big Picture   245
Before Writing   245
While Writing   248
After Writing   250

8   Developing Emotional Intelligence   253

CASE STUDY IN CRITICAL THINKING   After Math   254
Understanding Emotional Intelligence   255
Four Components of Emotional Intelligence   256
Knowing Your Own Emotions   257
Journal Entry 29   258

One Student's Story Lindsey Beck   258

Reducing Stress   259
What Is Stress?   259
What Happens when Stress Persists?   260
Unhealthy Stress Reduction   260
Healthy Stress Reduction   261
Choose Your Attitude   267
Journal Entry 30   268

One Student's Story Jaime Sanmiguel   268

Creating Flow   269
College and Flow   270
Work and Flow   271
Journal Entry 31   272

Emotional Intelligence (AT WORK)   273

►— **BELIEVING IN YOURSELF** Develop Self-Love   275

Design a Self-Care Plan   275

Journal Entry 32   278

One Student's Story **Wynda Allison Paulette**   279

Wise Choices in College Managing Money   280

Managing Money: The Big Picture   281
Increase Money Flowing In   281
Decrease Money Flowing Out   284

9   # Staying On Course to Your Success   289

Planning Your Next Steps   290

Assess Yourself, Again   290

Journal Entry 33   297

One Student's Story **Stephan J. Montgomery**   298

Bibliography   299
Index   303

Preface

On *Course* is intended for college students of any age who want to create success in college and in life. Whether students are taking a student success or first-year seminar course, a writing course, or an "inward-looking" course in psychology, self-exploration, or personal growth, *On Course* is an instruction manual for dramatically improving the quality of their outcomes and experiences. In each chapter, students learn essential study skills; however, that's just the beginning. Through self-assessments, articles, guided journals, case studies in critical thinking, and inspiring stories from fellow students, *On Course* empowers students with time-proven strategies for creating a great life—academic, personal, and professional. Students learn the techniques that have helped many thousands of students create extraordinary success!

I am grateful that in the years since its first publication in 1996, *On Course* has become a market leader in the crowded field of student success texts. Increasingly, educators are finding (as I have) that empowering students to become active, responsible learners produces significant increases in both student academic success and retention. My goal is to make this new edition of *On Course* even more helpful to the success of students and educators alike.

The retention results we are getting indicate the information in the text is impacting student behaviors. The students are applying the concepts and making changes in their thinking and practices. We just completed a student focus group of students who had formerly taken an FYE class. Student responses indicate they continue to apply what was learned in the FYE class to their thinking and actions into their 2nd semester.

Linda McMeen,
North Hennepin Community College

What's New in This Edition of *On Course*: Highlights

- **NEW! EXPANDED COVERAGE OF DIVERSITY.** Rather than simply adding one article about this important issue, information about diversity is incorporated in many places throughout the text. The intent of this approach is to emphasize that we are all different from others in many ways, and these differences often influence the choices we make, and thus the outcomes and experiences we create. By way of example, an article titled "Respecting Cultural Differences," beginning on page 161, will help students understand the growing diversity they will encounter in college and beyond, along with a number of strategies for showing respect for people different from themselves.

I appreciate the time, effort, and thoughtfulness that went into making these [diversity] additions. *On Course* has always been a fantastic textbook. I wasn't sure it could be better. But I have to say I can't wait to start teaching with the new edition.

Lory Conrad,
University of Arkansas - Fort Smith

- **NEW! ARTICLE ON THE CULTURE OF HIGHER EDUCATION.** The culture of higher education is unique and therefore challenging to many students. This article and the accompanying Journal Entry 2 on pages 18–20 will help students understand what a "culture" is, how their college or university culture is different from previous cultures they may have experienced (e.g., high school), and what choices they can make to thrive in the culture of higher education. Armed with this information, students will soon feel like natives of their new culture.

- **NEW! DISCUSSION OF ACADEMIC INTEGRITY.** Many educators are concerned about cheating in higher education. Woven into an article about personal integrity and self-respect, this discussion presents the author's own experiences with cheating and three powerful reasons why cheating is a bad choice for any college student to make.

- **NEW! ARTICLE ON DEVELOPING A LEARNING ORIENTATION TO LIFE.** Recent findings by psychologist Carol Dweck and others reveal the impact of growth and fixed mindsets on learning. This article presents the practical application of this important research, providing students with strategies for becoming effective lifelong learners (not to mention earning better grades).

- ***ONE STUDENT'S STORY*—FIVE NEW STORIES ADDED!** A popular feature in earlier editions, these short essays are authored by students who used *On Course* strategies to improve the quality of their college outcomes and experiences. All 25 stories show the positive and dramatic results possible when students apply what they learn in this course to overcome the multitude of challenges that can sabotage success in college, and beyond.

> I think these are very powerful stories. . . . It's good for students to hear that other students have faced the same struggles that they are going through and they have achieved success.
>
> *Kathryn Burk,*
> *Jackson Community College*

What's New in This Edition of *On Course*: Chapter by Chapter

Chapter 1

- New article and journal entry on understanding the culture of higher education, which includes a discussion of culture shock, the culture of higher education, and how culture informs choices we make, and features a new chart, "A Dozen Differences Between High School and College Culture"

- New *One Student's Story* by Kase Cormier, Asheville-Buncombe Technical Community College, North Carolina

- Revisions to the Self-Assessment:
  - Revised #30: My intelligence is something about myself that I can improve.

- Revised #36: I am aware of how to show respect to people who are different from me (race, religion, sexual orientation, age, etc.).
  - Revised #44: I seldom interact with people who are different from me.
  - Revised #62: Everyone is born with a certain amount of intelligence, and there's not really much you can do to change that.
- Revised Question 1 in Journal Entry 3
- New college customs exercises in *Wise Choices in College*: *College Customs* offers more practice and variety

Chapter 2

- Revised "Adopting a Creator Mindset" article and added section on "Responsibility and Culture" addressing cultural mindsets and Victim and Creator mindsets, with Rosa Parks presented as an example of someone with a Creator mindset
- Revised instructions and prompts for Journal Entries 5 and 8
- New section on stereotype threat within "Believing in Yourself: Change Your Inner Conversation" that addresses the "stinkin' thinkin'" that can affect cultural groups, with suggestions for reducing the negative impact of stereotype threats
- New *One Student's Story* and art by Freddie Davila, The Victoria College, Texas

Chapter 3

- New *One Student's Story* by James Terrell, Appalachian State University, North Carolina
- Revised "A Formula for Motivation" section to discuss how deep culture influences the value placed on achieving a college education and expectations of success in college
- Revised instructions for Journal Entries 11 and 12

Chapter 4

- New *One Student's Story* by Ashley Freeman, Copper Canyon College, California
- New "Time and Culture" section discusses how cultures differ in their beliefs and attitudes about time and what the college culture's expectations are about time
- Revised coverage in "Monthly Calendars" section to address new technologies on smart phones that help with time management
- New waiting-for list and project folder strategies for time management
- Revised instructions and additional prompts for Journal Entry 15

- New discussion about the skepticism some hold about visualizing in "Visualize Purposeful Actions" section
- Revised prompt 2 for Journal Entry 16

Chapter 5

- New information in "Creating a Support System" section that introduces individualistic and collectivist cultures and how the beliefs of these cultures impact students' decisions on independence versus interdependence
- New article and journal entry on "Respecting Cultural Differences," including a section on how to show respect to those who are different from us

Chapter 6

- New information in "Identifying Your Scripts" about how cultures contribute to our unconscious scripts and programming

Chapter 7

- Revised "Developing a Learning Orientation to Life" article discussing growth mindsets and fixed mindsets and how to develop a growth mindset
- Revised Journal Entry 25 with two choices for prompts about which to write
- Revised the terminology of learning styles to "preferred ways of learning," as well as the title of the self-assessment inventory to "Learning Preference Inventory"; additional explanation of preferred ways of learning is included as well.
- New coverage of academic integrity in "Believing in Yourself: Develop Self-Respect," including the costs of academic dishonesty and cheating

Chapter 8

- New *One Student's Story* and poem by Wynda Allison Paulette, National Park Community College, Arkansas

Chapter 9

- A retrospective pre-assessment added to the self-assessment. Self-assessments have the built-in problem of accuracy caused by the natural urge to choose answers that make us "look good." A retrospective pre-assessment allows students to identify at the end of the course where they believe they were at both the beginning of the course (retrospectively) and at the end. Such an assessment tends to make a comparison of pre- and post-test scores more valid.

Proven Features of *On Course*

The seventh edition includes all of the best features of *On Course*, updated and revised from the previous edition.

- **SELF-ASSESSMENT QUESTIONNAIRES.** *On Course* begins and ends with a self-assessment questionnaire. By completing the initial questionnaire, students can see areas of growth that need attention. By completing the concluding questionnaire, students see their semester's growth. Students have the option of completing the questionnaire either in the text or online, available on the College Success CourseMate for *On Course*. An advantage of the online version is that it gives an immediate printout of scores and assures that scores are accurate.

- **ARTICLES ON PROVEN SUCCESS STRATEGIES.** Thirty-three short articles explain powerful strategies for creating success in college and in life. Each article presents a success strategy from influential figures in psychology, philosophy, business, sports, politics, and personal and professional growth. In these articles, students learn the "secrets" of extraordinarily successful individuals.

- **CORE LEARNING SYSTEM.** All good learners employ four principles that lead to deep and lasting learning. Students learn how to use these four principles to create their own system for learning any subject or skill.

- **WISE CHOICES IN COLLEGE ADDRESSING STUDY SKILLS STRATEGIES.** To expand on the CORE Learning System, students are introduced to dozens and dozens of powerful strategies that they can use to improve their learning and raise their grades.

- **GUIDED JOURNAL ENTRIES.** A guided journal entry immediately follows each article, giving students an opportunity to apply the success strategy they just learned to enhance their results in college and in life. Numerous journal directions have been revised based on student and reviewer feedback, making the directions easier to follow and the writing more valuable for gaining personal and academic insights.

- **AN ARTICLE AND SEVEN CASE STUDIES ADDRESSING CRITICAL THINKING.** When polled, virtually every college educator agrees that critical thinking is essential for success in college and in life. Through *Case Studies for Critical Thinking* as well as an article and journal entry on critical thinking skills, students learn effective ways to solve challenging problems. They also learn valuable reasoning skills that help them create and analyze persuasive arguments. These skills sharpen their thinking ability and provide them with greater control over the quality of their lives.

The Wise Choice Process is one of the most valuable lessons from *On Course*. It provides students with the tools that help them make informed choices and think more critically about situations. I think that students are improving because the process helps them think through their options and analyze the results, which leads to positive changes.

Taunya Paul,
York Technical College

Journaling is the heart and soul of *On Course*. It helps me check the pulse of my students on a regular basis. I have countless testimonies from students who describe the journaling process as "life-changing." The most reluctant students who ultimately "give in" to journaling often become the most avid supporters of *On Course*.

Gail Janecka,
The Victoria College

I absolutely love these [*Case Studies for Critical Thinking*] and spend a lot of time with each of them. My favorite is "A Fish Story" and start my semester with this one. I get students thinking about professors' expectations, their own expectations, motivation, taking the initiative, being prepared for class, and being organized.

Cindy Thorp,
SUNY Alfred, College of Technology

The At Work sections give students a specific venue to see how the soft skills they acquire will transfer to career success. Semester after semester students will share how their work situation improved as a result of what they learned and tried from the At Work sections. These sections are a natural fit in the *On Course* chapters, and they are packed with pertinent information.

Gail Janecka,
The Victoria College

- *ON COURSE* **PRINCIPLES AT WORK.** These sections show how important the *On Course* success strategies are for choosing the right career, getting hired, and succeeding in the work world.
- **QUOTATIONS.** Marginal quotations express the timeless wisdom of famous and not-so-famous people regarding the success strategies under consideration throughout the text.

Support Materials for Students and Instructors

For additional information or for help with accessing support materials related to *On Course,* contact your Cengage Learning sales representative. If you need help finding your sales representative, visit http://academic.cengage.com and select "Find Your Rep" at the top of the page.

SUPPORT FOR STUDENTS

- **COLLEGE SUCCESS COURSEMATE.** *On Course* includes College Success CourseMate, a complement to your textbook. College Success CourseMate includes an integrated eBook as well as interactive teaching and learning tools, including an online version of the self-assessment, quizzes, Wise Choices, Respecting Differences, *One Student's Story* videos, and more. It also includes Engagement Tracker, a first-of-its-kind tool that monitors student engagement in the course. CourseMate is available as a bundle item with *On Course* or can be purchased separately by students at Cengage Learning's Online Bookstore, www.cengagebrain.com.

- **APLIA FOR *ON COURSE.*** Aplia is an online, auto-graded, and assignable homework system that improves learning by increasing student effort and engagement—without requiring more work from the instructor. Aplia for *On Course* helps students dive deeper into the concepts presented in the textbook. Engaging, interactive assignments ensure that students meet learning objectives, while automatically graded assignments offer immediate and constructive feedback. The problems and activities in Aplia for *On Course* guide students in developing the critical skills they need to earn better grades, achieve their potential, and chart a course for the future. To view a demo of Aplia for *On Course,* visit www.aplia.com/collegesuccess.

- **EBOOK.** An eBook is available for *On Course.* Students can download the complete *On Course* textbook at a cost savings at Cengage Learning's Online Bookstore, www.cengagebrain.com.

- **COLLEGE SUCCESS PLANNER.** Instructors can package the *On Course* textbook with this 12-month week-at-a-glance academic planner. The

College Success Planner assists students in making the best use of their time both on and off campus, and includes additional reading about key learning strategies and life skills for success in college. Ask your Cengage Learning sales representative for more details.

SUPPORT FOR INSTRUCTORS

- **NEW! ANNOTATED INSTRUCTOR'S EDITION.** To help guide instructors to the many ideas found within the Facilitator's Manual, the Annotated Instructor's Edition (ISBN: 9781133606857) provides specific cross-references directly in the margins to ideas and activities available in the Facilitator's Manual provided by Melanie Marine of the University of Wisconsin–Oshkosh and Catherine Eloranto of Clinton Community College.

- **REVISED FACILITATOR'S MANUAL.** The Facilitator's Manual, now offered both in a printed version (ISBN: 9781133606857) and online at the Instructor Companion Site (see below for more information), offers educators specific classroom activities and suggestions from Skip Downing for using *On Course* in various kinds of courses, and it endeavors to answer questions that educators might have about using the text. Additionally, the Facilitator's Manual now includes "best practices" provided by *On Course* instructors; additional study skills activities written by Melanie Marine of the University of Wisconsin–Oshkosh; new diversity activities provided by LuAnn Wood and Christina Davis, both of Century College; suggestions for teaching in an online environment written by Pratima Sampat-Mar of Pima Medical Institute; and a guide for how to successfully integrate the College Success Factors Index (CSFI) with *On Course* written by Gary Williams of Crafton Hills College. One of the most popular elements of the *On Course Facilitator's Manual* is the numerous in-class exercises that encourage students' active exploration of the success strategies presented in the text. These learner-centered exercises include role-playing, learning games, dialogues, demonstrations, metaphors, mind-mappings, brainstorms, questionnaires, drawings, skits, scavenger hunts, and many others.

- **UPDATED INSTRUCTOR COMPANION SITE.** This website (free to adopters) provides educators with many resources to offer a course that empowers students to become active, responsible, and successful learners. Read the Facilitator's Manual (which is also offered in a printed version, as explained above), download PowerPoint slides, view the content from the DVD *On Course: A Comprehensive Program for Promoting Student Academic Success and Retention*, and find a useful transition guide for educators who used previous editions of *On Course*. To access instructor digital resources, such as the Instructor Companion Site or instructor access for the College Success CourseMate site for *On Course*, follow these steps:

1. Visit **login.cengage.com**.

2. If you have not previously created a faculty account, choose "Create a New Faculty Account" and follow the prompts.

3. If you have created a faculty account previously, log in with your email address or user name and password.

4. Search for *On Course* to add the available additional digital resources to your bookshelf.

You will always need to return to **login.cengage.com** and enter your email address and password to sign in to access these resources. Use this space to write down your email address or user name and password below:

Email Address: _____

Password: _____

- **REVISED! POWER LECTURE CD-ROM FOR *ON COURSE*.** The Power-Lecture (ISBN: 9781133606871) contains a brand new test bank prepared by Stephanie Kratz of Heartland Community College in the ExamView test-generating software, enhanced instructor PowerPoint slides, revised by Lalanya Ennis of College of the Mainland, and a PDF of the Facilitator's Manual. Use the dynamic software to create customized exams specific to your class!

- ***ON COURSE: A COMPREHENSIVE PROGRAM FOR PROMOTING STUDENT ACADEMIC SUCCESS AND RETENTION* DVD.** This DVD (ISBN: 0547002173) provides instructors with an overview of the problems that keep today's capable students from being successful, complete with an explanation by Skip Downing about how *On Course* differs from other student success approaches. Additional features on this DVD include a description of the extensive *On Course* learner-centered resources, videos of three students presenting their *One Student's Story* essays that appear in the text, and a sample *On Course* learner-centered activity, facilitated by Skip Downing. Following the activity, college and university educators discuss how this same activity positively affected their students. Presented in short chapters, parts of this DVD are intended for instructors and other parts are perfect for showing to students. Content from this DVD is available for immediate viewing on the Instructor Companion Site.

- **WEBTUTOR™ ON WEBCT / WEBTUTOR™ ON BLACKBOARD.** Jump-start your course with customizable, rich, text-specific content within your course management system, including interactive quizzes, videos, an eBook, and more. Ask your Cengage Learning sales representative for more details.

- **ASSESSMENT TOOLS.** If you're looking for additional ways to assess your students, Cengage Learning has additional resources for you to consider. For more in-depth information on any of the following items, contact your Cengage Learning sales representative.

- **College Success Factors Index:** The College Success Factors Index (CSFI) 2.0, developed by Edmond Hallberg and Kaylene Hallberg, is an online survey that students complete to assess their patterns of behavior and attitudes in 10 key areas. These areas have been proven by research to affect student outcomes for success in higher education. Accessed online, the CSFI is a useful assessment tool for demonstrating the difference your college success course makes in students' academic success. At the start of the course, the CSFI helps assess incoming students and allows you to tailor your course topics to meet their needs. As a post-test, it provides an opportunity for you (and your students) to measure progress. In the new version, an Early Alert indicator flags students who are most at risk of getting off course in college. This information enables you to intervene at the beginning of the semester to increase students' likelihood of success—and improve retention rates. CSFI 2.0 also has text-specific remediation for *On Course* that guides students to appropriate pages in the textbook for added support. For more information about CSFI, visit our website at www.cengage.com/success/csfi2.

- **Noel-Levitz College Student Inventory:** *The Retention Management System™ College Student Inventory* (CSI; from Noel-Levitz) is an early-alert, early-intervention program that identifies students with tendencies that contribute to dropping out of school. Students can participate in an integrated, campus-wide program. Cengage Learning offers you three assessment options that evaluate students on 19 different scales: Form A (194 items), Form B (100 items), or an online etoken that provides access to Form A, B, or C (74 items). Advisors are sent three interpretive reports: the Student's Report, the Advisor/Counselor Report, and the College Summary and Planning Report.

- *The Myers-Briggs Type Indicator® (MBTI®) Instrument*[1]: The MBTI is the most widely used personality inventory in history—and it is also available for packaging with *On Course*. The standard Form M self-scorable instrument contains 93 items that determine preferences on four scales: Extraversion–Introversion, Sensing–Intuition, Thinking–Feeling, and Judging–Perceiving. Now offered online with the MBTI Complete®. Instructors do not need a certification to administer the MBTI Complete®. Students take the assessment on their own and automatically receive a complete interpretation of the results. In addition, you will receive *16 Paths to Student Success*, which includes lesson plans detailing how to incorporate MBTI® personality styles into your instruction on time management, communication, learning styles, and study skills.

---

[1]MBTI and Myers-Briggs Type Indicator are registered trademarks of Consulting Psychologists Press, Inc.

- **CENGAGE LEARNING'S TEAMUP FACULTY PROGRAM CONSULTANTS.** An additional service available with this textbook is support from **TeamUP Faculty Program Consultants.** For more than a decade, our consultants have helped faculty reach and engage first-year students by offering peer-to-peer consulting on curriculum and assessment, faculty training, and workshops. Our consultants are higher education professionals who provide full-time support in helping educators establish and maintain effective student success programs. They are available to help you to establish or improve your student success program and provide training on the implementation of our textbooks and technology. To connect with your TeamUP Faculty Program Consultant, call 1-800-528-8323 or visit www.cengage.com/teamup.

- **ON COURSE WORKSHOPS AND CONFERENCE.** Skip Downing, author of *On Course*, offers faculty development workshops for all educators who want to learn innovative strategies for empowering students to become active, responsible, and successful learners. These highly regarded professional development workshops are offered at conference centers across North America, or you can host a one- to four-day event on your own campus. An online graduate course (3 credits) is available as a follow-up to two of the workshops. Additionally, you are invited to participate in the annual *On Course* National Conference, where hundreds of learner-centered educators gather to share their best practices. For information about these workshops, graduate courses, and the national conference (including testimonials galore), go to www.oncourseworkshop.com. Questions? Email workshop@OnCourseWorkhop.com.

- ***ON COURSE* NEWSLETTER.** All college educators are invited to subscribe to the free *On Course* Newsletter. More than 50,000 educator-subscribers worldwide receive emails with innovative, learner-centered strategies for engaging students in deep and lasting learning. To subscribe, simply go to www.oncourseworkshop.com and follow the easy, one-click directions. Or you can email a request to workshop @oncourseworkshop.com.

Acknowledgments

This book would not exist without the assistance of an extraordinary group of people. I can only hope that I have returned (or will return) their wonderful support in kind.

At Cengage Learning, I would like to thank Shani Fisher, Marita Sermolins, Cathy Brooks, Lori Bradshaw, and Angela Hodge for their unflagging attention to details and encouraging guidance. At Baltimore City Community College, my thanks go to my former colleagues, the dedicated teachers of the College Success Seminar. At *On Course* Workshops, thanks to the extraordinary support and wisdom of my colleagues and friends Jonathan Brennan, Robin Middleton, Deb Poese, Eileen Zamora, Mark McBride, and Teresa Ward. Thanks also to the *On Course* Ambassadors, some of the greatest educators in the world who work tirelessly to introduce their students and colleagues to *On Course*. Many thanks to fellow authors and diversity experts Jean Moule and Lynn Spradlin for reviewing the diversity additions for accuracy and providing suggestions to improve the content. And especially Carol—your unwavering love and support keep me on course. You are my compass.

Numerous wise and caring reviewers have made valuable contributions to this book, and many contributed exercises to the Facilitator's Manual and I thank them for their contributions:

Marianne Auten, Paradise Valley Community College
Shelly Blackburn, Asheville-Buncombe Technical Community College
Kathryn Burk, Jackson Community College
Barbara Brownsmith Campbell, Asheville-Buncombe Technical
   Community College
Abla Christiansen, Solano College
Nagash Clark, Washtenaw Community College
Lory Conrad, University of Arkansas-Fort Smith
Martha Crise, Ozarks Technical Community College
Joseph Dobek, Broward College
Denise Dufek, Bay de Noc Community College
Katy Goforth, Tri-County Technical College
Jocelyn Harney, College of DuPage
Gail Janecka, The Victoria College
Xania Lawrence, Miami Dade College

Jocelyne Legrand, Miami Dade College
David Lerman, Piedmont Virginia Community College
Lea Beth Lewis, California State University, Fullerton
Sherry Lichte-Baird, Rio Salado College
Quakish Liner, Broward College
Kimberly Manner, Pierce College
Melanie Marine, University of Wisconsin, Oshkosh
Lisa Marks, Ozarks Technical Community College
Laura Marlow, Asheville-Buncombe Technical Community College
Joe Martinez, El Centro College
Louis Mays, Southern State Community College
Maureen McMahon, Paul Smith College
Linda McMeen, North Hennepin Community College
Dana Murphy, National Park Community College
Januwoina Nixon, Southern Adventist University
Eva O'Brian, Midlands Technical College
Sue Heath Olesiuk, Asheville-Buncombe Technical Community College
Taunya Paul, York Technical College
June Pomann, Union County College
Travis Ramage, Aurora University
Virginia Thompson, Grayson County College
Cindy Thorp, Alfred State College
Cheryl Tizio, Broward College
Cora Weger, IECC Lincoln Trail College
Burnierose Wilson, Chabot College
Marguerite Yawin, Tunxis Community College
Eileen Zamora, Southwestern College (emerita)

Finally, my deep gratitude goes out to the students who over the years have had the courage to explore and change their thoughts, actions, feelings, and beliefs. I hope, as a result, you have all lived richer, more personally fulfilling lives. I know I have.

Travel with Me

On Course is the result of my own quest to live a rich, personally fulfilling life and my strong desire to pass on what I've learned to my students. As such, *On Course* is a very personal book, for me and for you. I invite you to explore in depth what success means to you. I suggest that if you want to achieve your greatest potential in college and in life, dig deep inside yourself, where you already possess everything you need to make your dreams come true.

During my first two decades of teaching college courses, I consistently observed a sad and perplexing puzzle. Each semester I watched students sort themselves into two groups. One group achieved varying degrees of academic success, from those who excelled to those who just squeaked by. The other group struggled mightily; then they withdrew, disappeared, or failed. But, here's the puzzling part. The struggling students often displayed as much academic potential as their more successful classmates, and in some cases more. What, I wondered, causes the vastly different outcomes of these two groups? And what could I do to help my struggling students achieve greater success?

Somewhere around my 20th year of teaching, I experienced a series of crises in both my personal and professional lives. In a word, I was struggling. After a period of feeling sorry for myself, I embarked on a quest to improve the quality of my life. I read, I took seminars and workshops, I talked with wise friends and acquaintances, I kept an in-depth journal, I saw a counselor, I even returned to graduate school to add a master's degree in applied psychology to my doctoral degree in English. I was seriously motivated to change my life for the better.

If I were to condense all that I learned into one sentence, it would be this: **People who are successful (by their own definition) consistently make wiser choices than people who struggle.** I came to see that the quality of my life was essentially the result of all of my previous choices. I saw how the wisdom (or lack of wisdom) of my choices influenced, and often determined, the outcomes and experiences of my life. The same, of course, was true for my struggling students.

For two and a half decades, I have continued my quest to identify the inner qualities that empower a person to make consistently wise choices, the very choices that lead to success both in college and in life. As a result of what I learned (and continue to learn), I created a course at my college called the College Success Seminar. This course was a departure from traditional student success courses because instead of focusing primarily on study skills and campus resources, it focused on empowering students from the inside out. I had come to believe that most students who struggle in college are perfectly capable of earning a degree and that their struggles go far deeper than not knowing study skills or a failure to use campus resources. As a result, I envisioned a course that would empower students to develop their natural inner strengths, the qualities that would help them make the wise choices that would create the very outcomes and experiences they wanted in college . . . and in life. When I couldn't find a book that did this, I wrote *On Course*. A few years later, I created a series of professional development workshops to share what I had learned with other educators who want to see their students soar. Then, to provide an opportunity for workshop graduates to continue to exchange their experiences and wisdom, I started a listserv, and this growing group of educators soon named themselves the *On Course* Ambassadors, sharing *On Course* strategies with their students and colleagues alike. Later, I created two online graduate courses that further help college educators learn cutting-edge strategies for empowering their students to be more successful in college and in life. To launch the second decade of *On Course,* the *On Course* Ambassadors hosted the first of many *On Course* National Conferences, bringing together an overflow crowd of educators hungry for new ways to help their students achieve more of their potential in college and in life. Every one of these efforts appeals to a deep place in me because they all have the power to change people's lives for the better. But that's not the only appeal. These activities also help *me* stay conscious of the wise choices I must consistently make to live a richer, more personally fulfilling life.

Now that much of my life is back on course, I don't want to forget how I got here!

Skip Downing

Hello Everyone!

I am very excited about our new adventure. With that said, I want to quickly orient you to the layout of the book. There are two distinct authors, Tuesday S. Hambric (that's me ☺) and Skip Downing. I wrote Chapter Zero, and Skip Downing wrote the On Course chapters' one through nine. As you read, you will quickly see a difference in my writing voice and tone and that of Skip.

Chapter Zero's writing tone and style is conversational. This is deliberate. The idea behind the laid-back style is to communicate just that: relaxation. My writing voice and tone were inspired by tons of research, which asserts that people learn better when they are in a "happy place." For me, that means a happy place in our minds and our physical environments. I want you to converse with me, feel good about safely pondering as you read, and then write down your questions for your teacher to explore in class. When you do this, you, your teacher, and I together will have raised the bar for teaching and learning.

It is my prayer or hope (whichever applies) that this style of writing will encourage you to read the textbook before you come to class. Moreover, I want you to be prepared to have a lively discussion and application of the concepts learned. Therefore, I apologize up front if my tone is not what you expect for higher education. But, make no mistake about it, the content is significant and it works well when put into action! So, give it a chance; because there is nothing like smiling and having a little fun through the teaching and learning process!

Dr. Hambric/Mrs. Tuesday

Chapter Zero

"On Course"

Strategies for Creating Success in College and in Life through Critical Thinking Across Domains

----

By: Dr. Tuesday S. Hambric

Welcome to College...

The Foundation to College and Life Success

Learning Framework

Focus Question How will this course help you succeed both academically and socially? What will it take for you to apply what you will learn from this course to other courses and in other areas of your life?

Welcome to college! Know that you are in the right hands for both academic and life success. Now, this may sound boastful, but this claim is <u>supported</u> by students just like you: first-time-in-college students, students returning from the workforce to include both current and ex-military, and then there are our university students—the ones who prefer the smaller, more intimate learning environments that seem to be missing at the larger campuses. The list goes on and on.

Each and every one of you has unique circumstances. However, in *general*, students just like you have walked through theses doors, and, based on their testimonies, you are in the right hands for both academic and life success.

To put our claim to the test, this course has been evaluated with both qualitative and quantitative research. According to the data analysis report, *"In Their Own Voice"* (2010), 98% of former Learning Framework students expressed, in written statements, how the "Learning Framework course significantly changed their lives both academically and socially."

In support of what the students expressed in writing, the quantitative measures revealed that students entered this course with an average of 46% of the critical thinking skills needed to ensure academic and life success. However, those same students graduated the course with an average of 86% of the critical thinking skills needed in order to ensure success both academically and socially. (This information was collected and analyzed through the use of a pre- and post-course test.)

With all of that said, I think it is *safe* to say that this is one of the most important classes you will ever take during your academic career; so many blessings and good luck to you, on this first day of the rest of your life!

Academics and Life: What's the Real Connection?

The United States, more specifically, *your* state's educational system are consistently seeing a decline in its college graduation rates. With such a decline, who's going to lead our country? Did you know that people who do not graduate from college tend to find themselves making at least $1,000,000.00 less in their lifetime than someone who has graduated with a college degree (Longley, 2010)? So what are some of the major reasons why people do not finish their college journey? Why are so many people dropping out? The factors that impede academic success, influence the decline in graduation rates, and increase the dropout rates are (Hambric, 2011):

- Dysfunctional home environments.

- Student's lack of motivation.

- Students' **failure to choose wisely** due to their inability to reason, think critically, and systematically.

- Ineffective faculty, including one-dimensional teachers.

- Lack of economic resources.

- Expensive interventions with no accountability or proven research results.

Based on what you have read so far, what do you propose as a solution? If you said, "I just need to get motivated," or "They need to hire faculty that care and know how to teach," or even if you were a little distracted by my comment on students and critical thinking—and said, "I already know how to think critically!" either way, all answers are correct. However, I propose we work on ONE of the above factors. I propose that ONE factor can make a significant difference to all the other abovementioned factors, thus making a difference in both your academic and personal life's successes. How do I know? Ninety-eight percent (98%) of students just like you say so!

It all Starts with You the Individual—the Student

Have you ever heard a person say, "Things are only true if you believe they are true?" Or say, "Nothing in this world has meaning unless we give it meaning?" Well, the implication of those statements is that we have control over our thoughts (within reason, of course), and we therefore have control over our behavior, and we thus have control over our life outcomes. Do you believe this conclusion? Yes, or no and why? **Please note that it is very important, at this point, that you share your thoughts pertaining to this conclusion with your instructor. Because after your discussion with the professor, what you think and believe will determine whether or not you fully experience and embrace success. So, the question is "do you believe the implied conclusion from the two statements above?" These statements conclude that we have control over our thoughts, and therefore have control over our behaviors; thus, we have control over our life outcomes. Explain your answer below.

_____
_____
_____
_____
_____
_____

Here is the premise of this course, my solution to the declining graduation rates, and the decline in personal success. (As a side note, you do understand that I am invested in your success, right? If not, you will soon see.) My belief is that if we strengthen the individual—the student—then we can have a positive impact on all the other abovementioned factors that may impede both academic and life success. I claim that the foundation of success starts with you and how well you can CUSTOMIZE your thinking and how well you use that customization or process strategically. In order to customize your thinking, you must first learn how to maneuver your brain's way of processing information, and then you must learn how to intentionally use those maneuvers and processes to your advantage. The purpose of this is so that within any domain (i.e. situation or context), you will intentionally select a process of thinking that will increase, if not ensure, your academic and personal life success!

For example, let's take the first listed reason why students do not succeed in school—*The Dysfunctional Home Environment.* Using this fact, I will illustrate how changing *your* thinking can change your home environment. This change can be literal or simply how *you* perceive experiences (see them), thus changing how you respond to those experiences. Ultimately, changing your thinking changes the *reality in which you live.*

Dysfunctional Household:

James Thomas hates divorce. He lives with his mother and sister. His father remarried and started a new family. To make matters worse, James and his mother never agree on anything. Every conversation between James and his mother are fueled with anger and frustration.

James' mother often accuses him of having a bad attitude and disrespecting her authority. James on the other hand, thinks his mother is disrespecting him and is too lenient on his sister. The stress of the divorce is causing James to make bad decisions. He spends most of his time focusing on matters at home and has very little time for his studies. Needless to say, James is failing.

One day after a huge fight with his mother, James went in his room and reflected on the argument. He asked himself a couple of strategic questions. These questions helped him explore possible reasons why his mother accuses him of being disrespectful. Processing further, James recognizes his belief that he has to take his father's place as head of the household. Adding to these thoughts, James realizes he's angry at his father and holds a belief that his dad is not man enough to stick to his fatherly commitments. Finally, James understands why he takes on more responsibility around the house. He wants to show his mom and sister that he would never be like his father.

After intentionally searching his thoughts for deeper explanations, James concluded that his beliefs about being head of household and his anger at his father were causing him to make decisions that placed him in a position of superiority over his mother. James quickly identified his place as a young man – and rightfully so – while still under his mother's influence. He thinks differently now and appreciates his mother's strength to endure the hardships of divorce. He now knows his mom is doing the best she can, through it all, to raise him and his sister well. He thought back on how she had adapted financially and how she involved them in every decision that was made. Because *James changed* the way *he perceived* his life circumstances at home, he now has a new respect for his mother.

James spoke with his mother about his thoughts, both old and new. To his surprise, she thanked him and told him that she too wanted to apologize for not recognizing the stress that the divorce had placed on him. Needless to say, life for James was a lot better. Because he perceived his personal circumstances differently, he changed his reality. His home environment was no longer filled with stress. Less stress at home meant that James was better able to concentrate in other areas of his life, and thus he was better able to focus on school work and his actions toward success.

How did James' dysfunctional home environment affect his school work? What did James do that caused his life to be less stressful?

You have, to a certain degree, control over your own thinking. So, if you can deliberately restructure your thinking, then none of the impeding factors can stop your success (within reason) personally or academically. **Here's the bottom line:** If students learn to systematically reason and think critically, then they will increase their ability to make *Wise Choices*. By increasing your ability to make wise choices through systematic reasoning and critical thinking, you gain the ability to restructure your motivation, your ability to function successfully in spite of the classroom environment, and you gain the ability to seek out and use resources successfully. Ultimately, you increase your chances of academic and personal life success—as you define it!

Course Design, Student Learning Outcomes, Why it Matters...

This course is designed around student learning outcomes (SLO) that are taught through theories and then application of those theories (fig. 0.1). Be prepared to learn about different theoretical concepts at in-depth levels. You will then convert those theories into practical application through individual and cooperative group work. Finally, we challenge you to apply these concepts across other domains within your life to strive for success. In other words, you are expected to use what you learn in this class in other classes and in your personal life.

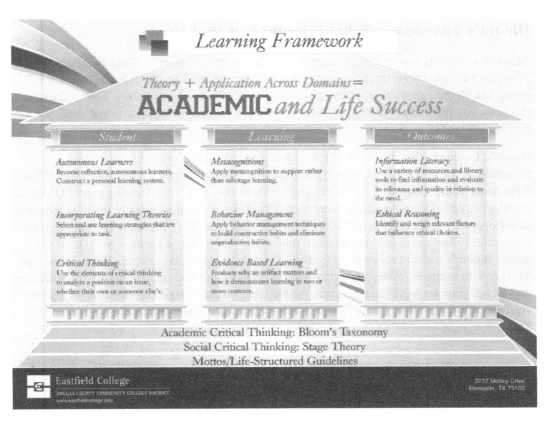

Learning Framework

Theory + Application Across Domains =

ACADEMIC *and Life Success*

Student	Learning	Outcomes
Autonomous Learners Become reflective, autonomous learners. Construct a personal learning system.	*Metacognitions* Apply metacognition to support rather than sabotage learning.	*Information Literacy* Use a variety of resources and library tools to find information and evaluate its relevance and quality in relation to the need.
Incorporating Learning Theories Select and use learning strategies that are appropriate to task.	*Behavior Management* Apply behavior management techniques to build constructive habits and eliminate unproductive habits.	*Ethical Reasoning* Identify and weigh relevant factors that influence ethical choices.
Critical Thinking Use the elements of critical thinking to analyze a position on an issue, whether their own or someone else's.	*Evidence Based Learning* Evaluate why an artifact matters and how it demonstrates learning in two or more contexts.	

Academic Critical Thinking: Bloom's Taxonomy
Social Critical Thinking: Stage Theory
Mottos/Life-Structured Guidelines

Eastfield College
DALLAS COUNTY COMMUNITY COLLEGE DISTRICT
www.eastfieldcollege.edu

3737 Motley Drive
Mesquite, TX 75150

"Course Design" **Figure 0.1**

The Course Foundation: On What Basis Are You Framing Your Academic and Life Success?

As I stated earlier, the key to your success, be it academic, personal or both depends entirely on your ability to reason strategically and think critically. Your success also depends on how well you are able to customize your thinking as it is appropriate for the context and task at hand.

In order to increase your chances of success, I have chosen three different theories that we will use to build your thinking platform, or *Learning Framework*, if you will. These theories are: Bloom's Taxonomy (primarily used for academic critical thinking), Stage Theory or Meta-Cognitions (primarily used for social/personal critical thinking), and then ABC theory, a variation of REBT originated by Dr. Albert Ellis (primarily used to assess and transform an individual's thinking as he or she sees fit). Your challenge is to synthesize all three of these theories and to used those often to create value-based thinking that influence successful behaviors, thus creating successful life outcomes.

Bloom's Taxonomy: What is it and how do I Use It?

Bloom's Taxonomy is very closely aligned with the Socratic Method of Dialectic or dialogue. When both are used together, you will see that it is through the Socratic dialogue that you will strengthen all three domains of learning within Bloom's Taxonomy (Whitely, 2006). Okay, at this point you should be wondering, "What is Bloom's Taxonomy and why is that important to me?"

Bloom's Taxonomy is a hierarchy of learning or a progression of critical thinking that is demonstrated in one or more domains. It is primarily used for academic critical thinking. These three domains are: Cognitive, Affective, and Psychomotor. Cognitive learning relates to critical thinking, affective learning relates to emotional intelligence and psychomotor learning relates to behaviors (see fig. 0.2) (Whitely, 2006). HERE IS THE SECRET: There are NO questions that fall outside of these areas and the levels of thinking within Bloom's Taxonomy. SO...if you master Bloom's way of processing information, you have mastered academia, for the most part. You know there are exceptions or extremes to everything, but rest assured that an overwhelming majority of your academic career rests in the knowing, the understanding, the using of, and the synthesis of Bloom's Taxonomy. I will show you later how to use and synthesize Bloom's Taxonomy; right now, let's focus on knowing and understanding.

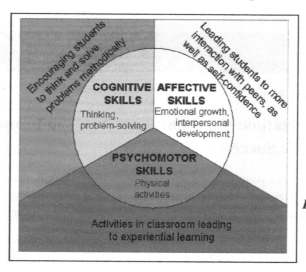

"Benjamin Bloom's Domains of Learning"
Figure 0.2.

All three areas of learning, cognitive, affective, and psychomotor, are very important to academic and personal life success, regardless to how *you* define success. In order for others to witness your success, to experience your idea that you are successful, you should demonstrate success...right? Isn't success *mostly* agreed upon if you see that a person is intelligent, happy, and/or is doing things that reinforce the idea of success? If yes, then you just comprehended the philosophy of Benjamin Bloom, the author of Bloom's Taxonomy. Benjamin says true learning reveals itself through improved thinking, improved emotional intelligence, and, finally, through improved action (Whitely, 2006). Consistent improvement towards your goal will eventually lead to success.

"Academic, Personal & Social Success through Bloom's Taxonomy: The Domains of Learning" **(Hambric, 2011). Figure 0.3.**

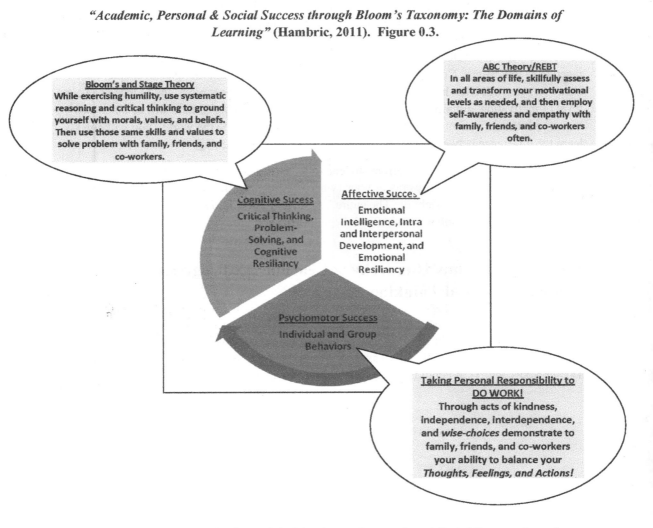

Stop for a moment and ponder figure 0.3: *"Academic, Personal, and Social Success through Bloom's Taxonomy: The Domains of Learning."* Looking at the figure you can easily see the philosophies behind the theories and how those theories can be applied to all areas of your life for major improvements. What are your ideas about success? Do you think a person needs to demonstrate that they are successful in order to be successful? How do your ideas of success fit or not fit with figure 0.3.

In this course, you will see that I place an equal amount of emphasis on all three areas. This is done by synthesizing all three philosophies and consistently applying those philosophies to each *"On Course"* chapter appropriately. As I continue, I will focus more on the cognitive domain within Bloom's Taxonomy through an introduction and application of his hierarchy of learning. After that, Stage Theory will be discussed to teach you the art of *Meta-cognitions*—thinking about your thinking. The affective domain will be addressed in chapter two and there you will be introduced to the ABC theory. The ABC theory will focus on assessing and changing your reaction to life events. Consequently, you will learn more about your thoughts in chapter two. However, you will learn how to use your thoughts to control your emotions and to increase your level of motivation. Finally, there is the psychomotor domain. This domain will be addressed throughout the entire semester—taking personal responsibility to do the work! You will quickly learn the difference between individual efforts and cooperative learning.

With all that you have read so far, from student success rates and course success rates to the course philosophies, I can only pray or hope (whichever applies) that you trust the data and are interested enough to jump right in. The entire Learning Framework faculty who teach this course in the Dallas County Community College District and I are committed to your achievements!

Bloom's Taxonomy Hierarchy of Learning: A Progression in Academic Critical Thinking

According to Benjamin Bloom, there are six levels of thinking in which we process information (see fig. 0.4) (Whitely, 2006). Using the following six levels, we will focus on three specific ways in which you can use Bloom's Taxonomy for academic success: 1) Asking Questions, 2) Taking Notes, and 3) In-depth Learning across domains.

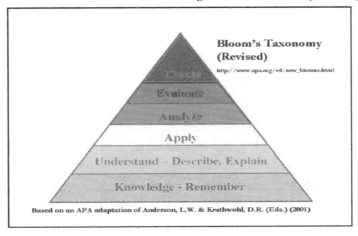

Figure 0.4 Six Levels of Bloom's Taxonomy

Following in the footsteps of Socrates, for many years teachers have strategically used all six levels of Bloom's Taxonomy to engage students in the art of teaching and learning (Whitely, 2006). When a class is not what you, the student, think it should be, can't you as a student do the same thing: engage your teachers in the art of teaching and learning? One of the most common complaints from students is, "My class is boring." Another common complaint is, "I like the class, but I'm not learning anything about the test. The teacher only talks about her children and their vacations." Well, Bloom's Taxonomy can not only help you engage in the class, but enjoy it as well—but wait...because the assumption here is that you as a student actually want to learn.

So how does this work? First let's look at what actions can be taken when you are engaged at the different levels of thinking and learning. In other words, if I wanted to think at the level of application, what would I be doing with information (the topic at hand) presented to me or the information that I have gathered? According to figure 0.5, you could *apply* the information to *solve* a problem. You could *sketch or illustrate* the information and so on (see fig. 0.5).

**"*Levels of Learning, Actions, and Outcomes*"—adopted from
Fattig, M. & Taylor, M.T. (2008). Figure 0.5**

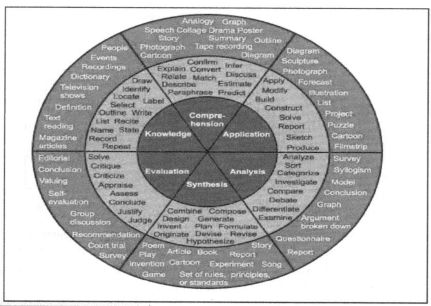

Hierarchy of Learning
The Six Levels of Thinking and Learning

Actions
Ways to Realize Materials Learned

Outcomes
As a Result of the Material Being Manipulated

Now that you have had time to review the different *action* words that are available in each level of thinking and learning, commit just a few of the *action* words from each level to memory. By doing this, you can quickly become a master at using information to craft questions that will give you answers or information that can be used to craft more questions. These questions will eventually lead to intellectual satisfaction. Well, that is the goal at least. Read the following story and think about how you can use Bloom's Taxonomy to not only engage in class, but to enjoy it as well.

The Chattering Teacher Who Seldom Teaches What's on the Test

Ms. Rodwhite entered class as she always did, very cheerful and with a smile. "Good morning," she said. "I take it you guys had a wonderful weekend?" A couple of students responded and the class was on its way. "Wow!" CJ thought. "Ms. Rodwhite is actually on subject today," he mumbled. The lecture was on molecules, atoms, and chemical measurements.

Ms. Rodwhite introduced the term *molecular form.* "*Molecular form* is when two or more of the same type of atoms is tightly bound together. The result is a package of atoms or a molecule that behaves in many ways as a single distinct object or unit, (Chemistry 101)," she stated and then paused giving students time to take notes.

Regrettably for CJ, the pause was just the amount of time Ms. Rodwhite needed to get off topic and to talk about her car. Ms. Rodwhite went on and on about how the car had given her trouble earlier that morning. CJ immediately became frustrated and then simply stared into la-la land...

Giving one final transition and a rushed definition, Ms. Rodwhite quickly brought her class to an end. Unfortunately for CJ and others in the class, the teacher only covered the definition of key terms with few elaborations.

Ms. Rodwhite taught her class at the level of knowledge and some comprehension. This is evident because of the definitions and the few elaborations she gave. However, CJ needs to be able to compare and contrast the different chemistry terms and maybe even evaluate them. Because Ms. Rodwhite spoke mostly of her car and other personal issues, CJ's work outside of class is harder than it has to be. He will have to, on his own, learn to analyze the different terms in chemistry, in particular the term *molecular form.* If you were CJ, how could you use Bloom's theory to re-engage the instructor and to keep her on task? What kind of questions could you craft?

Now using the *action* words that you have committed to memory from figure 0.5, craft three questions using the subject molecular form that CJ could have asked to get more in-depth information and study material. Remember, use figure 0.5 to help get you started.

1. _____

2. _____

3. _____

Hambric's Note-Taking w/Bloom's Taxonomy

Let me start by saying NO, we are not going to teach you how to take notes using the Cornell System, Outlining, or Concept Maps. You may already know how to put words on paper from your time in high school; and NO, we are not going to teach you how to take notes according to your learning style. Again, you may have learned this in college during a study skills class. HOWEVER... if you are not familiar with these strategies or do not already have the skills needed to take notes at the level of knowledge (which means to write down the lecture as close to exact as you can), then you can skip ahead to later chapters in the book (use the table of contents for specifics) and learn about note-taking, basic note-taking. When you have finished, turn back to this page in the textbook to learn the skills and techniques needed for advance note-taking—note-taking that require higher level thinking skills. Your instructor may choose to cover that information in detail now or later. But it will be his or her decision, hopefully, based on your needs.

Using Bloom's Taxonomy to take notes is, simply put, taking the definition of a word or a concept and rewriting it at higher level thinking, making sure that you always start with the original definition. Stated in Bloom's language, always start at the level of knowledge using given information. The KEY to taking notes using Bloom's Taxonomy is ensuring that you have the basic information as accurate or as truthful as possible. This will help to stabilize or ground your understanding of key terms, concepts, and theories, while you attempt to create variations of that same information when given to you via lecture notes, reading material, YouTube clips, etc.

Let's look at the term molecular form. As Ms. Rodwhite stated, molecular form is when two or more of the same type of atom is tightly bound together. The result is a package of atoms or a molecule that behaves in many ways as a single distinct object or unit. This information (the definition of the term molecular form) is considered information at the level of *knowledge*, basic information. In table 0.1, you will find an example that shows how that same information would look, when placed on note cards and written at higher levels of thinking in Bloom's Taxonomy.

Moreover, be conscious of the fact that there is more than one way of thinking within each level of Bloom's Taxonomy. That understanding is implied when you recognize that there is more than one *action* word within each level of Bloom's Taxonomy figure 0.5. Since there is more than one action word within a level, then is it safe to say *you* may come up with a different set of note cards for the term molecular form, cards that are different than the ones I have illustrated? Yes. Study the cards in table 0.1, and then choose an *action* word from each level of thinking in the wheel (the orange section only). See if you can come up with your own set of note cards using the term molecular form.

Table 0.1: *"Hambric's Note-taking Using Bloom's Taxonomy"* (Hambric, 2010).

Level of Note-Card and Action Word	Front Side of Note-Card Information being Studied	Back Side of Note-Card Information at different levels
Knowledge To *record* the facts	**Molecular Form**	When two or more of the same type of atom are tightly bound together. The result is a package of atoms or a molecule that behaves in many ways as a single distinct object or unit.
Comprehension To *explain*	**Molecular Form**	Because like atoms are bonded, they can work as one.
Application To *apply* the concept in a more familiar way	**Molecular Form**	This would be like four Michelin tires bound together by two axles and a frame, moving as a one vehicular unit or car.
Analysis To *examine/analyze* using hypothetical thinking (if this then what?)	**Molecular Form**	When two or more of the same type of atom are tightly bound together. The result is a package of atoms or a molecule that behaves in many ways as a single distinct object or unit.

As you can see from table 0.1, I used key *action* words from the Bloom's Taxonomy graph in figure 0.5. Those action words helped me to use the given information to craft notes at higher levels of thinking. It's the same for concepts and theories. When given a large amount of information about an idea or theory, simply deduce from the information what you think is the cornerstone concepts or the most important information that defines that theory or concept. In doing so, you will have acquired the basic the information that you need in order to create your note cards at the level of *knowledge,* and just as I have done in the earlier example, you too will rewrite what you have at the level of knowledge by converting the information into the levels of comprehension, application and analysis.

Now, at this point you should be thinking, *What about the other two levels?* I recommend that you master note-taking using the first four levels of Bloom's Taxonomy, because the ability to analyze information are skills that will propel you forward with ease to the last two levels of higher order thinking. The gate keeper skill for the last two levels is analysis. You CANNOT *create* or *evaluate* effectively without stellar analytical skills. Now let's practice!

Take out a book from one of your other classes; again, one that is different from this learning framework class/book. Next, take out a set of note cards or draw note cards on your paper. Now label the front side of each note card with one of the words *knowledge, comprehension, application, and analysis.* You should have four note cards on your desk or you should have drawn eight rectangles, every two representing the front and back of one note card, again for a total of eight note cards. Be sure they are large enough to hold written sentences.

Now, locate a term or concept in your chosen book. Once you have found the term, write the name of the term down on the front side of each labeled note cards. It should read: *knowledge/the term name* and so on. Next, you should write the definition of the term on which note card? You got it, on the card that reads knowledge. I think you've got it from here. Simply take the definition of the term and rewrite it at the different Bloom's Taxonomy levels using the actions words provided in figure 0.5 or research Bloom's Taxonomy and find even more action words to use. But the bottom line is for you to create four note cards, written at different levels in Bloom's Taxonomy that represent your chosen term. Don't stop here. I encourage you to do this for theories and concepts as well. It's a bit more of a challenge to take notes for concepts; however, it is very doable. In order to become a master at this, you must practice, practice, and practice until it becomes second nature to think in this fashion. Now that's note taking! And of course you would study this way, as well, right? Moving on…

Hambric's In Depth Learning w/Bloom's Taxonomy Across Curriculum

What does it mean to learn across curriculum? It means to use what you have learned in one class to help you relate or comprehend further what is being introduced in another class. It also means to synthesize what you have learned in one class with what you are being taught in another.

Let's take math for example. Oh, how the majority hates math; however, most of the problems that students have in math stem from students having a faulty mathematical foundation. Did I just say the biggest hurdle is having a faulty knowledge base? Wait: that sounds like Bloom's Taxonomy language. Yes, it is. Let's back up though. What are some of the facts about math that may help you be successful in math? We know it is comprehensive and that it has its own language. This means that math has some of its own words and terms that are conducive to math functions alone. So, let's deduce and draw a conclusion. If math is comprehensive, then in order to pass one level of math, we must know a sufficient amount of math language and functions from an earlier stage of math to experience success at the higher levels. Moreover, if math has its own language, one that is different to your everyday language, then one MAJOR step toward success in math would be to *read the math book*. The purpose of reading your math book is to learn the language of math, and by learning the language, you are adding to your *knowledge* base. That's right, you are building your pyramid of success—the Bloom's Taxonomy pyramid—from the bottom up. But there is more. You are not just reading the language, you are memorizing all the different terms and definitions, the formulae and their specific functions; and at this point, you are just gathering and committing to memory. We have not reached the point of asking "why" a formula functions a certain way. We just want to *record* the facts. Again we are simply *recording* and *memorizing*, and all of this is done at the level of *knowledge*.

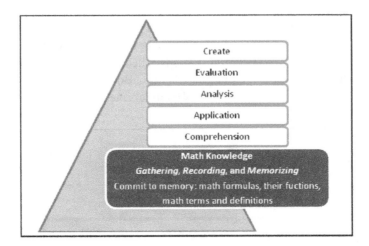

What do you think is next? If you said, "I need to understand what I have gathered," you are correct. Now according to the *action* words in figure 0.5, there are several ways to gain a deeper understanding of the math information that you gather or have gathered. But for the purposes of this example, we will make it simple and just say, take every term, definition and formula and their functions and rewrite or *explain* them in your own words. Even if you have to explain them in the form of cooking recipes, shopping sprees, or mechanical function, do whatever it takes to give yourself a greater and deeper understanding of the material. The word 'greater' refers to the number of ways in which you can recall information and the term 'deeper' means the quality with which you learn or how well you know something. Both are important and will be explained later when we talk about brain functions and neurological networks.

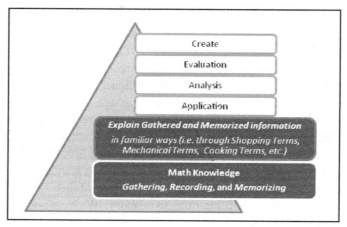

The next step is to take your new math *knowledge* and *comprehension*, and then *apply* that to actual math problems. But in doing so, you will work from two perspectives: you will first *apply* and then *analyze*. In other words, you will use the formula and then examine the process, checking to see if you used the formula properly. Again, you must practice, practice, and practice in order to become a master at this process. In order to strengthen your knowledge and comprehension, you may need to get tutoring. This is called employing interdependence (i.e. healthy support), which you will explore in later chapters. Bottom line, below is what it all looks like when you are doing math strategically using Hambric's method of seeing math through the eyes of Bloom's Taxonomy.

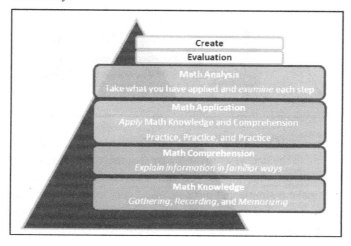

If you will recall the meaning of learning across the curriculum using Bloom's Taxonomy, then you can quickly recognize how combining what you learn in this Learning Framework class for deeper understanding in other classes (i.e. math class) is simply a way of synthesizing information from one class to another. Thus, you are learning across the curriculum using Bloom's Taxonomy!

Alone, it is not enough for me or your instructor to tell you how to use Bloom's Taxonomy across curriculum. To really learn the information and solidify your thoughts, you have to engage in this process yourself. So, take out a sheet of paper and explain, in writing, a well thought-out application of Bloom's Taxonomy to the writing process. In other words, write down how you would use Bloom's Taxonomy when PREPARING to write AND how you would use Bloom's Taxonomy during the *act* of writing a research paper.

Now that you know how to use and transform information, through active reading, you may have drawn several conclusions about the use of Bloom's Taxonomy. One conclusion in particular I hope you have drawn is that Bloom's Taxonomy is not only used for academics, it can also be applied to any type of information within all areas of your life. Bloom's Taxonomy is one of the three layered foundations in this Learning Framework course, and from this point forward, everything you learn in this class will be seen within the framework of Bloom's Taxonomy.

Stage Theory: A Theory of Intellectual Development—Social and Personal Critical Thinking (www.criticalthinking.org).

Keep Your Taxonomy of Learning Glasses on...

We have discussed critical thinking primarily from an academic perspective, but earlier I suggested that we, the professors, would help you succeed both academically and personally, right? No problem ☺

Just as it is important to direct your own thinking while in academia, it is also important to direct your own thinking in your personal life as well. According to Skip Downing, the author of *On Course*, thousands and thousands of students graduate every year without experiencing real change, doing nothing more than temporary learning. Echoing Skip's sentiment, Elder & Paul (2010) state that students "graduate from high school or even college and are still largely unreflective thinkers" (p.3). In other words, people are mostly unaware of the roles that thinking plays in their lives, and they are unaware of the processes of thinking. Therefore, they are unable to strategically manage their own thinking, and are thus unable to manage their own behaviors and life outcomes. In order to represent yourself, your family, me, your teacher, and this school very well, we need to set you up for success beyond academic thinking. You need to know how to govern and manage yourself, all according to your definition of success; and just like everything else I have spoken of in this book, this too is within reason. ☺

So, to maximize your chances at success and to ensure that you leave college not only aware of the thinking process, but that you are very well versed in it, I have relied on the experts—Linda Elder and Richard Paul. I have chosen their theory, Stage Theory, to address these two tasks and to teach you the process of thinking and ultimately how to govern your own thinking. Skip Downing will introduce the ABC theory in chapter 2 to teach you how to manage and transform your thinking when necessary. I will now attempt to pull out the meat and potatoes of Elder and Paul's theory; in other words, I will attempt to pull out the critical parts. However, to fully grasp their theory's foundation, concepts, assumptions, inferences, and conclusions, please visit Elder and Paul at www.criticalthinking.org and, to access a direct link to the article referenced in this chapter, visit http://www.criticalthinking.org/page.cfm?PageID=483&CategoryID=68. Alright, let's "DO WORK!" stated just as my former student, Shawn Ludwick, would say it.

Stage Theory is a theory of intellectual development through stages in which thinking is improved by systematically subjecting it to intellectual self-assessment (Elder & Paul, 2010). Stage Theory lays out six predictable, intellectual stages of development that one must pass through in order to develop as a critical thinker. The six stages of Stage theory are *Unreflective Thinker, Challenged Thinker, Beginning Thinker, Practicing Thinker, Advance Thinker,* and *Accomplished Thinker* (Elder & Paul, 2010). In an effort to cut down on confusion and to create distinct stages, I will cut back tremendously on the authors' verbiage.

So that you, the other students, and I can align our thinking, or, in other words, understand this theory from the same perspective, we need to understand the authors' assumptions. Stage Theory works from the assumptions that in order to develop as a critical thinker, 1) each person must advance through lower levels of development before reaching higher levels, 2) regression in thinking is possible, 3) commitment to systematic self-assessment is vital to advance intellectually, 4) subconscious intellectual advancements are not likely to happen without conscious practice, 5) a critical thinker is one who displays advanced and accomplished level thinking in most of the domains of his or her life, and 6) success is directly connected to a person's intellectual quality and work efforts (Elder & Paul, 2010).

From this point forward, I will explain each stage of intellectual development with distinctive traits. Elder & Paul (2010), created a section called "implications for instruction." I will change that to read *Some Implications for Self-Application.* The reason for the change is to enable you to become a true *Autonomous Learner*, with swift and in-depth passage from lower stages of intellectual development (in Stage Theory) to the higher stages. This way, you can actively participate by both following and leading in the teaching and learning process, regardless to how inspiring or uninspiring the teaching and learning environment.

I fully intend for all of you to represent yourselves, your family, me, your teacher, and the school very well outside of this classroom. In order to help you do so, your teachers and I want to hear about your active participation in other classes. We want to hear about both your successful and failed attempts at using both Stage Theory and Bloom's Taxonomy in other classes. It's a no brainer as to why we want to hear the success stories. Number one, we care, and number two, we'd like to brag as to how our Learning Framework course is making a real difference in the lives of our students ☺. Nonetheless, we want to hear about the failed attempts also. We want to hear these stories because we are invested in your progress. We want to *"help you help yourself,"* to help you improve your approach and/or try new strategies that will eventually lead to your success.

The Six Stages of Intellectual Development and Their

Implication for Self-Application (www.criticalthinking.org)

The Unreflective Thinker

Unreflective thinkers are people who do not consciously understand that thinking drives their behaviors (Elder & Paul, 2010). Unreflective thinkers spend the majority of their time reacting to life and they do not understand that there is a natural process to thinking.

Unreflective thinkers, have skills at the subconscious level, skills that they have no control over, which pose a problem. The problem is that they have flaws in their thinking, but they are unaware of those flaws. They are still unaware of the role thinking plays in their life; therefore, their successes are random and nor are they skillfully managed. With a lack of true awareness and strategic control, a false sense of security in their thinking causes their prejudices and misconceptions to go unchecked (Elder & Paul, 2010).

Some Implications for Self-Application: "We must recognize that in the present mode of instruction it is perfectly possible for students to graduate from high school, or even college, and still be largely unreflective thinkers" Elder & Paul, 2010, p. 3). If you want to avoid this, you must first embrace and/or partially agree with this theory's concepts and claims. You must become aware of the art of thinking and how that heavily influences one's life outcomes both positive and negative. Ask yourself the following question:

According to Stage Theory, what role does thinking play in your life and in the lives of others?

Did you know thinking has a natural process in which humans go through? It flows naturally as you gather knowledge and gain insights. On your own, try to identity two ways in which you seek information and gain insights. As you read further, see if how you think matches or fits what Elder and Paul identify as the natural process of thinking and learning.

Challenged Thinker

Because you have embraced (from above) the idea that thinking actually plays a role in your life's outcomes, you are now at the very least a challenged thinker. Challenged thinkers move to the 'challenged' stage when they become initially aware of their own positive and negative thinking. They realize that positive thinking is more likely to lead to positive outcomes and that negative thinking is more likely to lead to negative outcomes.

Challenged thinkers are aware that high quality thinking requires deliberate focus on their own thinking, but they make very little effort to change. They recognize that there are errors in their thinking, but they are not able to clearly identify those flawed elements within the natural thinking process. Also, they are not introduced to the ways in which thinking is assessed through checking for clarity, accuracy, precision, relevance, logicalness, etc. Like the unreflective thinker, challenged thinkers have developed some thinking skills, but they are inconsistent and can be deceiving to themselves (Elder & Paul, 2010; www.criticalthinking.org).

Some Implications for Self-Application: In order to move out of this stage, you have to challenge yourself. This challenge is probably one of the most difficult challenges you will face this early in your life. That is, you must admit that you have flaws in your thinking. Yes, I said it: you have flaws in your thinking. I have flaws in my thinking, your teacher has flaws in his or her thinking, your parents have flaws in their thinking and yes, you have flaws in your thinking. The most critical skill that you need to acquire at this stage is the skill of humility. Admitting that you are not always right demonstrates one type of humility.

To help with employing humility and exploring your thinking, you must monitor your thinking. Although you will struggle at this stage, you must get started by trying. You can try by writing down your logic. Write down the way in which you think, not necessarily what you think. In doing so, you can compare and contrast your way of thinking to what Elder and Paul have identified as a natural process of thinking; therefore, a more reliable way of thinking that can lead to success and propel you into the beginning thinker stage.

Paul and Elder (2010) identify the natural process of thinking as one that eventually leads to information and inquiry. When we collect or record information we gain knowledge and understanding. As we gain knowledge and understanding, we make inferences (i.e. we reason). As we gain knowledge and understanding, we create concepts in our minds that lead to implications, perspectives and then action or consequences.

1. Humble yourself.

2. Assess your way of thinking, not necessarily what you are thinking.

3. Compare and contrast your thinking with that of the natural process. Do this by asking yourself the following questions:

4. Does your thinking logically draw conclusions that originate from inquiries?

5. Does your thinking lead to knowledge and further understanding, which eventually leads to conclusions? Do these conclusions lead to concepts, which lead to implications and consequences that lead to further assessments?

If your answers to these questions are no, then make a commitment to begin actively assessing your thinking in at least one domain in your life. As you gain more skills, you can commit to assessing additional areas of your life. I suggest one at a time until you really become comfortable with the process of assessing your thinking. Here, you are not actively correcting your thinking; you are, however, becoming more familiar with the natural process of thinking and by making the commitment to do the work, you move into the beginning thinker stage.

The Beginning Thinker

Beginning thinkers are people who are aware that thinking drives behaviors. Often, they consciously try to control their thoughts in an effort to control their responses, but without a systemic way of assessing their thoughts or making changes, they have few successes and more failures. (Elder & Paul, 2010; www.criticalthinking.org). In my opinion, because they are beginning thinkers and are slowly committing to the act of assessing their own thinking with no clear plan, this causes them to continue to have basic problems in their thinking.

Beginning thinkers are conscious of the natural thinking process (i.e. thinking through concepts, assumptions, inferences, implications, points of view, etc.); and they understand the negative consequences that comes with egocentric thinking. Beginning thinkers realize that there is a natural process to thinking, and that natural thinking process can be assessed for improvements. Beginning thinkers grasp that, through systematic thinking, they can make improvements by employing clarity checks, inquiries for accuracy in their thinking and employing the act of weighing precision, relevance, and logicalness in their thinking. In this class, we will use the ABC theory in chapter 2 as the "go to" theory that we apply, when we systematically assess our thinking (Elder & Paul, 2010). The term beginning thinker speaks for itself. This group of thinkers is just in the beginning stages and they DO NOT have a systematic way of assessing their thinking.

Some Implications for Self- Application: To master this stage and to propel yourself forward to the next stage, you must build your self-confidence and gain a willingness to improve cognitively (Elder & Paul, 2010). To move forward to the practicing stage, you must follow at least one systematic way of assessing your thinking. The elements of thought will work well for this and/or the ABC Theory. ABC theory is introduced in chapter two. Both the ABC theory and the Elements of thought will give you greater insights as to what you are thinking and well you are thinking. So in order to change from a beginning thinker to a practicing thinker you need to do the following:

1. You must build up your intellectual confidence without evoking egocentrism.

2. You must commit to at least one systematic self-assessment that can be used in a variety of contexts.

3. You must commit to **not** becoming intellectually lazy or quitting on yourself.

The Practicing Thinker

Thinkers at this stage are clear about the flawed elements within their thinking. Unlike the unreflective and challenged thinkers, the practicing thinkers, to some extent, believe that they have control over their life outcomes. The practicing thinkers gain influence over their life outcomes through regular, **systematic** intellectual self-assessments. Mostly, practicing thinkers do this at low levels of satisfaction in their personal lives and slowly understand the global impact their thinking has on society.

With that said, the practicing thinkers are inconsistent with managing and transforming their thoughts and their thought processes globally. However, their skills are being strengthened every day due to their diligence and commitment to succeed intellectually; thus, striving to succeed in most areas of their lives (Elder & Paul, 2010; www.criticalthinking.org).

Some Implications for Self-Application: This is the part where your commitment has to be real. Work is involved here and it has to be consistent. But hey, it's worth it, because you are worth it!

1. You have to understand and **believe** that you have control over your thinking.

2. You have to be **persistent** and **committed.**

3. You have to, more often than not, deliberately engage in **systematic thinking** (i.e. examine your concepts, assumptions, inferences, implications, points of view, etc. and seek clarity, accuracy, precision, relevance, logicalness, etc.).

4. You must possess **humility**, be able to critique your own thinking, and attempt to correct it regularly.

5. You should now begin to **habitually monitor** your thinking processes (i.e. the elements of thoughts just mentioned in number two; Elder & Paul, 2010).

6. If all the above is applied, you will slowly become a critical thinker and possibly learn to transfer knowledge from one class and applying that understanding to another class (e.g. you would use the Learning Framework theories in your Government class, etc).

Now, before we move to the last two levels of intellectual thinking—the highest two levels, let's stop and process. So here is what I want you to do. I want you to ponder the following questions, and then write your answers on the lines below. I want to know what you're thinking right now.

1. There are six levels of intellectual development. You've been introduced to four of them. What do you think so far?

_____

_____

_____.

2. Have you identified with one of these levels? In other words, are you an unreflective, challenged, beginning, or practicing thinker? If you have identified with one of them, write it down on this line: _____.

3. If you identified yourself as one of the four thinkers, what will it take for you personally to master the next level? Write your answer below…

_____
_____
_____
_____
_____.

Good, good, good! Now, so far you've read about the unreflective, challenged, beginning, and practicing thinkers. Everything so far has been explained except what exactly is a system of thinking. So at this point, you might be asking yourself, "What is systematic thinking? She mentions that a lot." I'm glad you asked. ☺ One example of systematic thinking is to use the _Elements of Thought_ to help you identify and understand the different parts of communication. Below is an example of first, The Elements of Thoughts broken down into faulty thinking and then an example of The Elements of Thoughts broken down into reasoned elements of thinking.

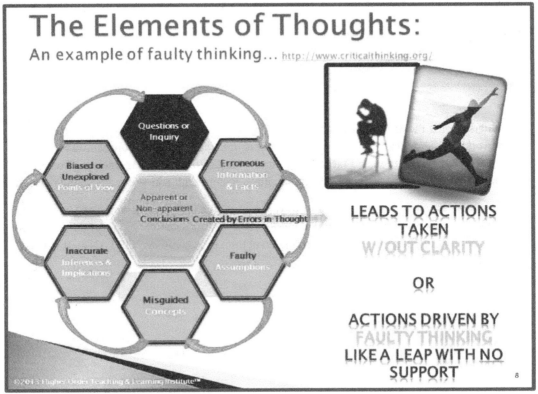

The Elements of Thoughts:
An example of faulty thinking… http://www.criticalthinking.org/

Questions or Inquiry

Biased or Unexplored Points of View

Erroneous Information & Facts

Apparent or Non-apparent Conclusions Created by Errors in Thought

Inaccurate Inferences & Implications

Faulty Assumptions

Misguided Concepts

LEADS TO ACTIONS TAKEN W/OUT CLARITY

OR

ACTIONS DRIVEN BY FAULTY THINKING LIKE A LEAP WITH NO SUPPORT

©2013 Higher Order Teaching & Learning Institute™

8

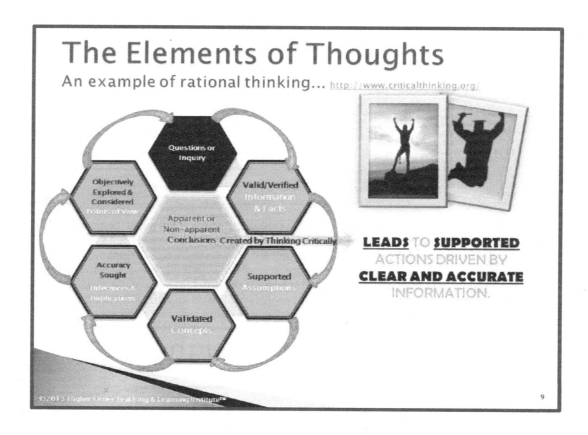

The Elements of Thoughts

An example of rational thinking... http://www.criticalthinking.org/

Questions or Inquiry

Objectively Explored & Considered Points of View

Valid/Verified Information & Facts

Apparent or Non-apparent Conclusions Created by Thinking Critically

Accuracy Sought Inferences & Implications

Supported Assumptions

Validated Concepts

LEADS TO SUPPORTED ACTIONS DRIVEN BY CLEAR AND ACCURATE INFORMATION.

©2013 Higher Order Teaching & Learning Institute™

By understanding the different parts of communication, you are then able to think within a framework—systematically. Systematic thinking is *thinking* that is structured in ways that will help you gather information and facts, help you see things from more than one perspective, help you seek unbiased clarity, help you weigh the pros and cons and help you make sound decisions.

There is more than one way to do this; however, we will focus on the Elements of Thought and later the ABC theory. Both will help you master level four—the practicing level thinker. It is Systematic thinking that makes the practicing level thinker SUPER IMPORTANT. It is what I call the Gatekeeper level. Let's analyze…

The practicing level thinker is the **gatekeeper level** of thinking. What does that mean in relation to the upper two levels and the lower three levels within Stage Theory?

_____
_____
_____
_____
_____
_____
_____
_____
_____
_____
_____
_____
_____
_____
_____
_____.

*Moving on...*The Advanced Thinker

Advance thinkers are constantly and consistently refining their thinking across domains which lead to successes in several areas of their lives. Advance thinkers consistently analyze their thought processes with the intentions of improving both their intrapersonal skills and interpersonal skills. They are able to use their understanding of others thinking to improve personal relationships and outcomes (Elder & Paul, 2010).

Some Implications for Self-Application: You must be willing to evaluate your core beliefs more often than not. Evaluating your core beliefs will allow you to have more in-depth and more insightful, intellectual self-assessments.

1. You must be willing to dive deep morally and assess your integrity.

2. You must be willing to allow others to have flaws in their thinking just as you have humbled yourself to accept your own intellectual flaws.

3. You must have courage!

Accomplished Thinker

The Advance thinkers are still working consciously at controlling their life outcomes; however, the Accomplished thinkers monitor, revise, and re-think strategies for continued improvement in their thinking both consciously and subconsciously. Advance thinkers are consistently successful even at the subconscious levels, because their thinking about their thinking has paid off. Their diligent and consistent intellectual monitoring have created successful scripts or habits that lead to positive outcomes. At this stage, egocentricism is managed well with little room for relapse (Elder & Paul, 2010).

Some Implications for Instructions: Wow! If you are here before you finished this semester, then you have accomplished a feat that takes most people a life-time, if they ever arrive here at all. However, your teacher and I want you to learn how to either stay here or to skillfully call on this level of thinking when you need it. Now remember…we can regress in our intellectual abilities, so, IF you want to stay here – and I say IF – because being here all the time in every domain of your life can be tiring. However, it is an AWESOME experience to solicit this stage of thinking when you need too. So, back to my point—if you want to stay at this stage of thinking, you must do the following:

1. If you are here, you must keep taking authority over the key concepts expressed in each of the lower stages.

2. In other words, you must deliberately analyze and critique your thoughts; monitor and transform the elements of your thoughts; and engage in thought assessment, intellectual humility, high levels of integrity, and morality all the time. If I had to quantify what I mean by *all the time*, I would arbitrarily say 95% to make a clear point.

3. Finally, at all times, you must have the courage it takes to endure without losing it. ☺

4. If you are still in the advanced thinker stage and looking ahead, this is very good. You must become highly skilled in the lower stages of thinking before you can reach this stage (www.criticalthinking.org).

Okay. Now that all six stages have been explained, I want you to really allow your brain to absorb the key information in each stage. Remember when I told you to keep on your Bloom's Taxonomy ◕—◕ glasses? Well, now I want you to use your knowledge and understanding of Bloom's Taxonomy to help you make better sense of Stage Theory.

Exercise:

Using the chart, first gather knowledge by *recording* the names of all six stages in Stage Theory. Then, go back and read each stage one at a time. As you do that, I want you to *summarize*, in your own words, what you are reading. Write your summaries next to the appropriate stage in the chart below. Please do not hesitate to revisit Bloom's Taxonomy if you need too. I want you to skip *application* for now: your instructors will give you assignments that will address the application of Stage Theory. I now want you to use the chart to *analyze* all six levels of Stage Theory. Choose one of the action words from the analysis portion of the wheel in figure 0.5. Use one or more of the analytical action words to help you analyze all six stages of Stage Theory.

Knowledge	Comprehension
Stage 1:	
Stage 2:	
Stage 3:	
Stage 4:	
Stage 5:	
Stage 6:	
My Analysis of Stage Theory:	

I am very optimistic, so I will say to you, "Good job on your efforts!" Humbly speaking, where in Stage Theory are you? During your class discussion and cooperative learning activities, your instructor and peers will help you further your insights as they relate to the different stages in Stage Theory and help you better assess where you are in Stage Theory (www.criticalthinking.org).

Moving On to *"On Course"*...

Now that you are ready to move on, just remember, this course is grounded in CRITICAL THINKING. That means that Bloom's Taxonomy and Stage Theory will be the thinking frameworks in which you will perceive each chapter.

So...at the beginning of every *"On Course"* chapter, put on your Bloom's Taxonomy glasses, which are primarily used for academic critical thinking, and your Stage Theory glasses, which are primarily used to improve your social and personal critical thinking. Combined and used well, they both will increase your chances of success in all your classes and in your life. From this point forward, read every chapter within the framework of Bloom's Taxonomy and Stage Theory. Here is an example of how that might be experienced:

> As you read each *"On Course"* chapter, you will gather *knowledge*. As you *comprehend* the material, in your own words, you will create *concepts* that will solicit *assumptions*. You will engage in one or more levels of *analysis*, which will lead you to a *conclusion*. A Practicing Thinker would conduct a personal exploration (gather knowledge) of their thoughts, with the intentions of *evaluating* errors in their thinking. They would also have the courage to *humble* themselves by admitting when they have fallen short of desired goals due to unproductive behaviors. This would bring them right back to Stage Theory, by giving them the opportunity to *systematically assess their own thinking* that led to the unproductive behavior. At this point the ABC theory would be employed to deeply examine values and beliefs to solicit change.

As a reminder, this section is designed to help you with personal and social critical thinking; however, it is also designed to help you become an *Autonomous Learner*. It is designed so you can move, with depth, from lower stages of intellectual development (in Stage Theory) to the higher stages (www.criticalthinking.org). This way, you can actively participate—both follow and lead—in the teaching and learning process, regardless to how inspiring or uninspiring the teaching and learning environment might be.

I hope that I have given you a clear and logical basis from which to learn and apply appropriate skills across the curriculum. Many blessings or good luck with the rest of the semester!

References:

Clark, D. (2010). *Bloom's Taxonomy of Learning Domains: The Three Types of Learning.* Retrieved on March 28, 2011, from http://www.nwlink.com/~donclark/hrd/bloom. html.

Downing, S. (2010). *On Course.* Cengage Publishing: Dallas, TX.

Elder, L. & Paul, R. (2010). *Critical Thinking A Development: Stage Theory.* Retrieved from, http://www.criticalthinking.org/articles/ct-development-a-stage-theory.cfm

Hambric, T. (2010). *Community college students perceived effects of their home environment on academic success.* Proquest, UMI: AAT 3423171

Longely, R. (2010). *Lifetime earnings soar with education: Masters degree worth 2.5 million in income.* About.com Guide, February 13, 2010.

Whitely, R. (2006). *Using the Socratic Method and Bloom's Taxonomy of the cognitive domain, to enhance online discussion, critical thinking, and student learning.* Development in Business Stimulation and Experiential Learning, Vol.33, pp. 65-70.

Getting On Course to Your Success

1

SUCCESSFUL STUDENTS ...	STRUGGLING STUDENTS ...
accept personal responsibility, seeing themselves as the primary cause of their outcomes and experiences.	**see themselves as victims**, believing that what happens to them is determined primarily by external forces such as fate, luck, and powerful others.
discover self-motivation, finding purpose in their lives by discovering personally meaningful goals and dreams.	**have difficulty sustaining motivation**, often feeling depressed, frustrated, and/or resentful about a lack of direction in their lives.
master self-management, consistently planning and taking purposeful actions in pursuit of their goals and dreams.	**seldom identify specific actions needed to accomplish a desired outcome**, and when they do, they tend to procrastinate.
employ interdependence, building mutually supportive relationships that help them achieve their goals and dreams (while helping others do the same).	**are solitary**, seldom requesting, even rejecting, offers of assistance from those who could help.

Taking the First Step

 Focus Questions What does "success" mean to you? When you achieve your greatest success, what will you have, what will you be doing, and what kind of person will you be?

Congratulations on choosing to attend college! With this choice, you've begun a journey that can lead to great personal and professional success.

WHAT IS SUCCESS?

I've asked many college graduates, "What did success mean to you when you were an undergraduate?" Here are some typical answers:

When I was in college, success to me was . . .

. . . getting all A's and B's.
. . . making two free-throws to win the conference basketball tournament.
. . . having a great social life.
. . . parenting two great kids and still making the dean's list.
. . . being the first person in my family to earn a college degree.

Notice that each response emphasizes *outer success:* high grades, sports victories, popularity, and college degrees. These successes are public, visible achievements that allow the world to judge one's abilities and worth.

I've also asked college graduates, "If you could repeat your college years, what would you do differently?" Here are some typical answers:

If I had a chance to do college over, I would . . .

. . . focus on learning instead of just getting good grades.
. . . major in engineering, the career I had a passion for.
. . . constantly ask myself how I could use what I was learning to enhance my life and the lives of the people I love.
. . . discover my personal values.
. . . learn more about the world I live in and more about myself . . . especially more about myself!

Notice that the focus some years after graduation often centers on *inner success:* enjoying learning, following personal interests, focusing on personal values, and creating more fulfilling lives. These successes are private, invisible victories that offer a deep sense of personal contentment.

Only with hindsight do most college graduates realize that, to be completely satisfying, success must occur both in the visible world and in the invisible spaces within our minds and hearts. This book, then, is about how to achieve both outer and inner success in college and in life.

To that end, I suggest the following simple definition of success: **Success is staying on course to your desired outcomes and experiences.** Maybe you'd

> College is a place where a student ought to learn not so much how to make a living, but how to live.
>
> *Dr. William A. Nolen*

like to earn a college degree or start your own business or marry and have six kids. Maybe you'd like to experience joy or confidence or love. Maybe you'd like to be seen by others as a "self-made" person who achieved success by your efforts alone. Maybe you'd prefer to experience being a valued member of a group that is loyal and committed to one another. Regardless of what your desired outcomes and experiences may be, following the time-tested strategies presented in *On Course* will help you achieve them.

As a college instructor, I have seen thousands of students arrive on campus with dreams, then struggle, fail, and fade away. I've seen thousands more come to college with dreams, pass their courses, and graduate, having done little more than cram their brains with information that's promptly forgotten after the final exam. They've earned degrees, but in more important ways they have remained unchanged.

Our primary responsibility in life, I suggest, is to realize the incredible potential with which each of us is born. All of our experiences, especially those during college, can contribute to the creation of our best selves.

> There is only one success—to be able to spend your life in your own way.
>
> *Christopher Morely*

On Course shows how to use your college experience as a laboratory experiment. In this laboratory you'll learn and apply proven strategies that help you create success—academically, personally, and professionally. I'm not saying it'll be easy, but you're about to learn strategies that have made a difference in the lives of thousands of students before you. So get ready to change the outcomes of your life and the quality of your experiences along the way! Get ready to create success as *you* define it.

To begin, consider a curious puzzle: Two students enter a college class on the first day of the semester. Both appear to have similar intelligence, backgrounds, and abilities. The weeks slide by, and the semester ends. Surprisingly, one student soars and the other sinks. One fulfills his potential; the other falls short. Why do students with similar aptitudes perform so differently? More important, which of these students is you?

Teachers observe this puzzle in every class. I bet you've seen it, too, not only in school, but wherever people gather. Some people have a knack for achievement. Others wander about confused and disappointed, unable to create the success they claim they want. Clearly, having potential does not guarantee success.

What, then, are the essential ingredients of success?

THE POWER OF CHOICE

The main ingredient in all success is wise choices. That's because the quality of our lives is determined by the quality of the choices we make on a daily basis. Successful people stay on course to their destinations by wisely choosing their beliefs and behaviors.

> The deepest personal defeat suffered by human beings is constituted by the difference between what one was capable of becoming and what one has in fact become.
>
> *Ashley Montagu*

Do beliefs cause behaviors, or do behaviors lead to beliefs? Like the chicken and the egg, it's hard to say which came first. This much is clear: Once you choose a positive belief or an effective behavior, you usually find yourself in a cycle of success. Positive beliefs lead to effective behaviors. Effective behaviors lead to success. And success reinforces the positive beliefs.

© Tee and Charles Addams Foundation.

Here's an example showing how the choice of beliefs and behaviors determines results. Until 1954, most track-and-field experts believed it was impossible for a person to run a mile in less than four minutes. On May 6, 1954, however, Roger Bannister of England ran a mile in the world-record time of 3:59.4. Once Bannister had proven that running a four-minute mile was possible, within months, many other runners also broke the four-minute barrier. In other words, once runners chose a new belief (a person *can* run a mile in less than four minutes), they pushed their physical abilities, and suddenly the impossible became possible. By the way, the present world's record, set in 1999 by Hicham El Guerrouj of Morocco, is an amazing 3:43.13. So much for limiting beliefs!

Consider another example. After a disappointing test score, a struggling student thinks, "I knew I couldn't do college math!" This belief will likely cause the student to miss classes and neglect assignments. These self-defeating behaviors will lead to even lower test scores, reinforcing the negative beliefs. This student, caught in a cycle of failure, is now in grave danger of failing math.

In that same class, however, someone with no better math ability is passing the course because this student believes she *can* pass college math. Consequently, she chooses positive behaviors such as attending every class, completing all of her assignments, getting a tutor, and asking the instructor for help. Her grades go up, confirming her empowering belief. The cycle of success has this student on course to passing math.

Someone once said, "If you keep doing what you've been doing, you'll keep getting what you've been getting." That's why if you want to improve your life (and why else would you attend college?), you may need to change some of your beliefs and behaviors. Conscious experimentation will teach you which ones are already working well for you and which ones need revision. Once these new beliefs and behaviors become a habit, you'll find yourself in the cycle of success, on course to creating your dreams in college and in life.

Life is a self-fulfilling prophesy . . . in the long run you usually get what you expect.

Denis Waitley

WRITE A GREAT LIFE

College offers the perfect opportunity to design a life worth living. A time-tested tool for this purpose is a journal, a written record of your thoughts and feelings, hopes and dreams. Journal writing is a way to explore your life in depth and discover your best "self." This self-awareness will enable you to make wise choices about what to keep doing and what to change.

Many people who keep journals do what is called "free writing." They simply write whatever thoughts come to mind. This approach can be extremely valuable for exploring issues present in one's mind at any given moment.

In *On Course*, however, you will write a guided journal. This approach is like going on a journey with an experienced guide. Your guide takes you places and shows you sights you might never have discovered on your own.

Before writing each journal entry, you'll read an article about proven success strategies. Then you'll apply the strategies to your own life by completing the guided journal entry that follows the article. Here are five guidelines for creating a meaningful journal:

- **Copy the directions for each step into your journal (just the bold print):** When you find your journal in a drawer or computer file 20 years from now, having the directions in your journal will help you make sense of what you've written. Underline or bold the directions to distinguish them from your answers.
- **Be spontaneous:** Write whatever comes to mind in response to the directions. Imagine pouring liquid thoughts into your journal without pausing to edit or rewrite. Unlike public writings, such as an English composition or a history research paper, your journal is a private document written primarily for your own benefit.
- **Be honest:** As you write, tell yourself the absolute truth; honesty leads to your most significant discoveries about yourself and your success.
- **Be creative:** Add favorite quotations, sayings, and poems. Use color, drawings, clip art, and photographs. Express your best creative "self."
- **Dive deep:** When you think you have exhausted a topic, write more. Your most valuable thoughts will often take the longest to surface. So, most of all—DIVE DEEP!

For easy reference, these five important guidelines are also printed on the inside back cover of this book.

Whether you handwrite your journal or compose it on a computer, I urge you to keep all of your journal entries together in one book or file. If you do, one day many years from now, you'll have the extraordinary pleasure of reading this autobiography of your growing wisdom about creating success in college and in life.

> Journal work is an excellent approach to uncovering hidden truths about ourselves.
>
> *Marsha Sinetar*

ASSESS YOURSELF

Before we examine the choices of successful students, take a few minutes to complete the self-assessment questionnaire on the next two pages. Your scores will identify behaviors and beliefs that support your success. They'll also point out behaviors and beliefs you may want to change to achieve more of your potential in college and in life. In the last chapter, you will have an opportunity to repeat this self-assessment and compare your two scores. I think you're going to be pleasantly surprised!

This self-assessment is not a test. There are no right or wrong answers. The questions simply give you an opportunity to create an accurate and current self-portrait. Be absolutely honest and have fun with this activity, for it is the first step on an exciting journey to a richer, more personally fulfilling life.

SELF-ASSESSMENT

Visit www.cengagebrain.com to access this self-assessment online through CourseMate for *On Course*.

Read the following statements and score each one according to how true or false you believe it is about you. To get an accurate picture of yourself, consider what IS true about you (not what you want to be true). Remember, there are no right or wrong answers. Assign each statement a number from 0 to 10, as follows:

Totally False ← 0 1 2 3 4 5 6 7 8 9 10 → **Totally True**

1. _____ I control how successful I will be.
2. _____ I'm not sure why I'm in college.
3. _____ I spend most of my time doing important things.
4. _____ When I encounter a challenging problem, I try to solve it by myself.
5. _____ When I get off course from my goals and dreams, I realize it right away.
6. _____ I'm not sure how I prefer to learn.
7. _____ Whether I'm happy or not depends mostly on me.
8. _____ I'll truly accept myself only after I eliminate my faults and weaknesses.
9. _____ Forces out of my control (such as poor teaching) are the cause of low grades I receive in school.
10. _____ I place great value on getting my college degree.
11. _____ I don't need to write things down because I can remember what I need to do.
12. _____ I have a network of people in my life that I can count on for help.
13. _____ If I have habits that hinder my success, I'm not sure what they are.
14. _____ When I don't like the way an instructor teaches, I know how to learn the subject anyway.
15. _____ When I get very angry, sad, or afraid, I do or say things that create a problem for me.
16. _____ When I think about performing an upcoming challenge (such as taking a test), I usually see myself doing well.
17. _____ When I have a problem, I take positive actions to find a solution.
18. _____ I don't know how to set effective short-term and long-term goals.
19. _____ I am organized.
20. _____ When I take a difficult course in school, I study alone.
21. _____ I'm aware of beliefs I have that hinder my success.
22. _____ I'm not sure how to think critically and analytically about complex topics.
23. _____ When choosing between doing an important school assignment or something really fun, I do the school assignment.
24. _____ I break promises that I make to myself or to others.
25. _____ I make poor choices that keep me from getting what I really want in life.
26. _____ I expect to do well in my college classes.
27. _____ I lack self-discipline.
28. _____ I listen carefully when other people are talking.
29. _____ I'm stuck with any habits of mine that hinder my success.
30. _____ My intelligence is something about myself that I can improve.

31. _____ I often feel bored, anxious, or depressed.
32. _____ I feel just as worthwhile as any other person.
33. _____ Forces outside of me (such as luck or other people) control how successful I will be.
34. _____ College is an important step on the way to accomplishing my goals and dreams.
35. _____ I spend most of my time doing unimportant things.
36. _____ I am aware of how to show respect to people who are different from me (race, religion, sexual orientation, age, etc.).
37. _____ I can be off course from my goals and dreams for quite a while without realizing it.
38. _____ I know how I prefer to learn.
39. _____ My happiness depends mostly on what's happened to me lately.
40. _____ I accept myself just as I am, even with my faults and weaknesses.
41. _____ I am the cause of low grades I receive in school.
42. _____ If I lose my motivation in college, I don't know how I'll get it back.
43. _____ I have a written self-management system that helps me get important things done on time.
44. _____ I seldom interact with people who are different from me.
45. _____ I'm aware of the habits I have that hinder my success.
46. _____ If I don't like the way an instructor teaches, I'll probably do poorly in the course.
47. _____ When I'm very angry, sad, or afraid, I know how to manage my emotions so I don't do anything I'll regret later.
48. _____ When I think about performing an upcoming challenge (such as taking a test), I usually see myself doing poorly.
49. _____ When I have a problem, I complain, blame others, or make excuses.
50. _____ I know how to set effective short-term and long-term goals.
51. _____ I am disorganized.
52. _____ When I take a difficult course in school, I find a study partner or join a study group.
53. _____ I'm unaware of beliefs I have that hinder my success.
54. _____ I know how to think critically and analytically about complex topics.
55. _____ I often feel happy and fully alive.
56. _____ I keep promises that I make to myself or to others.
57. _____ When I have an important choice to make, I use a decision-making process that analyzes possible options and their likely outcomes.
58. _____ I don't expect to do well in my college classes.
59. _____ I am a self-disciplined person.
60. _____ I get distracted easily when other people are talking.
61. _____ I know how to change habits of mine that hinder my success.
62. _____ Everyone is born with a certain amount of intelligence, and there's not really much you can do to change that.
63. _____ When choosing between doing an important school assignment or something really fun, I usually do something fun.
64. _____ I feel less worthy than other people.

Transfer your scores to the scoring sheets on the next page. For each of the eight areas, total your scores in columns A and B. Then total your final scores as shown in the sample on the next page.

SELF-ASSESSMENT SCORING SHEET

SAMPLE

A	B
6. _8_	29. _3_
14. _5_	35. _3_
21. _6_	50. _6_
73. _9_	56. _2_

_28_ + 40 − _14_ = 54

SCORE #1: ACCEPTING PERSONAL RESPONSIBILITY

A	B
1. ___	9. ___
17. ___	25. ___
41. ___	33. ___
57. ___	49. ___

___ + 40 − ___ = ___

SCORE #2: DISCOVERING SELF-MOTIVATION

A	B
10. ___	2. ___
26. ___	18. ___
34. ___	42. ___
50. ___	58. ___

___ + 40 − ___ = ___

SCORE #3: MASTERING SELF-MANAGEMENT

A	B
3. ___	11. ___
19. ___	27. ___
43. ___	35. ___
59. ___	51. ___

___ + 40 − ___ = ___

SCORE #4: EMPLOYING INTERDEPENDENCE

A	B
12. ___	4. ___
28. ___	20. ___
36. ___	44. ___
52. ___	60. ___

___ + 40 − ___ = ___

SCORE #5: GAINING SELF-AWARENESS

A	B
5. ___	13. ___
21. ___	29. ___
45. ___	37. ___
61. ___	53. ___

___ + 40 − ___ = ___

SCORE #6: ADOPTING LIFELONG LEARNING

A	B
14. ___	6. ___
30. ___	22. ___
38. ___	46. ___
54. ___	62. ___

___ + 40 − ___ = ___

SCORE #7: DEVELOPING EMOTIONAL INTELLIGENCE

A	B
7. ___	15. ___
23. ___	31. ___
47. ___	39. ___
55. ___	63. ___

___ + 40 − ___ = ___

SCORE #8: BELIEVING IN MYSELF

A	B
16. ___	8. ___
32. ___	24. ___
40. ___	48. ___
56. ___	64. ___

___ + 40 − ___ = ___

INTERPRETING YOUR SCORES

A score of . . .

0–39 Indicates an area where your choices will **seldom** keep you on course.

40–63 Indicates an area where your choices will **sometimes** keep you on course.

64–80 Indicates an area where your choices will **usually** keep you on course.

CHOICES OF SUCCESSFUL STUDENTS

SUCCESSFUL STUDENTS . . .	STRUGGLING STUDENTS . . .
accept personal responsibility, seeing themselves as the primary cause of their outcomes and experiences.	**see themselves as victims**, believing that what happens to them is determined primarily by external forces such as fate, luck, and powerful others.
discover self-motivation, finding purpose in their lives by discovering personally meaningful goals and dreams.	**have difficulty sustaining motivation**, often feeling depressed, frustrated, and/or resentful about a lack of direction in their lives.
master self-management, consistently planning and taking purposeful actions in pursuit of their goals and dreams.	**seldom identify specific actions needed to accomplish a desired outcome**, and when they do, they tend to procrastinate.
employ interdependence, building mutually supportive relationships that help them achieve their goals and dreams (while helping others do the same).	**are solitary**, seldom requesting, even rejecting, offers of assistance from those who could help.
gain self-awareness, consciously employing behaviors, beliefs, and attitudes that keep them on course.	**make important choices unconsciously**, being directed by self-sabotaging habits and outdated life scripts.
adopt lifelong learning, finding valuable lessons and wisdom in nearly every experience they have.	**resist learning new ideas and skills**, viewing learning as fearful or boring rather than as mental play.
develop emotional intelligence, effectively managing their emotions in support of their goals and dreams.	**live at the mercy of strong emotions**, such as anger, depression, anxiety, or a need for instant gratification.
believe in themselves, seeing themselves as capable, lovable, and unconditionally worthy human beings.	**doubt their competence and personal value**, feeling inadequate to create their desired outcomes and experiences.

FORKS IN THE ROAD

Why are these eight qualities so important? Because they shape many of the important choices we make. The road of life forks many times each day, and at every one we need to make a choice. Some of those choices are so significant they will literally change the outcomes of our lives. In college, students encounter opportunities such as work-study programs, majors, lunch with an instructor, study groups, social events, sports teams, new friends, study-abroad programs, romantic relationships, academic majors, all-night conversations, diverse cultures, challenging viewpoints, and field trips, among many others.

Other choices involve dealing with disappointing grades, homesickness, the death of a loved one, conflicts with friends, loneliness, health problems, endless homework, anxiety, broken romances, self-doubt, lousy class schedules, lost motivation, difficult instructors, academic probation, confusing tests, excessive drinking, frustrating rules, mystifying textbooks, conflicting work and school schedules, jealous friends, test anxiety, learning disabilities, and financial difficulties, to name a few.

In other words, college is just like life. There are always opportunities and obstacles, and the choices we make at each of these forks in the road determine whether we achieve our desired outcomes and experiences. It takes a lot more than potential to excel in college or in life. And you're about to find out how to succeed in both . . . despite inevitable challenges. You see, while life is generating a dizzying array of options, successful people are making one wise choice after another.

> I believe that choice—though it can be finicky, unwieldy, and demanding—is ultimately the most powerful determinant of where we go and how we get there.
>
> *Sheena Iyengar*

A FEW WORDS OF ENCOURAGEMENT

In this course, you'll be taking a personal journey designed to help you develop the empowering beliefs and behaviors that will help you maximize your potential and achieve the outcomes and experiences you desire. However, before we depart, let's see how you're feeling about this upcoming trip. Please choose the statement below that best describes how you feel right now:

1. I'm excited about developing the inner qualities, outer behaviors, and academic skills that have helped others achieve success in college and in life.

2. I'm feeling okay about this journey because I'll probably learn a few helpful things along the way.

3. I can't say I'm excited, but I'm willing to give it a try.

4. I'm unhappy, and I don't want to go!

In nearly every *On Course* group I've worked with, there have been some reluctant travelers. If that's you, I want to offer some personal words of encouragement. First, I can certainly understand why you might be hesitant. Frankly, I would have been a reluctant traveler on this journey when I was a first-year college student. I can tell you, though, I sure wish I'd known then what you're about to learn. Many students after completing the course have asked, "Why didn't they teach us this stuff in high school? It sure would have helped!" Even some of the most reluctant travelers have later said, "Every student should be required to take this course!"

I can't promise that you'll feel this way after finishing the course. But I can promise that if you do only the bare minimum or, worse yet, drop out, you'll never know if this course could have helped you improve your life. So, quite frankly, my goal here is to persuade you to give this course a fair chance.

Maybe you're thinking, *"I don't need this success stuff. Just give me the information and skills I need to get a good job."* If so, you're going to be pleased to discover that the skills you'll learn in this course are highly prized in the work world. In fact many companies pay corporate trainers huge fees to teach these same skills to their employees. Think of the advantage you'll have when you bring these skills with you to the job.

Or, perhaps you're thinking, *"I already know how to be successful. This is just a waste of my time."* I thought this, too, at one time. And I had three academic degrees from prestigious universities and a good job to back up my claim. Hadn't I already proven I could be a success? But when I opened myself to learning the skills that you'll discover in these pages, the quality of both my professional and personal life improved dramatically. I've also taught these skills to successful college educators (perhaps even your own instructor), and many of them have had the same experience I did. You see, there is success . . . and then there is SUCCESS!

Or, maybe you're thinking, *"I don't want to examine and write about myself. That's not what college should be about."* I understand this objection! When I was in college, self-examination was about the last thing on my to-do list (right after walking backwards to the North Pole in bare feet). Of course I had a "good" reason: Athletes like me didn't look inward. I labeled it "touchy feely" and dismissed self-exploration. I'm sure you have reasons for your reluctance: shyness, your cultural upbringing, or a host of other explanations that make you uncomfortable when looking within for the keys to your success. I urge you to overcome your resistance. You can learn now what it took me too many years to discover: Success occurs from inside out, not outside in. *You* are the key to your success. So, I hope you'll give this course your best effort. Most likely, it's the only one you'll ever take in college where the subject matter is YOU. And, believe me, if you don't master the content of this course, every other course you take (both in college and in the University of Life) will suffer. I wish you a great journey. Let the adventure begin!

> The battles that count aren't the ones for gold medals. The struggles within yourself—the invisible battles inside all of us—that's where it's at.
>
> *Jessie Owens, winner of four gold medals at the 1936 Olympics*

Journal Entry 1

In this activity, you will take an inventory of your personal strengths and weaknesses as revealed by your self-assessment questionnaire.

Remember: The five suggestions for creating a meaningful journal are printed on the inside back cover of *On Course*. Please review these suggestions before writing. Especially remember to copy the directions for each step (just the bold print) into your journal before writing.

> All glory comes from daring to begin.
>
> *Eugene F. Ware*

1. **In your journal, write the eight areas of the self-assessment and record your scores for each, as follows:**

_____ 1. Accepting personal responsibility

_____ 2. Discovering self-motivation

_____ 3. Mastering self-management

_____ 4. Employing interdependence

_____ 5. Gaining self-awareness

_____ 6. Adopting lifelong learning

_____ 7. Developing emotional intelligence

_____ 8. Believing in myself

Transfer your scores from the self-assessment to the appropriate lines above.

2. **Write about the areas on the self-assessment in which you had your highest scores.** Explain why you think you scored higher in these areas than in others. Were there any surprises? Were there any high scores you disagreed with? If so, why? How do you feel about your higher scores? Your entry might begin, "By doing the self-assessment, I learned that I . . . ."

> My journal from this course is the most valuable possession I own. I will cherish it always.
>
> *Joseph Haskins, student*

3. **Write about the areas on the self-assessment in which you had your lowest scores.** Explain why you think you scored lower in these areas than in others. Were there any surprises? Were there any low scores you disagreed with? If so, why? How do you feel about your lower scores? Remember the saying, "If you keep doing what you've been doing, you'll keep getting what you've been getting." With this thought in mind, write about any specific changes you'd like to make in yourself during this course. Your entry might begin, "By doing the self-assessment, I also learned that I . . . ."

One Student's Story

JALAYNA ONAGA
University of Hawaii-Hilo, Hawaii

It's amazing how fast someone can go from being excited about college to flunking out. A year and a half ago, I received a letter from the University of Hawaii at Hilo informing me that I was being dismissed due to my inability to maintain a GPA of at least 2.0. I wasn't surprised because I had spent the whole semester making one bad choice after another. I hardly ever attended classes. I didn't do much homework. I didn't study for tests. And I never asked anyone for help. Mostly I just hung out with friends who told me I didn't need to go to college. But, fast-forward to today and you'll see a woman who has clear goals for her future, the motivation to reach those goals, and a plan to carry her to her dreams. However, it took a lot of learning in order for me to make such a huge change in my life.

After taking courses for a while at a community college, I got permission to re-enroll at the university. I was so nervous! I worried that I'd get dismissed again and I'd never do anything with my life. A counselor suggested that I take the University 101 course, and I'm so thankful I did. While writing the *On Course* journals, I learned so much about myself and how I can succeed. I realized that when I first enrolled at the university, I was taking nursing courses because my parents wanted me to and I couldn't get motivated. This time I got inspired because my journals helped me look inside myself to figure out my own dreams for the future and to create a plan to reach them. For the first time, the plans I made were coming from my heart, not from someone telling me what I

should do. I realized that I really love kids and *my* dream is to teach second or third graders. That's when I made a personal commitment to attend every class and learn as much as I could. In later journals I learned that making a schedule and writing everything down helped me get the important things done. I even learned to ask for help, and when I was absent because my car broke down, I met with the teacher to find out what I had missed. Before tests, I found it inspiring to read over my journal because my own words reminded me of my dreams and why I should study hard to get them.

Best of all, my new choices really paid off. When the semester ended, I had three A's and a B+ and I made the dean's list. My University 101 course and the *On Course* textbook really changed me as a student and as a person. Not long ago, I was a student without a direction. Now I can envision myself in the near future teaching a class full of eager students, watching them learn and grow, just like I was able to do.

Understanding the Culture of Higher Education

 Focus Questions   What is the culture of higher education? How does understanding that culture increase your chances of success in college?

In some ways, enrolling in college is like moving to a foreign country. That's because the culture of higher education is different from other cultures you have known, even that of high school. Like an immigrant to any new land, you'll be successful in college to the degree that you learn and adapt to its unique culture.

Geert Hofstede, a Danish psychologist and anthropologist, has studied cultures all over the world. According to Hofstede, culture is "the collective programming of the mind that distinguishes the members of one human group from another."

In other words, what makes people different isn't just the physical characteristics you can see. In fact, much more significant is their unique cultural programming: the sum of customs and beliefs they've learned from family, friends, schools, religions, and other groups to which they belong. Every culture on Earth is programmed to operate by its own unique software. And this is true of higher education as well.

Some aspects of a culture are obvious and visible, whereas others are subtle and invisible. To understand the distinction between visible and invisible culture, Brooks Peterson, author of *Cultural Intelligence*, suggests picturing an iceberg (see Figure 1.1). Above the waterline are the elements of culture we can perceive with our five senses. "Surface" culture includes such things as food, fashions, language, gestures, games, art, music, and holidays.

Below the waterline you'll find the more stable and significant features of "deep culture." Most of these features are invisible to tourists and recent immigrants. Deep culture consists of the shared beliefs, attitudes, norms, rules, opinions, expectations, and taboos of a group of people. For natives, these deep-culture features are usually taken for granted until someone disobeys them. Here's a simple example. When you arrive at a ticket line, what do you do? If you're from mainstream North American culture, you automatically go to the end of the line. No sign is needed because everyone knows that's what you're supposed to do. You probably don't even think about it unless someone cuts in front of you. When someone defies a cultural rule, others get upset. Cultural programs help a group or society run smoothly by keeping people in line (literally and figuratively).

Culture, then, is the collection of surface- and deep-level customs and beliefs that get passed on from generation to generation. Each culture provides "approved" choices at significant, and even insignificant, forks in the road. Culture tells us, "This choice is normal and that one is strange." Or, "This choice is right and that one is wrong." Or, "This choice is good and that choice

> What we call customs rest on top and are most apparent. Deepest and least apparent are the cultural values that give meaning and direction to life. Values influence people's perceptions of needs and their choice between perceived alternative courses of action.
>
> *Benjamin Paul, Anthropologist*

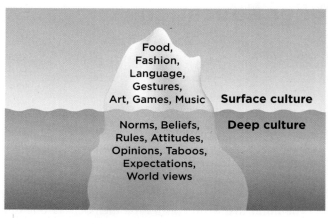

Figure 1.1 Cultural Iceberg

is bad." At each fork in the road, our inner programs give us a nudge in the culturally approved direction.

To put it succinctly, "Culture is the way we do things around here."

CULTURE SHOCK

What happens, then, when *they* don't do things the way *we* do? Or, what happens when *we* don't do things the way *they* do? In other words, what happens when different cultures clash?

Here's an example of surface cultures clashing: You're traveling with a group of American students in China. In the province of Guangdong, students from a local university invite your group to join them for a meal. You've saved your appetite for a grand feast, and after many tasty appetizers, your hosts proudly present the main dish. *What the heck is that? Oh my god . . . they're serving a barbequed dog!* Chances are, you've just experienced a clash of surface cultures. Your mind races with judgments about what is appropriate, right, or good to serve for dinner. In North American culture, dogs are pets. We all know the unwritten rule: People don't eat their pets (let alone serve them to guests).

Now, consider a clash of deep cultures. At your college, you join a math study group that includes Tariq, a young man from Saudi Arabia. You're explaining how you solved homework problem number three when Tariq excitedly interrupts: "What you are saying can also work for numbers four and five!" Tariq takes over the conversation, and you wait quietly until he finishes. Then you've barely begun explaining your approach to problem six when Tariq, with great enthusiasm, cuts you off again. A few minutes later, he butts in once more, and now you're steaming. You've just experienced a clash of deep cultures: judgments about what is appropriate, right, or good to do in a conversation. The unwritten rule in some cultures (e.g., United States, English-speaking Canada, and England) is that speakers take turns speaking. In other cultures (e.g., Middle East, Southern France, and Spain), interruptions are expected. In fact, if someone doesn't interrupt, others may assume the person doesn't care about the subject under discussion.

Culture shock is the upset and stress we experience when confronted with behaviors and beliefs that differ significantly from our own. Because we are quite sure that our way is right, a typical response to culture shock is judgment: Tariq is self-centered, inconsiderate, and rude. As judgments fly and our discomfort increases, typical responses are fight (*I'm not putting up with this!*) or flight (*I'm outta here!*) Seldom is either choice helpful in achieving our desired outcomes and experiences.

Which brings us to the importance of understanding the culture and traditions of higher education in North America.

THE CULTURE OF HIGHER EDUCATION

Because college is a unique culture, expect some challenges as you adapt. Most differences in surface culture will be pretty obvious. For example, like all cultures, higher education has its own language, so you'll probably hear words that

> Culture shock can take its toll on us. It can make us feel anxious, disoriented, and depressed. . . . Minimizing culture shock requires new knowledge and insights as well as a certain degree of flexibility.
>
> *Richard Bucher,*
> **Building Cultural Intelligence**

sound foreign to you. Suppose an instructor tells your class, "The directions for your first paper are posted on Moodle. Be sure to do it in MLA format." These directions make little sense if you don't know the lingo. But it's not really that complicated. Here's what those familiar with college culture know:

Moodle is a computer software program that allows colleges to offer class content on the Internet. (A similar program is called BlackBoard.) If your instructor doesn't provide directions for accessing course information posted on the Internet, contact the folks in your campus computer lab for help.

MLA format is a set of guidelines provided by the Modern Language Association (MLA) for how writers in the humanities should identify research sources. By the way, writers in the sciences use a different format, one provided by the APA (American Psychological Association). For more information about these formats, you can ask a librarian or do an Internet search for help.

To learn additional surface features of college culture, see "Wise Choices in College: College Customs" (pages 34–38). Following the suggestions there will help you avoid a number of bumps and potholes in your journey through higher education.

Now for a few words about deep culture. As suggested earlier, these differences will be less obvious. In fact, you may find yourself off course and not even realize that the cause is a clash of deep cultures. That's why the sooner you learn the culture of higher education in general, and the culture of your college in particular, the better you'll be able to make wise choices and stay on course to academic success.

Throughout *On Course* we will be exploring the deep culture of higher education in North America, but let's take a look at one example here. Keep in mind that statements about any culture are generalizations. As with all generalizations, they will likely vary for individual campuses and certainly vary for individual instructors. However, you can use the following example (and those presented throughout the book) to gage where your college—or an instructor—stands in regard to each of these mindsets and make your choices accordingly.

One element of deep college culture that's almost sure to be important at your college is a high regard for intellectual curiosity. I've asked literally thousands of educators, "What inner qualities would you like your students to have?" *Intellectual curiosity* is a near unanimous choice. Your instructors want you to be as curious about their subject as they are. Or at least curious about something. They want you to think deeply about life. They want you to ask thoughtful questions and pursue the answers with enthusiasm. Questions like *Why? How do you know? Who else believes this? What's the cause? What's another explanation? When might this not be so? How can I use this?* Bottom line: Intellectual curiosity is greatly prized in the deep culture of higher education.

A Dozen Differences Between High School and College Culture	
High School Culture—Assumes Immaturity	College Culture—Assumes Maturity
Students attend high school because they are required to by their parents or by law.	Students usually attend college because of a personal choice.
Teachers offer students many reminders to complete assignments.	Instructors give assignments and expect students to hand them in on time without reminders.
Teachers spend time disciplining students who create disruptions.	Instructors do not tolerate disruptive students and may bar them from the class.
Students typically spend 30 or more hours in class each week, and teachers cover the majority of course content during class.	Students typically spend 15 or fewer hours in class each week, and instructors expect students to learn the majority of course content outside of class.
Teachers and parents manage much of the students' time.	Students manage their own time.
Teachers are often pressured to "teach to the test" so that students can pass standardized assessments.	Instructors have more "academic freedom" in what and how they teach.
Academic standards are not always high, and savvy students often get good grades with little effort.	Academic standards are usually high, and all students need to figure out how to meet these challenging standards.
Family and friends provide students with advice or solutions for academic, social, and other problems.	Students solve their own problems or seek help at one of many support services provided by the college.
Students' choice of courses is relatively limited by graduation requirements.	Students have greater freedom to choose the courses they take and drop those they don't want to complete.
Teachers and parents minimize distractions that might otherwise hinder students' success.	Students must deal with distractions on their own, including parties, television, video games, Internet surfing, dating, sports, Facebook, drinking, road trips, and hanging out.
Educational costs are paid for by taxpayers, including text books.	Educational costs, including text books, are paid for by the student, the student's family, and/or by financial aid for which the student applies and, in some cases, must pay back.
Students have few choices.	Students have many choices.

So, how might a student clash with this aspect of deep college culture? Here's just one possibility. A student gets back a writing assignment, and the grade is lower than he expected. A *lot* lower. *Darn,* he thinks, *I spent hours writing that paper. What does the instructor expect anyway? This would have been at least a B in high school. Probably an A! What is she thinking!* For an answer, let's visit the instructor at home the night before where we catch her reading that very student's paper: *Darn, she thinks, this essay is so boring. It's as though the writer simply copied sentences from various Internet sites and strung them together as an essay. His main concern seems to be having enough words to fulfill the assignment. Where's the writer's curiosity, his passion, his quest for answers? What is he thinking!*

The student is discouraged, and the instructor is too. They both have good intentions yet neither may realize the problem: deep cultures clashing. He wants to get a good grade. She wants to see intellectual curiosity.

CHOICES AND CULTURE

The choices recommended in *On Course* exist as possibilities for every human being. However, here's a heads up: Sometimes an option presented in these pages may clash with your own cultural or individual programming. As such, you may judge them as inappropriate, wrong, or bad. For example, in Chapter 5 you'll read about the benefits of interdependence. This principle suggests that creating mutually supportive relationships can enhance your chances for success. However, if you've been raised in traditional North American culture, your default choice is likely to be independence. In fact, asking for help may feel so uncomfortable that pursuing your success alone may seem to be your only choice. There is certainly a time for *in*dependence, but what if choosing *inter*-dependence at the right time can improve your chances for success?

Here's another example. As you've learned, *On Course* presents success principles and practices. Then it asks you to reflect on these strategies by writing guided journal entries. If you've been raised in a working-class culture, and especially if you are young and male, your programming probably favors action over reflection. Thus, writing reflective journals may feel uncomfortable. There is certainly a time for action, but what if choosing reflection at the right time can improve your chances for success?

Here's the point: Empowered people appreciate having choices . . . as many as possible. Having options usually increases anyone's likelihood for success, especially when seeking success in a new culture. At each fork in the road, empowered people decide which choice—from among many—will most likely help them create the outcomes and experiences they want.

In this course you will learn much about the surface- and deep-culture rules of higher education. In the process, you'll come to understand what natives of this unique culture judge to be appropriate, right, and good (and, conversely, what they believe is inappropriate, wrong, and bad). At some point early in the process, you may feel that you don't belong in this culture . . . you might even feel unwelcome. Just know that this is a natural part of figuring out and fitting

> If all you have is a hammer, everything looks like a nail.
>
> *Carl Jung*

into any new culture. If your culture is very different from the culture of higher education, at some point you may even ask yourself, "How much of my culture do I need to give up in order to succeed in college?"

It's up to each of us to decide when to follow a choice of our culture, when to follow a choice of another culture, or when to honor a choice born of our own wisdom. Whatever their source, the more options you have to choose from, the more empowered you will be to create the life you want.

> *Life is the sum of all your choices.*
>
> **Albert Camus**

Journal Entry 2

In this activity you will explore various aspects of surface and deep culture that you have experienced in school.

1. **Contrast the surface culture of the last school you attended with that of your present school.** From the following list, choose two or more surface-level features that are different for the two schools. Then, in a separate paragraph for each feature, explain how the two schools are different.

Number of students in a class	Age of students
Race or ethnicity of students	Economic class of students
Courses offered	Amount of homework
Popular out-of-school activities	Teachers' treatment of students
Alcohol	Academic preparation of educators
In-groups	Religions
Clothes	Food
Languages spoken	Dialects spoken
Sports	Amount of writing assigned
Amount of reading assigned	Drugs
Architecture of buildings	Favorite music
Holidays observed	Out-groups
Attendance policy	Methods of teaching
Involvement of parents	Classrooms

> *The heart and soul of school culture is what people believe, the assumptions they make about how school works.*
>
> **Thomas Sergiovanni**

Here's how your journal entry might begin if you chose "Age of students":

"The ages of students at my high school ranged from about 14 to 18 years old. Here in college the ages of students range from about 17 to 40 or even older. In my math class this semester, I have a mother and daughter who are taking the class together. Overall, students here in college seem to average about 10 years older than students in high school. A couple of the older students that I've talked with went to college before and dropped out. These students seem to take their schoolwork more seriously than the younger students. They hardly ever miss a class or fail to turn in homework."

During elementary and second education, teachers and parents primarily guide students, for the most part students take classes with the same peers, homework assignments are checked often, notes to parents are often sent about good academic progress, and children are to some extent protected from distractions and competing alternatives to education. In postsecondary education, however, students are expected to exercise control of their conduct, maintain motivation, develop plans for the future, exercise delay of gratification, and put into effect goals and learning strategies.

Hefer Bembenutty

Journal Entry 2 *continued*

2. **Describe the deep culture of the last school you attended.** From the following list, choose two or more deep-culture features. Then, in a separate paragraph for each, describe the school's invisible beliefs, attitudes, opinions, expectations, norms, and/or taboos toward . . .

Maturity

Academic integrity (cheating and plagiarism)

Motivation

Civility (common courtesy to others)

Time

College education

Study groups (student collaboration)

Grades

Speaking and writing in Standard English ("correct" grammar)

Intellectual curiosity

People who are different (ethnicity, religion, sexual orientation, etc.)

Self-awareness

Learning

Academic standards (difficult/easy)

Importance of a college education

Formality

Choices

Punctuality

Homework

Contributing to class discussions

Quality of teaching

Emotions

Academic freedom (teachers choose what/how to teach)

Self-confidence

Studying

For example, suppose you chose to describe your high school's deep-culture belief about "college." Your paragraph might say:

"My high school had students from seven small towns. Five of the towns were fairly well off economically. Two of the towns were pretty poor. Students from the five richer towns—I was one of them—pretty much expected we would enroll in college after graduation. A lot of us had parents and older brothers and sisters who had gone to college. Although we didn't talk about it much, it was a given we'd go to college, too. I never even considered another option, and I think that was true for my friends as well. In junior year, our guidance counselors started helping us go through college catalogues and fill out applications. In our senior year, word got around fast when someone got a letter of acceptance to a college. Now that I think about it, I feel bad for the kids from the other two towns. I'm not sure if any of them went to college or not. I saw one of them a couple of weeks ago working at a mini-mart. I wonder if he was as sure he would *not* go to college as I was sure that I *would*. I had a couple of classes with him in high school, and he was no dummy. I bet he could get a college degree if he wanted to. As far as I know, he didn't even apply. *On Course* talks about making wise choices at a fork in the road. Sometimes it seems like the choice is decided by your culture before you even get to the fork."

Becoming an Active Learner

 Focus Questions   How does the human brain learn? How can you use this knowledge to develop a highly effective system for learning?

Successful athletes understand how to get the most out of their physical abilities. Likewise, to be a successful learner, you need to know how to get the most out of your mental abilities. Much has been discovered, especially in the last few decades, about how human beings learn. To benefit from these discoveries, let's take a quick peek into our brains.

HOW THE HUMAN BRAIN LEARNS

The human brain weighs about three pounds and is composed of trillions of cells. About 100 billion of them are neurons, and here's where much of our learning takes place. When a potential learning experience occurs (such as reading this sentence), some neurons send out spikes of electrical activity. This activity causes nearby neurons to do the same. When neurons fire together, they form what is called a "neural network." I like to picture a bunch of neurons joining hands in my brain, jumping up and down, and having a learning party. If this party happens only once, learning is weak (as when you see your instructor solve a math problem one day and can't recall how to do it the next). However, if you cause the same collection of neurons to fire repeatedly (as when you solve 10 similar math problems yourself), the result is likely a long-term memory. According to David Sousa, author of *How the Brain Learns,* "Eventually, repeated firing of the pattern binds the neurons together so that if one fires, they all fire, ultimately forming a new memory trace."

The human brain has the largest area of uncommitted cortex (no particular required function) of any species on earth. This gives humans extraordinary flexibility and capacity for learning.

Eric Jensen

Neurons before learning.

Neurons after learning.

In other words, if you want learning to stick, you need to create strong neural networks. In this way, learning literally changes the structure of your brain. Through autopsies, neuroscientist Robert Jacobs and his colleagues determined that graduate students actually had 40 percent more neural connections than those of high school dropouts. Jacobs's research joins many other brain studies to reveal an important fact: **To excel as a learner, you need to create as many neural connections in your brain as possible.**

THREE PRINCIPLES OF DEEP AND LASTING LEARNING

With this brief introduction to what goes on in our brains, let's explore how highly effective learners maximize their learning. Whether they know it or not, they have figured out how to create many strong neural connections in their brains. And you can, too.

How? The short answer is: **Become an active learner**. Learning isn't a spectator sport. You don't create deep and lasting learning by passively listening to a lecture, casually skimming a textbook, or having a tutor solve math problems for you. In order to create strong neural networks, you've got to participate actively in the learning process.

Now, here's the longer answer. Good learners, consciously or unconsciously, implement three principles for creating deep and lasting learning:

In a time of drastic change, it is the learners who inherit the future.

Eric Hoffer

1. **PRIOR LEARNING.** Brain research reveals that when you connect what you are learning now to previously stored information (i.e., already-formed neural networks), you learn the new information or skill faster and more deeply. For example, the first word-processing program I learned was Word Perfect. It took me a long time to learn because I had no prior knowledge about word processing; thus, my brain contained few, if any, neural networks relevant to what I was learning. First, I needed to learn what word processing can do (such as delete whole paragraphs) and then I needed to learn how to perform that function with Word Perfect. Later, when I was learning another word-processing program, Microsoft Word, I already knew what word processing can do, so I was able to learn this new program in a fraction of the time. Put another way, I already had neural networks in my brain related to word processing, and learning Microsoft Word got those neurons partying.

> When information goes "in one ear and out the other," it's often because it doesn't have anything to stick to.
>
> *Joshua Foer*

The contribution of past learning to new learning helps explain why some learners have difficulty in college with academic skills such as math, reading, and writing. If their earlier learning was shaky, they're going to have difficulty with new learning. They don't have strong neural networks on which to attach the new learning. It's like trying to construct a house on a weak foundation. In such a situation, the best option is to go back and strengthen the foundation, which is exactly the purpose of developmental (basic skills) courses. However, there's no point trying to learn these foundational skills the same way you learned them before. After all, how you learned them before didn't make the information or skills stick. So this time you'll need to employ different, more effective learning strategies, ones that will create the needed neural networks. If that's your situation, this time you'll have the advantage of employing the more effective strategies described here in *On Course*. And if you're a learner with a strong foundation, you'll find strategies here that will increase your effectiveness as a learner even more.

2. **QUALITY OF PROCESSING.** How you exercise affects your physical strength. Likewise, how you study affects the strength of your neural networks and therefore the quality of your learning. Some information (such as math formulas or anatomy terms) must be recalled exactly as presented. For such learning tasks, effective memorization strategies are the types of processing that work best. However, much of what you'll be asked to learn in college is too complex for mere memorization (though many struggling students try). For mastering complex information and skills, you'll want to use what learning experts call **deep processing.** These are the very strategies that successful learners use to maximize their learning and make it stick. You'll learn both effective memorization and deep-processing strategies in the "Wise Choices in College" sections in later chapters.

> Mathematics teachers . . . see students using a certain formula to solve problems correctly one day, but they cannot remember how to do it the next day. If the process was not stored, the information is treated as brand new again!
>
> *David A. Sousa*

Don't use just one deep-processing strategy, however. Successful athletes know the value of cross training, so they use a variety of training strategies. Similarly, successful learners know the value of employing *varied* deep-processing strategies. That's because the more ways you deep-process new learning, the stronger your neural networks become.

When you actively study any information or skill using *numerous and varied deep-processing strategies,* you create and strengthen related neural networks and your learning soars.

3. **QUANTITY OF PROCESSING.** The quality of your learning is significantly affected by how often and how long you engage in varied deep processing. This factor is often called "time on task," and the most effective approach is *distributed practice*. The human brain learns best when learning efforts are distributed over time. No successful athlete waits until the night before a competition to begin training. Why, then, do struggling students think they can start studying the night before a test? An all-night cram session may make a deposit in their short-term memories, perhaps even allowing them to pass a test the next day. However, even students who got good grades have experienced the ineffectiveness of cramming when they encounter "summer amnesia"—the inability to remember in fall-term classes what they learned during the previous school year. That's the result of not creating strong neural networks that make learning last. To create strong neural networks, you need to process the target information or skill with numerous and varied deep-processing strategies and do it *frequently.*

In addition to how frequently you use deep-processing strategies, also important is the *amount of time* you spend learning. Obviously, deep processing for 60 minutes generates more learning than deep processing for 5 minutes. So, highly effective learners put in **sufficient time on task.** The traditional guideline for a week's studying is two hours for each hour of class time. Thus, if you have 15 hours of classes per week, the estimate for your "sufficient time on task" is about 30 hours per week. Many struggling students neither study very often nor very long. However, some fool themselves by putting in "sufficient time," but spend little of it engaged in effective learning activities. They skim complex information in their textbooks. They attempt to memorize information they don't understand. Their minds wander to a conversation they had at lunch. They rummage through their book bags and dresser drawers and closets looking

Almost everyone has had occasion to look back upon his school days and wonder what has become of the knowledge he was supposed to have amassed during his days of schooling.

John Dewey

Three Principles of Deep and Lasting Learning

1. **Prior Learning.** Relate new information to previously learned information.
2. **Quality of Processing.** Use numerous and varied deep-processing strategies.
3. **Quantity of Processing.** Use frequent practice sessions of sufficient length distributed over time.

for their class notes. They play a video game or two. They phone a class-mate. They send a couple of text messages, and the next thing they know, it's time to go to bed. When they fail the test the next day, they complain, "But I studied *so long*!"

Some students have a chemical imbalance that prevents them from focusing for long periods of time and their learning suffers. If you think this may be true for you, make an appointment with your college's disability counselor to get help. But the reason most students struggle with learning is fully within their control. You don't need a genius IQ to be a good learner and do well in college. What you do need is a learning system that employs what we now know about how the human brain learns. Billions of neurons between your ears are ready to party. Let the festival of learning begin!

THE CORE LEARNING SYSTEM

Four general strategies are common to good learners. To remember these strate-gies, simply think of the word CORE (see Figure 1.2). CORE stands for **Collect, Organize, Rehearse,** and **Evaluate.** The CORE learning system is effective be-cause it automatically guides you to implement all three of the active learning prin-ciples discussed earlier. Thus, by applying what we know about how the human brain learns, the CORE learning system helps you create deep and lasting learning. Here's how it works:

Collect: In every waking moment, we're constantly collecting perceptions through our five senses. Without conscious effort, the brain takes in a mul-titude of sights, sounds, smells, tastes, and physical sensations. Most percep-tions disappear within moments. Some, such as our first language, stick for a lifetime. Thus, much of what we learn in life we do without intention. In col-lege, however, learning needs to be more conscious. That's because instructors expect you to learn specific information and skills. Then, of course, they want you to demonstrate that knowledge on quizzes, tests, exams, term papers, and other forms of evaluation. In college, two of the most important ways you'll

collect information and skills are through reading textbooks and attending classes. In Chapters 2 and 3, you'll learn proven strategies for maximizing the amount of high-quality information you collect in these ways.

Organize: Once we collect information, we need to make sense of it. When learning in everyday life, we tend to organize collected information in uncon-scious ways. We don't even realize that we're doing it. However, in a college course, you need to organize information systematically so it makes sense to you. In fact, making meaning from collected information is one of the most important outcomes of studying.

> Good learners, like everyone else, are living, squirming, questioning, perceiving, fearing, loving, and languaging nervous systems, but they are good learners precisely because they believe and do certain things that less effective learners do not believe and do. And therein lies the key.
>
> *Neil Postman*
> *& Charles Weingartner*

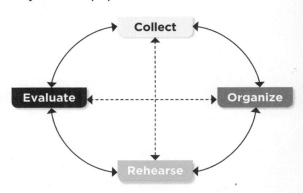

Figure 1.2 The CORE Learning System

In Chapters 4, 5, and 6, you'll learn proven strategies for organizing information into study materials that will lead to deep learning.

Rehearse: Once we collect and organize our target knowledge, we need to remember it for future use. Rehearsing (also called "practicing") strengthens neural networks and makes learning stick. When you solve 10 challenging math problems, you're rehearsing. Over time, the process of solving becomes easier and more natural. In Chapters 4, 5, and 6, you'll learn proven ways to rehearse information and skills so you can remember them for future use, whether on a test, in your career, or in your personal life.

Evaluate: Life is great at giving us informal feedback about the quality of our learning. Maybe you tell a joke and forget the punch line. You know immediately you have more learning to do. Higher education, however, provides us with more formal feedback. Yup, those pesky tests, term papers, quizzes, lab reports, essays, classroom questions, and final exams. Evaluation, both informal and formal, is an essential component of all learning because without feedback, we can never be sure if our learning is accurate or complete. Chapters 6 and 7 provide you with proven ways to assess what you have learned in your courses. Then you'll discover how to demonstrate that learning to instructors so you can maximize your grades in college.

Learning doesn't occur in a tidy, step-by-step fashion. At any moment while learning, you may need to jump to a different component in the CORE system. For example, while **Rehearsing,** you might realize that some information doesn't make sense to you, so you **Organize** it in a different way. At times you may engage two or more components simultaneously. For instance, when **Rehearsing** study materials, you're probably **Evaluating** your mastery of that knowledge at the same time. Thus, you can expect to use the four components of the CORE Learning System in any order and in any combination.

Although the CORE system is an effective blueprint for creating deep and lasting learning, not all learners prefer to **Collect, Organize, Rehearse,** and **Evaluate** in the same way. That's why you'll encounter many specific strategies in *On Course.* Your task is to experiment with and find the ones that work best for you. What you'll ultimately construct is a personalized learning system, one you can use for the rest of your life. In this way, you can be confident of your ability to learn anything you need to know on the path to achieving your goals and dreams in college and beyond.

When something is meaningful it is organized; when it is organized, it is simplified in the mind.

Robert Ornstein

Education which strengthens a person's ability to gather, organize and evaluate information, contributes to more accurate adult judgments.

Muriel James & Dorothy Joneward

Journal Entry 3

In this activity, you'll explore how you learned something (anything) using the approach of an active learner. Then you'll plan how you could use this same approach to improve your learning outcomes and experiences in college.

1. **Identify one thing you have learned simply because you enjoyed learning it.** It can be something you learned in school or anywhere else. If nothing comes immediately to mind, use the following questions to jog your memory. What do you know more about than most people (e.g., World War II or rare coins)? What are you good at (e.g., solving math problems or playing video games)? What skills have you mastered (e.g., using Excel spreadsheets or cooking)? What are your hobbies (e.g., vegetable gardening or reading mystery novels)? What have you spent a lot of time doing? (e.g., exercising or traveling)? To complete this step, simply write the completion of this sentence in your journal: "One thing I enjoyed learning is _____."

2. **With a focus on the information or skill identified in Step 1, write answers to each of the following questions. Use a separate sentence or paragraph for each answer.**

A. How did you gather the information or skills you needed to learn this? (Collect)

B. What did you do to learn the information or skills needed to learn this? (Organize)

C. What else did you do to learn this? (Rehearse—Variety)

D. How often did you engage in learning this? (Rehearse—Frequency)

E. When you engaged in learning this, how long did you usually spend? (Rehearse—Duration)

F. What feedback did you use to determine how well you had learned this? (Evaluate)

G. How did you feel when you engaged in learning this? (Motivating Experiences)

H. What were the rewards for learning this? (Motivating Outcomes)

3. **Write about the key points you have learned or relearned about learning and how you will use this knowledge to maximize your learning in college.** For example, your journal entry might begin, "By reading and writing about learning, I have learned/relearned that . . . . I will use this knowledge to maximize my learning in college by . . . ." Be specific!

Be sure to use the five suggestions printed on the inside back cover of *On Course. Especially remember to dive deep!* Diving deep changes the neurons in your brain and leads to deep and lasting learning. As you may have already realized, writing an in-depth journal entry is a powerful way to deep-process your experiences!

> I don't love studying. I hate studying. I like learning. Learning is beautiful.
>
> *Natalie Portman*

> Learning . . . should be a joy and full of excitement. It is life's greatest adventure; it is an illustrated excursion into the minds of noble and learned men, not a conducted tour through a jail.
>
> *Taylor Caldwell*

One Student's Story

KASE CORMIER
Asheville-Buncombe Technical Community College,
North Carolina

At the beginning of my first semester in college, I was overwhelmed. I had been out of school for more than 10 years and wasn't sure how to make the adjustment to being back in school after all that time. In previous attempts at school I had felt dumb; I had an awful memory and a learning disability that made writing and spelling difficult. While looking over the syllabi for my five classes, I had no idea how I was going to fit all that knowledge into my brain. The information for Anatomy and Physiology was enough by itself; adding in essays, computer projects, and reading assignments from other classes made my head spin. On top of all that, I was required to take a study skills class. A friend who had taken the class before told me it was worth it. Skeptical, I responded, "Are you kidding me? There is no way I'll get anything out of that class, and I have no more time."

The week before classes began, I decided to get a head start on the dizzying amount of reading I had to do. I picked up the *On Course* textbook and opened to Chapter 1. I skimmed the pages lazily until I got to the section on "Becoming an Active Learner." The information on creating "neural networks" piqued my interest, and I read about the three principles of deep learning:

connect new information to things you already know, use a lot of different study techniques, and study often. Although it was interesting at the time, I had too much to do to let it sink in; yet as the semester progressed, those three principles began popping into my head. I could practically feel my neurons firing off faster and faster as I learned new material, trying to find ways to process and retain everything I was being taught. Every class moved quickly, and I found that I only had a short amount of time to learn something. I kept applying those techniques, and as long as I connected new information back to what I already knew, found new and creative ways to learn it, and repeated those activities often, I could fit so much more information into my head. Better than simply cramming for a test, those principles enabled me to do more than just learn new information. They helped me retain it as well.

These three learning principles were extremely important for Anatomy and Physiology because of how much information we were responsible for. Cramming for the next test wouldn't work; every section was laying groundwork for the future, and I needed to retain that information. To create varied learning experiences, I tried out several

different study groups, each with a different style of learning, until I finally found a group that I connected with; afterward, I supplemented my primary study group with other groups to have some variety. I worked hard with each group, even making up silly games to explore different ways of learning the material. One game was "flashcard races." We put the names of the cranial nerves on flashcards, shuffled them, and then raced to see who could put them in order first. The more different ways I studied the information, the stronger my neural connections became. I took every opportunity to study in open lab, and in class, I asked lots of questions. My classmates joked with me, saying that I asked "Why?" too much, but I explained that it helped me relate the information to things I already knew. After our final lecture exam (which happened to be on neurons), my study buddies all gave me a hug and thanked me for improving the study sessions with my silly games and constant questioning. We all got A's!

The *On Course* principles may seem worthless at first, but don't be fooled. They stay with you and change the way you learn. I am grateful that I took the initiative to read that first chapter before my classes started. In high school I was a C student, but this semester I earned a 4.0! Connecting information to what I already knew, using a variety of study techniques, and studying often definitely helped make my first semester back in college a success.

Photo: Courtesy of Kase Cormier

On Course Principles

AT WORK

I think we have to appreciate that we're alive for only a limited period of time, and we'll spend most of our lives working.

Victor Kiam,
Chairman,
Remington Products

Applying the strategies you're going to learn in *On Course* will not only improve your results in college, it will also boost your success at work. You're about to explore dozens of proven strategies that will help you achieve your goals both in college and in your career.

This is no small matter. Career success (or lack of it) affects nearly every part of your life: family, income, self-esteem, people with whom you associate, where you live, your level of happiness, what you learn, your energy level, your health, and maybe even the length of your life.

Some students think, "All I need for success at work is the special knowledge of my chosen career." All that nurses need, they believe, are good nursing skills. All that accountants need are good accounting skills. All that lawyers need are good legal skills. These skills are called hard skills, the knowledge needed to perform a particular job. Hard skills include knowing where to insert the needle for an intravenous feeding drip, how to write an effective business plan, and what the current inheritance laws are. These are the skills you'll be taught in courses in your major field of study. They are essential to qualify for a job. Without them you won't even get an interview.

But, most people who've been in the work world a while will tell you this: Hard skills are essential to get a job but they are often insufficient to keep it or advance. That's because nearly all employees have the hard skills necessary to do the job for which they're hired. True, some may perform these skills a little better or a little worse than others, but one estimate suggests that only 15 percent of workers lose their jobs because they can't do the work. That's why career success is often determined by soft skills, the same strategies you'll be learning in this book. As one career specialist put it, "Having hard skills gets you hired; lacking soft skills gets you fired."

A U.S. government report confirms that soft skills are essential to job success. The Secretary of Labor asked a blue-ribbon panel of employers to identify what it takes to be successful in the modern employment world. This panel published a report in 1992 called the Secretary's Commission on Achieving Necessary Skills (SCANS). The report presents a set of foundation skills and workplace competencies that employers consider essential for work-world success, and the report's timeless recommendations continue to be a valuable source of information for employers and employees alike. No one familiar with today's work world will find many surprises in the report, especially in the foundation skills. The report calls for employees to develop the same soft skills that employers

On Course Principles **AT WORK**   *continued*

include in job descriptions, look for in reference letters, probe for in job interviews, and assess in evaluations of their workforce.

The SCANS report identifies the following soft skills as necessary for work and career success: taking responsibility, making effective decisions, setting goals, managing time, prioritizing tasks, persevering, giving strong efforts, working well in teams, communicating effectively, having empathy, knowing how to learn, exhibiting self-control, and believing in one's own self-worth. The Conference Board of Canada published a similar report called the *Employability Skills Profile: The Critical Skills Required of the Canadian Work Force*. Both reports identify these necessary soft skills but don't suggest a method for developing them. *On Course* will show you how.

Creators Wanted!

Candidates must demonstrate mastery of both the hard and soft skills necessary for career success.

Learning these soft skills will help you succeed in your first career after college. And, because soft skills are portable (unlike many hard skills), you can take them with you in the likely event that you later change careers. Most career specialists say the average worker today can expect to change careers at least once during his or her lifetime. In fact, some 25 percent of workers in the United States today are in occupations that did not even exist a few decades ago. If a physical therapist decides to change careers and work for an Internet company, he needs to master a whole new set of hard skills. But the soft skills he's mastered are the same ones that will help him shine in his new career.

So, as you're learning these soft skills, keep asking yourself, "How can I use these skills to stay on course to achieving my greatest potential at work as well as in college?" Be assured that what you're about to explore can make all the difference between success and failure in your career.

► BELIEVING IN YOURSELF

Develop Self-Acceptance

Focus Questions   Why is high self-esteem so important to success? What can you do to raise your self-esteem?

Roland was in his 40's when he enrolled in my English 101 class. He made insightful contributions to class discussions, so I was perplexed when the first two writing assignments passed without an essay from Roland. Both times, he apologized profusely, promising to complete them soon. He didn't want to make excuses, he said, but he was stretched to his limit: He worked at night, and during the day he took care of his two young sons while his wife worked. "Don't worry, though," he assured me, "I'll have an essay to you by Monday. I'm going to be the first person in my family to get a college degree. Nothing's going to stop me."

But Monday came, and Roland was absent. On a hunch, I looked up his academic record and found that he had taken English 101 twice before. I contacted his previous instructors. Both of them said that Roland had made many promises but had never turned in an assignment.

I called Roland, and we made an appointment to talk. He didn't show up. During the next class, I invited Roland into the hall while the class was working on a writing assignment.

"Sorry I missed our conference," Roland said. "I meant to call, but things have been piling up."

"Roland, I talked to your other instructors, and I know you never wrote anything for them. I'd love to help you, but you need to take an action. You need to write an essay." Roland nodded silently. "I believe you can do it. But I don't know if *you* believe you can do it. It's decision time. What do you say?"

"I'll have an essay to you by Friday."

I looked him in the eye.

"Promise," he said.

I knew that what Roland actually did, not what he promised, would reveal his deepest core beliefs about himself.

> The foundation of anyone's ability to cope successfully is high self-esteem. If you don't already have it, you can always develop it.
>
> *Virginia Satir*

> Self-esteem is the reputation we have with ourselves.
>
> *Nathaniel Branden*

SELF-ESTEEM AND CORE BELIEFS

So it is with us all. Our core beliefs—true or false, real or imagined—form the inner compass that guides our choices.

At the heart of our core beliefs is the statement *I AM ___*. How we complete that sentence in the quiet of our souls has a profound effect on the quality of our lives.

High self-esteem is the fuel that can propel us into the cycle of success. Do we approve of ourselves as we are, accepting our personal weaknesses along with our strengths? Do we believe ourselves capable, admirable, lovable, and fully worthy of the best life has to offer? If so, our beliefs will make it possible for us to choose wisely and stay on course to a rich, full life.

For example, imagine two students: one with high self-esteem, the other with low self-esteem. Picture them just after they get very disappointing test scores. What do they do next? The student with low self-esteem will likely choose options that protect his fragile self-image, options such as dropping the course rather than chancing failure. The student with high self-esteem, on the other hand, will likely choose options that move her toward success, options such as persisting in the course and getting additional help to be successful. Two students, same situation. One focuses on weaknesses. One focuses on strengths. The result: two different choices and two very different outcomes.

The good news is that self-esteem is learned, so anyone can learn to raise his or her self-esteem. Much of this book is about how you can do just that.

> Self-esteem is more than merely recognizing one's positive qualities. It is an attitude of acceptance and non-judgment toward self and others.
>
> *Matthew McKay & Patrick Fanning*

KNOW AND ACCEPT YOURSELF

People with high self-esteem know that no one is perfect, and they accept themselves with both their strengths and weaknesses. To paraphrase philosopher Reinhold Niebuhr, successful people accept the things they cannot change, have the courage to change the things they can change, and possess the wisdom to know the difference.

Successful people have the courage to take an honest self-inventory, as you began doing in Journal Entry 1. They acknowledge their strengths without false humility, and they admit their weaknesses without stubborn denial. They tell the truth about themselves and take action to improve what they can.

Fortunately for Roland, he decided to do just that. On the Friday after our talk, he turned in his English 101 essay. His writing showed great promise, and I told him so. I also told him I appreciated that he had let go of the excuse that he was too busy to do his assignments. From then on, Roland handed in his essays on time. He met with me in conferences. He visited the writing lab, and he did grammar exercises to improve his editing skills. He easily passed the course.

A few years later, Roland called me. He had transferred to a four-year university and was graduating with a 3.8 average. He was continuing on to

AS SMART AS HE WAS, ALBERT EINSTEIN COULD NOT FIGURE OUT HOW TO HANDLE THOSE TRICKY BOUNCES AT THIRD BASE.

graduate school to study urban planning. What he most wanted me to know was that one of his instructors had asked permission to use one of his essays as a model of excellent writing. "You know," Roland said, "I'd still be avoiding writing if I hadn't accepted two things about myself: I was a little bit lazy and I was a whole lot scared. Once I admitted those things about myself, I started changing."

Each of us has a unique combination of strengths and weaknesses. When struggling people become aware of a weakness, they typically blame the problem on others or they beat themselves up for not being perfect. Successful people, however, usually make a different choice: They acknowledge the weakness, accept it without self-judgment, and, when possible, take action to create positive changes. As always, the choices we make determine both where we are headed and the quality of the journey. Developing self-acceptance helps us to make those choices wisely.

> We cannot change anything unless we accept it.
>
> *Carl Jung*

 Journal Entry 4

In this activity, you will explore your strengths and weaknesses and the reputation you have with yourself. This exploration of your self-esteem will allow you to begin revising any limiting beliefs you may hold about yourself. By doing so, you will take a major step toward your success.

1. **In your journal, write a list of 10 or more of your personal strengths.** For example, mentally: *I'm good at math;* physically: *I'm very athletic;* emotionally: *I seldom let anger control me;* socially: *I'm a good friend;* and others: *I am almost always on time.*

2. **Write a list of 10 or more of your personal weaknesses.** For example, mentally: *I'm a slow reader;* physically: *I am out of shape;* emotionally: *I'm easily hurt by criticism;* socially: *I don't listen very well;* and others: *I'm a terrible procrastinator.*

3. **Using the information in Steps 1 and 2 and score #8 on your self-assessment, write about the present state of your self-esteem.** On a scale of 1 to 10 (with 10 high), how strong is your self-esteem? How do you think it got to be that way? How would you like it to be? What changes could you make to achieve your ideal self-esteem?

To create an outstanding journal, remember to use the five suggestions printed on the inside back cover of *On Course*. Especially remember to dive deep!

> Be what you is, not what you ain't, 'cause if you ain't what you is, you is what you ain't.
>
> *Luther D. Price*

Wise Choices in College

COLLEGE CUSTOMS

Keep reminding yourself that entering college is like crossing the border into another country. Each has new customs to learn. If you learn and heed the following college customs, your stay in higher education will be not only more successful but more enjoyable as well.

1. Read your college catalogue. Catalogues are usually available in the registrar's or counseling office, and many colleges post a copy of the catalogue on their website. This resource contains most of the factual information you'll need to plot a great journey through higher education. It explains how your college applies many of the customs discussed in this section. Keep a college catalogue on hand and refer to it often. It's an essential guidebook for your journey through higher education.

2. See your advisor. Colleges provide an advisor who can help you make wise choices. Sometimes this person is a counselor, sometimes an instructor. Find out who your advisor is, make an appointment, and get advice on what courses to take and how to create your best schedule. Ask your advisor to help you create a long-term academic plan that charts your path all the way to graduation. Students who avoid advisors often enroll in unnecessary courses or miss taking courses that are required for graduation. Your tuition has paid for a guide through college; use this valuable resource wisely.

3. Understand prerequisites. A "prerequisite" is a course that must be completed before you can take another course. For example, colleges require the completion of calculus before enrollment in more advanced mathematics courses. Before you register, confirm with your advisor that you have met all of the prerequisites. Otherwise you may find

yourself registered for a course you aren't prepared to pass. Prerequisites usually appear within each course description in your college catalogue.

4. Complete your general education requirements. Most colleges require students to complete a minimum number of general education credits. Typically, you need to take one or more courses from broad fields of study such as communication, natural science and technology, math, languages, humanities, and social and behavioral science. For example, to fulfill your requirement in science, you might need to complete 4 credits by taking any one of the following courses: biology, chemistry, astronomy, geology, or physics. Find a list of these required general education courses in your college catalogue, and check off each requirement as you complete it. Regardless of how many credits you earn, you can't graduate until you've completed the general education requirements. Depending on your college, general education requirements may be called core requirements, core curriculum, or general curriculum.

5. Choose a major wisely. You'll usually choose a major area of study in your first or second year. Examples of majors include nursing, early childhood education, biology, English, mechanical engineering, and art. You'll take the greatest number of courses in your major, supplemented by your general education courses and electives. Even if you've already picked a major, visit the career counseling center to see if other majors might interest you even more or be a better stepping stone to your chosen career. Your career counseling center can provide you with assessments to help you find a career that fits your interests and personality, and you can complete career inventories prior to choosing a major to help you narrow the best major for your intended career. For example, majoring in English is great preparation for a law degree. All majors and their required courses are available in your college catalogue. Until you've entered a major, you're wise to concentrate on completing your general education requirements.

6. Take a realistic course load. I once taught a student who worked full-time, was married with three small children, and had signed up for six courses in her first semester. After five weeks, she was exhausted and withdrew from college. There are only 168 hours in a week. Be realistic about the number of courses you can handle given your other responsibilities. Students often register for too many credits because of their mistaken belief that this choice will get them to graduation more quickly. Too often the actual result is dropped and failed classes, pushing graduation further into the future.

7. Attend the first day of class (on time). Of course it's wise to attend *every* day on time, but whatever you do, be present on the first day! On this day instructors usually provide the class assignments and rules for the entire semester. If you're absent, you may miss something that will come back to haunt you later. For example, find out each instructor's attendance policy and be sure you adhere to it. In some classes, it is possible to pass all tests and assignments and still fail a course because you didn't fulfill the attendance policy.

8. Sit in each classroom where you can focus on learning. Experiment. Try different places in the room. Many students focus best when sitting up front. Others prefer sitting on the side about halfway back, where they can see all of their classmates and the instructor during a discussion. Most students find that sitting in the back (especially in a large class) is the least desirable. Once you identify the place that best supports your learning, sit there permanently . . . unless you find that changing seats every day helps you learn better.

9. Study the syllabus. In the first class, instructors usually provide a syllabus (sometimes called a "first-day handout"). The syllabus is the single

most important handout you will receive all semester. Typically, it contains the course objectives, the required books and supplies, all assignments and due dates, and the method for determining grades. This handout also presents any course rules you need to know. Essentially, the course syllabus is a contract between you and your instructor, who will assume that you've read and understood this contract; be sure to ask questions about any part you don't understand.

10. Buy required course books and supplies as soon as possible. College instructors cover a lot of ground quickly. If you don't have your study materials from the beginning of the course, you may fall too far behind to catch up. To get a head start on their classes, some wise students go to their college bookstore or an online bookstore weeks before the semester or quarter begins and purchase course materials. If money is tight, check with the financial aid office to see if your college provides temporary book loans. Or, as a last resort, ask your instructors if they will put copies of the course texts on reserve at your college library. As you will see later, having your own books for each course makes it much easier to gather and organize the knowledge you will need to learn.

11. Introduce yourself to one or more classmates and exchange phone numbers and email addresses. After an absence, contact a classmate to learn what you missed. Few experiences in college are worse than returning to class and facing a test that was announced in your absence.

12. Inform your instructor before a planned absence. Think of your class as your job and your instructor as your employer. Professional courtesy dictates notifying your employer of an absence you know about in advance. The same is true with instructors. Usually a quick email will do, and most likely you'll find your instructor's email address in the course syllabus.

13. If you arrive late, slip in quietly. Don't make excuses. Just come in and sit down. If you want to explain your lateness, see the instructor after class.

14. Ask questions. If the question you don't ask shows up on a test, you're going to be upset with yourself. Your classmates are equally nervous about asking questions. Go ahead, raise your hand and ask one on the first day; after that, it'll be easier. Additionally, asking good questions demonstrates to your instructor that you have intellectual curiosity, which is a great reputation to have in higher education. Later, I'll show you how to arrive at each class with nifty questions to ask.

15. To hold an extended conversation with your instructors, make an appointment during their office hours. Most college instructors have regular office hours; these times are usually included in the course syllabus and may also be posted on the instructor's office door. You can make an appointment in person before or after class, or you can call the instructor's office. Be sure to show up on time (or call beforehand to reschedule). Arrive with a clear goal, such as clarifying a comment the instructor wrote on your English composition, or learning how to correct a math problem that you got wrong on the homework, or discussing how you could better prepare for your next test in history. You'll find most instructors very receptive to meeting you during their office hours. At a minimum, plan to make one appointment with all of your instructors each semester.

16. Get involved in campus life. Most colleges offer numerous activities that can broaden your education, add pleasure to your life, and introduce you to new friends. Consider participating in the drama club, school newspaper, intercultural counsel, student government, athletic teams, band or orchestra, literary magazine, yearbook committee, science club, or one of the many other organizations on your campus. There's probably a list of options in your college's catalog, student handbook or on its website. Such options are usually referred to as "extracurricular activities." "Extracurricular" simply means that the activities are not part of an academic class.

17. Know the importance of your grade point average (GPA). Your GPA is the average grade for all of the courses you have taken in college. At most colleges, GPAs range from 0.0 ("F") to 4.0 ("A"). Your GPA affects your future in many ways. At most colleges a minimum GPA (often 2.0, a "C") is required to graduate, regardless of how many credits you have accumulated. Students who fall below the minimum GPA are usually ineligible for financial aid and cannot play intercollegiate sports, or, in some cases, are in danger of academic dismissal, particularly for students who are already on academic probation. Academic honors (such as the dean's list) and some scholarships are based on your GPA. Finally, potential employers often note GPAs to determine if prospective employees have achieved success in college.

18. Know how to compute your grade point average (GPA). At most colleges, GPAs are printed on a student's transcript, which is a list of courses completed (with the grades earned). You can get a copy of your transcript from the registrar's office. Transcripts are usually free or available for a nominal charge. You can compute your own grade point average by using the formula in the following box. Or you can do it online at http://www.back2college.com/gpa.htm. Figuring your GPA could be tricky if you're taking one or more developmental courses. At many colleges, grades in developmental courses do not offer credits toward graduation, so they may not be used for calculating a GPA. For example, if you were taking three courses and two were developmental, your GPA would be determined by the grade you received in just the one non-developmental course. To check your school's policy about this issue, read your college catalog or ask a counselor or advisor.

Formula for Computing Your Grade Point Average (GPA)

$$\frac{(G1 \times C1) + (G2 \times C2) + (G3 \times C3) + (G4 \times C4) + \cdots (Gn \times Cn)}{\text{Total \# of Credits Attempted}}$$

In this formula, G = the grade in a course and C = number of credits for a course. For example, suppose you had the following grades:

"A" in Math 110 (4 Credits)   G1 ("A") = 4.0

"B" in English 101 (3 Credits)   G2 ("B") = 3.0

"C" in Sociology 101 (3 Credits)   G3 ("C") = 2.0

"D" in Music 104 (2 Credits)   G4 ("D") = 1.0

"F" in Physical Education 109 (1 Credit)   G5 ("F") = 0.0

Here's how to figure the GPA from the grades above:

$$\frac{(4.0 \times 4) + (3.0 \times 3) + (2.0 \times 3) + (1.0 \times 2) + (0.0 \times 1)}{4 + 3 + 3 + 2 + 1} = \frac{16 + 9 + 6 + 2 + 0}{13} = 2.54$$

19. If you stop attending a class, withdraw officially. Students are enrolled in a course until they're *officially* withdrawn. A student who stops attending is still on the class roster at semester's end when grades are assigned, and the instructor will very likely give the nonattending student an "F." That failing grade is now a permanent part of the student's record, lowering the GPA and discouraging potential employers. If you decide (for whatever reason) to stop attending a class, go directly to the registrar's office and follow the official procedures for withdrawing from a class. Make certain that you withdraw before your college's deadline. This date is often about halfway through a semester or quarter.

20. Talk to your instructor before withdrawing. If you're going to fail a course, withdraw to protect your GPA. But don't withdraw without speaking to your instructor first. Sometimes students think they are doing far worse than they really are. Discuss with your instructor what you need to do to pass the course and make a step-by-step plan. Be sure to discuss your plans with your advisor as well. He or she might have insights about what will be best for your general education or major requirements and when courses are available for you to retake. If you discover that failing is inevitable, withdraw officially.

21. Keep a file of important documents. Forms get lost in large organizations such as colleges. Save everything that may affect your future: course syllabi, completed tests and assignments, approved registration forms, scholarship applications, transcripts, and paid bills. If you're exempted from a college requirement or course prerequisite, get it in writing and add the document to your files.

22. Finally, some college customs dictate what you should *not* do. Avoiding the following behaviors shows respect for your classmates and instructors.

- Don't pack up your books or put on your coat until the class is over.

- After an absence, don't ask your instructor, "Did I miss anything?" (Of course you did.)

- Don't wear headphones during class.

- Don't let a cell phone disturb the class.

- Don't side-talk with a classmate while the instructor or another student is talking to the class.

- Don't read or send text messages during class.

- Don't make distracting noises in class (e.g., clicking pen, popping gum, drumming fingers, and so on).

COLLEGE CUSTOMS EXERCISES

1. Find someone who has been at your college much longer than you have. Ask him or her, "What is one thing you learned about college customs that you wish you had known on your first day? How has knowing this college custom helped you?" Be prepared to report your findings.

2. Figure out a student's GPA who got the following grades:

"C" in Math 110 (4 Credits)

"D" in English 101 (3 Credits)

"C" in Sociology 101 (3 Credits)

"B" in Music 104 (2 Credits)

"A" in Physical Education 109 (1 Credit)

You may assume that all of these courses count toward the student's GPA.

3. For class discussion:

- Which college custom surprises you most?

- Which custom do you think will be most challenging for you?

- Which custom would you like to hear more about?

Accepting Personal Responsibility

2

I accept responsibility for creating my life as I want it.

SUCCESSFUL STUDENTS...	STRUGGLING STUDENTS...
adopt a Creator mindset, believing that their choices create the outcomes and experiences of their lives.	**accept a Victim mindset**, believing that external forces determine the outcomes and experiences of their lives.
master Creator language, accepting personal responsibility for their results.	**use Victim language**, rejecting personal responsibility by blaming, complaining, and excusing.
make wise decisions, consciously designing the future they want.	**make decisions carelessly**, letting the future happen by chance rather than by choice.

Case Study in Critical Thinking

THE LATE PAPER

Professor Freud announced in her syllabus for Psychology 101 that final term papers had to be in her hands by noon on December 18. No student, she emphasized, would pass the course without a completed term paper turned in on time. As the semester drew to a close, **Kim** had an "A" average in Professor Freud's psychology class, and she began researching her term paper with excitement.

Arnold, Kim's husband, felt threatened that he had only a high school diploma while his wife was getting close to her college degree. Arnold worked the evening shift at a bakery, and his coworker **Philip** began teasing that Kim would soon dump Arnold for a college guy. That's when Arnold started accusing Kim of having an affair and demanding she drop out of college. She told Arnold he was being ridiculous. In fact, she said, a young man in her history class had asked her out, but she had refused. Instead of feeling better, Arnold became even more angry. With Philip continuing to provoke him, Arnold became sure Kim was having an affair, and he began telling her every day that she was stupid and would never get a degree.

Despite the tension at home, Kim finished her psychology term paper the day before it was due. Since Arnold had hidden the car keys and Professor Freud refused to accept assignments sent by email, Kim decided to take the bus to the college and turn in her psychology paper a day early. While she was waiting for the bus, **Cindy**, one of Kim's psychology classmates, drove up and invited Kim to join her and some other students for an end-of-semester celebration. Kim told Cindy she was on her way to turn in her term paper, and Cindy promised she'd make sure Kim got it in on time. "I deserve some fun," Kim decided, and hopped into the car. The celebration went long into the night. Kim kept asking Cindy to take her home, but Cindy always replied, "Don't be such a bore. Have another drink." When Cindy finally took Kim home, it was 4:30 in the morning. She sighed with relief when she found that Arnold had already fallen asleep.

When Kim woke up, it was 11:30 a.m., just 30 minutes before her term paper was due. She could make it to the college in time by car, so she shook Arnold and begged him to drive her. He just snapped, "Oh sure, you stay out all night with your college friends. Then, I'm supposed to get up on my day off and drive you all over town. Forget it." "At least give me the keys," she said, but Arnold merely rolled over and went back to sleep. Panicked, Kim called Professor Freud's office and told **Mary**, the administrative assistant, that she was having car trouble. "Don't worry," Mary assured Kim, "I'm sure Professor Freud won't care if your paper's a little late. Just be sure to have it here before she leaves at 1:00." Relieved, Kim decided not to wake Arnold again; instead, she took the bus.

At 12:15, Kim walked into Professor Freud's office with her term paper. Professor Freud said, "Sorry, Kim, you're 15 minutes late." She refused to accept Kim's term paper and gave Kim an "F" for the course.

Listed below are the characters in this story. Rank them in order of their *responsibility for Kim's failing grade in Psychology 101*. Give a different score to each character. Be prepared to explain your choices.

| Most responsible | → 1 2 3 4 5 6 ← | Least responsible |

_6_ **Professor Freud,** the instructor — 6

_1_ **Kim,** the psychology student — 1

_2_ **Arnold,** Kim's husband — 2

_3_ **Philip,** Arnold's coworker — 3

_4_ **Cindy,** Kim's classmate — 4

_5_ **Mary,** the administrative assistant — 5

▶ **DIVING DEEPER** Is there someone not mentioned in the story who may also bear responsibility for Kim's failing grade?

Adopting a Creator Mindset

 Focus Questions   What is self-responsibility? Why is it the key to creating the life you want?

When psychologist Richard Logan studied people who survived ordeals such as being imprisoned in concentration camps or lost in the frozen Arctic, he found they shared a common belief. They all saw themselves as personally responsible for creating the outcomes and experiences of their lives.

Ironically, responsibility has gotten a bad reputation. Some see it as a heavy burden they have to lug through life. Quite the contrary, personal responsibility is the foundation for creating success. Personal *response-ability* is the ability to respond wisely at each fork in the road, your choices moving you ever closer to your desired outcomes and experiences. The opposite is waiting passively for your fate to be determined by luck or powerful others. Whether your challenge is surviving an Arctic blizzard or excelling in college, accepting personal responsibility empowers you to make the most out of any situation.

I first met Deborah when she was a student in my English 101 class. Deborah wanted to be a nurse, but before she could qualify for the nursing program, she had to pass English 101. She was taking the course for the fourth time.

"Your writing shows fine potential," I told Deborah after I had read her first essay. "You'll pass English 101 as soon as you eliminate your grammar problems."

"I know," she said. "That's what my other three instructors said."

"Well, let's make this your last semester in English 101, then. After each essay, make an appointment with me to go over your grammar problems."

"Okay."

"And go to the Writing Lab as often as possible. Start by studying verb tense. Let's eliminate one problem at a time."

"I'll go this afternoon!"

But Deborah never found time: *No, really. . . . I'll go to the lab just as soon as I. . . .*

Deborah scheduled two appointments with me during the semester and missed them both: *I'm so sorry. . . . I'll come to see you just as soon as I. . . .*

To pass English 101 at our college, students had to pass one of two essays written at the end of the semester in an exam setting. Each essay, identified by social security number only, was graded by two other instructors. At semester's end, Deborah once again failed English 101. "It isn't fair!" Deborah protested. "Those exam graders expect us to be professional writers. They're keeping me from becoming a nurse!"

I suggested another possibility: "What if *you* are the one keeping you from becoming a nurse?"

> The best years of your life are the ones in which you decide your problems are your own. You do not blame them on your mother, the ecology, or the president. You realize that you control your own destiny.
>
> *Albert Ellis*

> The more we practice the habit of acting from a position of responsibility, the more effective we become as human beings, and the more successful we become as managers of our lives.
>
> *Joyce Chapman*

Deborah didn't like that idea. She wanted to believe that her problem was "out there." Her only obstacle was *those* exam graders. All her disappointments were *their* fault. *They* weren't fair. The *test* wasn't fair. *Life* wasn't fair! In the face of this injustice, she was helpless.

I reminded Deborah that it was *she* who had not studied her grammar. It was *she* who had not come to conferences. It was *she* who had not accepted personal responsibility for creating her life the way she wanted it.

"Yes, but ...," she said.

VICTIM AND CREATOR MINDSETS

Deborah had a problem that was going to keep her from ever passing English 101. But the problem wasn't the exam graders. The problem was her mindset.

A mindset is a collection of beliefs and attitudes. Like a lens, it affects the way you see a situation and influences your resulting choices. A **Victim mindset** keeps people from seeing and acting on choices that could help them achieve the life they want. A **Creator mindset** causes people to see multiple options, choose wisely among them, and take effective actions to achieve the life they want.

When you accept personal responsibility, you believe that you create *everything* in your life. This idea doesn't sit well with some people. "Accidents and natural disasters happen," they say. "There are muggings, murders, and wars. People are marginalized, oppressed, and brutalized simply because they are different. Blaming the victims is unfair. To say these people created the terrible things that happened to them is outrageous."

These observations are, as far as they go, true. At times, we *are* all affected by forces beyond our control. If a hurricane destroys my house, I am a victim (with a small "v"). In this case I am victimized by a force *outside* of me. But if I allow that event to ruin my life, I am a Victim (with a capital "V"). In this case I am victimized by a force *inside* of me. Whether I am victimized from the outside or from the inside is a crucial distinction. When I have a Victim mindset, I become my own oppressor. When I have a Creator mindset, I refuse to be oppressed.

Civil rights activist Rosa Parks is a perfect example of this distinction. On the evening of December 1, 1955, Parks was returning home on a Montgomery, Alabama, bus. She had just completed a long day as a seamstress in a department store. When the driver ordered her to give up her seat to a white passenger, Parks refused and was arrested. A few days later, outraged at her arrest, African Americans began a boycott of Montgomery buses that ended 381 days later when the law requiring segregation on public buses was finally lifted. As a result of choosing defiance, Parks has been called the "mother of the modern day civil rights movement." In an interview years later, Parks was asked why she choose to defy the bus driver's order to move. "People always say that I didn't give up my seat because I was tired," she said, "but that isn't true. I was not tired physically, or no more tired than I usually was at the end of a working day. I was not old, although some people have an image of me as being old then.

> Every time your back is against the wall, there is only one person that can help. And that's you. It has to come from inside.
>
> *Pat Riley, professional basketball coach*

> Which mistake do you think would be better to make . . . a) to believe you are in control of your life when you really might not be [or] b) to believe you are not in control of your life when you really might be?
>
> *Brooks Peterson*

I was forty-two. No, the only tired I was, was tired of giving in." In the face of an external oppression, Rosa Parks became an inspiring example of what one person with a Creator mindset can achieve.

So, is it outrageous to believe that you create everything in your life? Of course it is. But here's a better question: Would it improve your life to act *as if* you create all of the outcomes and experiences in your life? Answer "YES!" and watch a Creator mindset improve your life. After all, if you believe that someone or something out there causes all of your problems, then it's up to "them" to change. What a wait that can be! How long, for example, will Deborah have to wait for "those exam graders" to change?

The benefits to students of accepting personal responsibility have been demonstrated in various studies. Researchers Robert Vallerand and Robert Bissonette, for example, asked 1,000 first-year college students to complete a questionnaire about why they were attending school. They used the students' answers to assess whether the students were "Origin-like" or "Pawn-like." The researchers defined *Origin-like* students as seeing themselves as the originators of their own behaviors, in other words, Creators. By contrast, *Pawn-like* students see themselves as mere puppets controlled by others, in other words, Victims. A year later, the researchers returned to find out what had happened to the 1,000 students. They found that significantly more of the Creator-like students were still enrolled in college than the Victim-like students. If you want to succeed in college (and in life), having a Creator mindset gives you a big edge.

> I believe that we are solely responsible for our choices, and we have to accept the consequences of every deed, word, and thought throughout our lifetime.
>
> *Elisabeth Kübler-Ross*

RESPONSIBILITY AND CULTURE

In the 1950s, American psychologist Julian Rotter set out to study people's beliefs about who or what was responsible for the outcomes and experiences of their lives. He called it a study of "locus of control." *Locus* in Latin means "place" or "location." So, "locus of control" defines where people believe the power over their lives is located. Since Rotter's study, locus of control has been one of the

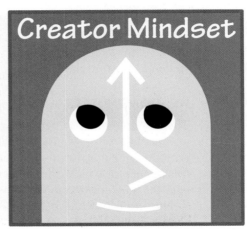

most examined aspects of human nature. What researchers discovered is that different cultures see locus of control differently.

People of some cultures believe they control their own destiny. Researchers call this mindset an *internal* locus of control. People with this mindset believe their outcomes and experiences depend on their own behaviors. This mindset is part of North American culture, where maturity is often defined as taking responsibility for one's own life. Not surprisingly, a strong part of the deep culture of North American higher education is a belief that college students are adults. As such, students are expected to make adult choices and be willing to accept responsibility for the consequences of those choices.

However, researchers found that people from some cultures assign responsibility for their fate to factors beyond their control. If you find that you are uncomfortable with the idea of personal responsibility, the cause may be found in your deep culture. For example, members of Latino culture, with roots in Catholicism, are likely to believe that a higher power is guiding their lives. The saying *Si Dios Quiere* ("If God Wants") reflects this belief. Muslims have a similar phrase in Arabic: *Insha'Allah* means "God willing" or "if God allows." Traditional Native Americans also value fate over self-determination. And members of working-class cultures—regardless of their ethnicity—may experience economic frustrations and doubt their ability to create the life of their dreams.

These differences in cultural mindsets highlight both the challenge and importance of deciding where our responsibilities begin and end. On the one hand, accepting too little responsibility is disempowering. We become little more than a feather floating on the breeze. On the other hand, accepting too much responsibility is disempowering as well. In some cases, we become like a pack mule crushed under the weight of problems not of our creation or in our control. The reality is that some choices truly are futile because of personal limitations or limitations imposed by fate or the will of others with more power. Like some kind of cosmic joke, one of our greatest responsibilities, then, is deciding what we are and are not responsible for, what we do and do not have control over. Worse, those decisions may change at the very next fork in the road. As a guideline to help you choose, in North American culture you'll usually be wise to adopt the philosophy of English poet William E. Henley, who in 1875 wrote: "I am the master of my fate; I am the captain of my soul." In fact, had Henley been a college student at the time, he might have added, "And I am the Creator of my GPA."

RESPONSIBILITY AND CHOICE

The key ingredient of personal responsibility is **choice.** Animals respond to a stimulus because of instinct or habit. For humans, however, there is a brief, critical moment of decision available between the stimulus and the response. In this moment, we make the choices—consciously or unconsciously—that influence the outcomes of our lives.

Numerous times each day, you come to a fork in the road and must make a choice. Even *not* making a choice is a choice. Some choices have a small impact: Shall I get my hair cut today or tomorrow? Some have a huge impact: Shall

---

Generally, European-American teachers believe in internal control and internal responsibility—that individuals are in control of their own fate, their actions affect outcomes, and success or failure in life is related to personal characteristics and abilities.

Jean Moule

By imposing too great a responsibility, or rather, all responsibility, on yourself, you crush yourself.

Franz Kafka

Figure 2.1 | Responsibility Model

> I do think that the greatest lesson of life is that you are responsible for your own life.
>
> *Oprah Winfrey*

I stay in college or drop out? The sum of the choices you make from this day forward will create the eventual outcome of your life. The Responsibility Model in Figure 2.1 shows what the moment of choice looks like.

In that brief moment between stimulus and response, we can choose a Victim mindset or a Creator mindset. When we respond as a Victim, we typically complain, blame, make excuses, and then repeat ineffective behaviors. When we respond as a Creator, we pause at each decision point and ask, "What are my options, and which option will best help me create my desired outcomes and experiences?"

The difference between responding to life as a Victim or Creator is how we choose to use our energy. When I'm blaming, complaining, and excusing, my efforts cause little or no improvement. Sure, it may feel good in that moment to claim that I'm a poor Victim and "they" are evil persecutors, but my good feelings are fleeting because afterward my problem still exists. By contrast, when I'm seeking solutions and taking actions, my efforts often (though not always) lead to improvements. At critical forks in the road, Victims waste their energy and remain stuck, whereas Creators use their energy for improving their lives. There is only one situation I can think of where blaming and complaining can be helpful. That's when you use them to generate energy that motivates you to take positive actions. My personal guideline: Up to 10 minutes for griping . . . then on to being a Creator and finding a solution.

> When you make the shift to being the predominant creative force in your life, you move from reacting and responding to the external circumstances of your life to creating directly the life you truly want.
>
> *Robert Fritz*

But, let's be honest. No one makes Creator choices all of the time. I've never met anyone who did, least of all me. Our inner lives feature a perpetual tug of war between the Creator part of us and the Victim part of us. My own experiences have taught me the following life lesson: The more choices I make as a Creator, the more I improve the quality of my life. That's why I urge you to join me in an effort to choose more often as a Creator. It won't be easy, but it's worth it. You may have to take my word for it right now, but if you experiment with the strategies in this book and continue using the ones that work for you, in a few months you'll see powerful proof in your own life of the value of making Creator choices.

"Oh, I get what you mean!" one of my students once exclaimed as we were exploring this complex issue of personal responsibility, "You're saying that living my life is like traveling in my car. If I want to get where I want to go, I better be the driver and not a passenger."

She was right. Personal responsibility is about taking hold of the steering wheel of our lives, about taking control of where we go and how we get there. Ultimately, each of us creates the quality of our life with the wisdom or folly of our choices.

I am a Shawnee. My forefathers were warriors. Their son is a warrior. . . . From my tribe I take nothing. I am the maker of my own fortune.

Tecumseh

Life is like a game of cards. The hand you are dealt is determinism; the way you play it is free will.

Jawaharlal Nehru

Journal Entry 5

In this activity, you will experiment with the Creator role. By choosing to take responsibility for your life, you will immediately gain an increased power to achieve your greatest potential.

1. **Write and complete each of the five sentence stems below.** For example, someone might complete the first sentence stem as follows: If I take personal responsibility for my education, *I will focus on really learning and not just getting good grades.*

1. If I take personal responsibility for my education . . .
2. If I take personal responsibility for my career . . .
3. If I take personal responsibility for my relationships . . .
4. If I take personal responsibility for my health . . .
5. If I take personal responsibility for all that happens to me . . .

2. **Make a choice: Write about one of the following:**

A. **What have you learned or relearned in this journal about personal responsibility, and how you will use this knowledge to improve your outcomes and experiences in college . . . and beyond?** If you are aware that accepting personal responsibility conflicts with your own cultural or personal beliefs, explore how you will deal with that difference. You might begin, *By reading and writing about personal responsibility, I have learned . . .*

B. **Share the details of a personal experience in which you did or did not take personal responsibility and explain the effects of this choice on your life.**

One Student's Story

BRIAN MOORE
Glendale Community College, Arizona

During my first semester in college, I was enrolled in a first-year English class. In high school I was usually able to pull off an A on my honors English papers without much work, and I thought I was a pretty good writer. So when I turned in my first college essay, I was expecting to get an A, or at worst a B. However, I was about to get a rude awakening. When we received our papers back a week later, I was shocked to see a C+ on my paper. I went to the instructor, and she said I just needed more practice and not to worry because I was in the class to learn. However, since I have high expectations for myself, those words weren't very comforting.

About that same time in my Strategies for College Success class, we were assigned to read a chapter in *On Course* about personal responsibility. The main idea is to adopt a "Creator" approach to problems, which I understood to mean basically seek solutions and not dwell on the negative. Then it clicked for me; I am responsible for my grades and I need to do whatever is necessary to get the ones I want. In high school, I could write one draft of an essay, turn it in, and I'd usually get an A, but that approach wasn't working in college. So, now I had to do something different. I started writing my papers before they were due and then meeting with my English teacher at least once a week to get her suggestions. Because I was a full-time student and also worked 17 to 20 hours a week in the cashier's office, sometimes I had to see her during times that were inconvenient. But I had to be flexible if I wanted her critique. During English class, we'd do peer editing, and I found that helpful, too. When I was in high school, I only spent about an hour or two writing an essay. Now I was spending at least three to five hours.

To my surprise, after some not-so-great increases in grades, I received what I had been waiting for: my first A on an essay. Although my final grade in English was a B, I learned a number of important lessons. It's really important to take your time with writing, to have your instructor or someone else read a rough draft and give you some suggestions, and then to write a final draft. I also learned that nobody can make the grade for you; you have to be responsible for yourself. I may not always get an A, but I learned to face a challenge, and no matter what grade I receive, knowing that I took responsibility as a "Creator" was the greatest lesson of all.

Mastering Creator Language

 Focus Question How can you create greater success by changing your vocabulary?

Have you ever noticed that there is almost always a conversation going on in your mind? Inner voices chatter away, offering commentary about you, other people, and the world. This self-talk is important because what you say to yourself determines the choices you make at each fork in the road. People with a Victim mindset typically listen to the voice of their Inner Critic or their Inner Defender.

> The world of self-criticism on the one side and judgment toward others on the other side represents a major part of the dance of life.
>
> *Hal Stone & Sidra Stone*

SELF-TALK

The Inner Critic

This is the internal voice that judges us as inadequate: *I'm so uncoordinated. I can't do math. I'm not someone she would want to date. I never say the right thing. My ears are too big. I'm a lousy writer.* The Inner Critic accepts too much responsibility and blames us for whatever goes wrong in our lives: *It's all my fault. I always screw up. I knew I couldn't pass biology. I ruined the project. I ought to be ashamed. I blew it again.* This judgmental inner voice can find fault with anything about us: our appearance, our intellect, our performance, our personality, our abilities, how others see us, and, in severe cases, even our value as a human being: *I'm not good enough. I'm worthless, I don't deserve to live.* (Although nearly everyone has a critical inner voice at times, if you often think toxic self-judgments like these last three, don't mess around. Get to your college's counseling office immediately and get help revising these noxious messages so you don't make self-destructive choices.)

Ironically, self-judgments have a positive intention. By criticizing ourselves, we hope to eliminate our flaws and win the approval of others, thus feeling more worthy. Occasionally when we bully ourselves to be perfect, we *do* create a positive outcome, though we make ourselves miserable in the effort. Often, though, self-judgments cause us to give up, as when I tell myself, *I can't pass math,* so I drop the course. What's positive about this? Well, at least I've escaped my problem. Freed from the pressures of passing math, my anxieties float away and I feel better than I have since the semester started. Of course, I still have to pass math to get my degree, so my relief is temporary. The Inner Critic is quite content to trade success in the future for comfort in the present.

Where does an Inner Critic come from? Here's one clue: Have you noticed that its self-criticisms often sound like judgmental adults we have known? It's as if our younger self recorded their judgments and, years later, our Inner Critic replays them over and over. Sometimes you can even trace a self-judgment back to a specific comment that someone made about you years ago. Regardless of its accuracy now, that judgment can affect the choices you make every day.

A loud, voluble critic is enormously toxic. He is more poisonous to your psychological health than almost any trauma or loss. That's because grief and pain wash away with time. But the critic is always with you—judging, blaming, finding fault.

*Matthew McKay
& Patrick Fanning*

Inner Critic   Inner Defender   Inner Guide

During discussions about Inner Critic voices, I have had students say that in their culture, parents routinely criticize their children. The parents say they do it to help. A Japanese-American student said that if he brought home a test with a grade of 98 his parents would tell him that wasn't good enough. A Chinese-American woman said if she gained a pound her mother would tell her she was fat and no man would ever want to marry her. A Jewish-American student made a vase in her ceramics class and gave it to her mother as a present. Her mother proudly displayed the vase on the dining table. The next day, she asked, "What grade did you get for the vase?" My student replied that she had gotten a "C." Soon after, the vase disappeared, never to be seen again. I'm inclined to give these parents the benefit of the doubt. I'm willing to believe they thought they were helping their children, even showing love. Whatever their intentions, though, it was clear these parents had given great power to their children's Inner Critics.

The Inner Defender

The flip side of the Inner Critic is the Inner Defender. Instead of judging ourselves, the Inner Defender judges others: *What a boring teacher. My advisor screwed up my financial aid. Those people [referring to a minority group] are not as good as we are. My roommate made me late to class. No one knows what they're doing around here. It's all their fault!* Inner Defenders accept too little responsibility and, thus, their thoughts and conversations are full of blaming, complaining, accusing, judging, criticizing, and condemning others.

Like Inner Critics, Inner Defenders have a positive intention. They, too, want to protect us from discomfort and anxiety. They, too, want us to feel more worthy. One way they do so is by judging others as wrong or bad or "less than." By tearing others down, the Inner Defender tries to make us feel better about ourselves. In this light, you can perhaps see that prejudice and bias are important tools of the Inner Defender.

Another way Inner Defenders try to help us is by blaming our problems on forces that seem beyond our control, such as other people, bad luck, the government, lack of money, uncaring parents, not enough time, or even too much time. The Inner Defender of a college student might say, *I can't pass math because my instructor is terrible. She couldn't teach math to Einstein. Besides that, the textbook stinks and the tutors in the math lab are rude and unhelpful. It's obvious this college doesn't really care what happens to its students.* If I'm that student, I breathe a sigh of relief because now I'm covered. If I drop the course, hey, it's not my fault. If I stay in the course and fail, it's not my fault either. And, if I stay in the course and somehow get a passing grade (despite my terrible instructor, lousy textbook, worthless tutors, and uncaring college), well, then I have performed no less than a miracle! Regardless of how bad things may get, I can find comfort knowing that at least it's not my fault. It's *their* fault!

And where did this voice come from? Perhaps you've noticed that the Inner Defender's voice sounds like judgmental adults we have known: *You can't trust those people. They're not as good as we are. They're lazy. All they want*

> What you're supposed to do when you don't like a thing is change it. If you can't change it, change the way you think about it. Don't complain.
>
> *Advice to Maya Angelou from her grandmother*

is a handout. They are the reason for our problem! At other times, the Inner Defender sounds like our own voice when we were scared little kids trying to defend ourselves from criticism or punishment by powerful adults. Remember how we'd excuse ourselves from responsibility, shifting the blame for our poor choices onto someone or something else: *It's not my fault. He keeps poking me. My dog ate my homework. What else could I do? I didn't have any choice. My sister broke it. He made me do it. Why does everyone always pick on me? It's all their fault!*

Notice what the Inner Critic and Inner Defender have in common. They are both voices of *judgment*. With the Inner Critic, we point the finger of judgment inward at ourselves. With the Inner Defender, we point the finger of judgment outward at someone or something outside of us. We pay a high price for listening to either our Inner Critic or Inner Defender. By focusing on who's to blame, we waste our energy on judgments instead of positive actions. We spin in place instead of moving purposely toward our desired outcomes and experiences. To feel better in the moment, we sabotage creating a better future.

Fortunately, another voice exists within us all.

The Inner Guide

This is the wise inner voice that seeks to make the best of any situation. The Inner Guide knows that judgment doesn't improve difficult situations. So instead, the Inner Guide objectively observes each situation and asks, *Am I on course or off course? If I'm off course, what can I do to get back on course?* Inner Guides tell us the impartial truth (as best they know it at that time), allowing us to be more fully aware of the world around us, other people, and especially ourselves. With this knowledge, we can take actions that will get us back on course.

Some people say, "But my Inner Critic (or Inner Defender) is *right*!" Yes, it's true that the Inner Critic or Inner Defender can be just as "right" as the Inner Guide. Maybe you really *are* a lousy writer and the tutors in the math lab actually *are* rude and unhelpful. The difference is that Victims expend all their energy in judging themselves or others, whereas Creators use their energy to solve the problem. The voice we allow to occupy our thoughts determines our

---

The object of teaching personal responsibility is to have the student substitute for the question "Who's to blame?" the question "What needs to be done?"

Nathaniel Branden

choices, and our choices determine the outcomes and experiences of our lives. So choose your thoughts carefully. As mentioned earlier, I allow myself up to 10 minutes to complain, blame, and make excuses. Then I redirect that energy and look for what I can do about the situation.

THE LANGUAGE OF RESPONSIBILITY

Translating Victim statements into the responsible language of Creators moves you from stagnant judgments to dynamic actions. In the following chart, the left-hand column presents the Victim thoughts of a student who is taking a challenging college course. Thinking this way, the student's future in this course is easy to predict . . . and it isn't pretty.

But, if she changes her inner conversation, as shown in the right-hand column, she'll also change her behaviors. She can learn more in the course and increase her likelihood of passing. More important, she can learn to reclaim control of her life from the judgmental, self-sabotaging thoughts of her Inner Critic and Inner Defender.

As you read these translations, notice two qualities that characterize Creator language. First, Creators accept ownership of their situation. Second, they plan and take actions to improve their situation. So, when you hear **ownership** and a **plan**, you know you're talking to a Creator. At any moment, you can choose either mindset . . . and that choice will shape your destiny.

> You must change the way you talk to yourself about your life situations so that you no longer imply that anything outside of you is the immediate cause of your unhappiness. Instead of saying, "Joe makes me mad," say, "I make myself mad when I'm around Joe."
>
> *Ken Keyes*

VICTIMS FOCUS ON THEIR WEAKNESSES	CREATORS FOCUS ON HOW TO IMPROVE
I'm terrible in this subject.	I find this course challenging, so I'll start a study group and ask more questions in class.
VICTIMS MAKE EXCUSES	**CREATORS SEEK SOLUTIONS**
The instructor is so boring he puts me to sleep.	The instructor's teaching style makes it difficult for me to pay attention in this class, so I'll challenge myself to pay attention and take at least one page of notes each class period.
VICTIMS COMPLAIN	**CREATORS TURN COMPLAINTS INTO REQUESTS**
This course is a stupid requirement.	I don't understand why this course is required, so I'm going to ask my instructor to help me see how it will benefit me in the future.
VICTIMS COMPARE THEMSELVES UNFAVORABLY TO OTHERS	**CREATORS SEEK HELP FROM THOSE MORE SKILLED**
I'll never do as well as John; he's a genius.	I need help in this course, so I'm going to ask John if he'll help me study for the exams.
VICTIMS BLAME	**CREATORS ACCEPT RESPONSIBILITY**
The tests are ridiculous. The professor gave me an "F" on the first one.	I got an "F" on the first test because I didn't read the assignments thoroughly. From now on I'll take detailed notes on everything I read.

> Excuses rob you of power and induce apathy.
>
> *Agnes Whistling Elk*

(Continues)

(Continued)

VICTIMS SEE PROBLEMS AS PERMANENT Posting comments on our class's Internet discussion board is impossible. I'll never understand how to do it.	**CREATORS TREAT PROBLEMS AS TEMPORARY** I've been trying to post comments on our class's Internet discussion board without carefully reading the instructor's directions. I'll read the directions again and follow them one step at a time.
VICTIMS REPEAT INEFFECTIVE BEHAVIORS Going to the tutoring center is no help. There aren't enough tutors.	**CREATORS DO SOMETHING NEW** I've been going to the tutoring center right after lunch when it's really busy. I'll start going in the morning to see if more tutors are available then.
VICTIMS TRY I'll try to do better.	**CREATORS DO** To do better, I'll do the following: Attend class regularly, take good notes, ask questions in class, start a study group, and make an appointment with the teacher. If all that doesn't work, I'll think of something else.
VICTIMS PREDICT DEFEAT AND GIVE UP I'll probably fail. There's nothing I can do. I can't . . . I have to . . . I should . . . I quit . . .	**CREATORS THINK POSITIVELY AND LOOK FOR A BETTER CHOICE** I'll find a way. There's always something I can do. I can . . . I choose to . . . I will . . . I'll keep going . . .

> I used to want the words "She tried" on my tombstone. Now I want, "She did it."
>
> *Katherine Dunham*

> Blaming . . . is a pastime for losers. There's no leverage in blaming. Power is rooted in self-responsibility.
>
> *Nathaniel Branden*

When people choose a Victim mindset, they complain, blame, and make excuses, and they have little energy left over to solve their problems. As a result, they typically remain stuck where they are, telling their sad story over and over to any poor soul who will listen. (Ever hear of a "pity party"?) In this way, Victims exhaust not only their own energy but often drain the energy of the people around them.

By contrast, when people choose a Creator mindset, they use their words and thoughts to improve a bad situation. First, they accept responsibility for creating their present outcomes and experiences, and their words reflect that ownership. Next, they plan and take positive actions to improve their lives. *Ownership* and a *plan*. In this way, Creators energize themselves and the people around them.

Whenever you feel yourself slipping into Victim language, ask yourself: What do I want in my life—excuses or results? What could I think, say, and do right now that would get me moving toward the outcomes and experiences I want?

Journal Entry 6

In this activity you will practice the language of personal responsibility. By learning to translate Victim statements into Creator statements, you will master the language of successful people.

1. Draw a line down the middle of a journal page. On the left side of the line, copy the 10 Victim statements found on this page and the next page.

2. On the right side of the line, translate the Victim statements into the words of a Creator. The two keys to Creator language are taking ownership of a problem and taking positive actions to solve it. *Ownership* and a *plan*. When you respond as if you are responsible for a bad situation, then you are empowered to do something about it (unlike Victims, who must wait for someone else to solve their problems). Use the translations on pages 51–52 as models.

3. Write what you have learned or relearned about how you use language: Is it your habit to speak as a Victim or as a Creator? Do you find yourself more inclined to blame yourself, blame others, or seek solutions? Be sure to give examples. What is your goal for language usage from now on? How, specifically, will you accomplish this goal? Your paragraph might begin, *While reading about and practicing Creator language, I learned that I . . .*

Remember to DIVE DEEP!

VICTIM LANGUAGE	CREATOR LANGUAGE
1. If they'd do something about the parking on campus, I wouldn't be late so often.	1.
2. I'm failing my online class because the site is impossible to navigate.	2.
3. I'm too shy to ask questions in class even when I'm confused.	3.
4. She's a lousy instructor. That's why I failed the first test.	4.
5. I hate group projects because people are lazy and I always end up doing most of the work.	5.

The way you use words has a tremendous impact on the quality of your life. Certain words are destructive; others are empowering.

Susan Jeffers

If you are in shackles, "I can't" has relevance; otherwise, it is usually a roundabout way of saying "I don't want to," "I won't," or, "I have not learned how to." If you really mean "I don't want to," it is important to come out and say so. Saying "I can't" disowns responsibility.

Gay Hendricks &
Kathlyn Hendricks

Journal Entry 6 *continued*

VICTIM LANGUAGE	CREATOR LANGUAGE
6. I wish I could write better, but I just can't.	6.
7. My friend got me so angry that I can't even study for the exam.	7.
8. I'll try to do my best this semester.	8.
9. The financial aid form is too complicated to fill out.	9.
10. I work nights so I didn't have time to do the assignment.	10.

One Student's Story

ALEXSANDR KANEVSKIY
Oakland University, Michigan

When I began college, I was unmotivated and chose to blame others for my problems and my shortcomings. I was so much smarter than everyone that I didn't need to do all the work that everyone else did; at least that's what I thought. My favorite pastime was staring blankly at a television, rather than attending lecture or doing assigned homework. I figured everything would take care of itself without my interference. I had carried this uninhibited laziness with me through high school and it, unfortunately, translated into my college career. It was then that the gravitas of my situation hit me; at my current rate I was going to be dismissed from school. I was placed on academic probation my sophomore year and unless I improved, I was out.

This was when I first laid my eyes and hands on the *On Course* book. I didn't think much of it at first; just another guide for the misguided, full of backwards theories and advice that wouldn't help me, or anyone else. But from the first reading, I noticed that this book was different. It used different language, language that didn't bore me or induce disinterest. What's funniest, though, was that one of the first journals that I was assigned had the most profound impact on my changing as a student. Just as *On Course* used innovative and interesting language to teach, this journal was all about changing my own language. Rather than use language that blames others or is blatantly negative, that journal taught me to use positive Creator language.

I needed to think and speak in a language that searched for answers and solutions, not a language that kept me unmotivated and helpless. When I rephrased my thinking and speaking, the rest of life followed. All of a sudden, responsibility was in my own hands and the solutions that I needed, but was afraid to search out, became much clearer. Now that I knew there were, in fact, answers and solutions, I didn't look to blame those around me. I realized that it was up to me to find these solutions, that they would not magically appear before my eyes and that nobody else would find them for me. My faults and shortcomings became more apparent than ever, and my arrogance was startling. I saw that I was not smart enough to be exempt from school and from the work of my fellow students. They all searched for solutions and held themselves responsible for these solutions; I never realized this because I had never yearned for these solutions, and therefore never had responsibility.

(Continues)

I stopped expecting solutions to come to me naturally and started to work, rather than fall asleep at the television. Positive Creator language was only the first step, but what I took from this first lesson carried through to every other lesson in class and in life. I found that I was newly interested in my classes; homework became a pleasure because each assignment was yet another opportunity to learn. Rather than fall asleep at the television, I now fell asleep after studying. And probation? That became a thing of the past. Even in basketball (my sport of choice) I started to take more of an interest in passing, rather than scoring, and helping my teammates, instead of blaming them for mistakes. Amongst my friends I am now known as the "problem solver," which is just as surprising to me as it is to them. They've noticed a definite change, and I am glad to advise them to read my *On Course* book so that maybe they too will find a lesson that sparks their own improvement. *On Course* provided me with valuable steppingstones that have made me into a student and person who cares enough to take responsibility for his language and his actions, doing what needs to be done in order to succeed in school and in the outside world.

Making Wise Decisions

Focus Questions How can you improve the quality of the decisions you make? How can you take personal responsibility for the outcomes and experiences in your life?

Life is a journey with many opportunities and obstacles, and each one requires a choice. Whatever you are experiencing in your life today is, to a great extent, the result of your past choices. More important, whatever you'll experience in the future will be fashioned greatly by the choices you make from this moment on.

This is an exciting thought. If we can make wiser choices, we can more likely create the future we want. On the road to a college degree, you will face important choices such as these:

Shall I . . .

- major in business, science, or creative writing?
- work full-time, part-time, or not at all?
- drop a course that bores me or stick it out?
- experiment with alcohol and drugs?
- study for my exam or go out with friends?

The sum of these choices, plus thousands of others, will determine your degree of success in college and in life. Doesn't it seem wise, then, to develop an effective strategy for choice management?

> The end result of your life here on earth will always be the sum total of the choices you made while you were here.
>
> *Shad Helmstetter*

THE WISE CHOICE PROCESS

In the face of any challenge, you can make a responsible decision by answering the six questions of the Wise Choice Process. This process, you might be interested to know, is a variation of a decision-making model that is used in many career fields. For example, nurses learn a similar process for helping patients that is abbreviated ADPIE. These letters stand for Assess, Diagnose, Plan, Implement, and Evaluate. Counselors and therapists in training may learn a similar process for solving personal problems. This process was described in 1965 by William Glasser in his book *Reality Therapy.*

And the *NASA Systems Engineering Handbook* says, "Systems engineering [. . .] consists of identification and quantification of system goals, creation of alternative system design concepts, performance of design trades, selection and implementation of the best design, verification that the design is properly built and integrated, and post-implementation assessment of how well the system meets (or met) the goals." In layperson's terms, systems engineers use their version of the Wise Choice Process to achieve their goals.

You are about to learn a system that will empower you to take greater responsibility for creating your life as you want it to be despite the inevitable challenges that life presents.

> My choice; my responsibility; win or lose, only I hold the key to my destiny.
>
> *Elaine Maxwell*

1. **WHAT'S MY PRESENT SITUATION?** Begin by identifying your problem or challenge, being sure to define the situation as a Creator, not as a Victim. The important information here is "What exists?" (not "Whose fault is it?"). Quiet your Inner Critic, that self-criticizing voice in your head: *I am a total loser in my history class.* Likewise, ignore your Inner Defender, that judgmental voice that blames everyone else for your problems: *My history instructor is the worst teacher on the planet.* Instead, rely on your Inner Guide, your wise, impartial inner voice that tells the truth as best it can. Consider only the objective facts of your situation, including how you feel about them. For example:

   I stayed up all night studying for my first history test. When I finished taking the test, I hoped for an A. At worst, I expected a B. When I got the test back, my grade was a D. Five other students got A's. I feel depressed and angry.

   By the way, sometimes when we accurately define a troublesome situation, we immediately know what to do. The problem wasn't so much the situation as our muddy understanding of it.

> I am the cause of my choices, decisions, and actions. It is I who chooses, decides, and acts. If I do so knowing my responsibility, I am more likely to proceed wisely and appropriately than if I make myself oblivious of my role as source.
>
> *Nathaniel Branden*

2. **HOW WOULD I LIKE MY SITUATION TO BE?** You can't change the past, but if you could create your desired outcome in the future, what would it look like?

   I get A's on all of my future tests.

3. **WHAT ARE MY POSSIBLE CHOICES?** Create a list of possible choices that you *could* do, knowing you aren't obligated to do any of them. Compile your list without judgment. Don't say, "Oh, that would never work." Don't even say, "That's a great idea." Judgment during brainstorming stops the creative flow. Move from judgments to possibilities, discovering as many creative options as you can. Give yourself time to ponder, explore, consider, think, discover, conceive, invent, imagine. Then dive even deeper. If you get stuck, try one

of these options. First, take a different point of view. Think of someone you admire and ask, "What would that person do in my situation?" Or, pretend your problem belongs to someone else, and he asks you what you should do. What advice would you offer? Third, incubate. That is, set the problem aside and let your unconscious mind work on a solution while you do other things. Sometimes a great option will pop into your mind while you are brushing your hair, doing math homework, or even sleeping. Your patience will often pay off with a helpful option that would have remained invisible had you accepted the first idea that came to mind or, worse, given up.

- *I could complain to my history classmates and anyone else who will listen.*
- *I could drop the class and take it next semester with another instructor.*
- *I could complain to the department head that the instructor grades unfairly.*
- *I could ask my successful classmates for help.*
- *I could ask the instructor for suggestions about improving my grades.*
- *I could read about study skills and experiment with some new ways to study.*
- *I could request an opportunity to retake the test.*
- *I could take all of the online practice quizzes.*
- *I could get a tutor.*

> A person defines and redefines who they are by the choices they make, minute to minute.
>
> *Joyce Chapman*

4. WHAT'S THE LIKELY OUTCOME OF EACH POSSIBLE CHOICE?

Decide how you think each choice is likely to turn out. If you can't predict the outcome of one of your possible choices, stop this process and gather any additional information you need. For example, if you don't know the impact that dropping a course will have on your financial aid, find out before you take that action. Here are the possible choices from Step 3 and their likely outcomes:

- *Complain to history classmates: I'd have the immediate pleasure of criticizing the instructor and maybe getting others' sympathy.*
- *Drop the class: I'd lose three credits this semester and have to make them up later.*
- *Complain to the department head: Probably she'd ask if I've seen my instructor first, so I wouldn't get much satisfaction.*
- *Ask successful classmates for help: I might learn how to improve my study habits; I might also make new friends.*
- *Ask the instructor for suggestions: I might learn what to do next time to improve my grade; at least the instructor would learn that I want to do well in this course.*
- *Read about study skills: I would probably learn some strategies I don't know and maybe improve my test scores in all of my classes.*
- *Request an opportunity to retake the test: My request might get approved and give me an opportunity to raise my grade. At the very least, I'd demonstrate how much I want to do well.*

> Destiny is not a matter of chance; it is a matter of choice. It is not a thing to be waited for; it is a thing to be achieved.
>
> *William Jennings Bryant*

- *Take all of the online practice quizzes: This action wouldn't help my grade on this test, but it would probably improve my next test score.*
- *Get a tutor: A tutor would help, but it would probably take a lot of time.*

5. **WHICH CHOICE(S) WILL I COMMIT TO DOING?** Now create your plan. Decide which choice or choices will likely create your desired outcome; then commit to acting on them. If no favorable option exists, consider which choice leaves you no worse off than before. If no such option exists, then ask which choice creates the least unfavorable outcome. And remember that not making a choice is a choice.

I'll talk to my successful classmates, make an appointment with my instructor and ask him to explain what I can do to improve, and I'll request an opportunity to retake the test. I'll read the study skills sections of On Course *and implement at least three new study strategies. If these choices don't raise my next test score to at least a B, I'll get a tutor.*

Each situation will dictate the best options. In this example, if the student had previously failed four tests instead of one, the best choice might be to drop the class. Or, if everyone in the class were receiving D's and F's, and if the student had already met with the instructor, a responsible option might be to see the department head about the instructor's grading policies.

6. **WHEN AND HOW WILL I EVALUATE MY PLAN?** At some future time you will want to assess your results. To do so, compare your new situation to how you want it to be (as you described in Step 2). If the two situations are identical (or close enough), you can call your plan a success. If you find that you are still far from your desired outcome, you have some decisions to make. You might decide that you haven't implemented your new approach long enough, so you'll keep working your plan. Or you may decide that your plan just isn't working, in which case you'll return to Step 1 and work through Step 5 to design a plan that will work better. However, you're not starting completely over because this time you're smarter than you were when you began: Now you know what doesn't work.

After my next history test, I'll see if I have achieved my goal of getting an A. If not, I'll revise my plan.

The principle of choice describes the reality that I am in charge of my life. I choose it all. I always have, I always will.

Will Schutz

Here's the bottom line: Our choices reveal what we *truly* believe and value, as opposed to what we *say* we believe and value. When I submissively wait for others to improve my life, I am being a Victim. When I passively wait for luck to go my way, I am being a Victim. When I make choices that take me off course from my future success just to increase my immediate pleasure (such as partying instead of studying for an important test), I am being a Victim. When I make choices that sacrifice my goals and dreams just to reduce my immediate discomfort (such as dropping a challenging course instead of spending extra hours working with a tutor), I am being a Victim.

However, when I design a plan to craft my life as I want it, I am being a Creator. When I carry out my plan even in the face of obstacles (such as when the campus bookstore runs out of a book that I need for class and I keep up with my assignments by reading a copy the instructor has placed on reserve in the library), I am being a Creator. When I take positive risks to advance my goals (such as asking a question in a large lecture class even though I am nervous), I am being a Creator. When I sacrifice immediate pleasure to stay on course toward my dreams (such as resisting the urge to buy a new cell phone so I can reduce my work hours to study more), I am being a Creator.

No matter what your final decision may be, the mere fact that you are defining and making your own choices is wonderfully empowering. By participating in the Wise Choice Process, you affirm your belief that you *can* change your life for the better. You reject the position that you are merely a Victim of outside forces, a pawn in the chess game of life. You insist on being the Creator of your own outcomes and experiences, shaping your destiny through the power of wise choices.

> One's philosophy is not best expressed in words; it is expressed in the choices one makes. In the long run, we shape our lives and we shape ourselves. The process never ends until we die. And, the choices we make are ultimately our own responsibility.
>
> *Eleanor Roosevelt*

Journal Entry 7

In this activity you will apply the Wise Choice Process to improve a difficult situation in your life. Think about a current problem, one that you're comfortable sharing with your classmates and teacher. As a result of this problem, you may be angry, sad, frustrated, depressed, overwhelmed, or afraid. Perhaps this situation has to do with a grade you received, a teacher's comment, or a classmate's action. Maybe the problem relates to a job, a relationship, or money. The Wise Choice Process can help you make an empowering choice in any part of your life.

1. Write the six questions of the Wise Choice Process and answer each one as it relates to your situation.

The Wise Choice Process

1. What's my present situation? (Describe the problem objectively and completely.)

2. How would I like my situation to be? (What is your ideal future outcome?)

3. What are my possible choices? (Create a long list of specific choices that might create your preferred outcome.)

4. What's the likely outcome of each possible choice? (If you can't predict the likely outcome of an option, stop and gather more information.)

5. Which choice(s) will I commit to doing? (Pick from your list of choices in Step 3.)

6. When and how will I evaluate my plan? (Identify the specific date and criteria by which you will determine the success of your plan.)

> When I see all the choices I really have, it makes the world a whole lot brighter.
>
> *Debbie Scott, student*

2. Write what you learned or relearned by doing the Wise Choice Process. Be sure to Dive Deep. You might begin, *By doing the Wise Choice Process, I learned that I . . .*

Remember, you can enliven your journal by adding pictures cut from magazines, drawings of your own, clip art, or quotations that appeal to you.

One Student's Story

FREDDIE DAVILA
The Victoria College, Texas

During my first semester of college I noticed a trend among my fellow students. Every time an assignment was due, many of them came to class with excuses instead of their completed work. I took this behavior personally because I had made time to complete all of my homework and prepare for class. I find it extremely disrespectful to the instructors and to those who come to class to learn whenever college students act like helpless children.

Also during my first semester, I happened to be taking "Strategies for Success," a class that introduced me to the *On Course* textbook. When I was invited to identify an important lesson worth sharing in a "One Page of Wisdom" assignment, I felt I needed to explain what I had learned throughout the semester the best way I knew how—through art. I looked back at The Wise Choice Process and the Responsibility Model for inspiration. As I did the preliminary sketches, I kept in mind the excuses I had heard students use over the last few months. I wanted my art to show that by making excuses, they were acting like Victims and were only hurting themselves.

I hope some of the students in my class saw themselves in the drawing; my goal was to make people think about their self-sabotaging habits and bad choices that stand in the way of their success. The road to success is filled with tough obstacles and tempting distractions, but by making wise choices at critical forks in the road, students on the journey will find success to be their ultimate destiny.

Courtesy of Freddie Davila

Photo: Courtesy of Freddie Davila

Personal Responsibility
AT WORK

I found that the more I viewed myself as totally responsible for my life, the more in control I seemed to be of the goals I wanted to achieve.

Charles J. Givens, entrepreneur and self-made multimillionaire

A student once told me she'd had more than a dozen jobs in three years. "Why so many jobs?" I asked. "Bad luck," she replied. "I keep getting one lousy boss after another." Hmmmm, I wondered, 12 lousy bosses in a row? What are the odds of that?

Responsibility is about ownership. As long as I believe my career success belongs to someone else (like "lousy" bosses), I'm being a Victim, and my success is unlikely. Victims give little effort to choosing or preparing for a career. Instead, they allow influential others (such as parents and teachers) or circumstances to determine their choice of work. They complain about the jobs they have, make excuses for why they haven't gotten the jobs they want, and blame others or their own permanent flaws for their occupational woes. By contrast, Creators know that the foundation of success at work (as in college) is accepting this truth: *By our choices, we are each the primary creators of the outcomes and experiences of our lives.*

Accepting responsibility in the work world begins with consciously choosing your career path. You alone can decide what career is right for you. That's why Creators explore their career options thoroughly, match career requirements with their own talents and interests, consider the consequences of choosing each career (such as how much education the career requires or what the employment outlook is), and make informed choices. Choose your career wisely because few things in life are worse than spending 8 hours a day, 50 weeks a year, working at a job you hate.

Taking responsibility for your work life also means planning your career path to keep your options open and your progress unobstructed. For example, you could keep your career options open in college by taking only general education courses while investigating several possible fields of work. Or you could eliminate a financial obstacle by getting enough education—such as a dental hygiene degree—to support yourself while pursuing your dream career—such as going to dental school.

In short, Creators make use of the power of wise choices. They believe that there is always an option that will lead them toward the careers they want, and they take responsibility for creating the employment they want. Instead of passively waiting for a job to come to them, they actively go out and look. One of my students lost a job when the company where she worked closed. She could have spent hours in the cafeteria complaining about her bad fortune and how she could no longer afford to stay in school. Instead she created employment for herself by going from store to store in a mall asking every manager for a part-time job until one said, "Yes." In the time she could have wasted in the cafeteria complaining about her money problems, she solved them with positive actions.

When it comes to finding a full-time career position, Creators continue to be proactive. They don't wait for the perfect job opening to appear in their local paper or on an

Personal Responsibility **AT WORK** *continued*

Creators Wanted!

Candidates must demonstrate personal responsibility, strong decision-making skills, and a solution-orientation to problems.

Internet job site. They don't wait for a call from an employment agency. They know that employers prefer to hire people they know and like, so Creators do all they can to get known and liked by employers in their career field. They start by researching companies that need their talents and for which they might like to work. Then, they contact potential employers directly. They don't ask if the employer has a job opening. Instead, they seek an informational interview: "Hi, I've just gotten my degree in accounting, and I'd like to make an appointment to talk to you about your company. . . . What's that? You don't have any positions open at this time? No problem. I'm just gathering information at this point, looking for where my talents might make the most contributions. Would you have some time to meet with me this week? Or would next week be better?" Creators go to these information-gathering interviews prepared with knowledge about the company, good questions to ask, and a carefully prepared résumé. At the end of the meeting they ask if the interviewer knows employers who might need their skills. They call all of the leads they get and use the referral as an opening for a job interview: "I was speaking with John Smith at the Ajax Company, and he suggested that I give you a call about a position you have open." A friend of mine got an information-gathering interview and wowed the personnel manager with her professionally prepared résumé and interviewing skills; even though the company "had no openings" when she first called, two days after the interview, she was offered a position.

Accepting responsibility not only helps you *get* a great job, it makes it possible to *excel* on the job. Employers love responsible employees. Wouldn't you? Instead of complaining, blaming, making excuses, and thus creating an emotionally draining work environment, responsible employees create a positive workplace where absenteeism is low and work production is high. Instead of repeating ineffective solutions to problems, proactive employees seek solutions, take new actions, and try something new. They pursue alternative routes instead of complaining about dead ends. Creators show initiative instead of needing constant direction, and they do their best work even when the boss isn't looking. Creators are willing to go the extra mile, and this effort pays off handsomely. As someone once said, "There is no traffic jam on the extra mile." If you run into a challenge while preparing for a career, seeking a job, or working in your career, don't complain, blame, or make excuses. Instead, ask yourself a Creator's favorite question: "What's my plan?"

► BELIEVING IN YOURSELF

Change Your Inner Conversation

Focus Question How can you raise your self-esteem by changing your self-talk?

Imagine this: Three students schedule an appointment with their instructor to discuss a project they're working on together. They go to the instructor's office at the scheduled time, but he isn't there. They wait 45 minutes before leaving. As you learn what they do next, which student do you think has the strongest self-esteem?

Student 1, feeling discouraged and depressed, spends the evening watching television while neglecting assignments in other subjects. Student 2, feeling insulted and furious, spends the evening complaining to friends about the horrible instructor who stood them up. Student 3, feeling puzzled about the mix-up, emails the instructor to see what happened and to set up another meeting; while waiting for a response, this student spends the evening studying for a test in another class.

Which student has the strongest self-esteem?

THE CURSE OF STINKIN' THINKIN'

How is it that three people can have the same experience and respond to it so differently? According to psychologists like Albert Ellis, the answer lies in what each person believes caused the event. Ellis suggested that different responses can be understood by realizing that the activating event (A) plus our beliefs (B) equal the consequences (C) (how we respond). In other words, $A + B = C$. For example:

Activating Event	+ Beliefs	= Consequence
Student #1: Instructor didn't show up for a scheduled conference.	My instructor thinks I'm dumb. I'll never get a college degree. I'm a failure in life.	Got depressed and watched television all evening.
Student #2: Same.	My instructor won't help me. Teachers don't care about students.	Got angry and spent the night telling friends how horrible the instructor is.
Student #3: Same.	I'm not sure what went wrong. Sometimes things just don't turn out the way you plan. There's always tomorrow.	Emailed the instructor to see what happened and to set up a new appointment; then studied for another class.

> It is the mind that maketh good or ill, That maketh wretch or happy, rich or poor.
>
> *Edmund Spencer*

> Self-esteem can be defined as the state that exists when you are not arbitrarily haranguing and abusing yourself but choose to fight back against those automatic thoughts with meaningful rational responses.
>
> *Dr. Thomas Burns*

Ellis suggests that our upsets are caused not so much by our problems as by what we *think* about our problems. When our thinking is full of irrational beliefs—what Ellis calls "stinkin' thinkin'"—we feel awful even when the circumstances don't warrant it. So, how we *think* about the events in our lives is the key issue. Problems may come and go, but our "stinkin' thinkin'" stays with us. As the old saying goes, "Everywhere I go, there I am."

Stinkin' thinkin' isn't based on reality. Rather, these irrational thoughts are the automatic chatter of the Inner Critic (keeper of Negative Beliefs about the self) and the Inner Defender (keeper of Negative Beliefs about other people and the world).

So what about our three students and their self-esteem? It's not hard to see that student 1, who got depressed and wasted the evening watching television, has low self-esteem. This student is thrown far off course simply by the instructor's not showing up. A major cause of this self-defeating reaction is the Inner Critic's harsh self-judgments. Here are some common self-damning beliefs held by Inner Critics:

> The Inner Critic keeps us feeling insecure and childlike. When it is operating, we feel like children who have done something wrong and probably will never be able to do anything right.
>
> *Hal Stone & Sidra Stone*

I'm dumb.	I'm unattractive.
I'm selfish.	I'm lazy.
I'm a failure.	I'm not college material
I'm incapable.	I'm weak.
I'm not as good as other people.	I'm a lousy parent.
I'm worthless.	I'm unlovable.

People dominated by their Inner Critic often misinterpret events, inventing criticisms that aren't there. A friend says, "Something came up, and I can't meet you tonight." The Inner Critic responds, "I screwed up again! I'll never have any friends!"

The activating event doesn't cause the consequence; rather, the judgmental chatter of the Inner Critic does. A strong Inner Critic is both a cause and an effect of low self-esteem.

What about student 2, the one who spent the evening telling friends how horrible the instructor was? Though perhaps less apparent, this student's judgmental response also demonstrates low self-esteem. The finger-pointing Inner Defender is merely the Inner Critic turned outward and is just as effective at getting the student off course. Here are some examples of destructive beliefs held by an Inner Defender:

> Everyone has a critical inner voice. But people with low self-esteem tend to have a more vicious and vocal pathological critic.
>
> *Matthew McKay & Patrick Fanning*

People don't treat me right, so they're rotten.
People don't act the way I want them to, so they're awful.
People don't live up to my expectations, so they're the enemy.
People don't do what I want, so they're against me.
Life is full of problems, so it's terrible.
Life is unfair, so I can't stand it.
Life doesn't always go my way, so I can't be happy.
Life doesn't provide me with everything I want, so it's unbearable.

People dominated by their Inner Defender imagine personal insults and slights in neutral events. A classmate says, "Something came up, and I can't meet you tonight." The Inner Defender responds, "Who do you think you are, anyway? I can find someone a lot better to study with than you!"

The activating event doesn't cause the angry response; rather, the judgmental chatter of the judgmental Inner Defender does. A strong Inner Defender is both a cause and an effect of low self-esteem.

Only student 3 demonstrates high self-esteem. This student realizes he doesn't know why the instructor missed the meeting. He doesn't blame himself, the instructor, or a rotten world. He considers alternatives: Perhaps the instructor got sick or was involved in a traffic accident. Until he finds out what happened and decides what to do next, this student turns his attention to an action that will keep him on course to another goal. The Inner Guide is concerned with positive results, not judging self or others. A strong Inner Guide is both a cause and an effect of high self-esteem.

DISPUTING IRRATIONAL BELIEFS

How, then, can you avoid stinkin' thinkin'?

First, you can become aware of the chatter of your Inner Critic and Inner Defender. Be especially alert when events in your life go wrong, when your desired outcomes and experiences are thwarted. That's when we are most likely to complain, blame, and excuse. That's when we substitute judgments of ourselves or others for the positive actions that would get us back on course.

Once you become familiar with your inner voices, you can begin a process of separating yourself from your Inner Critic and Inner Defender. To do this, practice disputing your irrational and self-sabotaging beliefs. Here are four effective ways to dispute:

- **Offer evidence that your judgments are incorrect:** *My instructor emailed me last week to see if I needed help with my project, so there's no rational reason to believe he won't help me now.*

- **Offer a positive explanation of the problem:** *Sure my instructor didn't show up, but he may have missed the appointment because of a last-minute crisis.*

- **Question the importance of the problem:** *Even if my instructor won't help me, I can still do well on this project, and if I don't, it won't be the end of the world.*

- **If you find that your judgments are true, instead of continuing to criticize yourself or someone else, offer a plan to improve the situation:** *If I'm honest, I have to admit that I haven't done well in this class so far, but from now on I'm going to attend every class, take good notes, read my assignments two or three times, and work with a study group before every test.*

According to psychologist Ellis, a key to correcting irrational thinking is changing a "must" into a preference. When we think "must," what follows in our thoughts is typically awful, terrible, and dreadful. For example, my Inner Defender's belief that an instructor "must" meet me for an appointment or he is an awful, terrible, dreadful person is irrational; I'd certainly "prefer" him to meet me for an

> Replacing a negative thought with a positive one changes more than just the passing thought—it changes the way you perceive and deal with the world.
>
> *Dr. Clair Douglas*

> Does it help to change what you say to yourself? It most certainly does.... Tell yourself often enough that you'll succeed and you dramatically improve your chances of succeeding and of feeling good.
>
> *Drs. Bernie Zilbergeld & Arnold A. Lazarus*

appointment, but his not meeting me does not make him horrible—in fact, he may have a perfectly good reason for not meeting with me. As another example, my Inner Critic's belief that I "must" pass this course or I am an awful, terrible, dreadful person is irrational; I'd certainly "prefer" to pass this course, but not doing so does not make me worthless—in fact, not passing this course may lead me to something even better. Believing irrationally that I, another person, or the world "must" be a particular way, Ellis says, is a major cause of my distress and misery.

STEREOTYPE THREAT

Social psychologist Claude Steele of Stanford University has identified a kind of stinkin' thinkin' that afflicts cultural groups: *stereotype threat*. A stereotype is a generalization about members of a particular group. For example, African Americans are all excellent in sports but they aren't good students . . . or women are all terrific at taking care of children but they are poor at math and science. Stereotype threat is a fear that your behavior in a particular situation—such as taking a math test—might confirm a negative stereotype about a cultural group to which you belong. The resulting anxiety causes a self-fulfilling prophesy, and you do, indeed, perform down to the stereotype rather than up to your ability.

As an example of the effect of stereotype threat, Steele and his colleagues showed that when race was emphasized, African-American college students did less well than their white classmates on a standardized test. However, when race was not emphasized, African-American students' scores were equivalent to those of white students. Further studies have shown that the academic success of many cultural groups fall prey to stereotype threat, including Latinos, females in math, and students of working-class backgrounds.

Here's how stinkin' thinkin' seems to contribute to stereotype threat. Let's say a female student sits down to take a math test. That's the activating event. Next come her beliefs: She knows the stereotype—women aren't good at math. She doesn't want to be lumped into or reinforce that stereotype. She becomes anxious, distracted, and can't remember all she studied. The result is a self-fulfilling prophesy. She doesn't do as well on the test as she is capable of, and the culprit is her stinkin' thinkin'.

Besides causing immediate problems in test situations, stereotype threat may even cause people to avoid the threat area altogether. A woman may avoid majoring in math and science. A white man may reject playing basketball. A working-class student may lose motivation and drop out of college.

The strategies for disputing that were mentioned earlier can also be applied to stereotype threat. A woman may **offer evidence that the stereotype is wrong**: *I did pretty well in math and science in high school . . . and I just read that four women recently won Nobel Prizes in science and mathematics.* A white man may **question the importance of the stereotype**: *I may not be the best player on the basketball team, but so what . . . it's great fun.* A working-class student may **offer a plan to address the stereotype**: *My English teacher told us her parents were migrant farm workers; I'm going to talk to her about how she kept herself motivated to get a college degree.*

Another way to reduce the negative impact of stereotype threat has been suggested by psychologists Michael Johns, Toni Schmader, and Andy Martens in a

> You mainly make yourself needlessly and neurotically miserable by strongly holding absolutist irrational beliefs, especially by rigidly believing unconditional shoulds, oughts, and musts.
>
> *Albert Ellis*

> Everyone experiences stereotype threat. We are all members of some group about which negative stereotypes exist, from white males and Methodists to women and the elderly.
>
> *Claude M. Steele*

study at the University of Arizona. They gave a math test to one group of students and found that female students performed worse than the men. Before giving the math test to a second group, they told students briefly about how stereotype threat could negatively affect the performance of women. Specifically, they announced, "It's important to keep in mind that if you are feeling anxious while taking this test, this anxiety could be the result of these negative stereotypes that are widely known in society and have nothing to do with your actual ability to do well on the test." In this second round of tests, female students did as well as the men. It seems that simply knowing about stereotype threat can reduce its power.

The guiding principle in this section is simple: Choose wisely the thoughts you allow to occupy your mind. Avoid letting automatic, negative thoughts or negative stereotypes undermine your self-esteem or your results. Evict stinkin' thinkin' and replace it with thoughts that empower.

Journal Entry 8

In this activity, you will practice disputing the judgments of your Inner Critic and your Inner Defender. As you become more skilled at seeing yourself, other people, and the world more objectively and without distracting judgments, your self-esteem will thrive.

1. **Write a sentence expressing a recent problem or event that upset you.** Think of something troubling that happened in school, at work, or in your personal life. For example, *I got a 62 on my math test.*

2. **Write a list of three or more criticisms your Inner Critic (IC) might level against you as a result of this situation. Have your Inner Guide (IG) dispute each one immediately.** Review the four methods of disputing described on page 65. You only need to use one of them for each criticism. For example,

IC: You failed that math test because you're terrible in math.

IG: It's true I failed the math test, but I'll study harder next time and do better. This was only the first test, and I now know what to expect next time.

3. **Write a list of three or more criticisms your Inner Defender (ID) might level against someone else or life as a result of this situation. Have your Inner Guide (IG) dispute each one immediately.** Again use one of the four methods for disputing. For example,

ID: You failed that math test because you've got the worst math instructor on campus.

IG: I have trouble understanding my math instructor, so I'm going to make an appointment to talk with him in private. John really liked him last semester, so I bet I'll like him, too, if I give him a chance.

Journal Entry 8 *continued*

4. **Make a choice: Write about one of the following:**

A. **Write what you have learned or relearned about changing your inner conversation.** Your journal entry might begin, *In reading and writing about my inner conversations, I have discovered that* . . . . Wherever possible, offer personal experiences or examples to explain what you learned.

B. One instructor said about this journal entry: "While I understand the importance of having students change their inner conversations, I don't think they ever actually apply what they write in their journals to the challenging situations in their lives. In other words, there's a big gap between what they learn and what they do." **Write a reply to this instructor expressing your opinion about her concern.**

One Student's Story

DOMINIC GRASSETH
Lane Community College, Oregon

Enrolling in college at the age of 28 was very intimidating to me. Having dropped out of high school at 15, I had a real problem with confidence. Even though I had a GED and was earning a decent living as a car salesman, I still doubted that I was smart enough to be successful in college. I finally took the leap and enrolled because I want a career where I don't have to work 12 hours a day, six days a week and never see my family. However, by the second week of the semester, I found myself falling back into old habits. I was sitting in the back of the classroom, asking what homework was due, and talking through most of the class. Negative thoughts constantly ran

through my mind: *The teachers won't like me. I can't compete with the 18-year-olds right out of high school. I don't even remember what a "verb" is. I can't do this.*

Then in my College Success class, we read Chapter 2 of *On Course* about becoming a Creator and disputing "stinkin' thinkin.'" I realized I had taken on the role of the Victim almost my whole life, and I was continuing to do it now. One day I was on my porch when I caught myself thinking my usual negative thoughts. It occurred to me that I was the only one holding me back, not the teachers, not the other students, not math, not English. If I wanted to be successful in college, I had to quit being scared.

I had to change my thinking. So I made a deal with myself that any time I caught myself thinking negatively, I would rephrase the statement in a way that was more positive. I started to truly pay attention to the thoughts in my head and question the negative things I was telling myself. After that I began sitting up front in my classes and participating more. I've always been kind of scattered, so I started using a calendar and a dry-erase board to keep track of what I had to do.

What amazes me is that I didn't really make that big of a change, yet I finished the semester with a 4.0 average! All I did was realize that what I was saying to myself was my underlying problem. I am responsible for my thoughts, and the choice about whether or not to succeed is mine. These days when I have a ridiculous thought going through my mind and I change it, I smile. It's very empowering.

Photo: Courtesy of Dominic Grasseth

Wise Choices in College

READING

The first step in the CORE Learning System is **Collecting** knowledge, and one of the most important ways you'll **Collect** knowledge in college is by reading. During your studies you can expect to read many thousands of pages. You'll read textbooks, reference books, journals, handouts, Web pages, and more. Most of the tests you'll take will be based on your reading. And so will the essays and research papers you'll write. Obviously, then, reading is one of the most important skills you can have for success in college.

Sadly, according, to American College Testing (ACT), many college-bound students lack this skill. Nearly half of the 1.2 million students who recently took the ACT college entrance test scored low in reading. This is bad news for those students. According to the ACT, the ability to read and understand complex texts is the skill that separates students who are ready for college from those who are not. And because of all of the reading that is required in college, even students with good reading skills will benefit from becoming more accomplished.

The learning strategies you'll encounter in this chapter have one thing in common: the ability to cure **mindless reading.** Mindless reading is the act of running your eyes over a page only to realize you don't recall a thing you read. The opposite of mindless reading is **active reading.** Active reading is characterized by intense mental engagement in what you are reading. This highly focused involvement leads to significant neural activity in your brain, assists deep and lasting learning, and (good news for students) leads to high grades.

READING: THE BIG PICTURE

When reading mindfully, you are actively **Collecting** key concepts, ideas (main and secondary)

Figure 2.2

and supporting details (major and minor). When placed by levels of significance, information you read looks like Figure 2.2.

A **key concept** is the main topic you are reading about. Examples of key concepts include *inflation*, *mitosis*, *World War II*, or *symbolic interactionism*.

Ideas that expand on concepts are divided into main and secondary ideas. A **main idea** (sometimes called a "thesis") is the most important idea the author wants to convey about a key concept. Two authors may write about the same key concept but present different main ideas. For example, they may both write about *inflation* but disagree about its cause. One might say, "The primary cause of inflation is war." The other may say, "The rising cost of production is the main cause of inflation."

A **secondary idea** (sometimes called a "topic sentence") elaborates on a main idea by answering questions that readers may have about it. For example, one question about inflation might be, "What effect do taxes have on rising costs?" Another might be "How do labor unions affect the cost of production?"

Each idea—main or secondary—is typically followed by **supporting details** such as examples, evidence, explanation, and experiences.

To illustrate the relationship of levels, imagine that your instructor asks your class the following. "In Chapter 2 of *On Course*, a key concept is personal responsibility. What is the main idea about it?" (Pause for a moment and decide how you would answer, because how well you answer provides feedback about your present reading abilities.)

Imagine one of your classmates replying, "The main idea in the second chapter of *On Course* is that personal responsibility is an important inner quality for creating academic, professional, and personal success."

"Well, done," your instructor says, "and what are some of the secondary ideas?"

Another student answers, "When we are being responsible we respond to life's challenges as Creators not as Victims. Another secondary idea is that our inner conversations affect whether or not we make responsible choices. And a third idea is that using a decision-making model called the Wise Choice Process helps us make responsible choices."

"Excellent," your instructor enthuses. "You've demonstrated you understand some of the important ideas of the chapter. Now, someone please elaborate on the Wise Choice Process." In response, a third student *explains* the six steps of the Wise Choice Process and then gives an *example* of how she used it to make a recent decision. By elaborating, she offers supporting details that answer the questions a thoughtful reader would have about the Wise Choice Process, such as "What is it and how can it be used?"

So as you look at the following learning strategies, keep in mind the big picture of reading: **Your goal is to Collect key concepts, important ideas, and supporting details.**

BEFORE READING

1. Approach reading with a positive attitude. Attitude is the foundation of your success because it influences the choices you make. Nowhere is this truer than in reading. Do you have negative attitudes about reading in general or reading specific subjects? Or do you harbor doubts about your ability to understand what you read? Do you think of any of your reading assignments as beyond your understanding, boring, worthless, or stupid? If so, replace negative attitudes with positive ones. Realize that reading offers you access to the entire recorded knowledge of the human race. With effective reading skills, you can learn virtually any information or skill you need in order to improve your life, but only if you approach each reading assignment with a positive attitude.

2. Create a distributed reading schedule. A marathon reading session before an exam is seldom helpful. Instead, spread many shorter sessions over an entire course. For example, plan to finish your 450-page history text by reading 30 to 40 pages each week. You can easily reach that goal by reading just five or six pages a day. A distributed schedule like this keeps you current with your assignments, helps you concentrate for your entire reading session, and increases how much you recall from what you read.

3. Review past readings. As a warm-up before you read, glance at pages you have previously read. Look at chapter titles and text headings to jog your memory and prepare for what you are about to read. Review any marks or comments you made when you read earlier assignments (see Strategy 11). Look over any notes you took (see Strategy 12). Reviewing like this takes advantage of one of the three principles of deep and lasting learning: prior learning. When you connect what you are reading now to previously stored information (i.e., already-formed neural networks), you learn the new information or skill faster and more deeply.

4. Preview before reading. Like observing a valley from a high mountain, previewing a reading assignment provides the big picture of what's to come. You'll see the important ideas and their organization, which increases understanding when you read.

At the beginning of a course, it's wise to preview the entire book. Most of the time, however, you'll be previewing a single chapter. Thumb through the pages, taking in chapter titles, chapter objectives, focus questions, text headings, charts, graphs, illustrations, previews, and summaries. Note any words that are specially formatted, such as with CAPITALS, **bold**, *italics*, and so on. In just a few minutes, you will have a helpful overview of what you are about to read. A chapter preview should take no longer than five minutes and include a quick look at some or all of the following features:

- **Table of Contents:** The fastest way to preview is to look at the table of contents because it provides an outline of your entire reading (for an example, see the table of contexts of this book on pages vii–xiv).

- **Chapter Objectives or Focus Questions:** Usually placed at the beginning of a chapter, these features identify what you can expect to learn from the chapter. Each section in *On Course* starts with one or more Focus Questions.

- **Chapter Titles and Headings:** Thumb through the pages you're about to read, and note the titles and headings. They provide a helpful overview of the topics you'll be reading about. For example, here are three levels of information presented in Chapter 2 of *On Course*:

  Accepting Personal Responsibility

  Adopting a Creator Mindset

  Victim and Creator Mindsets

  Responsibility and Culture

  Responsibility and Choice

- **Special Formatting:** Words in CAPITALS, **bold**, *italics*, or **color** put a spotlight on key concepts and ideas. When you see special formatting, you can be confident the author is giving you a hint: *This is important information!* A common use of specially formatted text is to call attention to special vocabulary. That is why **Creator mindset** and **Victim mindset** were bolded earlier in this chapter.

- **Visual Elements:** Charts, graphs, illustrations, cartoons, photographs, and diagrams are included to reinforce concepts in the text and improve readers' understanding. For example, the two drawings on page 22 illustrate how learning changes neurons in the brain. Captions for visual elements usually explain their significance.

- **Chapter Summaries:** Many college texts provide a summary at the end of a chapter. This summary typically identifies the important ideas in the chapter.

While it's taken quite a few words to describe these six options for previewing a reading assignment, once you get skilled, previewing will take you only a few minutes to do.

5. Identify the purpose of what you're reading.
To keep the big picture in mind, ask yourself, "What's the point of what I'm about to read?" For example, the "point" of every section of *On Course* is to present empowering beliefs and behaviors that you can add to your toolbox for success in college and in life. By keeping this purpose in mind as you read, you program yourself to **Collect** the most important ideas. The purpose of what you are reading at this moment is to identify strategies that may help you improve your reading comprehension and speed.

6. Create a list of questions. Create a list of questions. If the author provides focus questions, use them to start this list. Next, turn chapter titles or section headings into questions. For example, if the heading in a computer book reads "HTML Tags," turn this heading into one or more questions: *What is an HTML tag? How are HTML tags created?* If you see questions within the text, add them to your list. The process of reading for answers to questions, especially those you're really curious about, heightens your concentration, increases your active involvement, and improves your understanding.

WHILE READING

7. Read in chunks. Poor readers read one word at a time. Good readers don't read words; they read ideas, and ideas are found in groups of words, or chunks. For example, in the following sentence, try reading all of the words between the diamonds at once:

◆ If you read ◆ in chunks ◆ you will increase ◆ your speed ◆ and your comprehension. ◆

Like any new habit, this method will initially feel awkward. However, as you practice you'll find you can take in bigger chunks of information at increasingly faster rates of speed, like this:

◆ If you read in chunks ◆ you will increase your speed ◆ and your comprehension. ◆

Since much of your reading time occurs while you pause to take in words (called a "fixation"), the fewer times you pause, the faster you can read. In addition to taking in larger chunks of information, you can nudge yourself even faster by moving your fingers along the line of text as a speed regulator. As you get practiced at taking in more words in one fixation, you can increase the speed of your fingers and read even faster.

8. Concentrate on reading faster. In one experiment, students increased their reading speed up to 50 percent simply by concentrating on reading as fast as they could while still understanding what they were reading. You, too, can probably read faster by just *deciding* to.

9. Pause to recite. Have you ever finished reading an assignment only to realize you have no idea what you just read? Here's a remedy. Stop at the end of each section and summarize aloud what you understand to be the main ideas and supporting details. The more difficult the reading, the more often you'll want to pause to recite. Each recitation will give you instant feedback about how well you understand the author's ideas. When you can't smoothly recite the essence of what you have read, go back and read the passage again. Try reading aloud the words you have underlined or highlighted. Keep working actively with the ideas until you understand them completely.

10. Read for answers to questions on your list. If you've created a list of questions (Strategy 6), now is the time to cash in on that effort. For example, suppose you're about to read a chapter in your accounting book titled "The Double-Entry Accounting System." On your list of questions, you've written "What is a double-entry accounting system?" As you read the chapter, look for and underline the answer. Then write the question in the margin alongside. If you finish your reading assignment and still have unanswered questions on your list, ask your instructor for answers during class or office hours.

11. Mark and annotate your text. As you read, keep asking yourself: *What's the key concept . . . what are the main ideas about the concept . . . and what support is offered?* Identifying main and supporting ideas is usually easier after you've read a whole paragraph, or even a whole section. Once you decide what's important, underline or highlight these ideas in your book. As a guideline, mark only 10 to 15 percent of your text, selecting only what is truly important. Additionally, annotate what you read. To *annotate* means to add comments. Writing your own comments in the open spaces on each page helps you minimize mindless reading and maximize your understanding. Annotations could include summaries in your own words, diagrams, or questions for which you want answers. Later, when creating study materials, your marks and annotations will help you continue **Collecting** the most important ideas to learn.

12. Take notes. Many strategies exist for **Collecting** ideas from textbooks by taking notes in a separate binder or computer file, and in future chapters you'll learn a number of nifty strategies for doing just that. However, there is one option that is particularly suited for taking notes while reading a text, so we'll look at it here. Start by writing the chapter title at the top of your note page or computer file (this is usually the key concept). Beneath the chapter title, copy the first main heading from the chapter, thus recording a level 1 main idea. Add any subheadings from your book below the main heading, indenting a few more spaces to the right, thus recording level 2 secondary ideas). Here's what this would look like for Chapter 2 of *On Course*:

Structure	Example
Key Concept	Accepting Personal Responsibility
—Level 1 Main Idea	—Adopting a Creator Mindset
—Level 2 Secondary Idea	—Victim and Creator Mindsets
—Level 2 Secondary Idea	—Responsibility and Culture
—Level 2 Secondary Idea	—Responsibility and Choice
—Level 1 Main Idea	—Mastering Creator Language
—Level 2 Secondary Idea	—Self-Talk
—Level 2 Secondary Idea	—The Language of Responsibility
—Level 1 Main Idea	—Making Wise Decisions
—Level 2 Secondary Idea	—The Wise Choice Process

13. Look up the definition of key words. Use a dictionary when you don't know the meaning of a key word. Consider starting a vocabulary list in your journal. Or create a deck of index cards with new words on one side and definitions on the other. Online dictionaries, like Merriam-Webster's (http://www.m-w.com), offer an option that lets you hear the correct pronunciation of a word. Use your new words in conversations to lock them in your memory. Developing an extensive and eloquent vocabulary is a great success strategy. In case you want to set some goals for the size of your vocabulary, linguist David Crystal estimates that the average college graduate has an active vocabulary of 60,000 words and the ability to recognize an additional 75,000.

14. Read critically. Not all ideas in print are true. Learn to read critically by being a healthy skeptic. Look for red flags that may suggest a credibility problem. Who is the author? What are the author's credentials? What assumptions does the author hold? Does the author stand to gain (e.g., money, status, revenge) by your acceptance of his or her opinion? Are the facts accurate and relevant? Is the evidence sufficient? Are the author's positions developed with logic or only strong emotions? Are sources of information identified? Are they believable? Are they current? Are various sides of an issue presented, or only one? Given that anyone can post information on the Internet, reading critically is especially important when assessing information that you encounter online. You'll learn more about how to be a critical thinker in Chapter 7.

AFTER READING

15. Reflect on what you read. Upon finishing a reading assignment, lean back, close your eyes, and ask yourself questions that will help you see the big picture. For example . . .

- What are the key concepts?

- What are the main ideas about those concepts?

- What are the supporting details?

- What do I personally think and feel about the author's main ideas and supporting details?

16. Reread difficult passages. On occasion, every reader needs to revisit difficult passages to understand them fully. I recall one author whose writing made me feel like a dunce. However, somewhere around my fifth or sixth reading (and using strategies in this section), a light went on in my brain and I thought, "Oh . . . so that's what he means! That's not nearly as complicated as I thought!" Trust that by using the strategies presented here, you can comprehend any reading assignment if you stick with it long enough.

17. Recite the marked text. Read aloud the parts of the text you have underlined or highlighted. Attempt to blend the ideas into a flowing statement by adding connecting words between the words in your text. In effect, you'll be summarizing the key points of the material you just read.

18. Talk about what you read. Explain the main ideas and supporting details. Especially helpful is having this conversation with another student in your class who has read the same assignment. This study partner can give you feedback on where you may have misunderstood or left out something important.

19. Read another book on the same subject. Sometimes another author will express the same ideas more clearly. Ask your instructor or a librarian to suggest other readings. Or try a book on the same topic written for children. A book for younger learners may provide just the information or explanation you need to make sense of your college textbook.

20. Seek assistance. Still having problems understanding what you read? Ask your instructor to explain muddy points. Or see if your college has a reading lab or a tutoring center. For some subjects—such as math, science, and foreign languages—there may be dedicated personnel to help. If all else fails, see if your college has a diagnostician who can test you for a possible learning disability. Such a specialist may be able to help you improve your reading skills.

READING EXERCISE

Choose your most challenging textbook and rate your present comprehension of its content on a scale of 1 to 10 (with 10 indicating a deep and lasting understanding of what you read). Over the next week, apply new reading strategies when you read this challenging text. At the end of the week, again rate your understanding of the book on the 1-to-10 scale. Be prepared to explain why you think your rating went up, down, or stayed the same. In particular, is there one reading strategy that was most helpful in your quest to read this challenging text with greater comprehension?

Discovering Self-Motivation

3

Once I accept responsibility for creating my own life,
I must choose the kind of life I want to create.

*I'm motivated to create the outcomes
and experiences I've chosen for my life.*

SUCCESSFUL STUDENTS ...	STRUGGLING STUDENTS ...
create inner motivation, providing themselves with the passion and drive to persist toward their goals and dreams, despite all obstacles.	**have little sense of passion and drive**, often quitting when difficulties arise.
design a compelling life plan, complete with motivating goals and dreams.	**tend to invent their lives as they live them.**
commit to their goals and dreams, visualizing the successful creation of their ideal future.	**wander aimlessly from one activity to another.**

Case Study in Critical Thinking

POPSON'S DILEMMA

Fresh from graduate school, Assistant Professor Popson was midway through his first semester of college teaching when he began to get discouraged. Long gone were the excitement and promise of the first day of class. Now, only about two-thirds of his students were attending, and some of them were barely holding on. When Popson asked a question during class, the same few students answered every time. The rest stared off in bored silence. One student always wore a knit cap with a slender cord slithering from under it to an iPod in his shirt pocket. With 10 or even 15 minutes remaining in a class period, students would start stuffing notebooks noisily into their backpacks or book bags. Only one student had visited him during office hours, despite Popson's numerous invitations. And when he announced one day that he was canceling the next class to attend a professional conference, a group in the back of the room pumped their fists in the air and hooted with glee. It pained Popson to have aroused so little academic motivation in his students, and he began asking experienced professors what he should do.

Professor Assante said, "Research says that about 70 percent of students enroll in college because they see the degree as their ticket to a good job and fat paycheck. And they're right. College grads earn nearly a million dollars more in their lives than high school grads. Show them how your course will help them graduate and prosper in the work world. After that, most of them will be model students."

Professor Buckley said, "Everyone wants the freedom to make choices affecting their lives, so have your students design personal learning contracts. Let each one choose assignments from a list of options you provide. Let them add their own choices if they want. Even have them pick the dates they'll turn in their assignments. Give them coupons that allow them to miss any three classes without penalty. Do everything you can to give them choices and put them in charge of their own

education. Once they see they're in control of their learning and you're here to help them, their motivation will soar."

Professor Chang said, "Deep down, everyone wants to make a difference. I just read a survey by the Higher Education Research Institute showing that two-thirds of first-year students believe it's essential or very important to help others. Find out what your students want to do to make a contribution. Tell them how your course will help them achieve those dreams. Even better, engage them in a service learning project. When they see how your course can help them live a life with real purpose, they'll be much more interested in what you're teaching."

Professor Donnelly said, "Let's be realistic. The best motivator for students is grades. It's the old carrot and stick. Start every class with a quiz and they'll get there on time. Take points off for absences and they'll attend regularly. Give extra points for getting assignments in on time. Reward every positive action with points and take off points when they screw up. When they realize they can get a good grade in your class by doing what's right, even the guy with the iPod will get involved."

Professor Egret said, "Most people work harder and learn better when they feel they're part of a team with a common goal, so help your students feel part of a community of learners. Give them interesting topics to talk about in pairs and small groups. Give them team assignments and group projects. Teach them how to work well in groups so everyone contributes their fair share. When your students start feeling like they belong and start caring about one another, you'll see their academic motivation go way up."

Professor Fanning said, "Your unmotivated students probably don't expect to pass your course, so they quit trying. Here's my suggestion: Assign a modest challenge at which they can all succeed if they do it. And every student *has* to do it. No exceptions. Afterward, give students specific feedback on what they did well and what they can do to improve. Then give them a slightly more challenging assignment and repeat the cycle again and again. Help them *expect* to be successful by *being* successful. At some point they're going to say, 'Hey, I can do this!' and then you'll see a whole different attitude."

Professor Gonzales said, "Learning should be active and fun. I'm not talking about a party; I'm talking engaging students in educational experiences that teach deep and important lessons about your subject. Your students should be thinking, 'I can't wait to get to class to see what we're going to do and learn today!' You can use debates, videos, field trips, group projects, case studies, learning games, simulations, role plays, guest speakers, visualizations . . . the possibilities are endless. When learning is engaging and enjoyable, motivation problems disappear."

Professor Harvey said, "I've been teaching for 30 years, and if there's one thing I've learned, it's this: You can't motivate someone else. Maybe you've heard the old saying, 'When the student is ready, the teacher will arrive.' You're just wasting your energy trying to make someone learn before they're ready. Maybe they'll be back in your class in five or ten years and

they'll be motivated. But for now, just do the best you can for the students who *are* ready."

Listed below are the eight professors in this story. Based on your experience, rank the quality of their advice on the scale below. Give a different score to each professor. Be prepared to explain your choices.

Best advice ← 1 2 3 4 5 6 7 8 → Worst advice

3 **Professor Assante**   4 **Professor Egret**

8 **Professor Buckley**   7 **Professor Fanning**

1 **Professor Chang**   2 **Professor Gonzales**

6 **Professor Donnelly**   5 **Professor Harvey**

▶ **DIVING DEEPER** Is there an approach not mentioned by one of the eight professors that would be even more motivating for you?

Creating Inner Motivation

Focus Questions   How important do educators think motivation is to your academic success? What determines how motivated you are? What can you do to keep your motivation consistently high this semester . . . and beyond?

Recently, two extensive surveys asked college and university educators to rank factors that hinder students' success and persistence. These surveys were done by American College Testing (ACT) and the Policy Center on the First Year of College. In both surveys, educators identified *lack of motivation* as the number one barrier to students' success in college.

Lack of motivation has various symptoms: students arriving late to class or being absent, assignments turned in late or not at all, work done sloppily, appointments missed, offers of support ignored, and students not participating in class discussions or activities, to name just a few. But the most glaring symptom of all is the enormous number of students who vanish from college within their first year. According to ACT, about one-third of students in U.S. four-year public colleges and universities fail to return for their second year. In public two-year colleges, it's even worse: Nearly *half* of first-year students don't make it to a second year. Despite these grim statistics, you can be among those who stay and thrive in higher education!

There are three things to remember about education. The first is motivation. The second is motivation. The third is motivation.

Terrell Bell, former U.S. Secretary of Education

A FORMULA FOR MOTIVATION

The study of human motivation—exploring why we do what we do—is extensive and complex. However, one formula explains much about academic motivation: V × E = M.

In this formula, "V" stands for "value." In terms of your education, value is determined by the benefits you believe you'll obtain from seeking and obtaining a college degree. The greater the benefits you assign to college experiences and outcomes, the greater will be your motivation. The greater your motivation, the higher the cost you'll be willing to pay in terms of time, money, effort, frustration, inconvenience, and sacrifice. Take a moment to identify the score that presently represents the value you place on seeking and obtaining a college education. Choose a number from 0 to 10 (where "0" represents no perceived value and "10" represents an extremely high perceived value).

Having rated the value you place on achieving a college education, consider for a moment how your deep culture influenced your rating. Some cultural beliefs will boost your motivation, giving you staying power when the going gets rough. For example, most Chinese mothers place a high value on education, according to researcher Ruth K. Choa. They are quite willing to make big sacrifices to help their children succeed in school. Parents of middle- and upper-class students in North America are also known to place a high value on education. When parents in a culture demonstrate with words and deeds that they value education, the odds are great their children will as well.

Conversely, some cultures devalue formal education, thus lowering academic motivation. Working-class culture in North America often encourages its members to leave school in favor of a job and paycheck. Once the majority on campus, men now represent only about 43 percent of enrollment at North American colleges. It appears that to a growing number of men, "school is not cool." Some minorities, anthropologist John Ogbu observed, put little effort into academics in order to avoid the cultural stigma of acting "white." In a dominant culture that prizes education, such mindsets put members of these cultures in a painful dilemma. To do well in school goes against their culture, but to do poorly in school handicaps their future. Bottom line: To keep your motivation high, you'll need to have a clear sense of the personal value to you of a college degree.

In the formula V × E = M, the "E" stands for "expectation." In terms of your education, expectation is determined by how likely you think it is that you can earn a college degree with a reasonable effort. To make that calculation, you need to weigh your abilities (how good a student you are and how strong your previous education is) against the difficulty of achieving your goal (how challenging the courses are that you will need to take and how much you are willing to sacrifice to be successful). Take a moment to identify the score that presently represents your personal expectation of being able to complete a college degree with a reasonable effort. Choose a number from 0 to 10 (where "0" represents no expectation of success and "10" represents an extremely high expectation of success).

Today's theories about motivation emphasize the importance of factors within the individual, particularly the variables of expectancy and value. Students' motivations are strongly influenced by what they think is important (value) and what they believe they can accomplish (expectancy).

K. Patricia Cross

There is evidence that the time for learning various subjects would be cut to a fraction of the time currently allotted if the material were perceived by the learner as related to his own purposes.

Carl Rogers

Once again, consider how cultural influences may have swayed your expectations of success in college. If your rating is high, consider whether your score reflects the expectation of your parents or others in your culture. Studies show that many middle- and upper-class students in North America, as well as Asian-American students, have internalized high expectations for achieving academic success. However, members of other cultures may not have the same beliefs to lift their motivation. See if you can spot a self-defeating generalization about a group to which you belong because of your race, religion, sex, economic class, age, ethnicity, ability, or geographical region. For example, a young woman in my writing class once told me she knew she was going to fail. It was only the first day of the class and I asked her why she thought that. "I'm from the country," she said, "and people from the country can't write." I asked where she had learned that. "My fifth-grade teacher told us," she replied. And her tone said, "There, that *proves* it."

Research shows that teacher expectations influence students' own expectations of academic success. Fortunately, many teachers hold very high expectations for their students. Sadly, some instructors hold low expectations for all students, while some hold low expectations just for students of a particular culture. If you've had such a teacher, or encounter one in college, don't allow a Victim mindset to buy into disempowering stereotypes such as people from the country can't write, or women can't learn math, or students with learning disabilities aren't college material, or older students have lost the ability to learn. Instead, employ a Creator mindset, set your own high expectations, and live up to them.

In a nutshell, the V × E = M formula says that your level of motivation in college is determined by multiplying your value score by your expectation score. For example, if the value you place on a college degree is high (say, a 10), but your expectation of success in college is low (say, a 1), then your motivation score will be very low (10). Similarly, if you put little value on a college degree (say a 2), even if your expectation for success in college is high (say, a 9), then once more, your motivation score will be very low (18). In either case, your low score suggests that you probably won't do what's required to succeed in college: to make goal-directed choices consistently, to give a high-quality effort regularly, and to persist despite inevitable obstacles and challenges. Sadly, then, you'll join the multitude of students who exit college long before earning a degree.

Probably you see where all of this leads. To stay motivated in college, first, you need ways to raise (or keep high) the **value** you place on college, including the academic degree you'll earn, the knowledge you'll gain, and the experiences you'll have while enrolled. Second, you need ways to raise (or keep high) the **expectation** you have of being successful in college while making what you consider to be a reasonable effort. With our exploration of effective reading skills in Chapter 2, we've already identified some important academic skills that, when mastered, will contribute to your high expectations for success in college. Throughout *On Course*, you'll encounter literally hundreds of other skills, both academic and otherwise, that can raise your realistic expectation of success in college even higher.

Students tend to internalize the beliefs teachers have about their ability and they rise and fall in achieving the level of expectation of their teachers.

Lynn Kell Spradlin

For now, however, we are going to focus on value. Only you can determine how much value a college education holds for you, but let's look at some of the benefits that others have attributed to achieving a degree beyond high school.

VALUE OF COLLEGE OUTCOMES

One of the most widely recognized benefits of a college degree is increased earning power. According to recent U.S. Census Bureau data, high school graduates earn an average of $1.2 million dollars during their working lives. However, if you complete a two-year associate's degree, that lifetime total goes up another $400,000. If you complete a four-year bachelor's degree, you can add another $500,000. That means college graduates earn nearly one million dollars more in their lifetimes than those who end their formal education with a high school degree. Think what that additional money could do to help you and the people you love live a good life.

Not only does a college degree offer increased earnings, it also opens doors to employment in many desirable professions. Six out of every 10 jobs now require some postsecondary education and training, according to data reported by the ERIC Clearinghouse on Higher Education. The U.S. Department of Labor reports that the number of jobs requiring advanced skills now grows at twice the rate of those requiring only basic skills.

A college degree confers many additional benefits. According to the Institute for Higher Education Policy and the Carnegie Foundation, college graduates enjoy . . .

- higher savings levels.
- improved working conditions.
- increased personal and professional mobility.
- improved health and life expectancy.
- improved quality of life for offspring.
- better consumer decision making.
- increased personal status.
- more hobbies and leisure activities.

College grads also become more open-minded, more cultured, more rational, more consistent, and less authoritarian. As a bonus, these benefits are passed on to their children.

Additionally, attaining a college degree can bring personal satisfaction and accomplishment. I once had a 76-year-old student who inspired our class with her determination "to finally earn the college degree that I cheated myself out of more than 50 years ago." Another valuable outcome of a college degree is the pride and esteem that many enjoy when they walk across the stage to receive their hard-earned diploma. And for some, a college degree is an essential step toward fulfilling a personal vision; such was true for my college roommate who, for as long as he could remember, dreamed of being a doctor (and today he is one).

> For learning to take place with any kind of efficiency students must be motivated. To be motivated, they must become interested. And they become interested when they are actively working on projects which they can relate to their values and goals in life.
>
> *Gus Tuberville, former president,*
> *William Penn College*

Table 3.1   One Student's Desired Outcomes

Desired Outcomes	Value
Earn a grade point average (GPA) of 3.8 or better and make the dean's list this semester.	A high GPA will look great on my transcript when I apply for a job. Also, it will give me a real boost of self-confidence.
In my English class, write at least one essay that contains no more than two nonstandard grammar errors.	I want to be able to write without worrying that someone who reads my work is going to think I'm stupid or illiterate.
In my Student Success class, learn at least three strategies for managing my time more effectively.	I feel overwhelmed and stressed with all I need to do, and learning how to manage my time better will lower my stress level.
Get an A in my accounting class.	I want a career in accounting, so doing well in this course is the first step toward success in my profession.
Make three or more new friends.	My friends from high school all went to other colleges or they're working. I want to make new friends here so I'll have people to hang out with on the weekends.

For some people, long-term goals are too distant to be motivating. They do get fired up, however, by short-term goals they can nearly touch, such as outcomes they can create during this semester. Table 3.1 shows the short-term goals that one of my students chose for himself, along with his reasons why.

VALUE OF COLLEGE EXPERIENCES

Value isn't found only in outcomes; it's also found in experiences. In fact, all human beings manage their emotions by doing their best to maximize positive experiences and minimize negative ones. What, for example, is the value of playing an intramural sport, attending a movie, belonging to a fraternity or sorority, dancing, playing a video game, or hanging out with friends? Primarily, all are choices to manage our inner experiences. If done in excess, any one of these choices can get us off course from our desired outcomes. But done in moderation, all of these activities (and many others) can create a positive experience and contribute greatly to academic motivation. That's because if you're enjoying the journey called college, you're much more likely to persist until you reach the destination called graduation.

So, what are your desired experiences in college? If someday in the future you were to tell someone that college was one of the best experiences of your life, what specifically would you have experienced? Many will say "fun." Fair enough. Then make fun happen. Your challenge is to experience fun while staying on course to academic success. And you can do it! Consider these options for fun: Join a club, play a sport, get to know a classmate, attend a party, learn

> Setting specific goals helps learners in at least three ways: The goals focus attention on important aspects of the task; they help motivate and sustain task mastery efforts; and they serve an information function by arming learners with criteria that they can use to assess and if necessary adjust their strategies as they work.
>
> *Jere Brophy*

something new that really interests you. Here are other experiences that my students desired: respect, relaxation, connection, self-confidence, an open mind, quiet reflection, passion for learning, total engagement, full-out participation, inspiration, challenge, courage, spirit of the group, self-acceptance, joy, pride, freedom, and an "Aha."

One of the students in my college success class said he wanted to experience "creativity." As an alternative to the final project, he proposed to write a rap song about the success principles he'd learned in our class. I told him he had my permission as long as he agreed to "rap" his project to our class on the last day of the semester. Little did I know that he was a professional rapper with a couple of CDs to his credit. As promised, he (and his whole group) showed up on the last day of the semester, handed out the words to "The College Success Rap," and treated us all to a rousing course finale. Best of all, he did a great job of demonstrating that he had learned many of the key principles of success, helping his classmates learn them even more deeply. Afterward he said, "Man, that was great!"

Table 3.2 lists the desired experiences that another of my students identified for herself, along with her reasons why.

German philosopher Friedrich Nietzsche once said, "He who has a *why* to live for can endure almost any *how*." He affirms that few obstacles can stop us when we understand the personal value we place on the outcomes and experiences of our journey. Discover your own motivation and your chances for success soar!

> What ultimately counts most for each person is what happens in consciousness: the moments of joy, the times of despair added up through the years determine what life will be like. If we don't gain control over the contents of consciousness we can't live a fulfilling life.
>
> *Mihaly Csikszentmihaly*

> He who puts in four hours of "want to" will almost always outperform the person who puts in eight hours of "have to."
>
> *Roger von Oech*

Table 3.2   One Student's Desired Experiences

Desired Experiences	Value
Fun	My brother dropped out of college because he said it was all work and no play. I know I'm going to have to work hard in college, but I want to have fun, too. I think if I'm enjoying myself, that'll make all the assignments more bearable.
Academic confidence	I've never done particularly well in school, although my teachers have always said I could be a good student if I applied myself more. I want to feel just as smart as any other student in my classes.
Excitement about learning	I didn't really like my classes in high school. I want to get excited about learning in at least one course, so I look forward to the homework and sometimes the class time goes so fast I can't believe when it's over.
Personal confidence	I have always been a shy person, and I want to become more outgoing so I can do well on future job interviews and be more assertive in my career so I get the promotions I deserve.

Journal Entry 9

In this journal entry, you'll identify your desired outcomes and experiences for this course and/or this semester. Developing clarity on what you want to create this semester will help you stay motivated and on course until the end. Use the student examples earlier in this section as models, but of course record your own desired outcomes, experiences, and reasons.

1. In your journal, create an empty table like Table 3.1. Fill in three or more of your own desired *outcomes* for this course and/or this semester. Next to each, explain why you value achieving that outcome. Remember, "outcomes" are those things you will take *away* with you at the end of the semester (such as a grade or something you learn). At this point, you don't have to know HOW you will achieve these outcomes; you only need to know WHAT you want and WHY.

2. In your journal, create an empty table like Table 3.2. Fill in three or more of your desired *experiences* for this course and/or this semester. Next to each, explain why you value having that experience. Remember, "experiences" are those things you will have *during* this semester (such as fun or a sense of community). Once again, all that matters here is WHAT you would like to experience and WHY. At this time, you don't need to worry about HOW.

3. Using the formula of V × E = M, write about your level of motivation to be successful in college. Begin as follows: *The value I place on being a success in college is ____ [0–10] and my expectation of being a success in college is ____ [0–10]. Multiplied together, this gives me an achievement motivation score of ____ [0–100].* Then continue by explaining your score and identifying specific actions you can do to raise it (or keep it high).

Remember, dive deep. When you explore your motivation at a deep level, you improve your chances of having an important insight that can change your life for the better. So dive deep and discover what really motivates you.

> Success isn't a result of spontaneous combustion. You must set yourself on fire.
>
> *Arnold H. Glasow*

One Student's Story

CHEE MENG VANG
Inver Hills Community College, Minnesota

When I got to college, my biggest challenge was staying motivated. I was always going out clubbing with my friends, older sisters, and cousins. I was also shooting pool and hanging out with friends until late at night. I was lazy all the time and couldn't concentrate. I missed classes, fell behind in my homework, and tried to do everything at the last minute. This caused a lot of problems for me, like getting D's on my tests and quizzes. I felt like whatever happened to me was out of my control. I was feeling down and filled with dissatisfaction.

(Continues)

(Continued)

One night I was in a club, watching people drinking and dancing, and I thought, "This is getting boring. I'm tired and this isn't taking me anywhere at all." It was a good thing that College Success was part of my full-time student schedule. Our book was called *On Course*, and it helped me big time. It taught me to see myself as the primary cause of my outcomes and experiences and to find my desires that cause me to act. I was so stupid because my desire was right in front of me. There are so many reasons why it is important that I do well in college. My parents came to the United States from Laos, and all they ever wanted was a better life for their kids. It was hard for them in a new country, and we never had very much money. I realized I was being a loser and letting them down. Also, I am the first man in my family to go to college and my lovely five little brothers look up to me. I need to show them what a good role model their big brother can be. I want a career that will allow me to help my family, and when I have children, I don't want to be a dad working in McDonald's. My dream is to be a pharmacist, but I was headed in the wrong direction.

I come from a poor family, and I don't ever want to be like that in the future, so I had to make changes right away. I stopped going out to clubs and started taking responsibility. I became more outgoing in class. I studied two hours or more every day. I started getting A's and B's on my tests and quizzes. I finished the semester by raising my D grades to B's. As you can see, I've gone from being a lazy, unmotivated guy to a responsible, outgoing, I-control-my-destiny man. Now I don't feel like a victim any more. I've actually started to feel like a hero to my parents, my little brothers, and even to the small community where we live.

Designing a Compelling Life Plan

 Focus Questions If your life were as good as it could possibly be, what would it look like? What would you have, do, and be?

While growing up, Joan dreamed of becoming a famous singer. Following high school, she started performing in night clubs. She married her manager, and the two of them lived in a motor home, driving from town to town in pursuit of singing jobs. After exhausting years on the road, Joan recorded a song. It didn't sell, and her dream began to unravel. Marital problems complicated her career. Career problems complicated her marriage. Joan grew tired of the financial and emotional uncertainty in her life. Finally, in frustration, she divorced her husband and gave up her dream of singing professionally.

Although disappointed, Joan started setting new goals. She needed to earn a living, so she set a short-term goal to become a hairdresser. After graduating from cosmetology school, Joan saved enough money to settle some debts, buy a car, and pay for a new long-term goal. She decided to go to a community college (where I met her) and major in dental hygiene.

Two years later, Joan graduated with honors and went to work in a dentist's office. Lacking a dream that excited her, Joan chose another long-term goal: earning her bachelor's degree. Joan worked days in the dentist's office and at night she attended classes. After a few years, she again graduated with honors.

Your goals are the road maps that guide you and show you what is possible for your life.

Les Brown

Then, she set another long-term goal: earning her master's degree. Earlier in her life, Joan had doubted that she was "college material." With each academic success, her confidence grew. "One day I realized that once I set a goal, it's a done deal," Joan said.

This awareness inspired her to begin dreaming again. As a child, Joan had always imagined herself as a teacher, but her doubts had always steered her in other directions. Master's degree now in hand, she returned to our college to teach dental hygiene. A year later, she was appointed department chairperson. In only seven years, Joan had gone from a self-doubting first-year student to head of our college's dental hygiene department. Despite obstacles and setbacks, she continued to move in a positive direction, ever motivated by the promise of achieving personally valuable goals and dreams.

ROLES AND GOALS

According to psychologist Brian Tracy, many people resist setting life goals because they don't know how. Let's eliminate this barrier so you, like Joan, can experience the heightened motivation that accompanies personally meaningful goals.

First, think about the roles you have chosen for your life. A life role is an activity to which we regularly devote large amounts of time and energy. For example, you're presently playing the role of college student. How many of the following roles are you also playing: friend, employee, employer, athlete, brother, sister, church member, son, daughter, roommate, husband, wife, partner, parent, grandparent, tutor, musician, neighbor, volunteer? Do you play other roles as well? Most people identify four to seven major life roles. If you have more than seven, you may be spreading yourself too thin. Consider combining or eliminating one or more of your roles while in college. If you have identified fewer than four roles, assess your life again. You may have overlooked a role or two.

> The most important thing about motivation is goal setting. You should always have a goal.
>
> *Francie Larrieu Smith*

CATHY   **by Cathy Guisewite**

Once you identify your life roles, think about your long-term goals for each one. Identify what you hope to accomplish in this role in the next 2 to 5 or even 10 years. For example, in your role as a student, 10 years from now will you have a 2-year associate of arts (A.A.) degree? A four-year bachelor of arts (B.A.) or bachelor of science (B.S.) degree? Will you have attended graduate school to earn a master of arts (M.A.) or master of science (M.S.) degree? Or gone even farther to obtain a doctor of philosophy (Ph.D.) degree, a medical doctor (M.D.) degree, or a doctor of jurisprudence (J.D.) law degree? Any of these future academic goals could be yours.

HOW TO SET A GOAL

To be truly motivating, a goal needs five qualities. You can remember them by applying the DAPPS rule. "DAPPS" is an acronym, a memory device in which each letter of the word stands for one of five qualities: Dated, Achievable, Personal, Positive, and Specific.

Dated

Motivating goals have specific deadlines. A short-term goal usually has a deadline within a few months (like your semester's desired outcomes set in Journal Entry 9). A long-term goal generally has a deadline as far in the future as 1 year, 5 years, even 10 years (such as the goal you have for your most advanced academic degree). As your target deadline approaches, your motivation typically increases. This positive energy helps you finish strong. If you don't meet your deadline, you have an opportunity to examine what went wrong and create a new plan. Without a deadline, you might stretch the pursuit of a goal over your whole life, never reaching it.

Achievable

Motivating goals are challenging but realistic. It's unrealistic to say you'll run a marathon (26+ miles) next week if your idea of a monster workout has been opening and closing the refrigerator. Still, if you're going to err, err on the side of optimism. When you set goals at the outer reaches of your present ability, stretching to reach them causes you to grow. Listen to other people's advice, but trust yourself to know what is achievable for you. Apply this guideline: "Is achieving this goal at least 50 percent believable to me?" If so and you *really* value it, go for it!

Personal

Motivating goals are your own. They aren't thrust upon you by someone else. Be aware of pressure to conform to the expectations of others. Maybe you have a passion for graphic design but your parents want you to major in business so you can join the family business. Also be aware of subtle pressure to conform to the norms of your culture at the expense of what you want. For example, all cultures create expectations about what men and women *should*

One day Alice came to a fork in the road and saw a Cheshire cat in a tree. "Which road do I take?" she asked. "Where do you want to go?" was his response. "I don't know," Alice answered. "Then," said the cat, "it doesn't matter."

Lewis Carroll

Goals are dreams with a deadline.

Napoleon Hill

do, and, interestingly, gender-role stereotypes are similar across cultures. If you're a woman who wants to be an engineer, don't set a goal to be a dental hygienist. If you're a man who wants to be a kindergarten teacher, don't set a goal to be a lawyer. You don't want to be on your deathbed some day and realize you have lived someone else's life. Trust that you know better than anyone else what you want.

Positive

Motivating goals focus your energy on what you *do* want rather than on what you *don't* want. So translate negative goals into positive goals. For example, a negative goal not to fail a class becomes a positive goal to earn a grade of B or better. I recall a race car driver explaining how he miraculously kept his spinning car from smashing into the concrete racetrack wall: "I kept my eye on the track, not the wall." Likewise, focus your thoughts and actions on where you *do* want to go rather than where you *don't* want to go, and you, too, will stay on course.

Specific

Motivating goals state outcomes in specific, measurable terms. It's not enough to say, "My goal is to do better this semester" or "My goal is to work harder at my job." How will you know if you've achieved these goals? What specific, measurable evidence will you have? Revised, these goals become, "I will complete every college assignment this semester to the best of my ability" and "I will volunteer for all offerings of overtime at work." Being specific keeps you from fooling yourself into believing you've achieved a goal when, in fact, you haven't. It also helps you make choices that create positive results.

Through the years, I've had the joy of working with students who have had wonderful and motivating long-term goals: becoming an operating room nurse, writing and publishing a novel, traveling around the world, operating a refuge for homeless children, marrying and raising a beautiful family, playing professional baseball, starting a private school, composing songs for Aretha Franklin, becoming a college professor, swimming in the Olympics, managing an international mutual fund, having a one-woman art show, becoming a fashion model, getting elected state senator, owning a clothing boutique, and more. How about you? What do you *really* want?

DISCOVER YOUR DREAMS

Perhaps even more than goals do, dreams fuel our inner fire. They give our lives purpose and guide our choices. They provide motivating energy when we run headlong into an obstacle. When Candy Lightner's daughter was killed by a drunk driver, she transformed this tragedy into her dream to stop drunk driving, and her dream became the international organization Mothers Against Drunk Driving (MADD). I found my dream only after 20 years of college teaching: My passion is empowering students with the beliefs and behaviors essential for living

I always wanted to be somebody, but now I realize I should have been more specific.

Lily Tomlin

The future belongs to those who believe in the beauty of their dreams.

Eleanor Roosevelt

a rich and personally fulfilling life. Although it's difficult to define a dream, they're grand in size and fueled by strong emotions. Unlike goals, which usually fit into one of our life roles, dreams often take over our lives, inspire other people, and take on a life of their own. That's why I sometimes wonder if people have dreams or if dreams have people.

If you presently have a big dream, you know how motivating it is. If you don't have a big dream, you're certainly in the majority. Most people have not found a guiding dream, yet they can still have great lives. College, though, offers a wonderful opportunity to discover or expand your dreams. You'll be exposed to hundreds, even thousands, of new people, ideas, and experiences. With each encounter, be aware of your energy. If you feel your voltage rise, pay attention. Something within you is getting inspired. If you're fortunate enough to find such a dream, consider the pithy advice of philosopher Joseph Campbell: "Follow your bliss."

YOUR LIFE PLAN

Wise travelers use maps to locate their destination and identify the best route to get there. Similarly, Creators identify their goals and dreams and the most direct path there. In creating such a life plan, it helps to start with your destination in mind and work backwards. If you have a dream, accomplishing it becomes your ultimate destination. Or maybe your destination is the accomplishment of one or more long-term goals for your life roles. Because you can't complete a long journey in one step, your short-term goals become steppingstones, and each one completed brings you closer to the achievement of a long-term goal or dream.

Take a look at a page of a life plan that one student, Pilar, designed for herself. Although Pilar recorded her dream, not everyone will be able to do that. Her full life plan includes a page for each life role that she identified for herself, all of them with the same dream. Obviously, some life roles are going to make a more significant contribution to her dream than others. Notice that each long- and short-term goal adheres to the DAPPS rule.

> What is significant about a life plan is that it can help us live our own lives (not someone else's) as well as possible.
>
> *Harriet Goldhor Lerner*

MY DREAM: *I help families adopt older children (10 years old or older) and create home environments in which the children feel loved and supported to grow into healthy, productive adults.*

MY LIFE ROLE: *College student*

MY LONG-TERM GOALS IN THIS ROLE:

1. *I earn an associate of arts (A.A.) degree by June 2016.*
2. *I earn a bachelor of arts (B.A.) degree by June 2018.*
3. *I earn a master of social work (M.S.W.) degree by June 2020.*

MY SHORT-TERM GOALS IN THIS ROLE: *(this semester)*

1. *I achieve an A in English 101 by December 18.*

2. *I write a research paper on the challenges of adopting older children by November 20.*

3. *I achieve an A in Psychology 101 by December 18.*

4. *I learn and apply five or more psychological strategies that will help my family be happier and more loving by November 30.*

5. *I achieve an A in College Success by December 18.*

6. *I dive deep in every* On Course *journal entry, writing a minimum of 500 words for each one.*

7. *I learn five or more new success strategies and teach them to my younger brothers by November 30.*

8. *I take at least one page of notes in every class I attend this semester.*

9. *I turn in every assignment on time this semester.*

10. *I learn to use a computer well enough to prepare all of my written assignments by October 15.*

This is the first page of Pilar's six-page life plan. She wrote a similar page for each of her other five life roles: sister, daughter, friend, athlete, and employee at a group home for children.

Consciously designing your life plan, as Pilar did, has many benefits. A life plan defines your desired destinations in life and charts your best route for getting there. It gives your Inner Guide something positive to focus on when the chatter of your Inner Critic or Inner Defender attempts to distract you. And, like all maps, a life plan helps you get back on course if you get lost.

Perhaps most of all, a life plan is your personal definition of a life worth living. With it in mind, you'll be less dependent on someone else to motivate you. Your most compelling motivation will be found within.

> We . . . believe that one reason so many high-school and college students have so much trouble focusing on their studies is because they don't have a goal, don't know what all this studying is leading to.
>
> *Muriel James &*
> *Dorothy Jongeward*

> Many people fail in life, not for lack of ability or brains or even courage but simply because they have never organized their energies around a goal.
>
> *Elbert Hubbard*

Journal Entry 10

In this activity, you will design one or more parts of your life plan. To focus your thoughts, glance back at Pilar's life plan and use it as a model.

1. Title a new page in your journal: MY LIFE PLAN. Below the title, complete the part of your life plan for your role as a student.

My Dream: [If you have a compelling dream, describe it here. If you're not sure what your dream is, you can simply write, "I'm searching."]

My Life Role: Student

My Long-Term Goals in This Role: [These are the outcomes you plan to achieve as a student in the next 2 to 10 years, or even longer if necessary.]

My Short-Term Goals in This Role: [These are the outcomes you plan to achieve as a student this semester; each one accomplished brings you closer to your long-term goals as a student. To begin your list of short-term goals, you can write the same desired outcomes that you chose in Journal Entry 9; then add other short-terms goals as appropriate.]

Remember to apply the DAPPS rule, making sure that each long- and short-term goal is dated, achievable, personal, positive, and specific. With this in mind, you may need to revise the desired outcomes that you transfer here from Journal Entry 9.

If you wish, repeat this process for one or more of your other life roles: employee, parent, athlete, and so on. The more roles you plan, the more complete your vision of life will be. Taken together, these pages map your route to a rich, personally fulfilling life.

At this time you don't have to know how to achieve your goals and dreams, so don't even think about the method. All you need to know is what you want. In the following chapters, you'll learn dozens of powerful strategies for turning your life plan into reality. For now, keep your eye on your destination!

2. **Write about what you have learned or relearned by designing your life plan.** In particular, identify any impact this effort has had on your level of motivation to do well in college this semester, or do well in any other parts of your life.

> I started getting successful in school when I saw how college could help me achieve my dreams.
>
> *Bobby Marinelli, student*

Committing to Your Goals and Dreams

> Always bear in mind that your own resolution to succeed is more important than any one thing.
>
> *Abraham Lincoln*

 Focus Questions Do you start new projects (such as college) with great enthusiasm, only to lose motivation along the way? How can you keep your motivation strong?

Many people doubt they can achieve what they truly want. When a big, exciting goal or dream creeps into their thoughts, they shake their heads. "Oh, sure," they mumble to themselves, "how am *I* going to accomplish that?"

In truth, you don't need to know how to achieve a goal or dream when you first think of it. What you do need is an unwavering commitment, fueled by a strong desire. Once you promise yourself that you will do whatever it takes to accomplish your goals and dreams, you often discover the method for achieving them in the most unexpected ways.

COMMITMENT CREATES METHOD

A commitment is an unbending intention, a single-mindedness of purpose that promises to overcome all obstacles, regardless of how you may feel at any particular moment. During the summer between my sophomore and junior years in college, I learned the power of commitment.

That summer, I used all of my savings to visit Hawaii. While there, I met a beautiful young woman, and we spent 12 blissful days together.

One of my desires was to have a wonderful love relationship, so I promised to return to Hawaii during Christmas break. However, back in college 6,000 miles away, my commitment was sorely tested. I had no idea how, in just three months, I could raise enough money to return to Hawaii. Committed to my dream, though, I spent weeks inventing and rejecting one scheme after another. (Though I didn't realize it at the time, I was actually using the Wise Choice Process to find my best option.)

Then one day, I happened upon a possible solution. I was glancing through *Sports Illustrated* magazine when I noticed an article written by a student-athlete from Yale University. Until that moment, all I'd had was a commitment. When I saw that article, I had a plan. A long shot, yes, but a plan, nonetheless: Maybe the editors of *Sports Illustrated* would buy an article about the sport I played, lightweight football. Driven by my commitment, I worked on an article every evening for weeks. Finally, I dropped it in the mail and crossed my fingers.

A few weeks later, my manuscript came back, rejected. On the printed rejection form, however, a kind editor had handwritten, "Want to try a rewrite? Here's how you might improve your article. . . ."

I spent another week revising the article, mailed it directly to my encouraging editor, and waited anxiously. Christmas break was creeping closer. I had just about given up hope of returning to Hawaii in December.

Then one day my phone rang, and the caller identified himself as a photographer from *Sports Illustrated*. "I'll be taking photos at your football game this weekend. Where can I meet you?"

And that's how I learned that my article had been accepted. Better yet, *Sports Illustrated* paid me enough money to return to Hawaii. I spent Christmas on the beach at Waikiki, with my girlfriend on the blanket beside me.

Suppose I hadn't made a commitment to return to Hawaii? Would reading *Sports Illustrated* have sparked such an outrageous plan? Would I, at 20 years of age, have ever thought to earn money by writing a feature article for a national magazine? Doubtful!

What intrigues me as I recall my experience is that the solution for my problem was there all the time; I just couldn't see it until I made a commitment.

By committing to our dreams, we program our brains to look for solutions to our problems and to keep us going when the path gets rough. Whenever you're tempted to look for motivation outside yourself, remember this: Motivation surges up from a *commitment* to a passionately held purpose.

When you have a clear intention, methods for producing the desired results will present themselves.

Student Handbook, University of Santa Monica

Once a commitment is made without the option of backing out, the mind releases tremendous energy toward its achievement.

Ben Dominitz

VISUALIZE YOUR IDEAL FUTURE

Human beings seek to experience pleasure and avoid pain. Put this psychological truth to work for you by visualizing the pleasure you'll derive when you achieve your goals or dreams.

Cathy Turner explained how she visualized her way to winning two Olympic gold medals in speed skating: "As a little girl, I used to stand on a chair in front of the mirror and pretend I had won a gold medal. I'd imagine getting the medal, I'd see them superimposing the flag across my face just like they did on TV, and I would start to cry. When I really did stand on the podium, and they raised the American flag, it was incredible. I was there representing the United States, all of the United States. The flag was going up and the national anthem was being played, and there wasn't a mirror in front of me and it wasn't a chair I was standing on. I had dreamt that for so long. All my life. And my dream was coming true right then and there."

To make or strengthen your commitment to achieve success in college, do what Cathy Turner did. Visualize yourself accomplishing your fondest goal and imagine the delight you'll experience when it actually happens. Let this desired outcome and the associated positive experiences draw you like a magnet toward a future of your own design.

Some years ago, I happened to glance at a three-ring notebook carried by one of my students. Taped to the cover was a photo showing her in a graduation cap and gown.

"Have you already graduated?" I asked.

"Not yet. But that's what I'll look like when I do."

"How did you get the photo?"

"My sister graduated from college a few years ago," she explained. "After the ceremony, I put on her cap and gown and had my mother take this picture. Whenever I get discouraged about school, I look at this photo and imagine myself walking across the stage to receive my diploma. I hear my family cheering for me, just like we did for my sister. Then I stop feeling sorry for myself and get back to work. This picture reminds me what all my hard work is for."

A few years later at her graduation, I remember thinking, "She looks just as happy today as she did in the photo. Maybe happier."

Life will test our commitments. To keep them strong in times of challenge, we need a clear picture of our desired results. We need a motivating mental image that, like a magnet, draws us steadily toward our ideal future.

The power of visualizing makes sense when you remember that getting anywhere is difficult if you don't know where you're going. A vivid mental image of your chosen destination keeps you on course even when life's adversities conspire against you.

From my own experience, there is no question that the speed with which you are able to achieve your goals is directly related to how clearly and how often you are able to visualize your goals.

Charles J. Givens

I see a Chicago in which the neighborhoods are once again the center of our city, in which businesses boom and provide neighborhood jobs, in which neighbors join together to help govern their neighborhood and their city.

Harold Washington,
Chicago's first black mayor

HOW TO VISUALIZE

Here are four keys to an effective visualization.

1. **RELAX.** Visualizing seems to have the most positive impact when experienced during deep relaxation. One way to accomplish deep relaxation is to breathe deeply while you tighten muscle groups one by one from the tips of your toes to the top of your head.

2. **USE PRESENT TENSE.** Imagine yourself experiencing success *now*. Therefore, use the present tense for all verbs: *I am walking across the stage to receive my diploma.* OR *I walk across the stage.* (Not past tense: *I was walking across the stage;* and not future tense: *I will be walking across the stage.*)

3. **USE ALL FIVE SENSES.** Imagine the scene concretely and specifically. Use all of your senses. What do you see, hear, smell, taste, touch?

4. **FEEL THE FEELINGS.** Events gain power to motivate us when accompanied by strong emotions. Imagine your accomplishment to be just as grand and magnificent as you wish it to be. Then feel the excitement of your success.

> Visualization takes advantage of what almost might be called a "weakness" of the body; it cannot distinguish between a vivid mental experience and an actual physical experience.
>
> *Dr. Bernie Siegel*

Psychologist Charles Garfield notes that athletes have used visualizations to win sports events; psychologist Brian Tracy writes about salespeople using visualizations to succeed in the business world; and Dr. Bernie Siegel, a cancer specialist, has even chronicled patients improving their health with visualizations.

Finally, consider this: the act of *keeping* your commitment may be as important, if not even *more* important, than achieving a particular goal or dream. In this way, you raise your expectations for the success of future commitments, knowing that when you make a promise to yourself, you keep it.

So, create lofty goals and dreams. And, from deep within you, commit to their achievement.

 Journal Entry 11

In this activity, you will visualize the accomplishment of one of your most important goals or dreams. Once you vividly picture this ideal outcome, you will have strengthened your commitment to achieve it, and you will know how to do the same thing with all of your goals and dreams.

1. Write a visualization of the exact moment in the future when you are experiencing the accomplishment of your biggest goal or dream in your role as a *student*. Describe the scene of your success as if it is happening to you *now*. For example, if your desire is to graduate from a four-year university with a 4.0 average, you might write, *I am dressed in a long, blue robe, the*

Until one is committed there is hesitancy, the chance to draw back, always ineffectiveness. Concerning all acts of initiative (and creation), there is one elementary truth, the ignorance of which kills countless ideas and splendid plans: that the moment one definitely commits oneself, then Providence moves too. All sorts of things occur to help one that would never otherwise have occurred. A whole stream of events issues from the decision, raising in one's favour all manner of unforeseen incidents and meetings and material assistance, which no man could have dreamt would have come his way.

William Hutchison Murray,
Scottish mountaineer

Journal Entry **11** *continued*

tassel from my graduation cap tickling my face. I look out over the thousands of people in the audience, and I see my mother, a smile spreading across her face. I hear the announcer call my name. I feel a rush of adrenaline, and chills tingle on my back as I take my first step onto the stage. I see the college president smiling, reaching her hand out to me in congratulations. I hear the announcer repeat my name, adding that I am graduating with highest honors, having obtained a 4.0 average. I see my classmates standing to applaud me. Their cheers flow over me, filling me with pride and happiness. I walk. . . .

For visual appeal, consider also drawing a picture of your goal or dream in your journal. Or cut pictures from magazines and use them to illustrate your writing. If you are writing your journal on a computer, consider adding clip art that depicts your visualization. Allow your creativity to support your dream.

Remember the four keys to an effective visualization:

1. **Relax** to free your imagination.
2. Use **present-tense verbs** . . . describe the experience as if you are talking to someone on the phone at the very moment you are doing it. *I am going through the door. . . .*
3. Use all **five senses**. What do you see, hear, smell, taste, and feel (touch)?
4. Include **emotion**. Imagine yourself feeling great in this moment of grand accomplishment. You deserve to feel fantastic!

Read your visualizations often. Ideal times are right before you go to sleep and when you first awake in the morning. You may even wish to record your visualizations and listen to them often.

One Student's Story

JAMES TERRELL
Appalachian State University, North Carolina

Coming to Appalachian State University was a bit overwhelming for me. It meant that I would be seven hours away from my family. It also meant that I could not just go home whenever I wanted to. In the first week of school, I felt okay and was so glad to be on my own and making my own decisions. Things started to change quickly when I realized that I had to make some important decisions, the ones that my parents usually helped me make. In the back of my mind I kept thinking, I cannot ask them for help because I am on my own now. I began to get a little depressed because I missed my family, and things were not easy for me. I was ready to quit and enroll in a community college nearer home because I felt that the professors expected too much out of me. I was nearly at the point of telling my parents I was ready to come home because I really did not know why I was here.

That's when we began talking about Accepting Self-Responsibility in my Access Seminar class. In this lesson, things started to become clear to me. I learned about the different voices everyone has inside of them. I began to realize that it was my Inner Guide talking to me and helping me to stay on course when I was ready to give up. Also, I noticed it was my Inner Critic that was criticizing everything I did to try to stay on course. I had opposing forces trying to get to me.

I continued to listen to my Inner Guide, but I realized there was still something missing. The next week in the class we talked about Creating Inner Motivation. As we began this lesson, I realized that the reason I was struggling was because I lacked motivation. I did not have a goal in mind that would help me stay on track. This chapter helped me realize that I needed a goal and a dream to stay focused, and in class, we began to do activities that helped us visualize them. In addition to our written journals, our teachers told us to draw a picture of our dreams and to brainstorm obstacles that we might face on the way to our dreams. Before this, I knew I wanted to be a lawyer, and that was about it. Some people would be happy just knowing they wanted to be a lawyer when they finished college. I needed to know a little more, so I visualized various steps to becoming a lawyer. First, I pictured myself graduating from Appalachian State with a degree in political science, next I was graduating from Campbell University with a law degree, and then I saw myself moving to California, where I became a successful entertainment lawyer, living with my family in a nice neighborhood. As I visualized each part of my dream, everything became clear to me. I learned through reading this chapter and talking with the teachers that having our dreams written or drawn on paper can help us stay motivated.

I now feel more confident about staying in school. Every time I go into some of my hard classes, I just keep the mental picture of the day I enter law school and the dream I have plastered inside my head. Every time I get stressed or feel overwhelmed, I just look at the picture of my dream on the wall. I say to myself, "James, did you think this was going to be an easy road to your dream?" Every time the answer is "no," but now I know I'm not going to quit just because of obstacles. I look forward to the next four years of my life because I know that this course has taught me the basics of what I need to know to be a successful college student. I am now encouraged to help other people learn what I have learned, so they can be successful too.

Photo: Courtesy of James Terrell

Self-Motivation
AT WORK

PERSONAL SKILLS for CAREER SUCCESS TURN RIGHT

Figure out what kind of job would make you happiest because the kind that would make you happiest is also the one where you will do your best and most effective work.

Richard Bolles, career expert, author of What Color Is Your Parachute?

One of the most important choices you will ever make is whether to seek a job or a career. When you have a job, you work for a paycheck. When you have a career, you work for the enjoyment and satisfaction you earn from your daily efforts . . . and you also get paid, possibly very well. I've had both, and I assure you, a career makes life a whole lot sweeter. If you want to feel motivated to get up and go to work 50 weeks a year, you'll definitely want to choose a career.

College is a great place to prepare for a career. But, to stay self-motivated, you'll want to match your career choice and college major with your unique interests, talents, and personality. I once had a student who was majoring in accounting because he'd heard that accountants make a lot of money. He saw no problem with the fact that he hated math. He thought he was preparing for a career when in fact he was preparing for a job.

Some of the most motivated students in higher education are those who see college as the next logical step on the path to their

Self-Motivation **AT WORK**   *continued*

career goals. Sometimes these are younger students who are pursuing a lifelong dream of working in a particular profession. More often they are older students who've grown weary of working at uninspiring jobs and have come to college to prepare for rewarding careers. These self-motivated students are the ones who not only make the most of their education but who also enjoy the journey.

Creators Wanted!

Candidates must demonstrate self-motivation, a strong sense of purpose, and effective goal-setting abilities.

If you have a dream of a particular career, stay open to the possibility of finding something even more suited for you. If you're not yet sure what you want to do, keep exploring. The answer will probably reveal itself to you, and when it does, your life will change. One student I knew went from barely getting C's and D's to earning straight A's when she discovered her passion to be a kindergarten teacher.

Use your life-planning skills to design a motivating career path for yourself, identifying the long- and short-term goals that will act as steppingstones to your success. Using the DAPPS rule that you learned in this chapter, you might create a career path like this:

2 years: I've received my A.A. degree in accounting with high honors and, by thoroughly researching accounting firms nationally, I've decided on five firms that look promising to work for after earning my B.A. degree.

5 years: I've earned my B.A. in accounting with high honors, and I'm employed in an entry-level accounting position in a firm of my choice earning $50,000 or more per year.

10 years: I own my own accounting firm, and I'm earning $150,000 or more per year, contributing to the financial prosperity and security of my clients.

Keep in mind that there is more to choosing an employer than how much money you're offered. Choosing an employer whose purpose and values are compatible with your own will assist you greatly to stay motivated. By reading a company's mission statement, you can find out what it claims are its purpose and values. For example, suppose you wanted to work in retail sales or marketing for one of the giant office products companies. Here is the mission statement for Staples:

Slashing the cost and hassle of running your office! Our vision is supported by our core values: C.A.R.E.

- *Customers*—Value every customer
- *Associates*—Support them as valuable resources
- *Real Communications*—Share information with people when they need it
- *Execution*—Achieve our business goals

Now, here is the mission statement for a major competitor, Office Depot:

Office Depot's mission is to be the most successful office products company in the world. Our success is driven by an uncompromising commitment to:

- *Superior Customer Satisfaction:* A company-wide attitude that recognizes that customer satisfaction is everything.

▷

- *An Associate-Oriented Environment:* An acknowledgment that our associates are our most valuable resource. We are committed to fostering an environment where recognition, innovation, communication, and the entrepreneurial spirit are encouraged and rewarded.
- *Industry-Leading Value, Selection, and Services:* A pledge to offer only the highest-quality merchandise available at everyday low prices, providing customers with an outstanding balance of value, selection, and services.
- *Ethical Business Conduct:* A responsibility to conduct our business with uncompromising honesty and integrity.
- *Shareholder Value:* A duty to provide our shareholders with superior Return-On-Investment.

Based on their mission statements, which company do you think has a purpose and value system that would create a more motivating work environment for you?

Once you actually begin your search for a position in your chosen career, your goal-setting abilities and visualizing skills will help you stay motivated. You can expect to make dozens of contacts with potential employers for each one that responds with interest to your inquiry. One way to keep yourself motivated during your search is to set a goal of making a specific number of contacts each week. *Goal: I will send a letter of inquiry and my résumé to 10 or more potential employers each week.* In this way, you focus your energy on what you have control over—your own actions.

Additionally, take a few minutes each day to visualize yourself already in the career of your choice; see your office, your coworkers, and imagine yourself doing the daily activities of your career. This mental movie will reduce anxieties and remind you of the purpose for your hard work. Visualizing yourself in your ideal career will help keep you motivated when you encounter delays and disappointments on the path to your goal.

When you actually begin your career, self-motivation strategies will become extremely important to your success. You can't read many employment ads without noticing how many businesses are seeking employees who are "self-motivated." The ad might say "Must work well on own" or "Seeking a self-starter," but you know what such buzz words really mean. These employers want a worker who is able to take on a task and stick with it until completion despite obstacles or setbacks. Who wouldn't want a self-motivated worker? If you were an employer, wouldn't you?

Finally, your ability to set goals in your career is critical to your success. Goals and quotas are inevitable for those in sales positions, but many employers require all of their workers to set goals and create work plans. Your ability to set effective goals will not only help you excel at achieving goals for yourself, but also for your team, office, and company. As you move up in responsibility, your ability to coach others to set goals will be a great asset to the entire organization.

You will likely be working 30, 40, or even more years. Your ability to discover inner motivation will have a great deal to do with the quality of the outcomes and experiences you create during all of these years.

➤ BELIEVING IN YOURSELF

Write a Personal Affirmation

Focus Questions   What personal qualities will you need to achieve your dreams? How can you strengthen these qualities?

Certain personal qualities will be necessary to achieve your goals and dreams. For example, if you desire a happy family life, you'll need to be loving, supportive, and communicative. To discover the cure for cancer, you'll need to be creative, persistent, and strong-willed.

Think of the short- and long-term goals you have for your education. What are the personal qualities you'll need to accomplish them? Will you need to be intelligent, optimistic, articulate, responsible, confident, goal-oriented, mature, focused, motivated, organized, hard-working, curious, honest, enthusiastic, self-nurturing?

The potential for developing all of these personal qualities, and more, exists in every healthy human being. Whether a particular person fulfills that potential is another matter.

During childhood, a person's judgment of his or her personal qualities seems to be based mostly on what others say. If your friends, family, or teachers told you as a child that you're smart, you probably internalized this quality and labeled yourself "smart." But if no one said you are smart, perhaps you never realized your own natural intelligence. Worse, someone important may have told you that you are dumb, thus starting the negative mind chatter of your Inner Critic.

How we become the labels that others give us is illustrated by a mistake made at a school in England. A group of students at the school were labeled "slow" by their scores on an achievement test. Because of a computer error, however, their teachers were told these children were "bright." As a result, their teachers treated them as having high potential. By the time the error had been discovered, the academic scores of these "slow" students had risen significantly. Having been treated as if they were bright, the kids started to act bright. Perhaps, like these children, you have positive qualities waiting to blossom.

As adults, we can consciously choose what we believe. As one of my psychology professors used to say, "In your world, your word is law." In other words, my thoughts create my reality, and then I act according to that reality (regardless of its accuracy). For example, suppose I'm taking a large lecture class and I keep getting confused. Students sitting around me ask questions when they're confused, but I don't because, well, I've just never been comfortable asking questions in a large lecture hall—that's just the way I am. I'm shy. My Inner Defender is fine with this explanation because it protects me from doing something

We are what we imagine ourselves to be.

Kurt Vonnegut, Jr.

We continue to be influenced by our earliest interactions with our parents. We hear their voices as our own internal self-talk. Those voices function like posthypnotic suggestions. They often govern our lives.

John Bradshaw

uncomfortable. Or maybe it's part of my deep culture to refrain from questioning authority figures such as an instructor. The trouble is, the questions I don't ask keep popping up on tests, and I'm about to fail the course if I don't do something different.

Another part of me, my Inner Guide, knows I'd benefit from being bolder. In fact, if I want to pass this course, I *have* to be bolder! So I try an experiment. I start telling myself, *I am bold . . . I am bold . . . I am bold.* Of course, life keeps giving me chances to test my claim. A few class sessions later, I have another question, but I don't ask it. This time, though, I'm keenly aware of what I did: I took the wimpy way out. Undaunted, I continue my experiment, thinking, *I am bold . . . I am bold . . . I am bold.* The next time I have a question, I wait until after class and ask a fellow student. A little better, but still not *bold.* Then one day in class, I'm totally confused. *I am bold.* I shoot my hand in the air. Gulp. The professor calls on me, I ask my question, she answers, and, amazingly enough, I live to tell about it. Better yet, I get the answer correct on the next test. And best of all, my action finally corresponds with my claim. I came to a fork in the road (one I know so well), I consciously chose the bold path, I got the answer I needed, and I realize: My new thought generated new behaviors that, in turn, changed my outcomes and experiences for the better. And, if I did it once, I can do it again. Any time I need to. Any time I *choose* to!

> I was saying "I'm the greatest" long before I believed it.
>
> *Muhammad Ali*

CLAIMING YOUR DESIRED PERSONAL QUALITIES

An effective way to strengthen desired qualities is to create a personal affirmation, a statement in which we claim desired qualities as if we already have them in abundance. Here are some examples:

- I am a bold, joyful, loveable man.
- I am a confident, creative, selective woman.
- I am a spiritual, wise, and curious man, finding happiness in all that I do.
- I am a supportive, organized, and secure woman, and I am creating harmony in my family.

Affirmations help us breathe life into personal qualities that we choose to strengthen. One of my colleagues recalls that whenever she made a mistake as a child, her father would say, "I guess that proves you're NTB." "NTB" was his shorthand for "not too bright." Imagine her challenge of feeling intelligent when she kept getting that message from her father! Today, she doesn't even need her father around; her Inner Critic is happy to remind her that she's NTB. She could benefit from an affirmation that says, "I am VB (very bright)."

> To adopt new beliefs, we can now systematically choose affirming statements, then consciously live in them.
>
> *Joyce Chapman*

What limiting messages did you receive as a child? Perhaps others said you were "homely," "stupid," "clumsy," or "always screwing up." If so, today you can create an affirmation that empowers your desired qualities. For example, you could say, "I am a beautiful, intelligent, graceful woman, turning any mistake into a powerful lesson." Some people report that their positive affirmations seem like

"Mother, am I poisonous?"

lies. The negative messages from their childhood (chanted today by their Inner Critics) feel more like the truth. If so, try thinking of your affirmation as prematurely telling the truth. You may not feel beautiful, intelligent, or graceful when you first begin claiming these qualities, but, just as the "slow" children at the English school responded to being treated as bright, with each passing day you can behave your way into proving the truth of your chosen qualities. Using affirmations is like becoming your own parent: You acknowledge the positive qualities that no one has thought to tell you about . . . until now. And then, most important, you act on them, changing your outcomes and experiences in the process.

LIVING YOUR AFFIRMATION

Of course, simply creating an affirmation is insufficient to offset years of negative programming. Affirmations need reinforcement to gain influence in your life. Here are three ways to empower your affirmation: Repeat . . . Dispute . . . Align.

1. **REPEAT YOUR AFFIRMATION.** In this way you'll remember the qualities you have chosen to strengthen. One student repeated her affirmation during workouts on a rowing machine. The steady pace of the exercise provided the rhythm to which she repeated her affirmation. What would be a good occasion for you to repeat your affirmation?

2. **DISPUTE YOUR INNER CRITIC.** Realize that you already possess the qualities you desire. You already *are* creative, persistent, loving, intelligent . . . whatever. These are your natural human qualities waiting to be re-empowered. To confirm this reality (and quiet your Inner Critic), simply recall a specific event (or many) in your past when you displayed a quality that is in your affirmation.

3. **ALIGN YOUR WORDS AND DEEDS.** At each choice point, be what you affirm. If you say that you're "bold," make a bold choice. If you claim that you're "organized," do what an organized person does. If you assert that you're "persistent," keep going even when you don't feel like it. At some point, you'll have the evidence to assert, "Hey, I really am bold, organized, and persistent!" Your choices will prove the truth of your affirmation and your new outcomes and experiences will be the reward.

So, decide which personal qualities will help you stay on course to your goals and dreams and prepare to write a personal affirmation that will help you bring them forth!

My "Born to Lose" tattoo was written on my mind long before it was written on my arm. Now I'm telling myself I'm "Born to Win."

Steve R., student

Affirmations have to be supported by the behavior that makes them happen.

Charles Garfield

Journal Entry 12

In this activity, you will create a personal affirmation. If you repeat your affirmation often, it will help you make choices that will strengthen the personal qualities needed to achieve your goals and dreams.

1. **Write a one-sentence statement of one of your most motivating goals or dreams in your role as a student.** You can simply copy one that you wrote in Journal Entry 10 (or create a new one if you prefer).

2. **Write a list of personal qualities that would help you achieve this educational goal or dream.** Use adjectives such as *persistent, intelligent, hardworking, loving, articulate, organized, friendly, confident, relaxed,* and so on. Write as many qualities as possible.

3. **Circle the three qualities on your list that seem the most essential for you to achieve your goal or dream as a student (from Step 1).**

4. **Write three versions of your personal affirmation.** Do this by filling in the blanks in sentence formats A, B, and C below. Fill the blanks with the three personal qualities you circled in Step 3 above. NOTE: Use the same three personal qualities in each of the three formats.

   Format A: I am a _____, _____, _____ man/woman.
   Example: I am a strong, intelligent, persistent woman.
   Format B: I am a _____, _____, _____ man/woman, _____ing _____.
   Example: I am a strong, intelligent, persistent woman, creating my dreams.
   Format C: I am a _____, _____, _____ man/woman, and I _____.
   Example: I am a strong, intelligent, persistent woman, and I love life.
   Don't copy the examples; create your own unique affirmation.

5. **Circle or highlight the sentence from Step 4 that you like best.** Say or think your preferred affirmation to yourself until you can do so without looking at your written words. This repetition helps you to begin taking ownership of your affirmation and desired qualities.

6. **Write three paragraphs—one for each of the three qualities in your affirmation.** In each of these paragraphs, write about a specific experience when you displayed your desired quality. For example, if one of your desired qualities is persistence, tell a story about a time in your life when you were persistent (even a little bit!). Write the story like a scene from a book, with enough specific details that readers will feel as though they are seeing what you experienced. Your paragraph might begin, *The first quality from my affirmation is.... A specific experience in my life when I demonstrated that quality was....*

You can add creativity to your journal by writing your affirmation with colors, adding pictures or key words cut from magazines, drawings of your own, clip art, or quotations that appeal to you.

An affirmation is self-talk in its highest form.

Susan Jeffers

The practice of doing affirmations allows us to begin replacing some of our stale, worn out, or negative mind chatter with more positive ideas and concepts. It is a powerful technique, one which can in a short time completely transform our attitudes and expectations about life, and thereby totally change what we create for ourselves.

Shakti Gawain

One Student's Story

DONNA LUDWICK
Carteret Community College, North Carolina

Twenty-three years after dropping out of high school, I finally enrolled in college. In between, I got married, worked as a waitress, had three children, and adopted a fourth. My first baby got cancer and had three serious operations between the ages of two and five. What she and the other kids in the hospital went through touched my heart, and I knew I wanted to help kids who were dealing with serious illnesses. I had always thought that school was useless and that I didn't have the smarts to finish, but I started to see that the only way I was going to make something of myself was to go to college. When I was in my 30s, I got my GED and became a certified nursing assistant.

A few years later, I took the big step and came to college.

It was scary sitting in classes with people my daughter's age. They had such young minds and it all came so natural to them. One day while trying to do my math homework, I found myself saying, "I can't do this. I'm too stupid." Then I remembered my affirmation. We were reading *On Course* in my developmental English class, and the affirmation I wrote was, "I am a persistent, confident, hardworking woman, and I love to learn new things; I will be successful." At that moment, I felt like a boulder had been lifted off my shoulders. It took me four hours to finish that assignment, but I wouldn't quit. I passed the next math test, and

that made me feel more confident and work even harder. I applied my affirmation qualities in English, too. I knew what I wanted to say, but I couldn't put it on paper. I'd write, revise, tear it up, and start all over. But I wouldn't quit! I swear I worked more than one hundred hours on some of those essays, and pretty soon I started to turn my thoughts into what I really meant.

Sometimes it's a real struggle to work 35 hours a week, raise my kids, and go to school, too. Then I think, "This is going to get me what I want in life." I want to become a Licensed Practical Nurse, then go on for my RN degree and work in a hospital with those kids. I keep my affirmation on my refrigerator so I see it every day. With my affirmation staring me in the face, it reminds me I've come this far, and I'm not going to give up now. I really am a persistent, confident, hardworking woman, and I do love to learn new things. I *will* be successful!

Wise Choices in College

TAKING NOTES

In Chapter 2, we discussed the many hours you will spend in college **Collecting** information and skills from your reading assignments. In this chapter, we will examine the second most time-consuming way you will **Collect** information while in college: attending classes. In the pursuit of a four-year degree, students spend nearly 400 hours in a formal classroom. Students pursuing a two-year degree spend about half that time in class.

Your instructors, of course, expect you to learn what they cover in these class sessions. Unless you're motivated to take effective notes, however, most of what you hear in class will zip through your short-term memory and be quickly forgotten. More than one hundred years ago, Hermann Ebbinghaus conducted the first studies of memory and discovered that we lose about 75 percent of what we learn within twenty-four hours. That's why effective note-taking is an essential skill for achieving academic success in college.

Taking notes while attending a class is similar to taking notes while reading a textbook. However, taking notes during a class offers additional challenges. For one thing, as you mark or annotate a textbook, you stop reading. Thus, while reading you are in total control of how fast you receive new information. By contrast, when you take notes during a class, the speaker keeps talking. You have little or no control over the speed of information delivery. This situation places greater demands on your ability to identify key concepts, main ideas, and supporting details and write them down accurately and completely.

And that's not all. You're likely to encounter instructors who will provide their own unique obstacles to note-taking: They may speed talk until your head spins. Or . . . drone . . . on . . . so . . . sloooowly . . . you . . . have . . . trouble . . . staying . . . awake. They may be poorly organized. Or have accents that you have difficulty understanding. Some instructors may wander maddeningly from the topic or distract you with irritating mannerisms. Or all of the above.

A summary of research on note-taking compiled by Kenneth Kiewra reports sobering news. Lecture notes taken by first-year students contain, on average, only 11 percent of the critical ideas presented during a class. No matter how well you study, you can't pass tests if you are studying only 11 percent of the important ideas in a course.

You can choose to complain, blame, and make excuses for why it's impossible to take good notes in a class. Or, you can take full responsibility for your learning outcomes and experiences. Regardless of how many obstacles the instructor or the subject presents, it's your job to take effective notes. In this chapter you'll learn how.

TAKING NOTES: THE BIG PICTURE

To take effective class notes, you need to answer two key questions: *What* should I write in my notes and *how* should I write that information?

First, consider what to write in your notes. Despite a popular misconception, the answer is not "everything the instructor says." Even if you could write that fast, having a word-for-word transcript of a class is not the goal of note-taking. As with reading, the goal of note-taking is **Collecting** key concepts, main ideas, and supporting details. Thus, much of what you learned earlier about taking notes while reading also applies to taking notes in class. But you'll need some new strategies to compensate for the challenges of writing notes while someone is speaking.

As for how to write your notes, a number of note-taking systems have been invented, but essentially they all fit into one of two categories: linear or graphic. Examples of these methods will be explained in this chapter.

Many students worry about taking perfect class notes because they use their notes to study for tests. In the CORE Learning System, however, you do not study from either your class notes or your textbooks. Instead, as you'll learn in the next chapter, after **Collecting** key concepts, main ideas, and supporting details from all sources, you'll **Organize** this information into effective study materials. It is these materials that will help you create deep and lasting learning. For now, simply examine the note-taking strategies that follow and choose the ones that you think will best help you **Collect** important knowledge during each class. No single method of note-taking works best for everyone, so experiment and personalize a note-taking system that works best for you.

As you examine the following strategies, keep in mind that the big picture of note-taking is essentially the same as for reading: **You are Collecting key concepts, main ideas, and supporting details.**

BEFORE TAKING NOTES

1. Create a positive affirmation about taking notes. Some students hold negative beliefs about their ability to take good notes or the value of doing so. Create an affirming statement about taking notes. For example, *I take notes that record all of the main ideas and supporting details, making learning easy and fun.* Along with your personal affirmation, repeat this note-taking affirmation to motivate new learning attitudes and behaviors.

2. Assemble appropriate supplies. Experiment and decide on the best note-taking supplies for you. Find a pen you like writing with. Keep your notes in ring binders, composition books, spiral binders, or a laptop computer. Ring binders are handy because you can add and remove pages easily. This option is helpful when an instructor provides handouts or you revise your notes. If you use one binder for all of your classes, use tabs to separate the notes for each class. If you take class notes on a laptop computer, be sure to back up your files often to avoid the disaster of losing notes because of a hard-drive crash.

3. Complete homework assignments before class. Remember, neural networks created by prior learning make new learning easier. That's why completing assignments before class increases your ability to understand lectures and discussions. Also, you'll know what belongs in your notes. For example, you'll know if the instructor is repeating what was in the reading or adding new information. And, suppose the instructor's presentation style presents a challenge (such as speed talking). Because the information is already familiar, you'll more easily spot key concepts, main ideas, and supporting details. If your homework includes solving problems, complete them before class as well.

4. Prepare a list of questions. After completing homework assignments, write questions you have about the information. If you write them on binder paper, leave a space after each question for the answer. If you write questions on $3'' \times 5''$ cards, you can put answers on the other side. If you place questions in a computer file, it's easy to type in the answers. Bring these questions to class, study group meetings, tutoring sessions, or a conference with your instructor.

5. Attend every class. As obvious as this suggestion may seem, some students don't create good notes simply because they aren't in class. Sure, you can borrow notes from another student. But is it smart to bet your academic success on another student's note-taking skill? Remember, research reveals that first-year students' notes contain only 11 percent of the important ideas presented during a class. Your notes, after applying the strategies in this chapter, will be far more effective than that!

6. Be organized. At the end of each term, you'll have note pages galore for each course. To keep them organized, write some or all of the following information at the top of each note page:

- Course name
- Date of the class
- Topic of the class (usually listed in the course syllabus)
- Any associated reading assignments (also usually listed in the course syllabus)
- Page number (in case your notes get mixed up later)

WHILE TAKING NOTES

First, let's consider WHAT to write in your notes.

7. Listen actively for key concepts, main ideas, and supporting details. **C**ollecting this information *accurately* and *completely* takes active listening. When you listen actively, you're able to reflect back what a speaker says. In a conversation with a friend, you might reflect: *Sounds like you had an exciting time white water rafting last weekend.* Or in a music class, you might reflect, *So, you're saying a divertimento is a short musical piece that was popular during the Classical period.* When taking notes, you'd simply write an abbreviated version of this reflection: *Divertimento—a short musical piece popular during the Classical period.* Be aware that inner chatter competes with active listening, so quiet your Inner Critic and Inner Defender during class. Don't judge yourself: *I have no clue what she's talking about; I am such a dunce.* And don't judge others: *This jerk is the worst teacher on the planet.* Replace judgments with an active effort to hear all of the speaker's key concepts, main ideas, and supporting details. After all, if you don't **C**ollect the course information completely and accurately, then your entire learning effort is sabotaged from the start. See pages 158–159 for more suggestions to improve active listening.

8. Ask and answer questions. When you bring questions to class, raise your hand and ask. When your instructor asks a question, raise your hand and answer. When you don't understand an idea, raise your hand and ask: *Excuse me, Professor, what holds atoms together in a molecule?* Or, if you're too confused to formulate a question, simply request more information: *Would you please say more about Kant's idea that metaphysics can be reformed through epistemology?* If asking a question isn't an option, leave a space in your notes and write a question in the margin. Many options exist for later filling in the answer: Listen for the instructor to answer your question during the class. Visit the instructor during his or her office hours. Look for the missing information in your textbook. Ask a classmate or study group member for help. Seek assistance at your college's tutoring center.

9. Listen for verbal cues. Instructors will often provide verbal cues to introduce a main idea or supporting detail, thus helping you decide *what* to write in your notes. When you hear any of the following, get ready to record an important idea: *The point is . . . The following is very important . . . Be sure to write this next idea in your notes . . . On page 135 underline the following . . . Let me repeat that. . . The key here is . . . That's a great answer to my question . . . A third component is . . . The main symptom of this problem is . . . The next step for solving this problem is . . . If you remember only one thing from today's class, remember that . . . The key point here is . . .* (and the granddaddy of them all) *This will be on the test.* Also, instructors often give verbal cues before presenting supporting details. When you hear any of the following, get ready to record one or more supporting details: *To illustrate this point . . . Evidence for this includes . . . A good example is . . . To explain that idea further . . . This was proven in a study that showed . . .* Listen for additional kinds of supporting details such as personal experiences, experiments, dates, anecdotes, definitions, lists, names, facts, and data.

Now, we'll consider HOW to write your notes.

10. Take notes with an outline. Now that we've looked at ways to determine *what* to put in your notes, let's consider the second critical choice: *how* to write your notes. As mentioned earlier, the two general methods of note-taking are linear and graphic. First, we'll consider linear notes, which are the more common of the two. When you take notes in a linear fashion, you record ideas as much as possible in the order they are presented ("linear" means in a line). Outlines are good for this. They record ideas and supporting details on separate lines, using indentations to indicate levels of importance. You can view an example of an informal outline in Figure 3.1. Note the use of short phrases instead of full sentences to greatly condense what the speaker says. Here's how to take notes with an outline:

- Write a *key concept* at the top of a page. This information is usually expressed in a word or phrase. This might be the title of a chapter or a key word in the instructor's course outline. For example, the key concept in a history class might be "Causes of World War II," in a biology class it might be "Cell Communication," and in a psychology class it could be "Abraham Maslow."

- Record *main ideas (level 1)* beginning at the left margin. For a formal outline, start each level 1 line with a Roman numeral (e.g., I, II, III, IV).

- Under each main idea, indent a few spaces and record related *secondary ideas (level 2)*. For a formal outline, start each level 2 line with a capital letter (e.g., A, B, C, D).

- Under each secondary idea, indent a few more spaces and record any related *major supporting details (level 3)*. For a formal outline, begin each level 3 line with an Arabic numeral (e.g., 1, 2, 3, 4).

- If you need to add *minor supporting details (level 4)*, indent those lines a few more spaces

and, for a formal outline, begin those lines with small letters (e.g., a, b, c, d).

Outlines are most helpful when instructors present well-organized lectures. If your instructor provides printed lecture notes or uses PowerPoint slides, you've probably got an organized instructor. If, however, your instructor jumps from topic to topic and back again, all is not lost. That's when a concept map can ride to the rescue.

11. Take notes with a concept map. In this graphic note-taking method, *where* you place information (key concepts, main ideas, and supporting details) on the page shows both their level of importance and their relationship to one another. In general, ideas placed closer to the middle are more important than ideas placed farther away from the middle. Figure 3.2 shows an example of a concept map with content. Here's how to take notes with a concept map:

- Write the *key concept* in the middle of a page; then underline or draw a circle around it. This information is usually just a word or phrase. For example, if the topic of a class session is "Photosynthesis" or "Logical Fallacies" or "Abraham Maslow," that is what you would write in the middle of the page.

- Write *main ideas (level 1)* near the key concept, underline or circle them, and draw lines connecting them to the key concept.

- Write *secondary ideas (level 2)* near their related main idea, underline or circle them, and draw lines connecting them to the related main ideas.

- Write *major supporting details (level 3)* near their related secondary idea, underline or circle them, and draw lines connecting them to the related secondary idea.

- Write *minor supporting details (level 4)* near their related major supporting idea, underline or circle them, and draw lines connecting them to the related major supporting idea.

Concept maps are helpful when lecturers leap from idea to idea. They are also good for taking notes

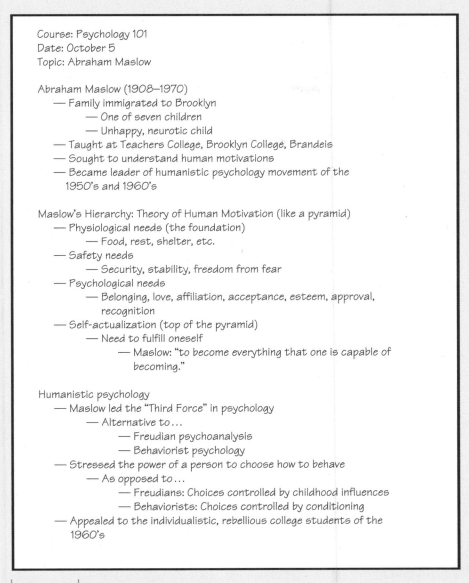

Course: Psychology 101
Date: October 5
Topic: Abraham Maslow

Abraham Maslow (1908–1970)
— Family immigrated to Brooklyn
— One of seven children
— Unhappy, neurotic child
— Taught at Teachers College, Brooklyn College, Brandeis
— Sought to understand human motivations
— Became leader of humanistic psychology movement of the 1950's and 1960's

Maslow's Hierarchy: Theory of Human Motivation (like a pyramid)
— Physiological needs (the foundation)
— Food, rest, shelter, etc.
— Safety needs
— Security, stability, freedom from fear
— Psychological needs
— Belonging, love, affiliation, acceptance, esteem, approval, recognition
— Self-actualization (top of the pyramid)
— Need to fulfill oneself
— Maslow: "to become everything that one is capable of becoming."

Humanistic psychology
— Maslow led the "Third Force" in psychology
— Alternative to…
— Freudian psychoanalysis
— Behaviorist psychology
— Stressed the power of a person to choose how to behave
— As opposed to…
— Freudians: Choices controlled by childhood influences
— Behaviorists: Choices controlled by conditioning
— Appealed to the individualistic, rebellious college students of the 1960's

| **Figure 3.1** | Informal Outline Example

Source: From Carol Kanar, *The Confident Student*, Third Edition, p. 353. Copyright © 1998 by Houghton Mifflin Company. Used by permission.

on class discussions that move back and forth between topics. As a speaker returns to an earlier idea, go to that part of the concept map, add the new information, circle or underline it, and draw a line connecting it to related information. The visual nature of a concept map makes it especially appealing to students who like a picture of what they are learning.

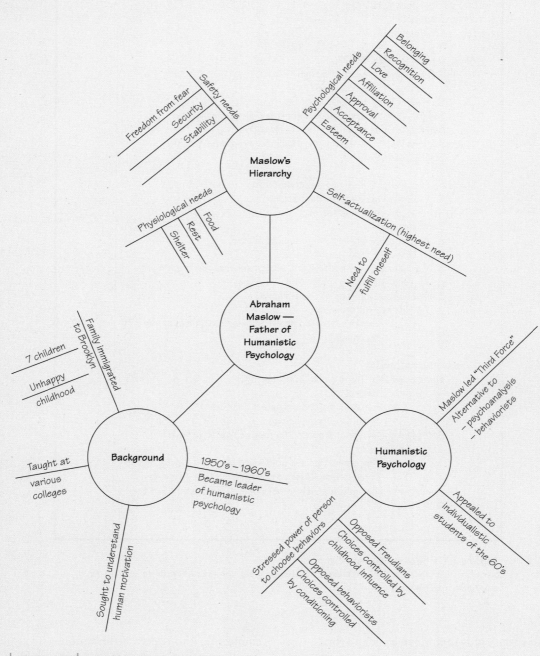

Figure 3.2 | Concept Map Example

12. Use three-column notes for mathematics. Since math instructors spend much class time demonstrating how to solve problems, a three-column approach is extremely helpful for **C**ollecting their methods. First, divide your note page into three columns. Title the left-hand column "Problem," the middle column "Solution," and the right-hand column "Explanation." When the instructor presents a problem, write it in the left column. As the instructor demonstrates how to solve the problem, write all steps in the middle column, making sure you understand each one. In the right-hand column, add any explanation that will help you understand how to solve similar problems. For example, you might add an explanation of each step or convert unfamiliar symbols into words.

Structure of Three-Column Math Notes

Problem	Solution	Explanation
The math problem as presented by the instructor	Step 1	Elaboration to explain steps of the solution
	Step 2	
	Step 3	
	Step 4	
	Step 5	
	Etc.	

You'll find an example of three-column math notes on page 145.

13. Speed up note-taking. Most speakers talk much faster than you can write (or even type, if using a computer), so here are three strategies for speeding up your note-taking:

- *Condense*: Instead of attempting to write everything, listen for a couple of minutes, identify the key concept, a main idea, and one or two secondary ideas, and then paraphrase them in your own words.

- *Leave a blank space*: When you miss something, skip down a few lines, and pick up writing what is being said now. As with unanswered questions, you can return later to fill in the blank space in a number of ways: ask the instructor

(in class, if appropriate, or during office hours), ask a classmate, ask a tutor, or review your reading assignment for the missing information.

- *Use abbreviations:* Create your own personal shorthand. The following are some possible abbreviations:

Ex	example	&	and
con't	continued	dept	department
imp	important	→	leads to
#	number	=	equals
1st	first	vs	versus
w/	with	w/o	without
nec	necessary	etc	and other things

14. Record the class. If you try the previous suggestions and still aren't happy with the quality of your notes, ask your instructor for permission to record the class. You can listen to the recording as many times as needed to fill in gaps in your notes or review difficult concepts. *Caution*: Don't procrastinate until you have forty-five hours of recorded class sessions to listen to and only twenty-four hours before the final exam. Instead, listen often to short segments. Each time, practice different note-taking strategies until you perfect your own personalized system.

AFTER TAKING NOTES

15. Polish your notes within twenty-four hours. As soon as possible after each class, make sure your notes are *accurate*, *complete*, and *understandable*. Do some or all of the following:

- Finish partial sentences.

- Expand on key words.

- Fill in spaces with missing information.

- Correct misspellings.

- Clarify unreadable words and confusing sentences.

- Delete unnecessary information.

- Revise drawings or charts.
- Correct steps in problem solving.

Afterward, if you still have gaps or confusion in your notes, meet with classmates, a tutor, or your instructor to address the problems. Not only does this action provide you with polished notes, it continues the active process of creating deep and lasting learning.

16. Compare notes. Compare your notes with those of your study group members or other motivated classmates. See if others have **Collected** important information that you missed. See where their notes may have different information and decide whose version is more accurate. This effort will help you all **Collect** additional information and further polish your notes.

NOTE-TAKING EXERCISE

In an upcoming class, take notes in a new way. Compare your experimental notes with those of a classmate, seeing which of you has recorded more complete and accurate information for later studying.

A BIT OF HERESY

In many study skills books, another method of note-taking is usually presented. Named for the university where it originated, the Cornell Method calls for note paper to be divided into three sections (see page 146 for the structure). Section A is used for recording notes from a reading assignment or class session. However, the Cornell Method offers no unique suggestions about *how* to record notes in that section. Sections B and C are employed later for adding key words, questions, and summaries, so they also offer no guidance about *how* to take notes. Thus, although the Cornell Method is usually presented as a note-taking system, it actually offers no strategies for *how* to take notes while reading or attending class (only *where* to record them). So, in the CORE Learning System, the Cornell Method is not considered a note-taking method. It is, however, a very powerful method for **Rehearsing** and **Evaluating** learning, so we will examine the use of this valuable learning strategy in Chapter 4.

Mastering Self-Management

4

Once I accept responsibility for choosing and creating the life I want, the next step is taking purposeful actions that will turn my desires into reality.

I am taking all of the actions necessary to achieve my goals and dreams.

SUCCESSFUL STUDENTS . . .	STRUGGLING STUDENTS . . .
act on purpose, choosing deeds that move them on course to their goals and dreams.	wait passively or wander from one unpurposeful activity to another.
employ self-management tools, regularly planning and carrying out purposeful actions.	live disorganized, unplanned lives, constantly responding to whims of the moment.
develop self-discipline, showing commitment, focus, and persistence in pursuing their goals and dreams.	quit or change course when their actions don't lead to immediate success.

Case Study in Critical Thinking

THE PROCRASTINATORS

Two students from Professor Hallengren's English composition class sat in the cafeteria discussing the approaching deadline for their fourth essay.

"There's no way I can get this essay done on time," **Tracy** said. "I've turned in every essay late, and I still owe him a rewrite on the second one. Professor Hallengren is going to be furious!"

"You think you're in trouble!" **Ricardo** said. "I haven't even turned in the last essay. Now I'm going to be two essays behind."

"How come?" Tracy asked. "I would have thought a young guy right out of high school would have all the time in the world."

"Don't ask me where my time goes," Ricardo answered, shrugging. "Deadlines keep sneaking up on me, and before I know it, I'm weeks behind. I live on campus, and I don't even have to commute. But something always comes up. Last weekend I was going to write that other English essay and then study for my sociology test, but I had to go to a wedding out of state on Saturday. I was having such a good time, I didn't drive back until Monday morning. Now I'm even further behind."

"So that's why you missed English class on Monday," Tracy said. "Professor Hallengren lectured us because so many students were absent."

"I know I miss too many classes. One time I stayed home because I didn't have my essay ready. And sometimes I stay up late talking to my girlfriend on the phone or playing video games. Then I can't get up in the morning."

"My situation is different," Tracy said. "I'm in my 30s and I'm a single mother. I have three kids: five, seven, and eight. I work 20 hours a week, and I'm taking four courses. I just can't keep up with it all! Every time I think I'm about to catch up, something goes wrong. Last week one of my kids got sick. Then my refrigerator broke, and I had to work overtime for money to get it fixed. Two weeks ago they changed my schedule at work, and I had to find new day care. All my professors act like their class is all I have to do. I wish! The only way I could do everything is give up sleeping, and I'm only getting about five hours a night as it is."

"What are you going to do?" Ricardo asked.

"I don't think I can make it this semester. I'm considering dropping all of my classes."

"Maybe I should drop out, too."

1. **Who do you think has the more challenging self-management problem, Ricardo or Tracy? Be prepared to explain your choice.**

2. **If this person asked for your advice on how to do better in college, what specific self-management strategies would you recommend that he or she adopt?**

▶ **DIVING DEEPER** Which person's situation, Ricardo's or Tracy's, is more like yours? Explain the similarities and identify what you do to keep up with all of the things you need to do.

Acting on Purpose

 Focus Questions   Have you ever noticed how much highly successful people accomplish? How do they make such effective use of their time?

Creators do more than dream. They have developed the skill of translating their desired outcomes into purposeful actions. They make a plan and then take one step after another . . . even when they don't *feel* like it . . . until they achieve their objective. Goals and dreams set your destination, but only persistent, purposeful actions will get you there.

Thomas Edison did more than dream of inventing the light bulb; he performed more than 10,000 experiments before achieving his goal. Martin Luther King, Jr., did more than dream of justice and equality for people of all races; he spoke and organized and marched and wrote. College graduates did more than dream of their diplomas; they attended classes, read books, wrote essays, conferred with instructors, rewrote essays, formed study groups, did library research, asked questions, went to support labs, sought out tutors, and more!

When we consider the accomplishments of successful people, we may forget that they weren't born successful. Most achieved their success through the persistent repetition of purposeful actions. Creators apply a powerful strategy for turning dreams into reality: **Do important actions first, *before* they become urgent**.

HARNESS THE POWER OF QUADRANT II

The significance of **importance** and **urgency** in choosing our actions is illustrated in the chart of the Quadrant II Time Management System® on the next page (from Stephen Covey's book *The 7 Habits of Highly Effective People*). This chart shows that our actions fall into one of four quadrants, depending on their importance and urgency.

Only you can determine the importance of your actions. Sure, others (such as friends and relatives) will have their opinions, but they don't really know what you value. If an action will help you achieve what you value, then it's *important* and you'd be crazy not to do it. Sadly, though, many people fill their time with unimportant actions, thus sabotaging their goals and dreams.

Likewise, only you can determine the urgency of your actions. Sure, others (such as instructors and counselors) will set deadlines for you, but these external finish lines won't be motivating unless you make them personally important. If meeting an approaching deadline will help you achieve something you value, it's *urgent* and you'd be crazy not to meet that deadline. Sadly, though, many people miss urgent deadlines, thus sabotaging their goals and dreams.

I've heard all sorts of excuses for why students "couldn't" get an assignment in on time. However, when I asked if they could have met the deadline if it was worth one million dollars, their answer was almost always, "Sure, but it wasn't." So now we know the real problem. It wasn't that they "couldn't" meet the deadline. They just didn't make the deadline valuable enough to do what needed to be done.

> Do not confuse a creator with a dreamer. Dreamers only dream, but creators bring their dreams into reality.
>
> *Robert Fritz*

> I am personally persuaded that the essence of the best thinking in the area of time management can be captured in a single phrase: organize and execute around priorities.
>
> *Stephen Covey*

Creators choose their own goals and meet deadlines (even those set by others) because it's what *they* want, because it's important to creating the life *they* desire.

As you read on about the four quadrants, ask yourself, "In which quadrant am I choosing to spend most of my time?" The choice you make will dramatically affect the outcomes and experiences you create.

> Not all of your daily activities are of equal importance, and your mission is to organize and prioritize all activities into a working plan.
>
> *Charles J. Givens*

- **QUADRANT I ACTIONS (Important and Urgent)** are important activities done under the pressure of nearing deadlines. One of my college roommates began his junior paper (the equivalent of two courses) just three days before it was due. He claimed that success in college was *important* to him, and the impending deadline certainly made this assignment *urgent*. He worked on the paper for 72 hours straight, finally turning it in without even proofreading. Although he squeaked by this time, he fell deeper and deeper into this pattern of procrastination, until in our senior year he failed out of college. Procrastination is the choice to do unimportant tasks while neglecting important tasks. It's a violation of your own priorities: acting on low priorities while neglecting high priorities. At the last minute, procrastinators dive desperately into Quadrant I to handle an action that has always been important but is now urgent. People who spend their lives in Quadrant I are constantly dashing about putting out brush fires in their lives. They frantically create modest achievements in the present while sacrificing extraordinary success in the future. Worse, Quadrant I is the one in which people experience stress, develop ulcers, and flirt with nervous breakdowns.

> It is not enough to be busy . . . the question is: What are we busy about?
>
> *Henry David Thoreau*

- **QUADRANT II ACTIONS (Important and Not Urgent)** are important activities done *without* the pressure of looming deadlines. When you engage in an important activity with time enough to do it well, you can create your greatest dreams. Lacking urgency, Quadrant II actions are easily postponed. Almost all of the suggestions in this book belong in Quadrant II. For example, you could postpone forever keeping a journal, using the Wise Choice

	Urgent	**Not Urgent**
Important	**Quadrant I** *Example:* Staying up all night cramming for an 8:00 A.M. Test.	**Quadrant II** *Example:* Creating a study group in the first week of the semester.
Not Important	**Quadrant III** *Example:* Attending a hastily called meeting that has nothing to do with your goals.	**Quadrant IV** *Example:* Mindlessly watching television until 4:00 A.M.

Process, adopting the language of Creators, discovering and visualizing your dreams, designing a life plan, and creating personal affirmations. However, when you do take purposeful actions such as these, you create a rich, full life. Quadrant II is where you will find Creators.

- **QUADRANT III ACTIONS (Not Important and Urgent)** are unimportant activities done with a sense of urgency. How often have you responded to the demand of your ringing phone only to be trapped in long, unwanted conversations? Or you agree to something because you can't bring yourself to say "no"? When we allow someone else's urgency to talk us into an activity unimportant to our own goals and dreams, we have chosen to be in Quadrant III.

- **QUADRANT IV ACTIONS (Not Important and Not Urgent)** are simply time wasters. Everyone wastes some time, so it's not something to judge yourself for, though your Inner Critic may try. Instead, listen to your Inner Guide. Become more conscious of your choices, and minimize wasting the irreplaceable hours of each day. A college professor I know surveyed his classes and found that many of his students watch more than 40 hours of television per week. That's the equivalent of a full-time job without pay or benefits!

A study in 1961 showed that students in higher education studied an average of 25 hours per week. Twenty years later, in 1981, college students' study time had dropped to 20 hours per week. By 2003, the average dropped again to only 13 hours of studying per week. These numbers help explain why so many capable students get off course in college. It's difficult to learn complex subjects with so little time in Quadrants I and II.

WHAT TO DO IN QUADRANTS I AND II

Creators spend as much time as possible in Quadrants I and II. In college, Creators attend class regularly. They take good notes. They do all assignments to the best of their ability. They schedule conferences with their instructors. They create study groups. They **Organize** their notes and study them often. They predict questions on upcoming tests and carry the answers on 3" × 5" study cards. No external urgency motivates them to take these purposeful actions. They create their own urgency by a strong commitment to their valued goals and dreams.

By contrast, Victims spend much of their time in Quadrants III and IV, where they repeat unproductive actions such as complaining, blaming, excusing, and wasting time. Not surprisingly, they move farther and farther off course each day.

If you want to know which quadrant you are in at any moment, ask yourself this question: "Will what I'm doing now positively affect my life one year from today?" If the answer is "yes," you are in Quadrant I or II. If the answer is "no," you are probably in Quadrant III or IV.

Creators say "no" to Quadrant III and Quadrant IV activities. Sometimes the choice requires saying "no" to other people: *No, I'm not going to be on your committee this semester. Thank you for asking.* Sometimes this choice requires saying "no" to themselves: *No, I'm not going to sleep late Saturday morning. I'm*

While it is true that without a vision the people perish, it is doubly true that without action the people and their vision perish as well.

Johnetta B. Cole, president,
Spelman College

A vision without a task is but a dream, a task without a vision is drudgery, a vision and a task is the hope of the world.

From a church in Sussex,
England, ca. 1730

going to get up early and study for the math test. Then I can go to the movies with my friends without getting off course.

When we say "no" to Quadrants III and IV, we free up time to say "yes" to Quadrants I and II. Imagine if you spent just 30 additional minutes each day taking purposeful actions. Think how dramatically that one choice could change the outcome of your life!

Journal Entry 13

In this activity, you will assess the degree to which you are acting on purpose. *Your* **purpose! As you spend more time in Quadrants I and II, you will notice a dramatic improvement in the results you are creating.**

Remember to reread the visualization of your dream (Journal Entry 11) often to help you stay motivated. Also, remember to say your affirmation (Journal Entry 12) each day to remind you of the personal qualities that will keep you on course to your dreams! These are both great Quadrant II actions.

1. **Write a list of 15 or more specific actions you have taken in the past two days.** (The actions are *specific* if someone could have recorded you doing them with a video camera.)

2. **Using an entire journal page, draw a four-quadrant chart like the example on page 114 .**

3. **Write each action from your list in Step 1 in the appropriate quadrant on your chart.** After each action, put the approximate amount of time you spent in the activity. For example, Quadrant IV might be filled with actions such as these:

1. Watched TV (2 hours)
2. Phone call to Terry (1 hour)
3. Watched TV (3 hours)
4. Went to the mall and wandered around (2 hours)
5. Hung out in the cafeteria (2 hours)
6. Played video game (4 hours)

4. **Write about what you have learned or relearned concerning your use of time.** Effective writing anticipates questions that a reader may have and answers these questions clearly. To dive deep in this journal entry, answer questions such as the following:

- What exactly did you discover after analyzing your time?
- In which quadrant do you spend the most time?
- What specific evidence did you use to draw this conclusion?
- If you continue using your time in this way, are you likely to reach your goals and dreams? Why or why not?
- What most often keeps you from taking purposeful actions?
- How do you feel about your discoveries?
- What different choices, if any, do you intend to make about how you use time?

One Student's Story

JASON POZSGAY
Oakland University, Michigan

When I started college as a freshman engineering student, I knew I would have a little trouble with the transition from high school to college. What I didn't know was that my main challenge would come from distractions. There's a mall only five minutes from campus, and when my friends wanted to hang out there, I wouldn't say no. Other times we'd play video games, or go out to dinner, or watch television. There was always something to distract me and no one to tell me to get to work. I was an A/B student in high school, and I was used to things coming easy to me. In college there's a lot more work and it's definitely not work you can do in five minutes and be done like in high school. I always found some excuse not to do my work, and then I'd try to do it the day it was due. I remember waiting until about 30 minutes before my first chemistry test to start studying. When my grades started dropping, I realized I needed to change but I wasn't sure how.

That's when we read about self-management in the *On Course* book. In class we did an activity where we divided a paper into four quadrants. Then we put what we had done the last two days onto those quadrants. I only had a few things in Quadrants I and II (Important). But Quadrant IV (Unimportant) was full. I realized I was studying only about 3 hours a week, but I was going to the mall about 5 hours, watching movies and television about 6 to 10 hours, playing video games about 20 hours, and surfing the Internet about 30 hours. I had never had a high-speed connection before, and things like YouTube and Facebook were consuming a good part of my life.

Now that I had figured out my problem, I needed a solution. I started by hanging up the quadrants in my room with my wasted time on them. I then put up another blank quadrant chart next to it. I decided to try new ways to manage my time over the next week and keep track of how I spent my time every day. I set a goal to reduce my time in Quadrants III and IV to no more than 20 hours per week and increase my time in Quadrants I and II up to 30 or 40 hours. At first I tried to completely cut out everything that was a waste of time, but I found myself stressed out. I was studying so much I thought my brain would explode, and I couldn't remember what I was studying. Then I tried getting all of my work done before I did anything that could be seen as a waste of time. But, again I was unable to focus on my work. Then I found the strategy that has helped. I put my schedule on a dry erase board and I adjust it to what I have going on that week. I make sure that I put both work and leisure time on the schedule. Also, if I have something important going on, like a test, I write it on my schedule in bold letters so I don't forget. Essentially I have made a reusable planner.

This strategy has helped me out a lot since I put it into effect. When I filled in the quadrants at the end of the first week, I was about halfway to my goals. Toward the end of the semester, I tracked my time again, and I reached my goals. My new system makes me more aware of what I'm choosing to do. I spend less time on the Internet, and I learned to say no. I remember when a bunch of my friends wanted to go to the movies the night before I had a math test. They asked me to go at least 10 times, but I stayed home and studied. I actually did really well on the test. Probably the best choice I made was taking my video games home. Since I started writing my important work on the white board, I've missed almost no assignments and my grades have improved in every class. I have found a strategy that arranges my time so that I can get my important work done and still have time for fun things. My reusable planner has helped me a lot in my freshman year, and I plan to keep using it throughout college.

Photo: Courtesy of Jason Pozsgay

Creating a Leak-Proof Self-Management System

 Focus Question   How can you devote more time to creating the outcomes and experiences that matter most to you?

At the beginning of a class, I asked my students to pass in their assignments. A look of panic came over one man's face. "What assignment?" he moaned. "You mean we had an *assignment* due today?" On another day, I overheard a student ask a friend: "Did you study for the math test today?" "No," the friend replied, "I didn't have time." Not long ago, a student told me, "I'm doing fine in my classes, but that's because I'm letting the rest of my life go down the drain."

Do these situations sound familiar? Do important actions leak through your hands like water? Do you sometimes give a half-hearted effort on important tasks . . . or finish them late . . . or not even do them at all? Do you neglect one important role in your life to do well in another? It's no easy matter getting everything done, especially if you're adding college to an already demanding life. But there are proven tools that can help you work more effectively and efficiently.

Typically these are called *time management* tools, but the term is misleading because no one can actually manage time. No matter what we mortals do, time just keeps on ticking. What we *can* manage, however, is ourselves. More specifically, we can manage the choices we make within the time we have every day.

TIME AND CULTURE

As with so many aspects of life, cultures differ in their beliefs and attitudes about time. In some cultures, such as Latino and Native American cultures, people tend to be relaxed and informal about time. In such a culture, arriving late for an appointment may not be considered a blunder or an insult. However, members of mainstream North American culture—including higher education—usually view time differently. A common saying is "Time is money." Both are saved, budgeted, invested, spent, and wasted. Time is considered a valuable resource, and how you use it shapes not only your outcomes and experiences but the judgments that others make of you as well.

A wise choice in college is to assume that your instructors take a serious view of time-sensitive choices such as attending classes, completing homework, and keeping appointments. Instructors will often list in their course syllabus the penalties for offenses. Even if your grade isn't lowered by such choices, you can assume that your reputation with the instructor has been harmed.

One of the keys to your success in college, then, is having a leak-proof self-management system. This is the system in which you record, organize, prioritize, and store all of your important actions. Then you complete one important task after another to the best of your ability. In short, **the secret to effective**

Time is the coin of your life. It is the only coin you have, and only you can determine how it will be spent.

Carl Sandburg

Unlike many people in dominant culture who may find their days and their lives driven by appointment books, calendars, and to-do lists, Latino cultural values do not emphasize rigid adherence to schedules.

Lynn Kell Spradlin

self-management is making choices that maximize the time you spend in Quadrants I and II. These are the quadrants, you'll recall, where all of your actions are important for achieving your desired outcomes and experiences.

Understand that there's no self-management system that is right for everyone. Rather, there are many tools with which to experiment. You'll know you've found your best self-management system when you start achieving more of your desired outcomes and experiences with less stress. As a bonus, when you find the self-management approach that feels right for you, your expectations of success in college (and elsewhere) will go up because now you'll be confident you can get the required work done. Here are five of the best tools for making sure you spend the bulk of your time creating a great future.

MONTHLY CALENDAR

Some important actions need to happen on a specific day and maybe even at a specific time. For such actions, a **monthly calendar** (page 124) provides a chronological list of your upcoming Quadrant I and II commitments, appointments, and assignments. Use it to record recurring classes, labs, work hours, and study group meetings, as well as one-time events such as a tutoring session or conference with an instructor. Also put on your calendar the due dates of tests, research papers, final exams, projects, lab reports, and quizzes. A monthly planner is an easy and effective self-management tool to use all by itself. In a glance, you can see what you're scheduled to do in the days, weeks, even months to come.

In place of paper calendars, many people keep their appointment schedule on a smart phone such as a Blackberry or iPhone. Smart phones are actually handheld computers that can do a lot more than merely store your calendar. Depending on the model, a smart phone can also record contact information (address and phone numbers), play music, send and receive text messages, take photos and videos, surf the Internet, and allow you to download and respond to email. A smart phone can even be programmed to send you a reminder about an appointment or deadline. Free electronic calendars are offered by a number of Internet sites (simply do an Internet search for "online calendar"). A unique advantage of these services is that most allow you to create calendars that can be accessed and updated by members of a group. So, if you have a project group, a study team, or a large family, an online calendar service might be just the right tool for managing your collective schedules.

Scheduling purposeful actions on your calendar is one thing; actually doing them is quite another. Once you have chosen your priorities, let nothing keep you from completing them except a rare emergency or

I think that learning about and using time is a very complicated kind of learning. Many adults still have difficulty with it.

Virginia Satir

© Hallmark/Dan Regan

special opportunity. Make a habit of saying "no" to unscheduled, low-priority alternatives found in Quadrants III and IV.

NEXT ACTIONS LIST

Some important actions don't need to happen on a specific day. They just need to be done as soon as possible. A **next actions list** (page 125) records everything you need to do "next" (as opposed to a calendar, where you schedule actions on a particular day or at a particular time). Whenever you have some free time that you might otherwise waste, your next actions list provides Quadrant I or II actions to complete. Here's how to use one:

(page 125)

1. Write your life roles and corresponding goals, which you defined in Chapter 3, in the shaded boxes. This first step makes your next actions list more effective than a mere to-do list by ensuring that your actions are directed at the accomplishment of all of your important goals.

2. List Quadrant I (Important and Urgent) actions for each of your goals. For example, if your short-term goal for Math 107 is to earn an A, your list might contain actions like these:

   Role: Math 107 student

   Goal: Grade A

   - *Read pages 29–41 and do problems 1–10 on page 40.*
   - *Study 2 hours or more for Friday's test on Ch's 1–3.*

   Each of these actions is **important,** and each is relatively **urgent.** As with a goal set with the DAPPS rule, be specific. Vague items such as *Do homework* provide little help when the time comes to take action. Much more helpful are specific tasks such as *Read pages 29–41 and do problems 1–10 on page 40.*

3. List Quadrant II (Important and Not Urgent) actions under each of your goals. For example, your list for Math 107 might continue with actions like these:

   - *Make appointment with Prof. Finucci and ask her advice on preparing for Friday's test.*
   - *Reschedule appointment with math lab tutor.*
   - *Meet with study group and compare answers on practice problems.*

These Quadrant II behaviors are the sorts of activities that struggling students seldom do. You could go through the entire semester without doing any of these purposeful actions because none of them is urgent. But when you consistently choose Quadrant II actions, this decision makes a big difference in the results you create.

Whenever you have free time during the day, instead of slipping unconsciously into Quadrants III or IV, check your next actions list for purposeful actions. As you complete an action, cross it off your list. As you think of new

In college I learned how to manage more tasks than anyone could possibly finish. Literally. We learned how to keep a lot of balls in the air at the same time. You couldn't study for every class every day, so you had to decide what could be put off till later. The experience taught us to set priorities.

Dennis Hayes, Hayes Microcomputer Products

Asking "What's the next action?" undermines the victim mentality. It presupposes that there is a possibility of change, and that there is something you can do to make it happen.

David Allen

important actions, add them to your list under the appropriate role. A bonus of keeping a next actions list is that it eliminates the burden of remembering numerous small tasks, freeing your brain to do more creative and critical thinking.

TRACKING FORM

Some goals are achieved by repeating particular actions consistently over time. The third self-management tool, a **tracking form** (on page 126), helps you coordinate many oft-repeated actions that are all directed at a common goal. Elite athletes typically use some form of this tool to plan and monitor their training. In college, a tracking form is ideal for helping you plan and take actions that will help you succeed in a challenging course. Suppose, for example, you decide to use a tracking form to help you gain a deep understanding of sociology and earn an A in the course. One helpful outer (physical) action might be "Read the textbook one or more hours." A possible inner (mental) action is "Say my affirmation five or more times." So, you write these two actions in the appropriate left-hand column, and put the dates of the next 14 days at the top of the check-box columns.

All the best work is done the way ants do things—by tiny untiring and regular additions.

Lefcadio Hearn

Each day that you take these actions, you check the appropriate box, and at the end of 14 days, you'll see exactly what you have (or have not) done to achieve your goal. One of my students commented, "Before I used the tracking form, I thought I was studying a lot. Now I realize I'm not studying enough." She started studying more, and her grades improved dramatically. A tracking form keeps your Inner Defender from fooling you into thinking you're doing what's necessary to stay on course when, in fact, you're not.

WAITING-FOR LIST

Your progress toward a goal will sometimes stall while you wait for someone else to get back to you. Maybe you're waiting to hear from a librarian about when a book you need has become available. Maybe you're waiting to hear from friends about whether they're going to join you at the basketball game on Friday night. Maybe you're waiting for an instructor to tell you whether you can change the topic of your term paper. Each of these items should go on your **waiting-for list**, along with the date it's added. Glance over the list daily. When an item has been on the list a while, contact the appropriate person and give them a nudge. With this tool, you'll dramatically reduce the number of times your goals get stuck waiting for someone else to take action on something important to you.

How much of human life is lost in waiting?

Ralph Waldo Emerson

PROJECT FOLDER

Some goals take many actions to achieve. For each multi-step project, create a separate **project folder**. Suppose your speech instructor assigns a group presentation. Everything related to that large task goes in one folder: the handout describing the assignment, the names and contact information for all group members, a next actions list for this project, assignments for each group member, the email address of someone you heard about who knows how to make great PowerPoint slides, research materials you've collected for your part of the presentation, a list of helpful websites, and YouTube videos that might enliven your presentation. Every time you get more information related to this presentation, it goes in the project folder. Never again will you utter those woeful words: "I know it's here somewhere."

THE REWARDS OF EFFECTIVE SELF-MANAGEMENT

> When the seniors in the College Board study were asked what contributed to a successful and satisfying career in college, 73 percent said the "ability to organize tasks and time effectively."
>
> *Tim Walter & Al Siebert*

Some people resist using a written self-management system. "These forms and charts are for the anally retentive," one student objected. "Everything I need to do, I keep right here in my head." I know this argument well, because I used to make it myself. Then one day, one of my mentors replied, "If you can remember everything you need to do, I guess you're not doing very much." Ouch.

I decided it wouldn't kill me to experiment with self-management tools. Over time, I came up with my own combination of the tools we've been examining. In the process I became aware of how I had been wasting precious time. With my old self-management system (mostly depending on my memory, with an occasional "note to self"), the best I did was remember to do what was important and urgent. The worst I did was forget something vital, then waste time cleaning up the mess I had made. With my new self-designed system, now I not only complete my Quadrant I actions, I also spend large chunks of time in Quadrant II, where I take important actions before they become urgent. I'm better at keeping commitments to myself and others. I'm less likely to go off course. Relieved of remembering every important task I need to do, my mind is free to think more creatively and boldly. And, most of all, my written self-management system helps me carry out the persistent, purposeful actions necessary to achieve my goals and dreams.

> When people with whom you interact notice that without fail you receive, process, and organize in an airtight manner the exchanges and agreements they have with you, they begin to trust you in a unique way.
>
> *David Allen*

If you're already achieving all of your greatest goals and dreams, then keep using your present self-management system because it's working! However, if your Inner Guide knows you could be more successful than you are now, then maybe it's time to implement a new approach to managing your choices. You'll rarely meet a successful person who doesn't use some sort of written self-management system, whether in the world of work or in college. In fact, researchers at the University of Georgia found that students' self-management skills and attitudes are even better predictors of their grades in college than their Scholastic Aptitude Test (SAT) scores.

Consistently using a written self-management system is a habit that takes time to establish. You may begin with great energy, only to find later that a week has gone by without using it. Avoiding self-judgment, simply examine where you went astray and begin your plan anew. Experiment until you find the system that works best for your personality and creates the outcomes and experiences you desire. In time, your skills in using your personally designed written self-management system will excel. And then watch how much more you accomplish!

Journal Entry 14

In this activity, you'll explore how you could improve your present self-management system. By becoming more effective and efficient in the use of time, you'll complete a greater number of important actions and maximize your chances of attaining your goals and dreams.

1. **Write about the system (or lack of system) that you presently use to decide what you will do each day.** There is no "wrong" answer, so don't let your Inner Critic or Inner Defender get involved. Consider questions such as how you know what homework to do, when to prepare for tests, what classes to attend, and what instructor conferences to go to. How do you track what you need to do in other roles, such as your social or work life? Why do you currently use this approach? How well is your system working (giving examples wherever possible)? How do you *feel* while using this approach to self-management (e.g., stressed, calm, energized, frantic, etc.)?

2. **Write about how you *could* use or adapt the five self-management tools in this chapter to create a leak-proof self-management system and improve your outcomes and experiences. Or, if you do not want to use or adapt any of these tools, explain why.** Consider the monthly calendar, the next actions list, the tracking form, the waiting-for list, and the project folder. How might you use them separately or in combination? How could you use a smart phone, computer, or other technology in your self-management system? How might you use written self-management tools not mentioned here that you may know about? In short, invent your own system for managing your choices that you think will maximize the quality of your outcomes and experiences. Should you need them, copies of a monthly calendar, a next actions list, and tracking form are available at www.cengagebrain.com, where you can access online resources for *On Course*.

> I used to wonder how other students got so much done. Now that I'm using a planner, I wonder how I settled for doing so little.
>
> *John Simmons, student*

Monthly Calendar

Monday	Tuesday	Wednesday	Thursday	Friday	Saturday	Sunday

Month _____

Next Actions List

Role:									
Goal:									

Role:									
Goal:									

Role:									
Goal:									

Role:									
Goal:									

Role:									
Goal:									

Telephone calls

Miscellaneous actions

Role:									
Goal:									

Tracking Form

Role:

Dream:

Long-term goal:

Short-term goals (to be accomplished this semester):

     1.

     2.

     3.

     4.

OUTER (Physical) Action Steps

Dates:

INNER (Mental) Action Steps

Dates:

One Student's Story

ALLYSA LEPAGE
Sacramento City College, California

When the fall semester began, I wasn't sure how I was going to fit everything into my schedule. In addition to taking three college courses, I was waitressing 24 hours a week, taking dance classes, teaching dance classes to kids, spending time with my boyfriend, doing housework and errands, hanging out with friends from three different groups (high school, college, and church), and rehearsing two evenings a week for an annual December musical at Memorial Auditorium, an event that draws thousands of people. I'd stay up late to get my homework done, then wake up exhausted. I was struggling in math, and in my heart I knew I could be doing better in my other classes. I'd forget to turn in homework, I was skimping on preparation for my dance classes, I wasn't calling friends back, and I'd forget to bring costumes and makeup to rehearsals for the musical. I was sick all the time with colds and headaches. I was seriously stressed and not doing full justice to anything.

Before I lost all hope, my Human Career Development class went over self-management tools. I developed my own system and started writing down everything I needed to do. I keep a big calendar by my bed so I see it in the morning, and I carry a smaller calendar in my purse. My favorite tool is a list of everything I have to do put into categories. I make a new list every day and put important things at the top so it's okay if I don't get to the ones on the bottom. My system helps me see what my priorities are and get them done first so I don't feel so scattered.

By doing important things first, I began having more focus, not rushing as much, and getting more done. Of course I had to let a few lower-priority things go for a while, like doing housework and spending as much time with some of my friends. I started getting more sleep, completing my homework, and getting A's on all of my tests while doing everything else that I needed to do. After a while, I began to accomplish so much more and I realized that I *do* have enough time to fit all of the important things into my schedule. In fact, every once in a while now I actually find myself with a luxury I haven't had in a long while—free time.

Developing Self-Discipline

Focus Questions   Do you find yourself procrastinating, even on projects that mean a great deal to you? How can you keep taking purposeful actions even when you don't feel like it?

Every semester perfectly capable students abandon their goals and dreams. Somewhere along the path, they get distracted and stop . . . or they wander off in another direction.

"Hey," their instructors want to shout, "you're going the wrong way. The goals and dreams you say you want are over here! Keep coming this way. You can do it!"

Maybe these students believe college is a sprint, over in a flash. Not so. Like most grand victories, college is a marathon with many hurdles along the way. It may take only 30 seconds to stride proudly across the stage to receive your college diploma, but it will have taken you thousands of persistent small steps taken over years to get there.

Self-discipline is self-caring.

Dr. M. Scott Peck

In a word, success takes self-discipline—the willingness to do whatever has to be done, whether you feel like it or not, until you reach your goals and dreams. Every January, athletic clubs are wall-to-wall with people who made New Year's resolutions to get in shape. You know what happens. A month later, the crowds are gone, reminding us that getting and staying in shape takes commitment, focus, and persistence.

So it goes with every important goal we set. Our actions reveal whether we have the self-discipline to stay on course in the face of tempting alternatives. Most students want to be successful, but *wanting* and *doing* are worlds apart. Hanging out with friends is easier than going to class. Watching television is easier than reading a challenging textbook. Partying is easier than doing research at the library.

Many people choose instant gratification. Few choose the far-off rewards of persistent and purposeful actions. Many begin the journey to their dreams; few finish. Yet all we need to do is put one foot in front of the other . . . again and again and again. A journey of a thousand miles may begin with a single step, but many more better follow.

Self-discipline has three essential ingredients: **commitment**, **focus**, and **persistence**. In Journal Entry 11, you explored how to strengthen your commitment. Now we'll take a look at focus and persistence.

> To be disciplined or nondisciplined is a choice you make every minute and every hour of your life. Discipline is nothing more than the process of focusing on any chosen activity without interruption until that activity is complete.
>
> *Charles J. Givens*

STAYING FOCUSED

Distractions constantly tug at our minds, and, like an unruly child, the unfocused mind dashes from one distraction to another. Everyone has experienced losing focus for a minute, an hour, even a day. But struggling students lose focus for weeks and months at a time. They start arriving late, skipping classes, doing sloppy work, ignoring assignments. They take their eyes off of the prize and forget why they are in college.

For many students, the time to beware of losing focus is at midterm. The excitement of the new semester has been replaced by the never-ending list of assignments. That's when Inner Defenders start offering great excuses to quit: *I've got boring teachers; my schedule stinks; I'm still getting over the flu; next semester I could start all over.* And Inner Critics chime in with practiced self-judgments: *I never could do math; I'm not as smart as my classmates; I'm too old; I'm too young; I'm not really college material.*

> You always have to focus in life on what you want to achieve.
>
> *Michael Jordan*

Your Inner Guide, however, knows that winners stay focused and finish strong. They complete the semester with a bang, not a snivel. Their efforts go up as the semester winds down. Your Inner Guide can help you regain focus by addressing one question: *What are my goals and dreams?* If you need a reminder, revisit your life plan in Journal Entry 10 and the visualization of your biggest academic goals or dream in Journal Entry 11. If your goals and dreams don't motivate you to keep taking purposeful actions right to the finish line, then perhaps you need to rethink where you want to go in life.

Calvin and Hobbes

by Bill Watterson

BEING PERSISTENT

If focus is self-discipline in thought, then persistence is self-discipline in action. Here's the question your Inner Guide can ask when you slow down or quit: "Do I love myself enough to keep going?" After all, you are the one who'll benefit most from the accomplishment of your goals and dreams . . . and you're the one who will pay the price of disappointment if you fail.

Here's the thing, though. Although failure is certain if you quit, success isn't guaranteed simply because you persist. Sometimes wisdom requires more than simply repeating the same thing over and over expecting a better result. If Plan A isn't working, don't quit. But also don't keep doing what isn't working! Change your approach. Move on to Plan B. Or C or D if necessary.

One of my students learned just how powerful persistence and a willingness to try something different can be. When Luanne enrolled in my English 101 class, she had taken and failed the course three times before. She had actually developed some good writing skills, but she definitely needed to master Standard English to pass the course. "I know," she said, "that's what all my other teachers told me." She paused, took a deep breath and added, "At least I'm not a quitter."

I asked Luanne why she was going to college. As she told me about her dream to work in television, her eyes sparkled. I asked if mastering standard grammar would help her achieve her dream. She hesitated, perhaps nervous about where her answer might lead.

Finally she said, "Yes."

"Great! So, what's one action that, if repeated every day for a month or more, would improve your grammar?" She needed to discover a Quadrant II activity and make it a new habit.

"Probably studying my grammar book."

Perhaps the most valuable result of all education is the ability to make yourself do the thing you have to do, when it ought to be done, whether you like it or not; it is the first lesson that ought to be learned; and however early a man's training begins, it is probably the last lesson that he learns thoroughly.

Thomas Henry Huxley

I handed her a **32-Day Commitment Form** (see page 133). "Okay, then, I'm inviting you to make a commitment to study your grammar book for 32 days in a row. You can put a check on this form each day that you keep your promise to yourself. Will you do it?"

"I'll try."

"C'mon, Luanne. You've been *trying* for three semesters. My question is, 'Will you commit to studying grammar for 30 minutes every day for the next 32 days?'"

She paused again. Her choice at this moment would surely affect her success in college, and probably the outcome of her life.

"Okay," she said, "I'll do it."

And she did. Each time I passed the writing lab, I saw Luanne working on grammar. She was there so often the tutors started joking about charging her rent.

But that's not all Luanne did. She attended every English class. She completed every writing assignment. She met with me to discuss her essays. She created flash cards, writing problem sentences on one side and corrections on the other. In short, Luanne was taking the persistent actions of a self-disciplined student.

As mentioned earlier, to receive a passing grade in English 101, students had to pass one of two exit exam essays graded by other instructors. The first exam that semester brought Luanne some good news: She had gotten her highest score ever. But there was the usual bad news as well: Both exam graders said her grammar errors kept them from passing her.

Luanne was at another important choice point. Did she have the self-discipline to persist in the face of discouraging news? Would she quit or finish strong?

"Okay," she said finally, "show me how to correct my errors." We reviewed her essay, sentence by sentence. The next day she went to the writing lab earlier; she left later. She rewrote the exam essay for practice, and we went over it again. Applying self-discipline, Luanne's mastery of standard grammar continued to improve.

That semester, the second exit exam was given on the Friday before Christmas. In order to finalize grades, all of the English 101 instructors met that evening to grade the essays. I promised to call Luanne with her results.

The room was quiet except for rustling papers as two dozen English instructors read one essay after another. At about 10 o' clock that night, I received my students' graded essays. I looked quickly through the pile and found Luanne's. She had passed! As I dialed the phone to call her, Luanne's previous instructors told others about her success.

"Merry Christmas, Luanne," I said into the phone, "you passed!"

I heard her delight, and at that moment, two dozen instructors in the room began to applaud.

The major difference I've found between the highly successful and the least successful is that the highly successful stick to it. They have staying power. Everybody fails. Everybody takes his knocks, but the highly successful keep coming back.

Sherry Lansing, chairman,
Paramount Pictures

A dream doesn't become reality through magic; it takes sweat, determination, and hard work.

Colin Powell

Journal Entry 15

In this activity, you will apply self-discipline by planning and carrying out a 32-day commitment that will help you achieve a goal in college. Making and keeping a 32-day commitment has a number of benefits. First, it guarantees that you spend significant time on task, which is essential to college success. Second, a 32-day commitment automatically provides distributed practice, one of the keys to deep and lasting learning. And third, it helps you make visible progress toward your goal, thus raising your expectations of success and your motivation to persist.

1. From your life plan in Journal Entry 10, copy one of your most important and challenging short-term goals from your role as a *student*.

2. Write and complete the following sentence stem three or more times: **I WOULD MOVE STEADILY TOWARD THIS GOAL IF EVERY DAY I . . . .**

Write three or more different physical actions that *others can see you do* and that you can do every day of the week, including weekends. So you wouldn't write, "be motivated" or "attend class." Others cannot see your motivation, and you can't attend class every day for 32 days straight. Instead, if your short-term goal is to earn an A in English, you might complete the sentence with specific actions such as these:

1. **I WOULD MOVE STEADILY TOWARD THIS GOAL IF EVERY DAY** *I spend at least 15 minutes doing exercises in my grammar book.*

2. **I WOULD MOVE STEADILY TOWARD THIS GOAL IF EVERY DAY** *I write at least 200 words in my journal.*

3. **I WOULD MOVE STEADILY TOWARD THIS GOAL IF EVERY DAY** *I revise one of my previous essays, correcting the grammar errors that my teacher marked.*

Chances are, all of these actions will fall in Quadrant II.

3. On a separate page in your journal, create a 32-Day Commitment Form or attach a photocopy of the one on page 133. Complete the sentence at the top of the form ("Because I know. . . .") with ONE action from your list in Step 2. For the next 32 days, put a check beside each day that you keep your commitment.

4. Make a choice: Write about one of the following:

A. **Describe your thoughts and feelings as you begin your 32-day commitment.** Develop your journal paragraphs by asking and answering readers' questions, such as, How self-disciplined have you been in the past? What is your goal? What were some possible actions you considered? What action did you choose for your 32-two-day commitment? How will this action, when performed consistently, help you reach your goal? What challenges might you experience in keeping your commitment? How will you overcome these challenges? How do you feel about undertaking this commitment? What is

My Daddy used to ask us whether the teacher had given us any homework. If we said no, he'd say, "Well, assign yourself." Don't wait around to be told what to do. Hard work, initiative, and persistence are still the nonmagic carpets to success.

Marian Wright Edelman

Becoming a world-class figure skater meant long hours of practice while sometimes tolerating painful injuries. It meant being totally exhausted sometimes, and not being able to do all the things I wanted to do when I wanted to do them.

Debi Thomas

Journal Entry 15 *continued*

your prediction about whether or not you will succeed in keeping your 32-day commitment? If you miss a day, what will be your inner conversation?

B. Imagine that your *On Course* class has an anonymous online discussion board. (That is, students can post messages online for the class to read, but no one can tell who wrote them unless they sign their name.) One student posts, "I missed day four of my 32-day commitment, and now I feel terrible about myself. I'm great about keeping promises to everyone else, but I'm not so good about keeping commitments to myself." A second student writes, "I missed two days already, but it doesn't bother me at all. It's just a stupid homework assignment. What difference does it make?" Write a response that you imagine your instructor might write to the two anonymous students.

IMPORTANT: If you miss a day on your 32-Day Commitment Form, don't judge yourself or offer excuses. Simply ask your Inner Guide what got you off course, learn the lesson that is available, renew your commitment to yourself, and start over at Day 1.

One Student's Story

HOLT BOGGS
Belmont Technical College, Ohio

I was a first-year student and enjoying college, but I was having a hard time in my electronics class. The teacher lectured about things like current, watts, volts, and resistance, and even though I read the book, took notes in class, and asked questions, I still wasn't understanding what I needed to. When I got back my first test, I didn't fail but I did pretty badly. I was scared because, if this is what the first test was like, how hard would the rest of them be? This was a new experience for me because I never had to study much to do well in school. I knew that I had to try something different if I was going to pass electronics.

In my Student Learning and Success class, I read about the 32-day commitment, and I decided to give it a try. I decided to read one section from my electronics book twice every day for 32 days. I figured that if I read the section twice, maybe I would understand it better the second time around. However, as the semester went on, I still wasn't doing so hot. At times I felt like quitting my commitment because, even though I was reading every section twice, I still wasn't getting it. By midterm, I was ahead of the class in the book, and when the instructor taught the section, it was all review for me. Then one day he was putting examples on

the board, and I realized, "Hey, I know this stuff." Since I already understood most of the material, I had time to focus on the things that I didn't understand. Everything that was still blurry to me he made clear. On the next chapter test, I got a 93, and in the end I passed the class with a B.

It's amazing what doing one little thing for 32 days can do for you. I never would have thought committing 32 days to reading a section from my book twice would help so much. Before, I'd say, "Yeah, I read it," but I was only skimming. When I read it a second time, I picked up things that I missed the first time through and I really understood what I was reading. In the end, the 32-day commitment was able to help me pass my electronics class, but even more important, this experience gave me a lot more confidence. Now I know that I can pass all of the challenging classes on the way to my degree.

32-Day Commitment

Because I know that this commitment will keep me on course to my goals, I promise myself that every day for the next 32 days I will take the following action:

_____

_____

_____

Day 1		Day 17	
Day 2		Day 18	
Day 3		Day 19	
Day 4		Day 20	
Day 5		Day 21	
Day 6		Day 22	
Day 7		Day 23	
Day 8		Day 24	
Day 9		Day 25	
Day 10		Day 26	
Day 11		Day 27	
Day 12		Day 28	
Day 13		Day 29	
Day 14		Day 30	
Day 15		Day 31	
Day 16		Day 32	

As we make and keep commitments, even small commitments, we begin to establish an inner integrity that gives us the awareness of self-control and the courage and strength to accept more of the responsibility for our own lives. By making and keeping promises to ourselves and others, little by little, our honor becomes greater than our moods.

Stephen Covey

Self-Management

AT WORK

As it is in college, success in the workplace means converting your goals into a step-by-step plan and having the self-discipline to spend the majority of your time doing what is important, preferably before it becomes urgent. Here in the realm of action, doers separate themselves from dreamers. Folks in business often refer to this aspect of success as "doing diligence."

In college, "doing diligence" is wise because the effort usually nets you good grades, and a high GPA impresses potential employers with both your intelligence and your work ethic. But getting good grades isn't all you can do in college to stand out in a job interview. Here are some other Quadrant II actions that will look great on your résumé:

Success in business requires training and discipline and hard work. But if you're not frightened by these things, the opportunities are just as great today as they ever were.

David Rockefeller, former chairman, The Chase Manhattan Bank

- Gain experience in your career field through part-time jobs, volunteer work, internships, or cooperative-education experiences.

- Demonstrate leadership qualities through your involvement with the student government; create a portfolio of your best college work.

- Join clubs or activities that relate to your future career.

Wise choices like these offer employers something that distinguishes you from all the other applicants for the job.

When it comes time to search for a position in your field, your effective self-management skills will once more serve you well. Consider using the **tracking form** to direct your outer and inner action steps toward your employment goal. The **next actions list** is a great tool for keeping track of essential one-time actions such as returning calls or sending thank-you notes after an interview. **Monthly calendars** help you avoid the embarrassment of arriving late or having to cancel a job interview because of a scheduling conflict. **Waiting-for lists** enable you to follow up with requests you have made, such as a reference letter you haven't received. A **project folder** for each job you apply for keeps all of the information about that position in one place. All of these tools will allow you to monitor your use of time, assuring that you spend the bulk of your time productively in Quadrants I and II.

As you begin your career search, consider doing the following outer action steps.

- Develop a list of careers that interest you.
- Make a list of potential employers in each career.
- Attend a résumé-writing workshop.

Self-Management AT WORK   *continued*

- Write a résumé and cover letter to showcase the talents and experiences you offer an employer.
- Personalize each cover letter to fit the job you're applying for.
- Develop your telephone skills.
- Participate in mock interviews where others ask you likely questions.

Your college's career center or a career development course can help you take these job-search actions effectively.

Searching for employment can get discouraging, and you would be wise to take some inner actions to maintain a positive attitude. You could create an affirmation as a mental pick-me-up. For example, "I am enthusiastically taking all of the actions necessary to find the ideal position to start my career." Or "I optimistically send out 10 job inquiries each week." If you find an important action difficult to do (such as calling employers to see if they have unadvertised openings), you could visualize yourself doing it and having the experience go extraordinarily well.

Once you move into your career, your self-management skills will become essential for accomplishing all you have to do. Notice how many people at your workplace carry planners, either paper or electronic. If you don't already have a planner that works for you, experiment to see if one will help you to manage the avalanche of tasks that will come your way in a new position. There's no one-size-fits-all self-management system for everyone, but there is one self-management system that will fit you. And it's your responsibility to find or invent it.

At the beginning of your career, tasks will likely take you twice as long to do as they will after a few years of practice. So not only do you need to manage your next actions list, you'll also need to make some sacrifices to get them all done. People with a "job" mentality sometimes stop short of getting all of their work done because work inevitably leaks into their personal time. They work only until their "shift" is over. On the other hand, people with a "career" mentality know that sometimes they'll need to stay late or take work home. They have the discipline to work until the task is done. Of course, these folks have to find a balance that allows them to have a personal life as well. One important thing to know is that the workload is always heavy at the beginning of a career, and this is the time when you establish your reputation as someone who can be counted on to get the job done.

Creators Wanted!

Candidates must demonstrate effective self-management, self-discipline, and the ability to manage complex actions to achieve goals.

▶ BELIEVING IN YOURSELF

Develop Self-Confidence

Focus Questions   In which life roles do you feel most confident? In which do you experience self-doubt? What can you do to increase your overall self-confidence?

On the first day of one semester, a woman intercepted me at the classroom door.

"Can I ask you something?" she said. "How do I know if I'm cut out for college?"

"What's your opinion?" I asked.

"I think I'll do okay."

"Great," I said.

She stood there, still looking doubtful. "But . . . my high school counselor said. . . ." She paused.

"Let me guess. Your counselor said you wouldn't do well in college? Is that it?"

She nodded. "I think he was wrong. But how do I know for sure?"

Indeed! How *do* we know? There will always be others who don't believe in us. What matters, however, is that we have confidence in ourselves. Self-confidence is the core belief that *I CAN*, the unwavering trust that I can successfully do whatever is necessary to achieve my realistic goals and dreams.

Ultimately, it matters little whether someone else thinks you can do something. It matters greatly whether *you* believe you can. Luck aside, you'll probably accomplish just about what you believe you can. In this section we'll explore three effective ways to develop greater self-confidence.

CREATE A SUCCESS IDENTITY

Are you confident that you can tie your shoes? Of course. And yet there was a time when you weren't. So how did you move from doubt to confidence? Wasn't it by practicing over and over? You built your self-confidence by stacking one small victory upon another. As a result, today you have confidence that you can tie your shoes every time you try. By the same method, you can build a success identity in virtually any endeavor.

The life of Nathan McCall illustrates the creation of a success identity under difficult circumstances. It also shows how a Creator mindset can help you overcome any feelings you have of being "different," such as not being part of the mainstream culture. McCall grew up in a Portsmouth, Virginia, ghetto where he faced prejudice and racism. His involvement with crimes and violence led to imprisonment. After his release, McCall attended college and studied

---

If people don't feel good about themselves and believe that they'll win a championship, they never will.

Tara VanDerveer, former head coach of the NCAA Championship Stanford University women's basketball team

---

Success brings its own self-confidence.

Lillian Vernon Katz

journalism. As you might imagine, one of his greatest challenges was self-doubt. But he persevered, tackling each challenge as it came—one more test passed, one more course completed. After graduation, he got a job with a newspaper, and over the years he steadily rose to the position of bureau chief. Recalling his accumulated successes, McCall wrote in his journal, "These experiences solidify my belief that I can do anything I set my mind to do. The possibilities are boundless." Boundless indeed! McCall went from street-gang member and prison inmate to successful and respected reporter for the *Washington Post,* later author of a New York Times bestseller, and then became a faculty member at Emory University in Georgia.

Genuine self-confidence results from a history of success, and a history of success results from persistently taking purposeful actions. That's why a 32-day commitment (Journal Entry 15) is not only an effective self-management tool but also a great way to start building a success identity. After we experience success in one area of our lives, self-confidence begins to seep into every corner of our being, and we begin to believe *I CAN.*

> Research studies show that people who have high self-esteem regularly reward themselves in tangible and intangible ways. . . . By documenting and celebrating their successes, they insure that these successes will reoccur.
>
> *Marsha Sinetar*

CELEBRATE YOUR SUCCESSES AND TALENTS

A friend showed me a school assignment that his eight-year-old daughter had brought home. At the top of the page was written: *Nice job, Lauren. Your spelling is very good. I am proud of you.* What made the comments remarkable is this: The teacher had merely put a check on the page; Lauren had added the compliments herself.

At the age of eight, Lauren has much to teach us about building self-confidence. It's great when someone else tells us how wonderful our successes and talents are. But it's even more important that we tell ourselves.

One way to acknowledge your success is to create a success deck: Every day, write at least one success (big or small) on an index card. Add it to your growing stack of successes and read through the deck every day. Or post the cards on a wall where you'll be reminded often of your accomplishments: *Got an 86 on history test. . . . Attended every class on time this week. . . . Exercised for two hours at gym.* In addition to acknowledging your successes, you can celebrate them by rewarding yourself with something special—a favorite dinner, a movie, a night out with friends.

> Peak performers develop powerful mental images of the behavior that will lead to the desired results. They see in their mind's eye the result they want, and the actions leading to it.
>
> *Charles Garfield*

VISUALIZE PURPOSEFUL ACTIONS

We can also strengthen our self-confidence, as well as our abilities, by visualizing purposeful actions done well, especially actions outside our comfort zone. Psychologist Charles Garfield once performed an experiment to determine the impact of visualizations on a group of people who were afraid of public speaking. These nervous speakers were divided into three subgroups:

Group 1 read and studied how to give public speeches, but they delivered no actual speeches.

Group 2 read about speechmaking and also gave two talks each week to small audiences of classmates and friends.

Group 3 read about effective speaking and gave one talk each week to small groups. This group also watched videotapes of effective speakers and, twice a day, *mentally rehearsed* giving effective speeches of their own.

Experts on public speaking, unaware of the experiment, evaluated the effectiveness of these speakers both before and after their preparation. Group 1 did not improve at all. Group 2 improved significantly. Group 3, the group that had visualized themselves giving excellent speeches, improved the most.

When I first introduce the idea of visualizing to my students, many are skeptical. In particular, young male students are often outspoken. "That's just *stupid*," one basketball player said. Two things helped change the minds of many. First, they were intrigued to learn that world-class athletes use mental imagery to improve their skills. Three examples are basketball legend Michael Jordan, golf great Tiger Woods, and tennis superstar Roger Federer. Second, like me, many skeptics became believers after they gave visualization a serious try. My conversion occurred after I dramatically improved my backhand in racquetball. I got a book with still pictures showing each step of a perfect backhand. For weeks, I imagined those steps in my mind . . . and then practiced them on the court. My "aha" came the day that one of my backhands smacked the front wall with the crack of a pistol (instead of my usual marshmallow hitting a pillow).

Mentally rehearsing purposeful actions will not only help you improve your ability to do the action but will also reduce associated fears. Suppose you're feeling anxious about an upcoming test. Your Inner Critic is probably visualizing a disaster: *As soon as I walk into the exam room, my pulse starts racing, I start sweating, I start feeling weak, and my mind goes totally blank. I fail!*

What if you visualized a more positive experience? You could imagine yourself taking the test confidently, creating an ideal outcome. Your revised mental movie might look like this: *I walk into the exam fully prepared. I've attended all of my classes on time, done my very best work on all of my assignments, and studied effectively. Feeling confident, I find a comfortable seat and take a few moments to breathe deeply, relax, and focus myself. I concentrate on the subject matter of this test. I release all my other cares and worries, feeling excited about the opportunity to show how much I have learned. The instructor walks into the room and begins handing out the exams. I know that any question the instructor asks will be easy for me to answer. I glance at the test and see questions that my study group and I have prepared for all semester. Alert and aware, I begin to write. Every answer I write flows easily from the storehouse of knowledge I have in my mind. I work steadily and efficiently, and, after finishing, I check my answers thoroughly. I hand in the exam with a comfortable amount of time remaining, and as I leave the room, I feel a pleasant weariness. I am confident that I have done my very best.*

Because you choose the movies that play in your mind, why not choose to star in a movie in which you successfully complete purposeful actions?

Mental practice is also referred to as "visualization" or "imagery rehearsal." We start with 20 to 30 minutes of relaxation training, followed by the visualization of some aspect of the athlete's game that needs improvement. It's the mental equivalent of physical practice.

Dr. Richard Suinn, Sports Psychologist to Olympic athletes

If we picture ourselves functioning in specific situations, it is nearly the same as the actual performance. Mental practice helps one to perform better in real life.

Dr. Maxwell Maltz

Creators know there are many choices that will strengthen self-confidence. When we consciously choose options such as creating a success identity, celebrating our successes and talents, and visualizing the successful completion of purposeful actions, we will soon be able to say with supreme confidence: *I CAN.*

Journal Entry 16

In this activity, you will practice ways to increase your self-confidence. Self-confident people *expect* success, which in turn strengthens their motivation and fuels their energy. If what they are doing isn't working, they don't quit. Instead, they switch to Plan B (or C or D) and persist. Then they finish strong, consistently giving their best to achieve their goals and dreams! In this way, the very success they want and expect often becomes a reality.

1. **List the successes you have created in your life.** The more successes you list, the more you will strengthen your self-confidence. Include small victories as well as big ones.

2. **List your personal skills and talents.** Again, the longer your list, the more you will strengthen your self-confidence. What are you good at doing? What would your friends say are your skills and talents? Don't overlook talents that you use daily. No talent is too insignificant to acknowledge. If listing your personal skills and talents makes you uncomfortable, recall the old saying, "It ain't bragging if it's true!"

3. **List positive risks that you have taken in your life.** When did you stretch your comfort zone and do something despite your fear?

4. **List important actions that you presently have some resistance about doing.** What purposeful actions cause anxious rumblings in the pit of your stomach? For example, maybe you fear asking a question in your biology lecture or you're nervous about going to a scheduled job interview.

5. **Write a visualization of yourself successfully doing one of the actions you listed in Step 4.** Remember to use the four keys to effective visualizing discussed in Journal Entry 11:

  1. **Relax.**
  2. **Use present-tense verbs.**
  3. **Be specific and use many senses.**
  4. **Feel the feelings.**

As a model for your writing, reread the positive visualization on page 138.

> I wanted to be the best dentist that ever lived. People said, "But she's a woman; she's colored," and I said, "Ha! Just you wait and see."
>
> *Bessie Delany, dentist and author*

> If you have no confidence in self, you are twice defeated in the race of life. With confidence, you have won even before you have started.
>
> *Marcus Garvey*

One Student's Story

ASHLEY FREEMAN
Copper Canyon College, California

Have you ever walked into a classroom feeling like everyone is staring at you? When you get called upon to read aloud to the class, does your heart beat like a bass drum that you hope others can't hear? When someone talks to you, do you sweat and stumble over your words and end up feeling like a complete fool? I never wanted to admit that lack of confidence was a problem for me, but in school I was always the person who was extremely shy and quiet, always keeping to myself, trying to be invisible. When someone asked me a question, I would attempt to answer, but I would lower my eyes and my voice would get very quiet, making it hard to hear what I was saying. The other person probably thought I was rudely ignoring them. The first day of class in college, as I was looking around at all of the students coming in, I realized the biggest obstacle I had to face was me. My low self-confidence, low self-esteem, and my extreme quietness were going to be a huge challenge.

When I had decided to attend college, I was a little scared, but I had plenty of love and support from my family and was excited to attend. I knew my grades wouldn't be a problem, as I have really good study habits. Due to health issues, I attended high school through an independent study program. I was able to graduate with good grades,

but I never had to be around anyone except my teacher. I lacked social skills with people my own age, but I always had my homework done early and for all of my hard work, I graduated three months early. The first day in college, however, I was a nervous wreck, wondering if I had made a huge mistake by enrolling. The teachers announced that we would be doing group activities, partnering with others, reading aloud, and forming study groups to strengthen our skills. I panicked, and all I could do was tell myself not to give up. As the days passed, I said little or nothing during my classes. In my English class, I partnered with Annette, a woman who befriended me the first day despite my quietness. The class uses the *On Course* book, and we started learning strategies that could help us. I was still nervous, but after reading about some of the strategies, I decided to take more actions to get the most out of my college education and experience. I became determined to prove to myself and everyone else that I could succeed in college.

In order to create what *On Course* calls a "success identity," I made a 32-day commitment to be more outspoken. One promise I made was to talk to at least three people every day. Another was to read out loud in front of the class without having to be asked by my teachers.

I also decided to volunteer more in class and share more of my work without being embarrassed. I decided to ask more questions during and after class as well as offer help to my classmates. I even asked my teachers and classmates for written feedback about my efforts to be more self-confident and participate actively in class. Not only did they give me this feedback, some even wrote me inspirational praise.

I'm very proud of myself for all of the changes I've made and that I'm still making every day. I am inspired to continue to grow and reach my full potential, and I'm grateful to all of the people who have been so kind to me and helped me see that I can do it. During the semester, we were asked to write an essay about what we had learned in the course, and my teacher announced that students would be able to read their essays in front of the Copper Mountain College Board of Trustees. I was so proud of the progress I had made that I was the second student in the class to volunteer. As I read my speech, I felt my confidence growing and was even able to make a good amount of eye contact with my audience. After my speech was done, I thanked everyone and as I walked back to my spot I started crying, knowing I had accomplished my goal. Thanks to learning *On Course* strategies and receiving encouragement and motivation from my family, teachers, friends, and classmates, today I have stronger self-confidence and a more positive outlook on my future than ever before.

Photo: Courtesy of Ashley Freeman

Wise Choices in College

ORGANIZING STUDY MATERIALS

To pass the many quizzes, tests, and exams they will take in college, students obviously need to know how to study. But, many do not.

In fact, the study methods of many students—even those who were "good" students in high school—are only marginally effective in college. Even when they pass tests, many students understand and remember only a fraction of what they studied. Imagine the problems this missing knowledge causes when it's needed later in the course. Or later in a more advanced course. Or even later in a career. Relying on ineffective study skills leads to shallow and short-lived learning. Such ineffective learning is a sure-fire way to undermine academic, professional, and even personal success.

You're about to explore a number of strategies that will help you *learn in a deep and lasting way.* Mastering these strategies will provide you with the ability to improve your learning outcomes and experiences for the rest of your life. And, yes, your grades in college will almost surely go up as well.

ORGANIZING STUDY MATERIALS: THE BIG PICTURE

Recall from Chapter 1 that effective learners take advantage of three principles that contribute to deep and lasting learning. First is **prior learning**—relating new information to what you already know. Second is the **quality of processing**—creating many different kinds of deep-processing strategies. And third is the **quantity of processing**—using frequent practice sessions of sufficient length distributed over time.

In this chapter we will examine study strategies that address the *quality of processing.* Quality processing leads to a deep understanding of what we are learning. To develop deep understanding, we begin by **Organizing** the knowledge we have **Collected** from all course materials. Our goal is the creation of many different kinds of effective study materials. Later in Chapter 5, we will look at strategies for **Rehearsing** these study materials in order to take advantage of the third learning principle: *quantity of processing.* Using this combined approach will create learning that is both deep and lasting.

So, experiment with the many study strategies that follow and continue personalizing your own CORE Learning System. As you do, keep in mind the big picture of this step in studying: **You are Organizing the information and skills you have Collected from all course resources, and your goal is the creation of many different kinds of effective *study materials*. Engaging actively in this process greatly enhances your understanding of what you are learning.**

BEFORE ORGANIZING STUDY MATERIALS

1. Adopt a growth mind-set. Having positive beliefs about the value of studying improves your learning outcomes. According to psychologist Carol Dweck, one important belief is that *the ability to learn can be improved.* Dweck calls this belief a "**growth mind-set.**" The opposite mind-set is that you're stuck with whatever learning ability you were born with (which is stinkin' thinkin'). To begin developing a growth mind-set about learning, create an affirming statement about the value of using high-quality study strategies. For example, *My CORE Learning System makes learning more effective and fun.* Along with your personal affirmation, repeat this learning affirmation in order to make new choices about studying.

2. Create an ideal study space. Having one comfortable place where you usually study has many advantages. Your learning resources are always close at hand. You aren't distracted by unfamiliar sights or sounds. And your mind becomes accustomed to shifting into learning gear whenever you enter your study area. Design your study area so you enjoy being there. Minimum requirements include a comfortable chair, plenty of light, room to spread out your course materials, and space to store your books and supplies. Personalize your study area to make it even more inviting. For example, display pictures of loved ones or add plants. Do whatever it takes to create a space you look forward to entering.

3. Arrange to be undisturbed. Do whatever is necessary to minimize interruptions while you study. Schedule regular study times and ask friends and relatives not to contact you during those times. Put a Do-Not-Disturb sign on your door. Let voice mail take telephone calls. Resist checking emails or text messages. If necessary, study where no one can easily disturb you, such as at your campus library. Protect the sanctity of your study time.

4. Create a distributed study schedule. As you know, active learners engage in numerous study sessions spread over time. So refer to your calendar where you have recorded all of the announced tests for your classes (you *have* done this, right?). Then choose a date before each test when you will begin serious studying. As a guideline, start seven days before a regular test and up to fourteen days before a major exam. Plan to use one quarter to one third of the days for creating study materials (as you will learn to do in this chapter). Use the remaining days to **Rehearse** these materials using the strategies you'll learn in Chapter 5. A tracking form is ideal for creating a distributed study schedule.

5. Gather all course materials. Start with your textbooks (marked and annotated) and your class notes. Add to them all other course documents, such as handouts, study guides, graded tests and essays, and study group notes.

WHILE ORGANIZING STUDY MATERIALS

6. Condense course materials. Since you have already marked and annotated all of your reading assignments and taken detailed notes in class, you will have a large **Collection** of information and skills. As a result, you may think you have all you need for studying. Not true. Learning from these raw materials is seldom effective. Instead, good learners condense all of these materials into the key concepts, main ideas, and supporting details of the course. Then they **Organize** this condensed knowledge into effective *study materials.* But one thing at a time. Here's an effective way to condense:

- Read through the markings, annotations, and notes you added to your course materials. As you do, place a star beside key concepts, main ideas, and supporting details.

- Now, reread only the information you marked with a star, find the most important ideas within those, and put a second star beside them.

- Finally, reread just the ideas you have marked with two stars, identify the most important of these, and put a third star beside them.

- Read through all starred information one more time and circle the key concepts.

By doing this process, you should have condensed your course materials by at least half (preferably more) and identified various levels of information:

- Key concepts (circled)
- Level 1: main ideas (three stars)
- Level 2: secondary ideas (two stars)
- Levels 3 and 4: supporting details—major and minor (one star)

Now your goal is to **Organize** this condensed information in ways that will help you understand it thoroughly. The **Organizing** options described next fall into one of two broad categories: *linear* or *graphic* (just as with note taking). Experiment to find which options work best for you. Keep in mind that while a particular **Organizational** approach may work well for one subject (e.g., sociology), a different approach may be better for another (e.g., mathematics).

7. Create outlines (linear organizer). Using the key concepts, ideas, and supporting details you have just identified with circles and stars, you can now create an outline using the process described on page 106. However, an even easier way to craft an outline for study purposes is to copy your textbook's table of contents to a blank page. Sometimes you can find the book's table of contents on the publisher's or author's website. Then you can simply copy and paste it into your own study document. Once you have the table of contents converted into an outline, add to it starred information from *all* of your course materials. It's likely that you will have some starred information (e.g., lecture notes) that does not fit into the outline created from the textbook. In that case, simply create a new section in the outline and add the new information. Outlines make particularly valuable study materials when preparing for essay tests or writing a paper (composition) to demonstrate your learning.

8. Create test questions (linear organizer). Put yourself in the mind of the instructor preparing a test. What information or skill does she expect you to learn? Write questions that will reveal your understanding of that target knowledge. Although any questions about the key concepts and main ideas of the course make helpful study materials, they are most effective when you know the kinds of questions that will be on the test. The best way to find out is to ask. "*Professor, what kinds of questions will be on the midterm exam? True/false? Multiple choice? Matching? Short answer? Essay? Word problems? Translations?*" Some instructors will tell you exactly what to expect. Others won't answer your question directly but may offer hints, provide sample questions, or even give you copies of past tests. Here are additional ways to generate test questions:

- Turn headings from your textbook into questions.
- Turn chapter learning objectives and/or summaries into questions.

- Find questions in your class notes that the instructor asked during class.
- Find concepts (circled) and main ideas (starred) in your textbook or class notes and turn them into questions.
- Make a list of key terms and turn them into questions.
- See if your textbook has practice problems either in the book or on a related website.
- Exchange possible test questions with study group members.

It's a great feeling to begin a test and find that you have practiced answering nearly every question on it.

9. Create flash cards (linear organizer). On one side of an index card, write a question that your instructor might ask on a test. On the back of the card, write the answer. Examples include a. . . .

- date and what happened on that date
- word and its definition
- graph and its meaning
- person's name and what he or she is noted for
- math problem and its solution
- quotation and who said it

Show your flash cards to your instructor or a tutor. Ask them to verify the appropriateness of the questions and the accuracy of the answers. Carry flash cards with you everywhere. Pull them out for a quick review whenever you have a few extra minutes. If you study them only twenty minutes per day, that's over two extra hours of studying each week. A number of free Internet sites allow you to create flash cards and even play games with the content. To find such a site, simply type "flash cards" into an Internet search engine. (Be cautious about using flash cards created by other students, as their answers may be incorrect.) Flash cards make valuable study materials in courses where you expect objective tests

Front

Problem: Add polynomials

$$2y^2 - 3y + 9$$
$$+ \;\; -3y^2 \quad\;\; - 2$$

Back

Solution: Combine like terms

$$2y^2 - 3y + 9$$
$$+ \;\; -3y^2 \quad\;\; - 2$$
$$\overline{\quad -y^2 - 3y + 7 \quad}$$

Sample Problem-Solution Flash Cards

Front

What are the five keys to
setting effective goals?

Back

Use the Dapps Rule

Make all goals: <u>D</u>ated,
<u>A</u>chievable, <u>P</u>ersonal,
<u>P</u>ositive, and <u>S</u>pecific

Sample Question-and-Answer Flash Card

Source: From Carol Kanar, *The Confident Student*, Third Edition, p. 353.
Copyright © 1998 by Houghton Mifflin Company. Used by permission.

such as true/false, definitions, matching, multiple
choice, fill in the blank, and some kinds of math
problems. See examples of flash cards shown
above.

10. Create concept maps (graphic organizer). In
Chapter 3, you learned how to take class notes using a concept map. Whether or not you choose to
take class notes with concept maps, strongly consider them for creating study materials. You'll see
an example of a concept map on page 108 and the
steps for creating one on page 106. Concept maps
have a number of benefits when used as study
materials. First, they clearly show the relationship
among levels of information (i.e., key concepts,
main ideas, and supporting details). They aid
learning by combining the left brain's verbal and
analytical skills with the right brain's spatial and
creative abilities. Concept maps are simple to expand, so you can easily add new information from
various sources. And they are especially useful
when preparing for an essay test or term paper.

**11. Create three-column study charts for
math (graphic organizer):** If you took math notes
using three-column charts (see page 145), you
are well on your way toward **Organizing** helpful
study materials for that course. If not, simply
begin now by dividing blank pages into three
columns and titling them: Problem, Solution, and
Explanation. Now add one problem at the top of
the left-hand column of each page; include problems representing different levels of difficulty:

- **Easy problems:** These could be problems your
  instructor solved in class that you immediately
  "got." These might be problems you correctly
  solved on a test or homework assignment. Or
  they could even be problems you initially did
  wrong but have since learned how to solve.

- **Challenging problems:** These might be problems
  that you got wrong on a test or homework assignment and still don't understand how to solve. Or
  they might be problems your instructor solved in
  class but continue to baffle you. Or, they could be
  sample problems you haven't tried to solve, but just
  looking at them, you doubt whether you can. These
  challenging practice problems could come from
  sources such as class notes, homework, tests, the
  tutoring center, or the website for your textbook.

Problem	Solution	Explanation
Find an equation of the line with slope 4 that contains the point (2, −1).	Step 1: $y = 4x + b$	Substitute 4 for the "m" in $y = mx + b$; "m" is the slope.
	Step 2: $-1 = 4(2) + b$	Replace x with 2 and y with −1 in the equation.
	Step 3: $-1 = 8 + b$	In ordered pairs, the first value is for x, the second is for y.
	Step 4: $-9 = b$	Multiply to simplify.
	Step 5: Equation: $y = 4x - 9$	Solve for b by subtracting 8 from both sides.
	Step 6: $-1 = 4(2) - 9$ Is this true?	Replace the "b" with −9 in the equation $y = 4x + b$.
	Step 7: $-1 = 8 - 9$ YES	Check the answer by substituting the x and y values in the answer.

Figure 4.1 | Three-Column Study Chart for Math

Now do your best to solve each problem in the middle column, while writing explanations (e.g., directions, key terms, and rules) in the right-hand column. Because you are creating study materials, it is essential that you understand each step in the solution as well as its explanation. If you get stuck on a problem, set it aside and save it. You'll learn how to deal with these challenging problems in Chapter 5. For now, include as many solved problems as you can. Figure 4.1 shows an example of a three-column study chart for math.

12. Create Cornell study sheets. Walter Pauk, an educator at Cornell University, devised a simple and helpful way to organize study materials. Cornell study sheets are very useful later on when you **Rehearse** and **Evaluate** the target knowledge, as you'll learn to do in Chapter 5. Here's how to construct one:

- Create a blank Cornell study sheet by drawing lines on notebook paper to create the three sections depicted in Figure 4.2. If working on a computer, use the table feature in your word processing program. Simply create a table with two rows and two columns. Drag the middle vertical line to the left to widen Section A and narrow Section B. Drag the middle horizontal line toward the bottom to lengthen Section A. Then merge the bottom two columns to create Section C.

- In Section A, copy study materials you have already created, especially outlines and concept maps.

- Compose questions about the information found in Section A. Write each question in Section B alongside its answer in Section A.

- Circle or underline key concepts in Section A. Write each key concept in Section B alongside its definition or explanation in Section A.

- In Section C, write a summary of the key concepts, main ideas, and supporting details that appear in Section A.

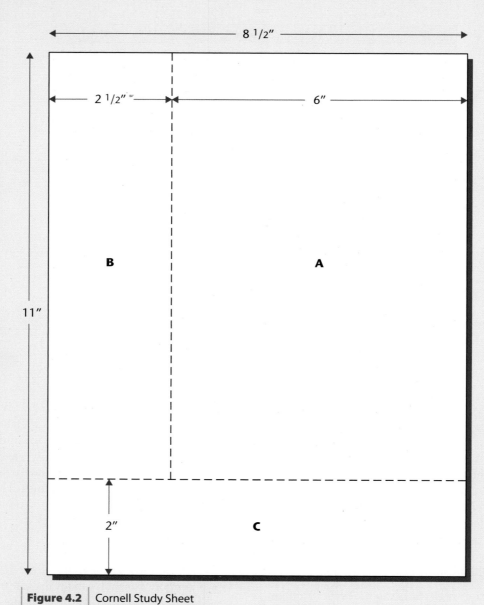

Figure 4.2 Cornell Study Sheet

Source: From Walter Pauk, *How to Study in College*, Sixth Edition, p. 205. Copyright © 1997 by Houghton Mifflin Company. Used by permission.

See Figure 4.3 for an example of a completed Cornell study sheet. Note that Section A (the largest section) contains an informal outline that was created (as described in Strategy 7), polished, and then copied onto the study sheet.

AFTER ORGANIZING STUDY MATERIALS

13. Read more on the same subject. Are you having difficulty understanding the information in your notes? Consider **Collecting** more. Ask your instructor, tutor, or a librarian to suggest

	Course: Psychology 101
	Topic: Abraham Maslow
	Abraham Maslow (1908–1970)
	— Family immigrated to Brooklyn from Russia
	— One of seven children
	— Unhappy, neurotic child
What was the psychological movement that Maslow led?	— Taught at Teachers College, Brooklyn College, Brandeis
	— Sought to understand human motivations
When did he become leader of this movement?	— Became leader of humanistic psychology movement of the 1950s and 1960s.
What are the five levels of motivation, according to Maslow's Hierarchy?	Maslow's hierarch: theory of Human Motivation (like a pyramid)
	— Physical (the foundation)
	— Food, water, air, rest, health, exercise, etc.
What are examples of each level?	— Safety needs
	— Security, stability, shelter, freedom from fear
	— Social needs
	Love, belonging, connection, affiliation
	— Psychological needs
	— self-esteem, power, approval, recognition, confidence
Self-actualization	— Self-actualization (top of the pyramid)
	— Need to fulfill oneself, creation
	— Maslow: "To become everything that one is capable of becoming."
	Humanistic psychology
	— Maslow led the "Third Force" in psychology
	— Third Force—alternative to other approaches of psychology
How does humanistic psychology differ from Freudian and behavioral psychology regarding "choice" in human behavior?	— Freudian psychoanalysis
	— Behaviorist psychology
	— Stressed the power of a person to choose how to behave
	— Other approaches minimized the importance of conscious choice
	— Freudians: Choices controlled by childhood influences
	— Behaviorists: Choices controlled by conditioning
	— Appealed to the individualistic, rebellious college students of the 1960s

Abraham Maslow became the leader of the humanistic psychology movement in the 1950's and 60's. Unlike Freudian and behavioral psychologists, humanists believe people have the power to choose their own behaviors. Maslow is most noted for his efforts to identify forces that motivate human beings. His "hierarchy" proposes that some needs must be addressed before others. The most primary needs are physical (air, water, food). Next comes safety (freedom from fear, shelter from cold). Then social needs such as love and belonging. Next, psychological needs such as self-esteem, power, approval, recognition and confidence. Self-Actualization sits a top Mazlow's pyramid of motivation.

Figure 4.3 | Cornell Study Sheet Completed Example

additional reading materials. Sometimes another author will express the same idea in a way that will flip a switch in your head and get your neurons firing. This extra information may clarify muddy areas or fill in gaps in your study materials. If you have difficulty understanding your textbook, look for a book on the same subject written for younger students. It may present the same information in a way that is easier to comprehend. After reading this simpler version, you can return to your study materials with an improved understanding.

14. Get feedback on your study materials. Show them to classmates and study group members. Show them to a tutor. Show them to your instructor. Ask for their suggestions to improve the accuracy, completeness, and organization of your study materials.

15. Seek help. If you don't understand something you're studying or need more one-on-one explanations, make an appointment with your instructor. You can also go to the tutoring center on your campus to get assistance. If the first tutor you see isn't much help, ask for a different tutor the next time. Keep seeking help until you understand the information or skill well enough to create well-**Organized** study materials.

STUDYING EXERCISE

Interview successful students and ask for their favorite ways to create effective study materials. See if you can discover additional strategies not on the list presented here. However, be ready to hear that many students don't create study materials. Rather, they skip this step of learning and study directly from their unorganized class notes or textbook markings. Now you need never make this mistake again.

A NOTE ABOUT CORNELL STUDY SHEETS

As mentioned in Chapter 3, many study skills books suggest writing all of your notes from reading assignments and class sessions directly on Cornell-formatted pages. This approach is usually called the "Cornell note-taking system." By contrast, I recommend that you take your reading and class notes on regular paper or a computer. Next, do three things to deep process the information you have **Collected**:

1. Polish your notes, making sure they are complete and accurate.
2. Condense your notes, identifying key concepts, ideas, and supporting details.
3. **Organize** the condensed notes, creating effective study materials (e.g., outlines, concept maps) that include information from *all* course materials.

Now, if you wish, copy your polished, condensed, and organized study materials onto a Cornell study sheet.

Here's why I urge you to wait to create Cornell study sheets until you have thoroughly processed your original notes. If you write your original notes on Cornell study sheets, you will be tempted to study from them without polishing, condensing, or **Organizing** the information. This means you will be skipping essential steps necessary for creating deep and lasting learning. But suppose you resist the temptation and you do polish, condense, and **Organize** the notes you took on Cornell-formatted pages. Now you'll need to write them on other pages anyway, so there was no real purpose for taking them on Cornell-formatted pages to begin with. Here's the bottom line: The best use for Cornell-formatted pages is for **Rehearsing** and **Evaluating** (not **Collecting**) what you are learning, and you will learn how to do this in Chapter 5.

Employing Interdependence

5

Once I accept responsibility for taking purposeful actions to achieve my goals and dreams, I then develop mutually supportive relationships that make the journey easier and more enjoyable.

I am developing mutually supportive relationships.

SUCCESSFUL STUDENTS ...	STRUGGLING STUDENTS ...
develop mutually supportive relationships, recognizing that life is richer when giving to and receiving from others.	**remain dependent, codependent, or independent** in relation to others.
strengthen relationships with active listening, showing their concern for the other person's thoughts and feelings.	**listen poorly**, demonstrating little desire to understand another person's perspective.
respect cultural differences, understanding how to achieve success in a world of increasing diversity.	**judge those who are different** as inappropriate, lacking, wrong, or bad.

Case Study in Critical Thinking

PROFESSOR ROGERS' TRIAL

Professor Rogers thought her Speech 101 students would enjoy role-playing a real court trial as their last speech for the semester. She also hoped the experience would teach them to work well in teams, a skill much sought after by employers. So, she divided her students into groups of six—a team of three defense attorneys and a team of three prosecuting attorneys—providing each group with court transcripts of a real murder case. Using evidence from the trial, each team would present closing arguments for the case, after which a jury of classmates would render a verdict. Each team was allowed a maximum of 24 minutes to present its case, and all three team members would receive the same grade.

After class, **Anthony** told his teammates, **Sylvia** and **Donald**, "We'll meet tomorrow at 4:00 in the library and plan a defense for this guy." Sylvia felt angry about Anthony's bossy tone, but she just nodded. Donald said, "Whatever," put headphones on, and strolled away singing louder than he probably realized.

"Look," Anthony said to Sylvia at 4:15 the next day, "we're not waiting for Donald any more. Here's what we'll do. You go first and take about 10 minutes to prove that our defendant had no motive. I'll take the rest of the time to show how it could have been the victim's brother who shot him. I want an A out of this."

Sylvia was furious. "You can't just decide to leave Donald out. Plus, what about the defendant's fingerprints on the murder weapon! We have to dispute that evidence or we'll never win. I'll do that. And I'll go last so I can wrap up all the loose ends. I want to win this trial."

The defense team met twice more before the trial. Donald came to only one of the meetings and spent the entire time reading the case. He said he wasn't sure what he was going to say, but he'd have it figured out by the day of the trial. Anthony and Sylvia argued about which evidence was most important and who would speak last. At one point, another student threatened to call security when Sylvia lost her temper and started shouting at Anthony that no one had elected him the leader.

The day before the trial, Anthony went to Professor Rogers. "It's not fair that my grade depends on my teammates. Donald couldn't care less what happens, and Sylvia is always looking for a fight. I'll present alone, but not with them."

"If you were an actual lawyer," Professor Rogers replied, "do you think you could go to the judge and complain that you aren't getting along with your partners? You'll have to figure out how to work as a team. The trial goes on as scheduled, and all three of you will get the same grade."

On the day of the trial, the three student prosecutors presented one seamless and persuasive closing argument. Then Anthony leapt up, saying, "I'll go first for my team." He spoke for 21 minutes, talking as fast as he could to present the entire case, including an explanation of how the defendant's fingerprints had gotten on the murder weapon. Sylvia, greatly flustered, followed with a seven-minute presentation in which she also explained how the defendant's fingerprints had gotten on the murder weapon. At that point, Professor Rogers announced that the defense was already four minutes over their time limit. Donald promised to be brief. He assured the jury that the defendant was innocent and then read three unconnected passages from the transcript as "proof." His presentation took 75 seconds. The jury of fellow students deliberated for five minutes and unanimously found the defendant guilty. Professor Rogers gave all members of the defense team a D for their speeches.

Listed below are the characters in this story. Rank them in the order of their responsibility for the group's grade of D. Give a different score to each character. Be prepared to explain your answer.

Most responsible	←	1	2	3	4	→	Least responsible

___ **Professor Rogers**　　___ **Sylvia**

___ **Anthony**　　___ **Donald**

▶ **DIVING DEEPER** Imagine that you have been assigned to a group project in one of your college courses and that the student whom you scored above as most responsible for the group's grade of D (Anthony, Sylvia, or Donald) is in your group. What positive actions could you take to help your group be a success despite this person?

Creating a Support System

 Focus Question How could you make accomplishing your success a little easier and a lot more fun?

What part will others play in your quest to achieve your goals and dreams? And what part will you play in theirs?

How you answer these questions will affect your level of success in college and beyond. As with so many aspects of life, your culture has programmed you to make its approved choices. And there is probably no other area where cultures are more clearly different than in their beliefs about the role that people play in one another's lives.

At one end of this spectrum are **individualistic** cultures. These cultures have an "I/me" orientation, and independence is highly regarded. At the other end of this spectrum are **collectivistic** cultures. These cultures have a "we/us" orientation and interdependence is highly regarded. Look back at the *On Course* Self-Assessment in Chapter 1 and note your score for "Employing Interdependence." If it was low, you likely have an individualistic mindset. If your score was high, you likely have a collectivistic mindset.

Mainstream North American culture has a strongly individualistic mindset, according to researcher Geert Hofstede. In this culture, rugged individualism and personal success are highly regarded, and each person is seen as a unique individual. When children reach adulthood, they are expected to strike out on their own and compete for success. Individualistic cultures admire people who "stand on their own two feet," who "pull themselves up by their boot straps," who "stand out in a crowd," and who are "self-made" men and women. Feeling good about oneself is related to one's personal accomplishments.

By contrast, other cultures—Latino, Asian, and Native American cultures among them—have a collectivistic mindset. These cultures value social harmony and family honor. They respect those who fit in and enhance the welfare of the group. Whereas individualistic cultures believe "the squeaky wheel gets the grease," collectivistic cultures believe "The goose that honks gets shot" or "The nail that sticks up gets pounded down." Family unity, honor, and respect are vital parts of collectivistic cultures. The importance of family is demonstrated by lifelong caring for both immediate and extended family members. Three or even four generations of family members may live near, or even with, one another. Feeling good about oneself is related to one's contribution to others, including family, workplace, and culture.

Each of these cultural perspectives has advantages and disadvantages. Creators, however, see beyond their cultural programming. They know there is a time to be independent and a time to be interdependent. With this perspective, they multiply the number of options they have at each new fork in the road. My experience is that most students choose independence far more

> Ask yourself: When making a choice, do you first and foremost consider what you want, what will make you happy, or do you consider what is best for you *and* the people around you? . . . Where we fall on this continuum is very much a product of our cultural upbringing and the script we are given for how to choose. . . .
>
> *Sheena Iyengar*

> Even as people take pride in their national independence, we know we are becoming more and more interdependent.
>
> *Bill Clinton*

often than interdependence. As a result, they can benefit from using more of the resources their colleges provide to help them succeed. Let's consider some choices you could make to create a support system that will help you not only achieve your goals in college but make the journey less stressful.

SEEK HELP FROM YOUR INSTRUCTORS

Building positive relationships with your college instructors is a powerful Quadrant II action that can pay off handsomely. Your instructors have years of specialized training. You've already paid for their help with your tuition, and all you have to do is ask.

Find out your professors' office hours and make an appointment. Arrive prepared with questions or requests, and you'll likely get good help. As a bonus, by getting to know your instructors, you may find a mentor who will help you in college and beyond.

GET HELP FROM COLLEGE RESOURCES

Nearly every college spends a chunk of tuition money to provide support services for students, but these services go to waste unless you use them. Do you know what support services your college offers, where they are, and how to use them?

Confused About Future Courses to Take?

Get help from your advisor or someone in the counseling center. They can help you decide on a major and create a multiyear academic plan that includes all of your required courses and their prerequisites.

Academic Problems?

Get help at one of your college's tutoring labs. Many colleges have a writing lab, a reading lab, and a math lab. Other sources of academic assistance might include a science learning center or a computer lab. Your college may also have a diagnostician who tests students for learning disabilities and suggests ways of overcoming them.

Money Problems?

Get help from your college's financial aid office. Money is available in grants and scholarships (which you don't pay back), loans (which you do pay back, usually at low interest rates), and student work programs (which offer jobs on campus). Your college may also have a service that can locate an off-campus job, perhaps one in the very career field you want to enter after graduation. In Chapter 8, you'll find detailed information about addressing your money problems (see pages 280–288).

> For every one of us that succeeds, it's because there's somebody there to show you the way out. The light doesn't always necessarily have to be in your family; for me it was teachers and school.
>
> *Oprah Winfrey*

Personal Problems?

Get help from your college's counseling office. Trained counselors are available at many colleges to help students through times of emotional upset. It's not unusual for students to experience some sort of personal difficulty during college; Creators seek assistance.

Health Problems?

Get aid from your college's health service. Many colleges have doctors who see students at little or no cost. Health-related products may be available inexpensively or even for free. Your college may even offer special health insurance for students.

Problems Deciding on a Career?

Get help from your college's career office. There you can take aptitude tests, discover job opportunities, learn to write or improve your résumé, and practice effective interviewing skills.

Problems Getting Involved Socially at Your College?

Request assistance from your college's student activities office. Here you'll discover athletic teams, trips, choirs, dances, service projects, student professional organizations, the college newspaper, the campus literary magazine, clubs, and more, just waiting for you to get involved.

CREATE A PROJECT TEAM

If you're tackling a big project, why not create a team to help? A project team is formed to accomplish one particular task. In business, when a project needs attention, an *ad hoc* committee is formed. *Ad hoc* in Latin means "toward this." In other words, an *ad hoc* committee comes together for the sole purpose of solving one problem. Once the task is complete, the committee disbands.

One of my students created a project team to help her move. More than a dozen classmates volunteered, including a fellow who provided a truck. In one Saturday morning, the team packed and delivered her possessions to a new apartment. Without the help of a team, how long would the move have taken her, how much would it have cost, and how much stress would it have caused her?

What big project do you have that would benefit from the assistance of others? The only barrier standing between you and a project team is your unwillingness to ask for help.

START A STUDY GROUP

In the late 1970s and early 1980s, a mathematics graduate student at the University of California, Berkeley, showed the value of academic study groups. Uri Treisman had noticed that students who succeeded in calculus met outside of class and, among other things, talked about solving math problems. Struggling

Alone we can do so little; together we can do so much.

Helen Keller

We are all interdependent. Do things for others—tribe, family, community—rather than just for yourself.

Chief Wilma Mankiller

My driving belief is this: great teamwork is the only way to reach our ultimate moments, to create the breakthroughs that define our careers, to fulfill our lives with a sense of lasting significance.

Pat Riley, former professional basketball coach

students didn't. As a result of this observation, Treisman created a program for struggling calculus students. His approach encouraged these students to gather for the purpose of talking about mathematics and solving challenging problems. The program was so successful that it has since been offered at many other colleges and universities. You can create a variation of Triesman's program in any course you want. Simply start a study group with some of your classmates. A study group differs from a project team in two ways. First, a study group is created to help everyone on the team excel in a particular course. Second, a study group meets many times throughout a semester. In fact, some study groups are so helpful that their members stay together throughout college.

Study groups offer a number of benefits. Participation increases your active involvement with the course content, which in turn leads to deeper learning and higher grades. The resulting academic success raises your expectations for success and increases your level of motivation. Study group participation helps you develop the skill of working with a group, a skill much sought after by employers. And some study group members may become your lifelong friends. Here are three suggestions for maximizing the value of your study group:

1. **CHOOSE ONLY CREATORS.** As the semester begins, make a list of potential study group members: classmates who attend regularly, come prepared, and participate actively. Also watch for that quiet student who doesn't say much but whose occasional comments reveal a special understanding of the subject. After the first test or essay, find out how the students on your list performed and invite three or four of the most successful to study with you.

2. **CHOOSE GROUP GOALS.** Regardless of potential, a study group is only as effective as you make it. Everyone should agree upon common goals. You might say to prospective study group members, "My goal in our math class is to master the subject and earn an A. Is that what you want, too?" Team up with students whose goals match or exceed your own.

3. **CHOOSE GROUP RULES.** The last step is establishing team rules. Pat Riley, one of the most successful professional basketball coaches ever, had his players create a "team covenant." Before the season, they agreed on the rules they would follow to stay on course to their goal of a championship. Your team should do the same. Decide where, how often, and at what time you'll meet. Most important, agree on what will happen during the meetings. Many study groups fail because they turn into social gatherings. Yours will succeed if you adopt rules like these:

Rule 1: *We meet in the library every Thursday afternoon from one o'clock to three o'clock.*

Rule 2: *All members bring their favorite study materials, including 20 new questions with answers and sources (e.g., textbook page or class notes).*

Love thy neighbor as thyself, but choose your neighborhood.

Louise Beal

If people around you aren't going anywhere, if their dreams are no bigger than hanging out on the corner, or if they're dragging you down, get rid of them. Negative people can sap your energy so fast, and they can take your dreams away from you, too.

Earvin (Magic) Johnson

Rule 3: *All study materials are discussed and all written questions are asked, answered, and understood before any socializing.*

One student I know took this advice and started a study group in his anatomy and physiology class, a course with a notoriously high failure rate. At the end of the semester, he proudly showed me a thank-you card signed by the other four members of his group. "We couldn't have done it without you," they wrote. "Thanks for *making* us get together!" Defying the odds, everyone in the group had passed the course.

Whom you spend time with will dramatically affect your outcomes and experiences in college. If you hang out with people who place little value on learning or a college degree, it's challenging to resist their negative influence. However, if you associate with highly committed, hard-working students, their encouragement can motivate you to stay on course to graduation even when the road gets rough. One of my students actually moved to a new apartment when he realized that "friends" from his old neighborhood spent most of their time putting down his efforts to get a college degree. When it comes to selecting your "group" in college, be sure to choose people who want out of life what you do.

> Until recently, the "old girls" did not know how the "old boys" network operated. . . . Women now know that, besides hard work and lots of skill, the move to the top requires a supportive network.
>
> *June E. Gabler*

Many people collaborate only with others who are like them. One of the greatest benefits of your college experience is meeting people of diverse backgrounds, with different cultures, beliefs, customs, ideas, skills, experiences, abilities, and resources. Be sure to network with those who are older or younger than you, who are from different states or countries, who are of different races or cultures, and who have different religions or political preferences. Exposure to such differences will expand your horizons and enhance your life.

Start a contact list of the people you meet in college. You might even want to write a few notes about them: their major or career field, names of family members, hobbies, interests, and especially their strengths. Keep in touch with these people during and after college.

Creators develop mutually supportive relationships in college that continue to support them for years—even for a lifetime. Don't get so bogged down with the daily demands of college that you fail to create an empowering support network.

Ed ARNO

© Estate of Ed Arno

Journal Entry 17

In this activity, you will explore the creation of a support system. Afterward, you may decide to start networking more to help you achieve your greatest goals and dreams.

1. Write and complete the following sentence stems:

1. An outer obstacle that stands between me and my success in college is . . . (Examples of *outer* obstacles are a lack of time to study or a teacher you don't understand.)

2. Someone besides me who could help me overcome this outer obstacle is . . .

3. How this person could help me is by . . .

4. An inner obstacle that stands between me and my success in college is . . . (Examples of *inner* obstacles are shyness or a tendency to procrastinate.)

5. Someone besides me who could help me overcome this inner obstacle is . . .

6. How this person could help me is by . . .

7. The most challenging course I'm taking in college this semester is . . .

8. This course is challenging for me because . . .

9. Someone besides me who could help me overcome this challenge is . . .

10. How this person could help me is by . . .

2. **Write about two (or more) choices you could make to create a stronger support system for yourself in college.** Consider the choices you could make to overcome the challenges and obstacles to your success that you identified in Step 1. Consider also any resistance you may have about taking steps to create a support system. Dive deep as you explore each choice fully.

Individually, we are one drop.
Together, we are an ocean.

Ryunosuke Satoro

Nobody but nobody can make it out here alone.

Maya Angelou

One Student's Story

JASON MATTHEW LODEN
Avila University, Missouri

During my first semester in college, I struggled in my Calculus class. I didn't understand anything my instructor taught, and his mathematical terms bounced off me like a foreign language. I dreaded going to class and frequently zoned out when I did. After class, I attempted to teach myself the material, but I couldn't understand the confusing terms. I started turning in my homework late and incomplete, and my first two test grades were in the low 60s. I knew I needed help, but I was too independent to admit it.

One day, in my freshman seminar class, my instructor began discussing independent individuals. He informed us that it takes a strong person to be independent, but what

he went on to say hit me like a brick: "It takes a stronger individual to be *inter*dependent." I stared at him for a while, pondering his last few words. That night, I cracked open the *On Course* textbook and began to read through Chapter 5. It stressed that people who are interdependent (rely on others as well as themselves) are often happier and have greater success in life than those who are independent (rely only on themselves). Persuaded by the readings, I met with my Calculus instructor and arranged twice-a-week tutoring sessions. I also formed a calculus study group with my friends Joey and Amy, and we began meeting every Friday.

At the beginning of each tutoring session, my instructor gave me

a quiz. Then we would focus on one specific element of calculus, such as derivatives as they relate to velocity. In my study group, we dove into our homework, sharing our answers along with the processes we used to solve them. At first, I was very frustrated, but after a month of hard work and interdependent studying, I started to grasp the whole idea of calculus. By the end of the semester, I had become a Quadrant II student in calculus. I no longer worried about my homework or stressed over class because I prepared a little each day with the help of my instructor and friends. My grade steadily improved throughout the semester, leading to a fabulous 94 on my final, which allowed me to achieve an A for the course. Before this experience, I knew that I had a good chance of success in life as an independent individual. Now that I know the power of a support group, there's no stopping me!

Strengthening Relationships with Active Listening

Focus Questions   Do you know how to strengthen a relationship with active listening? What are the essential skills of being a good listener?

Once we have begun a mutually supportive relationship, we naturally want the relationship to grow. Books on relationships abound, suggesting untold ways to strengthen a relationship. At the heart of all of these suggestions is a theme: We must show that we value the other person professionally, personally, or both.

Many ways exist to demonstrate another's value to us. Some of the most powerful methods include keeping promises, giving honest appreciation and approval, resolving conflicts so that both people win, staying in touch, and

> When people talk, listen completely. Most people never listen.
>
> *Ernest Hemingway*

speaking well of someone when talking to others. However, for demonstrating the high esteem with which you value another person, there may be no better way than active listening.

Few people are truly good listeners. Too often, we're thinking about what we want to say next. Or our thoughts dash off to our own problems, and we ignore what the other person is saying. Or we hear what we *thought* the person was going to say rather than what he or she actually said.

Good listeners, by contrast, clear their minds and listen for the entire message, including words, tone of voice, gestures, and facial expressions. No matter how well one person communicates, unless someone else listens actively, both the communication and the relationship are likely to go astray. Imagine the potential problems created if good listening skills are absent when an instructor says to a class, "I need to change the date of the final exam from Monday to the previous Friday. I just found out that I need to turn in my final grades on Monday." Suppose a student assumes that the instructor said the exam will be moved to the *following* Friday (instead of the *previous* Friday). When that student shows up on the "following" Friday, not only will the exam be long over, but the instructor will have turned in the final course grades as well. Talk about an unpleasant surprise!

Listening actively means accepting 100 percent responsibility for receiving the same message that the speaker sent, uncontaminated by your own thoughts or feelings. That's why active listening begins with empathy, the ability to understand the other person as if, for that moment, you *are* the other person. To empathize doesn't mean that you necessarily agree. Empathy means understanding what the other person is thinking and feeling. And you actively reveal this understanding.

With active listening, you send this message: *I value you so much that I am doing my very best to see the world through your eyes.*

HOW TO LISTEN ACTIVELY

Active listening is a learned skill. You will become an excellent listener if you master the following four steps:

Step 1: Listen to Understand

Listening isn't effective when you're simply waiting for the first opportunity to insert your own opinion. Instead, focus fully on the speaker, activate your empathy, and listen with the intention of fully understanding what the other person thinks and feels.

Step 2: Clear Your Mind and Remain Silent

Don't be distracted by judgmental chatter from your Inner Critic and Inner Defender. Clear your mind, stay focused, and be quiet. Let your mind listen for thoughts. Let your heart listen for the undercurrent of emotions. Let your

---

For the lack of listening, billions of losses accumulate: retyped letters, rescheduled appointments, rerouted shipments, breakdowns in labor management relations, misunderstood sales presentations, and job interviews that never really get off the ground.

Michael Ray & Rochelle Myers

Active listening, sometimes called reflective listening, involves giving verbal feedback of the content of what was said or done along with a guess at the feeling underneath the spoken words or acts.

Muriel James & Dorothy Jongeward

intuition listen for a deeper message hidden beneath the words. Let your companion know that you are actively listening. Sit forward. Nod your head when appropriate. Offer verbal feedback that shows you are actively listening: "Mmmmm . . . I see . . . Uh huh. . . . "

Step 3: Ask the Person to Expand or Clarify

Don't make assumptions or fill in the blanks with your own experience. Invite the speaker to share additional information and feelings:

- *Tell me more about that.*
- *Could you give me an example?*
- *Can you explain that in a different way?*
- *How did you feel when that happened?*
- *What happened next?*

Step 4: Reflect the Other Person's Thoughts and Feelings

Don't assume you understand. In your own words, restate what you heard, both the ideas and the emotions. Then verify the accuracy of your understanding:

- To a classmate: *Sounds like you're really angry about the instructor's feedback on your research paper. To you, his comments seem more sarcastic than helpful. Is that it?*
- To a professor: *I want to be clear about the new date for the final exam. You're postponing the exam from Monday to the following Friday. Have I got it right?*

Notice that reflecting adds nothing new to the conversation. Don't offer advice or tell your own experience. Your goal is merely to understand.

USE ACTIVE LISTENING IN YOUR COLLEGE CLASSES

Active listening not only strengthens relationships with people, it strengthens our understanding of new concepts and helps us learn. In class, successful students clear their minds and prepare to hear something of value. They reflect the instructor's ideas, confirming the accuracy of what they heard. When confused, they ask the instructor to expand or clarify, either in class or during the instructor's conference hours. Using a Creator mindset, these students actively listen to understand. And, ultimately, they record their understanding in their notes. Obviously, the more accurate the information is in your class notes, the more you will learn when studying.

So, choose today to master active listening. You'll be amazed at how much this choice will improve your relationships, your learning, and your life.

If I were to summarize in one sentence the single most important principle I have learned in the field of interpersonal relations, it would be this: Seek first to understand, then to be understood.

Stephen Covey

What few people realize is that failure to be a good listener prevents us from hearing and retaining vital information, becoming a roadblock to personal and professional success.

Jean Marie Stine

If there is any one secret of success, it lies in the ability to get the other person's point of view and see things from his angle as well as your own.

Henry Ford

Dr. Eliot's listening was not mere silence, but a form of activity. Sitting very erect on the end of his spine with hands joined in his lap, making no movement except that he revolved his thumbs around each other faster or slower, he faced his interlocutor and seemed to be hearing with his eyes as well as his ears. He listened with his mind and attentively considered what you had to say while you said it. . . . At the end of an interview the person who had talked to him felt that he had his say.

Henry James about Charles W. Eliot, former president of Harvard University

Journal Entry 18

In this activity, you will practice the skill of active listening by writing out a conversation with your Inner Guide. As discussed earlier, thoughts are dashing through our minds much of the time. Writing a conversation with your Inner Guide applies this knowledge in a new and powerful way. First, it helps us become more aware of the thoughts that are guiding our choices. Second, writing this conversation encourages us to sort through confusion and find a positive solution. Third, it reminds us that we are not our thoughts and we can change them whenever doing so would benefit us. And, finally, writing this conversation with our Inner Guide gives us practice with an important mental skill used by highly intelligent and adaptive people: *metacognition*. Metacognition is the skill of thinking about our thinking. Developing metacognition helps us see where our thinking is flawed. It allows us to change our thinking to achieve better outcomes and experiences. If you've ever talked to yourself while working on a problem, you were probably using metacognition. You may find writing this dialogue to be a new (and perhaps unusual) experience. However, the more you practice, the more you'll see what a valuable success skill it is to have a conversation with yourself as an active listener. And, of course, becoming an active listener with others will strengthen those relationships immeasurably.

1. Write a conversation between you (ME) and your Inner Guide (IG) about a problem you are facing in college. Label each of your IG's responses with the listening skill it uses: silence, expansion, clarification, reflection (remember to reflect feelings as well as thoughts). Let your IG demonstrate the skills of active listening without giving advice.

Here's an example of such a conversation:

ME: I've been realizing what a difficult time I have asking for assistance.

IG: Would you like to say more about that? **(Expansion)**

ME: Well, I've been having trouble in math. I know I should be asking more questions in class, but . . . I don't know, I guess I feel dumb because I can't do the problems myself.

IG: You seem frustrated that you can't solve the math problems without help. **(Reflection)**

ME: That's right. I've always resisted that sort of thing.

IG: What do you mean by "that sort of thing"? **(Clarification)**

ME: I mean that ever since I can remember, I've had to do everything on my own. When I was a kid, I used to play alone all the time.

IG: Uh-huh. . . . **(Silence)**

ME: As a kid, I never had anyone to help me. And I don't have anyone to help me now.

IG: So, no one is available to help you? Is that how it seems? **(Reflection)**

ME: Well, I guess I could ask Robert for help. He seems really good in math, but I'm kind of scared to ask him.

IG: What scares you about asking him? **(Expansion)** . . . etc.

Imagine that the conversation you create here is taking place over the phone. Don't hang up until you've addressed all aspects of the problem and know what your next action step will be. Let your Inner Guide demonstrate how much it values you by being a great listener.

2. **Write what you learned or relearned about active listening during this conversation with your Inner Guide.** Remember to dive deep to discover a powerful insight. When you think you have written all you can, see if you can write at least one more paragraph.

Respecting Cultural Differences

 Focus Question   What are some keys to achieving success in a world of increasing diversity?

Virtually anywhere you go these days, you encounter people different from you. And that's a trend you can expect to grow. The Pew Research Center predicts major changes in race and ethnicity in the United States between 2005 and 2050. Whites will decrease from 67 to 47 percent of the population. Latino/a Americans will increase from 14 percent to 29 percent. African Americans will remain constant at 13 percent. And Asian Americans will increase from 5 percent to 9 percent. Other ethnicities such as Native Americans and Arab Americans will add even more to the growing diversity of North America.

College enrollment already reflects these changes, according to the *Chronicle of Higher Education*. In the past 40 years, entering White students decreased from 90.9 to 73.1 percent. Simultaneously, African American students increased from 7.5 to 11 percent. Four decades ago, Asians and Latinos/as combined made up only 0.6 percent of new students in higher education, but today the percent of Asians has increased to 8.9 and Latinos to 9.7.

Visible differences such as skin color are relatively easy to identify. Others may be less obvious but no less important. These differences include religion, economic class, mental and physical ability, sexual orientation, age, military experience, and learning preferences, to name just a few. If you add deep-culture differences in beliefs, values, attitudes, and norms, the list of possible differences between any two people is long, indeed.

Much has been written about the challenges of interacting effectively with people who are different. If you search "diversity" at Amazon.com, you'll get links to nearly 17,000 books. If you search "diversity" at Google.com, you'll get

> I am an American; free born and free bred, where I acknowledge no man as my superior, except for his own worth, or as my inferior, except for his own demerit.
>
> *Theodore Roosevelt*

more than 230 million results! The complexity of creating harmony in diverse populations has also been explored in college courses, professional journals, newspapers, magazines, conferences, and workshops. The problems explored in these forums range from misunderstandings stemming from differences in cultural beliefs, attitudes, norms, and rules to the horrors of hate crimes, ethnic cleansings, and genocide.

Addressing the complexities of deeply ingrained prejudice and oppression of minorities is beyond the scope of a book about college success. My hope is that people empowered by the strategies in this book, like you, will find satisfaction in living up to their potential instead of tearing down the lives of others. And if you are a student who faces prejudice and unfair treatment, my hope is that you will feel empowered to stand in opposition to such injustices. Whether you consider yourself a member of a cultural majority or minority, your success very likely depends on your ability to interact effectively with people who are different from you. In higher education, for example, someone different from you may be your instructor, tutor, counselor, advisor, or classmate. In the workplace, someone different from you may be your employer, supervisor, manager, customer, or coworker.

By themselves, differences are not a problem. But add to them the human tendency to judge, fear, and (in some cases) harm people who are different, and you have the perfect recipe for conflict between individuals, groups, and nations. The antidote is to replace judgments with respect.

There are certainly moral arguments to be made for treating everyone with respect, but there is a very practical reason as well. Today, more than ever before, everyone's success is affected by their ability to interact effectively with people who are different from them. Judgments lead to fear, misunderstanding, conflict, discrimination, oppression, and even war. By contrast, respect leads to cooperation, compassion, learning, empowerment, success, and peace. Your choice either to judge or show respect will have a profound effect on the outcomes and experiences of your life and those with whom you interact.

> Tolerance, inter-cultural dialogue and respect for diversity are more essential than ever in a world where peoples are becoming more and more closely interconnected.
>
> *Kofi Annan, Former Secretary-General of the United Nations*

SHOWING RESPECT

Here are some ways you can show respect to people who are different from you. They range from the simple to the complex.

1. **PRONOUNCE NAMES CORRECTLY.** There are few things more personal to us than our names. In her book, *Stealing Buddha's Dinner*, Bich Minh Nguyen tells of her shame when Americans pronounced her Vietnamese name "bitch" instead of "Bick." The internationalization of sports is helping mainstream North Americans hear the pronunciation of unfamiliar names such as Yani Tseng (Taiwanese professional golfer), Daisuke Matsuzaka (Japanese professional golfer), Siyar Bahadurzada (Afghan mixed martial artist), and Ndamukong Suh (professional football player whose father is from Cameroon). When you meet someone

with an unfamiliar name, simply say, "I want to be sure I'm pronouncing your name correctly. Would you please say it for me?"

2. **USE THE PREFERRED TERM FOR A PERSON'S CULTURAL GROUP.**
Close in importance to our names is the name of our cultural group. Thus, using preferred terminology conveys the same sort of respect as does pronouncing a person's name correctly. Complicating the issue, members of some cultures may differ in their preference. So, once again, if in doubt, ask.

For example, *Latino* and *Latina* are terms preferred by many members of this cultural group. However, some may prefer "Hispanic," a term that others reject as having been thrust upon them by the U.S. Census Bureau. Also, avoid using terminology that excludes a group. For example, if you say to a group of people, "You're welcome to bring your husband or wife," you have excluded gay people and singles living together. Instead, simply say "husband, wife, or partner." When it comes to people with disabilities, remember that the disability is not the person, so separate the two by presenting the person first. Instead of a "disabled person," say "a person with differing abilities." Some members of majority groups get annoyed by this extra effort to come up with the preferred terminology, and they judge it as "political correctness." However, like our personal names, the terms we prefer for our cultural groups are personal as well, and honoring that preference shows respect.

> [E]thnic group members pay very serious attention to the ways in which they label themselves and are labeled by others. Finding out what term is preferable is a matter of respect. . . .
>
> *Jerry V. Diller*

3. **LEARN NONVERBAL BEHAVIORS.** Experts in communication say that as much as 90 percent of the message we send is conveyed nonverbally. That's why it's essential to know that two nonverbal languages can be as different as two verbal languages. Here are a few examples.

Gestures: Circling your thumb and forefinger in North America means "Everything is great . . . A-Ok." In some South American countries, however, this is an obscene gesture. A two-handed handshake in North America emphasizes one's pleasure of greeting someone. But in Saudi Arabia such a gesture is offensive because Saudis consider one's left hand to be unclean.

> When it comes to nonverbal language, we often mistakenly assume that our systems of communicating nonverbally are all the same.
>
> *David Matsumoto and Linda Juang*

Space: In North American culture, we tend to stand about three to four feet apart when speaking to most people. However, people in some South American and Arabic cultures stand much closer to one another in conversation. I once saw two male students talking after class. One was from Saudi Arabia, the other from the United States. Every time the Saudi student stepped closer, the American stepped back. During a 5-minute conversation, they covered about 15 feet in their cross-cultural dance. It was humorous to watch, but I wonder if either or both felt disrespected with no idea why.

Eye Contact: For many North Americans, eye contact during a conversation generally conveys interest and respect. However, in Asian cultures such as Korea and Japan, eye contact is considered rude and disrespectful. Imagine the potential misunderstandings in a conversation between an instructor and student from these different cultures.

So, whether the difference is in gestures, space, eye contact, or other body language, we can be respectful by realizing that others may speak a different nonverbal language.

4. **SEE PEOPLE AS INDIVIDUALS (NOT STEREOTYPES).** The human mind is a pattern-making device. We want to generalize about life to understand, explain, and predict. Knowing that a particular instructor is "easy" or "hard," for example, helps us make decisions about such things as how much to study for a final exam. Unfortunately, once our minds grab onto a generalization, we want to apply it even if it's wrong or doesn't apply in this situation. This is the problem with stereotypes. A stereotype is a generalization about a group of people based on limited or even faulty evidence. Once we accept a generalization as true, we have a tendency to apply it to all individuals we encounter from that group. If you want to see examples of stereotypes you hold about others, simply complete the following sentence stems with the first thought that comes to mind:

> It is nearly impossible to grow up in a society and not take on its prejudices. Consequently, it is not a matter of whether one is biased. We all are. Rather, it is a question of what negative racial attitudes one has learned so far and what, from this moment on, one is willing to do about them.
>
> *Jean Moule*

Women are. . .	Southerners are. . .
Republicans are. . .	White men are. . .
Jews are. . .	Asians are. . .
Black men are. . .	Rich people are. . .
Muslims are. . .	College instructors are. . .

Stereotypes about any group disrespect individuals from that group, denying them their uniqueness. Knowing cultural tendencies—for example, whether a culture is individualistic or collectivistic—may help to explain why a member of that culture did what he or she did. But using a stereotype to try to predict what a person will do insults that person's uniqueness. As one example of how to employ this idea, don't assume someone either fits a stereotype or can speak for a whole culture: "Emiko, you people are all good in math, right?" Ouch. Instead of stereotyping, see each person for the unique individual he or she is. Just like you.

5. **AVOID THE RIGHT/WRONG GAME.** Human beings are judgment machines. We think what we do is right, so anything different must be wrong. When we play the Right/Wrong Game with people whose culture is different from ours, it has a fancy name: *ethnocentrism*. Ethnocentrism is the belief that the way *we* do things is superior to the way *they* do things.

Sheena Iyengar, a Columbia University business professor, tells of an experience she had with ethnocentrism. At a restaurant in Japan, she ordered green tea with sugar. The waiter replied, "One does not put sugar in green tea." She replied that she knows Japanese people do not put sugar in their green tea, but she likes to put sugar in her green tea. Because of her insistence, the waiter passed on her request to the restaurant manager. After a few minutes, the manager came to her table, apologized, and explained that the restaurant could not serve green tea with sugar because it had no sugar. Because she could not have her green tea the way she preferred, Dr. Iyengar ordered a cup of coffee. The coffee was delivered along with two packets of sugar! Sure, there's a certain humor to the story . . . but beneath it all, there's disrespect. My way is better than your way . . . I'm right . . . you are wrong! How often do we disrespect—or even harm—someone because we insist on being right?

6. **AVOID MICROAGGRESSIONS.** You think of yourself as a good person. You'd never participate in acts of blatant racism. Yet you may unintentionally disrespect people who are different from you through microaggressions. Microaggressions are brief slights and insults that send demeaning messages to members of minority groups. Jean Moule, an African American professor at Oregon State University, shares some personal examples: "A man saw my face as I walked into the store and unconsciously checked his wallet. On the street, a woman catches my eye a half a block away and moves her purse from the handle of her baby's stroller to her side as she arranges the baby's blanket. In the airport, a man signals to his wife to move her purse so it is not over the back of her chair, adjacent to the one I am moving toward. . . . I believe these are examples of 'blink of the eye' racism." The hidden message in each person's response is that African Americans are criminals.

> I see a huge irony. While hate crimes receive the most attention, the greatest damage to the life experiences of people of color is from racial microaggression.
>
> *Derald Wing Sue*

Here's another example. A female student is in a math study group with three men who ignore her efforts to contribute to the discussion of homework problems. The hidden message is that women can't do math. Asian American college professor Derald Wing Sue notes that he is often complimented for speaking English so well. A third-generation American, Sue replies, "I hope so. I was born here." The hidden message is that he will always be a foreigner in the country of his birth.

What makes microaggressions challenging to address is two-fold. The senders are often unaware of their bias and the receivers aren't sure if the slight was deliberate. If you believe you were the recipient of a microaggression, use the assertiveness skills you'll learn later in this chapter to address the insult. And if someone tells you that he or she was insulted by something you said or did (a microaggression), set your Inner Defender aside. Use the listening skills you practiced earlier to learn how you can be more respectful of others.

7. **ADVOCATE FOR RESPECT.** Oppression comes in many guises. Sometimes it shows up as a joke that makes fun of someone who is different. Sometimes oppression escalates to a bigoted comment about

something like someone's race, religion, or sexual orientation. Realize that your silence will be interpreted as agreement with these prejudiced views. Be a voice for respect by letting others know that you don't approve of such comments. (You'll learn some great strategies for being assertive later in this chapter.)

Sadly, oppression will sometimes escalate to acts of cruelty and violence. Recent examples on college campuses include a swastika scrawled on a bathroom wall near a Jewish studies center, signs in bathrooms that said "Death to Fags," and the stabbing of a Nigerian-born student body president. No one can—or should have to—learn in an environment of fear. College offers an opportunity to encounter many points of view so that you can choose the ones that will best support you to create a great life. Don't allow others to deny you or your fellow students of that opportunity because of their prejudices and biases. If you witness or are the target of such hate crimes, report them to campus officials. Follow up to see that something is done. And, in the spirit of interdependence, consider requesting help from a group that has experience dealing with hate crimes, such as the Southern Poverty Law Center and the Anti-Defamation League. These and other groups that promote social justice can be found via an Internet search.

Interacting effectively with people from different cultures can be challenging. However, in a world that is becoming more diverse with each passing day, showing respect for others—and insisting upon it for yourself—will help you achieve your goals and dreams while helping others to do the same.

> All that is necessary for the triumph of evil is that good men do nothing.
>
> *Edmund Burke*

> You demand respect and you'll get it. First of all, you give respect.
>
> *Mary J. Blige*

Journal Entry 19

1. **Describe a time when you felt disrespected**. Present the experience as if it is a scene from a novel. Describe the setting of where the event took place. Explain who was there. Show what they did and said. Explain how you felt.

2. **Describe the same experience a second time, but this time revise what people said and did in a way that would have left you feeling fully respected.** In this revision of history, have everyone speak and behave in ways that would have changed the outcomes and experiences for the better, leaving you feeling fully respected.

Interdependence

AT WORK

PERSONAL SKILLS for CAREER SUCCESS TURN R'GHT

Over 90 percent of us who work for a living do so in organizations, and the ability to function effectively as a member of a team is usually an imperative of success.

Nathaniel Branden, psychologist

You may have noticed that many employment ads say, "Looking for a team player" or "Must relate well to others." Few abilities have more impact on your success at work than your ability to interact well with supervisors, peers, subordinates, suppliers, and customers. And enhancing this ability starts now.

Someday you'll probably ask former professors or employers to write you a letter of recommendation. What they write on that future day will depend on the relationships you're building with them now. Are you someone who works well with others? Someone who completes assignments and does them with excellence? Attends classes regularly and on time? Is respectful of others? Self-aware? Responsible?

A former student called me with a request that I write her a recommendation. After much thought, I said no. Based on her performance in my class, I could not honestly write anything that would help her chances of getting hired. Sadly, when she was "blowing off" my course, she hadn't anticipated the day when she would need me to speak well of her to a potential employer.

In the work world, most people must interact well with others to keep their jobs or to advance. In college, one way to continue developing effective interdependence is by participating actively in study groups. Learning to work collaboratively now will contribute to your success tomorrow (not to mention that your grades will likely be higher).

As you begin a search for your ideal job, one of the best sources of information about what a career is *really* like is someone who is doing it now. By conducting information-gathering interviews with enough people who are working in your chosen profession, you'll learn about qualifications, employment outlook, work conditions, and salaries. If you don't know anyone in the career of your choice, be a Creator and ask people you know for referrals. If that fails, try the Yellow Pages. Call a company you find there, ask for the Public Information Office, and explain the information you're seeking. Besides the information you may uncover, who knows who might be impressed with your professional approach to job hunting!

Creators Wanted!

Candidates must demonstrate interdependence, a team-orientation, and a strong ability to work cooperatively with others.

The same information-gathering strategy is helpful when it comes to learning important information about a particular employer you may be considering. Talk to people who work at the company and find out from the inside what it's really like. For example, if you find the company's mission statement appealing, ask employees if the company backs up those words with actions. Of course, it's important to talk to a number of people to avoid being swayed by one or two biased opinions.

Many people limit their job search to employment agencies and advertised positions, jobs listed in the "visible" marketplace. However, some career specialists estimate that as many as 85 to 90 percent of the available jobs are unlisted and found only by uncovering them in the "invisible" marketplace. Creators discover these unpublished openings by networking. Do that by seeking informational interviews with possible employers, and ask them if they know of others who might have a job for which you'd qualify. Additionally, you can ask friends and acquaintances if they know of positions that are available where they work. Ask professors if they've heard of job openings. Ask at church and club meetings. Ask all of these folks to spread the word that you're looking for a position. You never know who might help you discover an opening that would be ideal for you. A great job might become visible only because you asked a friend who asked a coworker who asked his sister who asked her boss who said, "Sure, we've got a job like that. Have the person call me."

EMPLOY TEAMWORK

Another great strategy during a job search is to develop a support group, especially one made up of other job seekers. Support groups not only provide emotional support when disappointments (and your Inner Critic) strike, they can also give you helpful suggestions and practice at essential skills. For example, support groups can critique your résumé and cover letters. They can help you practice your interviewing skills. Someone in your support group may share an experience that can teach you a valuable lesson. For instance, if someone reports going blank when an interviewer asked, "Do you have any questions for me?" you'll learn to prepare questions to ask at your own interviews.

Okay, let's say you've gotten your dream position in the company you wanted. Teamwork continues to have a big impact on your work life. The *Harvard Business Review* reported a study that discovered why some scientists at Bell Labs in New Jersey were considered "stars" by their colleagues. Interestingly, the stars had done no better academically than their less successful colleagues. In fact, the study found that the stars and their coworkers were very similar when measured on IQ and personality tests. What distinguished the stars was their strong networks of important colleagues. When problems struck, the stars always had someone to call on for advice, and their requests for help were responded to quickly. Interdependence transformed good scientists into stars.

I once asked a very successful investment banker (he retired at the age of 35) how important networking was in his profession. "Well, there's networking up here," he said, holding his hand as high as he could reach, "and then there's everything else down here." He dropped his hand to within inches of the floor. "In this business, you either build relationships or you fail."

One last suggestion about interdependence could apply anywhere on your career path, but is particularly important once you are in your job: Find a mentor. A mentor is someone further along in his or her career development and willing to guide and help newer employees like you. Keep your eyes open for someone successful whose qualities you admire. You can create an informal mentoring relationship by making choices that put you into frequent contact with this person, or you can create a formal relationship by actually asking the person to be your mentor. With wisdom born of experience, a mentor can help keep you on course to career success.

> # ► **BELIEVING IN YOURSELF**

Be Assertive

 Focus Question How can you communicate in a style that strengthens relationships, creates better results, and builds strong self-esteem?

On rare occasions, we may encounter someone who doesn't want us to achieve our goals and dreams. Much more often, though, we run across folks who are too busy, too preoccupied, or couldn't care less about helping us. Meeting such people is especially likely in a bureaucracy such as a college or university. How we communicate our desires to them has a profound impact not only on the quality of the relationships and results we create, but on our self-esteem as well.

According to family therapist Virginia Satir, the two most common patterns of ineffective communication are **placating** and **blaming.** Both perpetuate low self-esteem.

- **PLACATING.** Victims who placate are dominated by their Inner Critic. They place themselves below others, protecting themselves from the sting of criticism and rejection by saying whatever they think will gain approval. Picture placators on their knees, looking up with a pained smile, nodding and agreeing on the outside, while fearfully hiding their true thoughts and feelings within. *"Please, please approve of me,"* they beg as their own Inner Critic judges them unworthy. To gain this approval, placators often spend time in Quadrant III doing what is urgent to others but unimportant to their own goals and dreams. Satir estimated that about 50 percent of people use placating as their major communication style.

- **BLAMING.** Victims who blame are dominated by their Inner Defender. They place themselves above others, protecting themselves from disappointment and failure by making others fully responsible for their problems. Picture them sneering down, a finger jabbing judgmentally at those below. Their Inner Defender snarls, *"You never . . . Why do you always . . . ? Why don't you ever . . . ? It's your fault that. . . ."* Satir estimated that about 30 percent of people use blaming as their major communication style.

Either passively placating or aggressively blaming keeps Victims from developing mutually supportive relationships, making the accomplishment of their dreams more difficult. The inner result is damaged self-esteem.

LEVELING

What, then, is the communication style of Creators? Some have called this style *assertiveness:* honestly expressing opinions and requests. Satir calls this

Once a human being has arrived on this earth, communication is the largest single factor determining what kinds of relationships she or he makes with others and what happens to each in the world.

Virginia Satir

Learning to perceive the truth within ourselves and speak it clearly to others is a delicate skill, certainly as complex as multiplication or long division, but very little time is spent on it in school.

Gay & Kathlyn Hendricks

communication style *leveling*. Leveling is characterized by a simple, yet profound, communication strategy: asserting the truth as you see it.

Creators boldly express their personal truth without false apology or excuse, without harsh criticism or blame. Leveling requires a strong Inner Guide and a commitment to honesty. Here are three strategies that promote leveling:

1. **COMMUNICATE PURPOSEFULLY.** Creators express a clear purpose even in times of emotional upset. If a Creator goes to a professor to discuss a disappointing grade, she will be clear whether her purpose is to (1) increase her understanding of the subject, (2) seek a higher grade, (3) criticize the instructor's grading ability, or accomplish some other option. By knowing her purpose, she has a way to evaluate the success of her communication. The Creator states purposefully, *When I saw my grade on this lab report, I was very disappointed. I'd like to go over it with you and learn how to improve my next one.*

2. **COMMUNICATE HONESTLY.** Creators candidly express unpopular thoughts and upset feelings in the service of building mutually supportive relationships. The Creator says honestly, *I'm angry that you didn't meet me in the library to study for the sociology test as you agreed.*

3. **COMMUNICATE RESPONSIBLY.** Because responsibility lies within, Creators express their personal responsibility with I-messages. An I-message allows creators to take full responsibility for their reaction to anything another person may have said or done. An effective I-message has four elements:

A statement of the situation:	*When you . . .*
A statement of your reaction:	*I felt/thought/decided . . .*
A request:	*I'd like to ask that you . . .*
An invitation to respond:	*Will you agree to that?*

Let's compare Victim and Creator responses to the same situation. Imagine that you feel sick one day and decide not to go to your history class. You phone a classmate, and she agrees to call you after class with what you missed. But she never calls. At the next history class, the instructor gives a test that was announced the day you were absent, and you fail it. Afterward, your classmate apologizes: "Sorry I didn't call. I was swamped with work." What response do you choose?

Placating: *Oh, don't worry about it. I know you had a lot on your mind. I probably would have failed the test anyway.*

Blaming: *You're the lousiest friend I've ever had! After making me fail that test, you have some nerve even talking to me!*

Leveling: *I'm angry that you didn't call. I realize that I could have called you, but I thought I could count on you to keep your word. If we're going to be friends, I need to know if you're going to keep your promises to me in the future. Will you?*

I speak straight and do not wish to deceive or be deceived.

Cochise

We should replace our alienating, criticizing words with "I" language. Instead of, "You are a liar and no one can trust you," say, "I don't like it when I can't rely on your words—it is difficult for us to do things together."

Ken Keyes

Notice that the leveling response is the only one of the three that positively addresses the issue, nurtures a relationship of equals, and demonstrates high self-esteem.

MAKING REQUESTS

Making effective requests is another demonstration of both assertiveness and high self-esteem. Creators know they can't reach their greatest goals and dreams alone, so they ask for help. The key to making effective requests is applying the DAPPS rule. Whenever possible, make your requests **D**ated, **A**chievable, **P**ersonal, **P**ositive, and (above all) **S**pecific. Here are some translations of vague Victim requests to specific, clear Creator requests:

Victim Requests	Creator Requests
1. I'm going to be absent next Friday. It sure would be nice if someone would let me know if I miss anything.	1. John, I'm going to be absent next Friday. Would you be willing to call me Friday night and tell me what I missed?
2. I don't suppose you'd consider giving me a few more days to complete this research paper?	2. I'd like to request an extension on my research paper. I promise to hand it in by noon on Thursday. Would that be acceptable?

When you make specific requests, the other person can respond with a clear "yes" or "no." If the person says "no," all is not lost. Try negotiating:

1. *If you can't call me Friday night, could I call you Saturday morning to find out what I missed?*

2. *If Thursday noon isn't acceptable to you, could I turn my paper in on Wednesday by 5:00?*

A Creator seeks definite yes or no answers. Victims often accept "maybe" or "I'll try" for fear of getting a "no," but it's better to hear a specific "no" and be free to move on to someone who will say "yes."

One of my mentors offered a valuable piece of advice: "If you go through a whole day without getting at least a couple of 'no's,' you aren't asking for enough help in your life."

SAYING "NO"

Saying "no" is another tool of the assertive Creator. When I think of the power of saying "no," I think of Monique. One day after class she took a deep breath, sighed, and told me she was exhausted. She complained that everyone at her job kept bringing her tasks to do. As a result, she had virtually no social life, and she was falling behind in college. She wanted advice on how to manage her time better.

If you go to somebody and say, "I need help," they'll say, "Sure, honey, I wish I could," but if you say, "I need you to call so-and-so on Tuesday, will you do that?" they either will say yes or they'll say no. If they say no, you thank them and say, "Do you know someone who will?" If they say yes, you call on Wednesday to see if they did it. You wouldn't believe how good I've gotten at this, and I never knew how to ask anybody for anything before.

Barbara Sher

"Sounds like you're working 60 hours a week and doing the work of two people," I observed. She nodded modestly. "Here's an outrageous thought: The next time someone at work brings you more to do, say 'no.'"

"That sounds so rude."

"Okay then, say, 'I'm sorry, but my schedule is full, and I won't be able to do that.'"

"What if my boss asks? I can't say 'no' to her."

"You can say, 'I'll be glad to take that on. But since I have so many projects already, I'll need you to give one of them to someone else. That way I'll have time to do a good job on this new project.'"

Monique agreed to experiment with saying "no." The next time I saw her, she was excited. "I sent my boss a memo telling her I had too much work and I couldn't take on the latest project she had assigned me. Before I'd even talked to her about the memo, one of my coworkers came by. He said our boss had sent him to take over some of my projects. Not only did I not get the new project, I got rid of two others. I just might be able to finish this semester after all."

Monique's voice had a power that hadn't been there before. With one "no" she had transformed herself from exhausted to exhilarated. That's the power of a Creator being assertive.

> When two people are relating maturely, each will be able to ask the other for what he or she wants or needs, fully trusting that the other will say "no" if he or she does not want to give it.
>
> *Edward Deci*

Journal Entry 20

In this activity, you will explore assertiveness. This powerful way of being creates great results, strengthens relationships, and builds self-esteem.

1. Make a choice: Write about one of the following (A or B):

A. **Write three different responses to the instructor described in the following situation.** Respond to the instructor by (1) placating, (2) blaming, and (3) leveling. For an example of this exercise, refer to the dialogues on page 170.

Situation: You register for a course required in your major. It is the last course you need to graduate. When you go to the first class meeting, the instructor tells you that your name is NOT on the roster. The course is full, and no other sections of the course are being offered. You've been shut out of the class. The instructor tells you that you'll have to postpone graduation and return next semester to complete this required course.

Remember, in each of your three responses, you are writing what you would actually say to the instructor—first as a placator, second as a blamer, and third as a leveler.

B. **Think about one of your most challenging academic goals. Decide who could help you with this goal. Write a letter to this person and request assistance.** You can decide later whether or not you will send the letter.

Here are some possibilities to include in your letter:

- Tell the person your most challenging academic goal for this semester.
- Explain how this goal is a steppingstone to your dream.
- Describe your dream and explain its importance to you.
- Identify your obstacle, explaining it fully.
- Discuss how you believe this person can help you overcome your obstacle.
- Admit any reluctance or fear you have about asking for assistance.
- Request *exactly* what you would like this person to do for you and persuade him or her to give you helpful assistance.

Remember, for effective requests, use the DAPPS rule.

2. **Write what you have learned or relearned about being assertive.** How assertive have you been in the pursuit of your goals and dreams? How has this choice affected your self-esteem? What changes do you intend to make in communicating (placating, blaming, leveling), making requests, and saying "no"? Be sure to dive deep!

> When things really get difficult, all I can say is, ask for help.
>
> *Dr. Bernie Siegel*

One Student's Story

AMY ACTON
Southern State Community College, Ohio

I returned fall quarter feeling broken. I had hoped some time off would help my marriage and my mental state. But I felt exhausted and overwhelmed. I barely slept or ate. I was grinding my teeth and having nightmares. In class, I daydreamed because I didn't really want to be there. I already have a bachelor's degree from Wilmington College, but I'm back in school because I want to be a nurse. In the past, my GPA has always been high. But because of challenges in my marriage, studying was no longer on my A list. Maybe not even on my B or C list. I had to read an assignment several times to get it, and I was definitely not doing my best work. When I got a C on the first test in Anatomy and Physiology, I panicked. The worst part was pretending everything was okay. I couldn't ask for help or admit the level of suffering. Not me. Instead, I smiled my best Pollyanna grin and went through the motions to keep up the appearance of a healthy life.

I was taking PYSC 108: College Success because the previous term someone had come into my English class and raved about it. *That sounds like a course I could use*, I thought. In the first week, I took the self-assessment. Ouch. Kick a girl while she's down. I scored remarkably low in interdependence. I was shocked that creating a support system was so important. I'd always valued my independent nature. But I knew I had to do something different. I had to start somewhere.

So I started by asking for help. At first, it made me feel like vomiting. But it got easier. I trusted *On Course* and decided there must be benefits to interdependence. With practice, it got more comfortable. Now, it's wonderful. I began by asking students who were doing well in Anatomy and Physiology to start a study group. We would meet and go over what we covered in class. They told me about strategies they use to memorize all the bones we had to know. We made study cards and I carried them everywhere. I even started asking for help from coworkers at the hospital where I work. I usually did all of the patient charting, but I started asking others to share the task.

Next, I practiced the art of saying "no." I was raised to say "yes," followed by "please." Saying "no" took some work. I literally broke out in hives at first. I took allergy medicine and kept trying. I've gotten so good at it that now I say it every day, usually followed by "thank you." My mom is famous for calling me and asking me to pick up something at the store. I finally told her I had to choose activities that were important to my goals, like studying my nursing courses. I even said "no" to cleaning my house all the time. I prefer a clean house, but saying no to cleaning means I can say yes to more important things. The results have been life changing.

I also made a conscious effort to tell people how I truly feel. Living as my authentic, quirky self feels right. Many relationships where I was doing all the work have disappeared. For example, I asked my husband to help more around the house. He got angry at first, but I told him how important it is to me to get help so I can succeed in school and become a nurse. Now he helps more than he used to. I've finally made living the life that I want a priority, and the people who really care about me are glad.

I am so happy and grateful that I signed up for this course. Also, that I took it seriously and dove deep. I was off course in September, but the New Year is looking brighter. When I got my grades at the end of the quarter, I had all A's. My marriage is way better and my husband tells me I've changed. He doesn't say how, but I can tell that he likes me better now. This process didn't happen overnight. The journal entries were a valuable tool to inspire healing. While writing the journals, I felt very reserved at first. But soon I realized that I had something to say. I was hearing my voice again . . . *my* voice! Hearing my voice was like running into an old friend. There was a moment when I giggled. I thought, "I remember you. I like you. Where have you been my old friend?"

Photo: Courtesy of Amy Acton

Wise Choices in College

REHEARSING AND MEMORIZING STUDY MATERIALS

No matter how good your study materials are, if you can't remember what you're learning, you're going to fail. This outcome is likely whether the test is given by an instructor, an employer, or by life itself. That's why the ability to understand *and* remember what you learn is essential to success.

In Chapter 4, we explored strategies for developing a deep and lasting *understanding* of what we want to learn. To do so, we gathered all of the knowledge we had **Collected** from reading assignments and class sessions. Then we **Organized** that knowledge to create a variety of helpful study materials. In this way we continued to build the neural networks that store our knowledge for future use.

In this chapter, we'll take these efforts another step toward creating deep and lasting learning. We'll look at strategies to *remember* what we are learning. To do so, we'll explore effective ways to **Rehearse** study materials. Here is the learning principle that guides our efforts: *To strengthen neural networks, use many different kinds of* **Rehearsal** *strategies and distribute these efforts over time.*

As may be obvious, *understanding* and *remembering* reinforce one another. Thus, efforts to remember also help you understand, just as efforts to understand help you remember. That's why it is so important to include in your CORE Learning System both **Organizing** for understanding and **Rehearsing** for remembering. In fact, I hope you are experiencing confidence that you can rightfully have in your ability to learn virtually any information or skill. The key is choosing effective study strategies and spending sufficient time on task. You are not only fully responsible for your learning; you are also completely up to the challenge!

REHEARSING AND MEMORIZING STUDY MATERIALS: THE BIG PICTURE

Rehearsal is a term that learning researchers use for mental efforts to remember something. **Rehearsal** strategies generally fall into one of two kinds—elaborative and rote. In this chapter, we will look at both. In most cases, however, **elaborative rehearsal** will better serve your learning goals in college. These strategies use deep processing that strengthens both understanding *and* remembering. They do so by focusing on meaning, by showing relationships between ideas, and by connecting new knowledge with old. As such, elaborative rehearsal enhances deep and *lasting* learning.

By contrast, **rote rehearsal** is more about remembering than understanding. As such, it employs surface processing such as memorizing by sheer repetition. There is both good news and bad about rote rehearsal. The good news is that memorized facts and details can be valuable. For example, rote rehearsal is probably how you learned both the alphabet and multiplication tables, and they have certainly come in handy over the years. But there's bad news as well. Mindlessly memorizing information can fool you into thinking you understand something when you don't. Then you stroll into a test feeling prepared . . . only to discover how wrong you were. And even if you do pass the test, the knowledge you memorized without understanding will probably be gone when you need it later on.

So, experiment with the many **Rehearsal** strategies in this chapter. As you do, continue personalizing a CORE Learning System that helps you create deep and, in particular, *lasting* learning. As a bonus, most **Rehearsal** strategies perform double duty. As you **Rehearse**, you also generate feedback that allows you to **Evaluate** your learning. For example, when you **Rehearse** by quizzing yourself and get a wrong answer, that's valuable feedback. It prompts you to **Collect** more information, **Organize** it differently, and/or keep **Rehearsing**.

While examining the following strategies, keep in mind the big picture of **Rehearsing** your study materials. **First, use *elaborative* Rehearsal strategies to learn and remember complex ideas; use *rote* Rehearsal strategies to memorize facts and details. Second, schedule frequent Rehearsal sessions of sufficient length distributed over time. Third, use all feedback to Evaluate and, if needed, revise your approach to learning.**

BEFORE REHEARSING AND MEMORIZING STUDY MATERIALS

1. Form a study team. Many of the following learning strategies are enhanced by doing them with others. That's why teaming up with fellow Creators can increase the effectiveness of your study time. Follow the suggestions on page 154 to ensure that your study team functions at top form.

2. Create a distributed study schedule. Remember: *Learning is enhanced by frequent practice sessions of sufficient length distributed over time.* Here's an example. Suppose two classmates each study a total of twenty hours for a final exam. One classmate crams twenty hours of studying into the twenty-four hours before the test. The other distributes her effort by studying two hours each day for ten days before the test. The second student will almost always experience deeper and longer lasting learning. If you began the distributed study schedule suggested in Chapter 4, you devoted the first 25 to 33 percent of your total study time to **Organizing** a variety of effective study materials. Now, use the remaining time to deep-process those study materials using the **Rehearsal** strategies that follow. Your payoff will be improved learning, not to mention better grades.

3. Assemble all study materials. In Chapter 4, you learned to create a great variety of study materials. Have them all handy as you begin the second stage of your study efforts. You will understand and remember more of what you study if you **Rehearse** different kinds of study materials. For example, you might **Rehearse** with an outline one day, a concept map the next, and flash cards the next.

WHILE REHEARSING AND MEMORIZING STUDY MATERIALS

4. Review your study materials. *Reviewing* means reading over your study materials silently and with great concentration on the meaning. To avoid mindless reviewing, do the following three steps:

- Review a section of your study materials.

- Look away and ask yourself, *What are the key concepts, main ideas, and supporting details of what I just read?* Think through complete answers to those questions.

- Look back at your study materials to confirm the accuracy of your thinking.

Keep repeating these three steps with additional sections of your study materials. Reviewing in this way causes you to make sense of and remember what you have just read. This process also provides immediate feedback on how well you understand the content of your study materials.

5. Recite your study materials. *Reciting* is similar to reviewing but is done *aloud*. You've probably used reciting when you met a person for the first time. Perhaps you said the person's name aloud to help you remember it. "It's nice to meet you, *Clarissa*. I've never met anyone named *Clarissa* before. Is *Clarissa* a family name?" As you read aloud from your study materials, add any related information that comes to mind. Now look away from your study materials and do your best to say the same information again. Pretend you are explaining the information to someone who isn't in the course but is interested in the information.

Look back at your study materials and compare the information there with what you have been saying. Repeat the process with each section of your study materials. Continue doing this look-away technique until what you recite captures the essence of what is in your notes. By reciting aloud, you engage multiple senses (sight and sound), thus creating stronger neural networks.

6. Use Cornell study sheets. (See page 147 for an example.) Remember that Section A of a Cornell study sheet contains information you have **Organized** in your preferred way (e.g., outlines or concept maps). Section B contains key words and questions about the information in Section A. And Section C contains a summary of the key concepts and main ideas in Section A. To **Rehearse** information on Cornell study sheets, do the following:

- Study the content of Section A using either reviewing or reciting. Keep rehearsing the content in Section A until you feel confident that you understand it fully.

- Now cover Section A with a blank sheet of paper and look at Section B. There you will see the key words and questions you have written. Explain the key words and answer the questions as thoroughly as you can. Afterward, uncover the information in Section A and check the accuracy of your responses.

- Finally, cover the whole page and write a summary of the information in Section A. Then, uncover Section C on your Cornell study sheet and compare summaries. As your learning deepens, you may find that your latest summary is even better than the one you wrote earlier.

Note how this process offers both an excellent study technique and an instant **Evaluation** of your learning. If you can't explain the key concepts or answer the questions in Section B, you know you have more studying to do. The same is true if you can't create a summary as good as—or better than—the one you originally wrote in Section C.

7. Test yourself. Get out the list of possible test questions you prepared earlier (see page 143 for how to prepare questions). Taking a practice test is a great way to both **Rehearse** and **Evaluate** your knowledge. Think of a self-test as a dress **Rehearsal** for the real thing. To that end, do your best to duplicate the actual test situation. For example, practice answering the kinds of questions that will be on the real test (e.g., multiple choice, short answer, true/false, essay, problems). If the test will be timed, time your own practice test. If possible, test yourself in the room where the real test will be given. If you expect distractions during the test, reproduce them as well. As a bonus, when you excel in a practice test, confidence will replace self-doubts. After taking the practice test, get feedback on your answers. The best person to provide this feedback is your instructor. Others to ask include tutors in the learning center, friends who already took the class and did well, and classmates.

8. Hold a study team quiz. Here's a variation on a self-test. Ask study team members to bring questions to a meeting and quiz each other. Don't move on until everyone agrees on an answer. If needed, find the correct answer in your course materials (e.g., textbook or class notes). Or set it aside to ask your instructor. To add fun to your efforts, search the Internet for sites that allow you to create learning games such as *Jeopardy* (the television quiz show). For those motivated by friendly competition, make a game out of the quiz by awarding points for correct answers. Perhaps the person with the highest score gets treated to lunch by the others. This competition is one in which everyone wins by enhancing their learning.

9. Study three-column math charts. (See page 145 for an example.) The key to studying mathematics is solving problems, solving problems, and solving more problems. Here's where the three-column math charts you created are so helpful. Take a blank sheet of paper and place it over Column 2 (Solution) and Column 3 (Explanation). Now all you can see is the problem in Column 1. Solve the problem on the blank sheet of paper (which is covering the Solution and Explanation columns). If you have difficulty solving the problem, give yourself hints by uncovering part of the solution or explanation. After solving the problem, uncover Columns 2 and 3. Then check both your solution and your understanding of the process. If a problem continues to stump you, seek help from your instructor, a tutor, or classmates who excel in math. Trust that with enough practice and enough help, you'll be able to solve even the most difficult problems. Remember, you don't learn to solve math problems by only watching your instructor solve them. You don't even learn to solve math problems by only reading how. You learn to solve math problems by *solving* math problems.

10. Study with flash cards. (See page 143 for suggestions on creating flash cards.) Carry a deck of rubber-banded flash cards with you at all times. Pull them out for a quick review whenever you have a few extra minutes. If you study your flash cards just fifteen minutes per day (say in three sessions of five minutes each), that's nearly two extra hours of studying each week! The process is simple. Look at the front side of a flash card and recite the answer you believe is on the back. Turn it over and look. If you got the answer correct, put a dot in the upper right hand corner of the answer side. Now place the card on the bottom of your deck and keep repeating the process, perhaps shuffling the deck now and then. When you place the third dot on a card (meaning you got it correct three times), transfer that card to a second deck. Keep studying Deck 1 until all cards are moved to Deck 2. Review Deck 2 occasionally to keep your learning fresh. Flash cards are great study tools when preparing for short-answer tests, such as multiple choice and fill in the blank.

11. Memorize by chunks. Occasionally you may find it desirable—or even required—to memorize something for a course (e.g., a poem, a formula, or a summary from your Cornell study sheets). An important thing to know about memorizing is that *reading* information and *recalling* information

strengthen different neural connections. Since you need to *recall* the information on a test, you want to strengthen the neural networks that manage recall (not reading). That's why simply reading something over and over is an ineffective way to memorize it. Here is one way to create strong neural networks for recalling information. If you memorize the words with a full understanding of their meaning, you'll be engaged in *elaborative* **Rehearsal**. However, if all you do is memorize the words like a parrot, you're using *rote* **Rehearsal**.

- Recite the entire text you want to memorize (e.g., poem, formula, summary, etc.)

- Recite the first chunk of information (e.g., line, string of symbols, sentence, etc.) from the text.

- Recite the first chunk without looking at the text.

- Recite the first *and* second chunks of information while looking at the text.

- Recite this longer chunk aloud without looking at the text.

- Keep adding chunks until you can correctly recite the entire text aloud five times without looking at it.

- Take a ten-minute break and again recite the entire text aloud from memory until you do it correctly five times in a row.

- Thereafter, recite daily the entire text from memory; give extra practice to sections that are a challenge for you to recall.

If you wish, you can substitute writing for reciting in any of the steps. In fact, you'll probably find it helpful to alternate back and forth between reciting and writing.

12. Memorize with acronyms. An acronym is a word made from the first letters of other words that you want to remember. For example, in Chapter 4 of *On Course*, you encountered the DAPPS Rule, an acronym that helps you remember the qualities of an effective goal: **D**ated, **A**chievable, **P**ersonal,

Positive, **Specific**. If you want to remember the names of the Great Lakes, you can use the acronym HOMES: **Huron**, **Ontario**, **Michigan**, **Erie**, **Superior**. In this way, remembering one word (the acronym) cues you to recall all of the other words represented by the individual letters. Acronyms can be real words (HOMES) or made-up words (DAPPS).

13. Memorize with acrostics. Acrostics are sometimes called sentence acronyms. Like acronyms, acrostics are made from the first letters of other words you want to memorize. However, instead of creating a new word from the initial letters, you create a sentence. For example, biology students may be required to know the taxonomic classifications: kingdom, phylum, class, order, family, genus, species. Taking the first letter of each word in this list, you can create the sentence **"King Peter came over for grape soda."** Music students can recall the notes on the lines of a musical staff (E-G-B-D-F) by the sentence **"Every good boy does fine."** To remember the order of operations for math (parentheses, exponents, multiply, divide, add, and subtract), remember the acrostic of **"Please excuse my dear Aunt Sally."** Notice that an acrostic is an especially helpful tool when you need to remember items in a particular order.

14. Memorize with associations. When you associate something new with something you already know, the new information is easier to recall. Suppose you want to remember the name of your new mathematics teacher, Professor Getty; you could associate his name with the Battle of Gettysburg that you studied in American history. You might even visualize him wearing a uniform and carrying a musket. Now you'll remember his name. Have you ever thought of something important in the middle of the night but you can't recall it in the morning? Try tossing a pillow (or some other item) into the middle of your room and consciously associating that item to the important thought. When you see the pillow in the morning, you'll usually remember.

15. Memorize with the loci technique. The loci (pronounced *low´-sigh*) technique is a variation of association. *Loci* is Latin for "places," so with this strategy, you associate items you want to memorize with familiar places. Suppose you're studying parts of the brain and you want to remember the *amygdala*, which plays an important role in processing and remembering emotional reactions. Think of a familiar place, such as your living room. Picture your television turned to your favorite talk show and the host introducing an angry woman wearing a bright red dress. The host is saying, "Please welcome Amy G. Dala." Review this mental image several times a day for two or three days. When you need to recall the *amygdala*, mentally visit your living room, turn on the television, and there's angry ol' Amy G. Dala waiting to be introduced. You can now associate other parts of the brain with additional places in your living room. Say, isn't that a neo-cortex sitting on your couch?

AFTER REHEARSING AND MEMORIZING STUDY MATERIALS

16. Review, Review, Review. Repetition strengthens memory. Shortly after a study period, spend a few minutes reviewing your outlines, graphic organizers, flash cards, Cornell study sheets, or whatever study materials you prefer. Two hours later review again. For the next three days, review your study materials daily. Next, review them weekly. I've found that reviewing before going to sleep helps me to remember. But the ideal time to review is any time you can. Repeated review takes little effort but creates much learning.

17. Teach what you learn. If you ask your instructors when they achieved a deep and lasting understanding of their subject, most will say it was when they started teaching it. Explaining a complex idea requires a thorough understanding. And stumbling over an explanation is clear evidence of incomplete learning. So find people to teach. Say, "Let me tell you something fascinating that I learned in one of my classes." Teaching is also a great activity to do in a study group. Suppose each time your group met, each member gave a five-minute lecture on something important they had learned in the course that week. Other teaching possibilities are only limited by your imagination. One student I knew put her children to bed each night in a most ingenious way. She donned hand puppets and delivered animated lectures to her children about what she had learned in college that day. Every night her kids couldn't wait

for Professor Hand to tuck them in. Now that is a Creator!

MEMORIZING EXERCISE

Suppose you were asked to memorize all of the memory strategies you just read about. How would you go about it? Fully describe your methods.

Gaining
Self-Awareness

6

Despite all of my efforts to create success in college and in life, I may still find myself off course. Now is the perfect time to identify and revise the inner obstacles to my success.

I am consciously choosing core beliefs and habit patterns that support my success.

SUCCESSFUL STUDENTS . . .	STRUGGLING STUDENTS . . .
recognize when they are off course.	**wander through life unaware of being off course**.
identify their self-defeating patterns of thought, emotion, and behavior.	**remain unaware of their self-defeating patterns of thought, emotion, and behavior**.
rewrite their outdated scripts, revising limited core beliefs and self-defeating patterns.	**unconsciously persist in making choices based on outdated scripts**, finding themselves farther and farther off course with each passing year.

Case Study in Critical Thinking

STRANGE CHOICES

"Do your students make really strange choices?" **Professor Assante** asked.

The other professors looked up from their lunches. "What do you mean?" one asked.

"At the beginning of each class, I give short quizzes that count as 50 percent of the final grade," Professor Assante replied. "One of my students comes late to every class, even though I keep telling her there's no way she can pass the course if she keeps missing the quizzes. But she still keeps coming late! What is she thinking?"

"That's nothing," **Professor Buckley** said. "I've got a really bright student who attends every class and offers great comments during discussions. But the semester is almost over, and he still hasn't turned in any assignments. At this point, he's too far behind to pass. Now that's what I call a strange choice."

"You think that's strange," **Professor Chen** said, "I'm teaching composition in the computer lab. Last week I sat down next to a woman who was working on her essay, and I suggested a way she could improve her introduction. I couldn't believe what she did. She swore at me, stormed out of the room, and slammed the door."

Professor Donnelly chimed in. "Well, I can top all of you. In my philosophy class, participation counts for one-third of the final grade. I've got a student this semester who hasn't said a word in 12 weeks. Even when I call on him, he just shakes his head and says something under his breath that I can't hear. One day after class, I asked him if he realized that if he didn't participate in class discussions, the best grade he could earn is a D. He just mumbled, 'I know.' Now there's a choice I don't get!"

"How about this!" **Professor Egret** said. "I had a student last semester with a B average going into the final two weeks. Then he disappeared. This semester, I ran into him on campus, and I asked what happened. 'Oh,' he said, 'I got burned out and stopped going to my classes.' 'But you only had two more weeks to go. You threw away 13 weeks of work,' I said. You know what he did? He shrugged his shoulders and walked away. I wanted to shake him and say, 'What is wrong with you?'"

Professor Fanning said, "Talk about strange choices. Last week I had four business owners visit my marketing class to talk about how they promote their businesses. Near the end of the period, a student asked if the business owners had ever had problems with procrastination. While the panelists were deciding who was going to answer, I joked, 'Maybe they'd rather answer later.' Okay, it was weak humor, but most of the students chuckled, and then one panelist answered the question. The next day I got a call from the dean. The student who'd asked about procrastination told him I'd mocked her in front of the whole class, and now she's going to drop out of college. I had videoed the class, so I asked her if she'd be willing to watch the recording. Later she admitted I hadn't said what she thought I had, but she still dropped out of school. What is it with students today and their bizarre choices?"

Listed below are the six professors' students. Choose the one you think made the strangest choice and speculate on why this student made the choice. Dive deeper than obvious answers such as "He's probably just shy." Why do you suppose he is shy? What past experiences might have made him this way? What might the inner conversation of his Inner Critic and Inner Defender sound like? What emotions might he often feel? What beliefs might he have about himself, other people, or the world? In what other circumstances (e.g., work, relationships, health) might a similar choice sabotage his success?

← 1 2 3 4 5 6 →

___ **Professor Assante's** student

___ **Professor Buckley's** student

___ **Professor Chen's** student

___ **Professor Donnelly's** student

___ **Professor Egret's** student

___ **Professor Fanning's** student

▶ **DIVING DEEPER** Recall a course you once took in which you made a choice that your instructor might describe as "strange." Explain why you made that choice. Dive deep, exploring what *really* caused your choice.

Recognizing When You Are Off Course

Focus Questions   In which of your life roles are you off course? Do you know how you got there? More important, do you know how to get back on course to your desired outcomes and experiences?

Take a deep breath, relax, and consider your journey so far.

You began by accepting personal responsibility for creating your life as you want it. Then you chose personally motivating goals and dreams that give purpose and direction to your life.

Next, you created a self-management plan and began taking effective actions. Most recently, you developed mutually supportive relationships to help you on your journey. Throughout, you have examined how to believe in yourself.

Despite all these efforts, you may still be off course—in college, in a relationship, in your job, or somewhere else in your life. You just aren't achieving your desired outcomes and experiences. Once again, you have an important choice to make. You can listen to the blaming, complaining, and excusing of your Inner Critic and Inner Defender. Or you can ask your Inner Guide to find answers to important questions such as . . .

- What habits do I have that sabotage my success?
- What beliefs do I have that get me off course?
- How can I consistently make wise choices that will create a rich, personally fulfilling life?

> Consider this: If at first you don't succeed, something is blocking your way.
>
> *Michael Ray & Rochelle Myers*

THE MYSTERY OF SELF-SABOTAGE

Self-sabotage has probably happened to everyone who's set off on a journey to a better life. Consider my student Jerome. Fresh from high school, Jerome said his dream was to start his own accounting firm by his 30th birthday. He set long-term goals of getting his college degree and passing the C.P.A. (certified public accountant) exam. He set short-term goals of earning A's in every class he took during his first semester. He developed a written self-management system and demonstrated interdependence by starting a study group. But at semester's end, the unthinkable happened: Jerome failed Accounting 101!

Wait a minute, though. Jerome's Inner Guide has more information. You see, Jerome made some strange choices during his first semester. He skipped his accounting class three times to work at a part-time job. On another day, he didn't attend class because he was angry with his girlfriend. Then he missed two Monday classes when he was hungover from weekend parties. He was late five times because parking was difficult to find. Jerome regularly put off doing homework until the last minute because he was so busy. He didn't hand in an

> Progressively we discover that there are levels of experience beneath the surface, beneath our consciousness, and we realize that these may hold the key both to the problems and the potentialities of our life.
>
> *Ira Progoff*

important assignment because he found it confusing. And he stopped going to his study group after the first meeting because . . . well, he wasn't quite sure why. As the semester progressed, Jerome's anxiety about the final exam grew. The night before, he stayed up late cramming, then went to the exam exhausted. During the test, his mind went blank.

Haven't you, too, made choices that worked against your goals and dreams? Haven't we all! We take our eyes off the path for just a moment, and some invisible force comes along and pulls us off course. By the time we realize what's happened—if, in fact, we ever do—we can be miles off course and feeling miserable.

What's going on around here, anyway?

UNCONSCIOUS FORCES

One of the most important discoveries in psychology is the existence and power of unconscious forces in our lives. We now know that experiences from our past linger in our unconscious minds long after our conscious minds have forgotten them. As a result, we're influenced in our daily choices by old experiences we don't even recall.

Dr. Wilder Penfield of the Montreal Neurological Institute found evidence that our brains may retain nearly every experience we have ever had. Dr. Penfield performed brain surgery on patients who had local anesthesia but were otherwise fully awake. During the operation, he stimulated brain cells using a weak electric current. At that moment his patients reported re-experiencing long-forgotten events in vivid detail.

Further research by neuroscientist Joseph LeDoux suggests that a part of our brains called the amygdala stores emotionally charged but now unconscious memories. The amygdala, like a nervous watchman, examines every present experience and compares it to past experiences. When a key feature of a present event is similar to a distressing event from the past, it declares a match. Then, *without our conscious knowledge*, the amygdala hijacks our rational thought processes. It causes us to respond to the present event as we learned to respond to the past event. The problem is, the outdated response is often totally inappropriate in our present situation. By the time the amygdala loosens its grip on our decision-making power, we may have made some very bad choices.

If many of the forces that get us off course are unconscious, how can we spot their sabotaging influence? By analogy, the answer appears in a fascinating discovery in astronomy. Years ago, astronomers developed a mathematical formula to predict the orbit of any planet around the sun. However, one planet, Uranus, failed to follow its predicted orbit. Astronomers were baffled as to why Uranus was "off course." Then the French astronomer Leverrier proposed an ingenious explanation: The gravitational pull of an invisible planet was getting Uranus off course. Sure enough, when stronger telescopes were invented, the planet Neptune was discovered, and Leverrier was proven correct.

In the entire history of science, it is hard to find a discovery of comparable consequence to the discovery of the power of unconscious belief as a gateway—or an obstacle—to the hidden mind, and its untapped potentialities.

Willis Harman

We know from surgical experiences that electrical stimulation delivered to the temporal area of the brain elicits images of events that occurred in the patient's past. This is confirmation that such memories are "stored," but in most instances they cannot be voluntarily recollected. Thus, all of us "know" more than we are aware that we know.

Richard Restak, M.D.

Here's the point: Like planets, we all have invisible Neptunes tugging at us every day. For us, these invisible forces are not in outer space. They exist in inner space, in our unconscious minds. As with Uranus, the first clue to spotting the existence of these unconscious forces is recognizing that we are off course. So, be candid. Where are you off course in your life today? School? Relationships? Work? Health? Finances? Elsewhere? What desired outcomes and experiences are you moving away from instead of toward? What goals and dreams seem to be slipping away? Self-awareness allows you to identify that you are off course. Only then can you start making wiser choices that will get you back on course to the life you want to create.

> I learned that I could not look to my exterior self to do anything for me. If I was going to accomplish anything in life I had to start from within.
>
> *Oprah Winfrey*

Journal Entry 21

Everyone gets off course at times, but only those who are self-aware can make a course correction to improve their lives.

1. **Write about a time when you were off course and took effective actions to get back on course.** Examples include ending an unhealthy relationship, entering college years after high school, changing careers, stopping an addiction, choosing to be more assertive, or changing a negative belief or bias you held about yourself, other people, or the world. Dive deep in your journal entry by asking and answering questions such as the following:

- In what area of my life was I off course?
- What choices had I made to get off course?
- What changes did I make to get back on course?
- What challenges did I face while making this change?
- What personal strengths helped me make this change?
- What benefits did I experience as a result of my change?
- If I hadn't made this change, what would my life be like today?

2. **Write about an area of your life in which you are off course today.** If you need help in identifying an area, review your desired outcomes and experiences from Journal Entry 9 and your goals and dreams from Journal Entry 10. Explain which area of your life is furthest from the way you would like it to be. What choices have you made that got you off course? What will be the effect on your life if you continue to stay off course?

The fact that you've made positive changes in the past is a good reminder that you have the personal strengths to make similar changes whenever you wish. All you need is the awareness that you're off course and the motivation to make new choices.

> The truth is that our finest moments are most likely to occur when we are feeling deeply uncomfortable, unhappy, or unfulfilled. For it is only in such moments, propelled by our discomfort, that we are likely to step out of our ruts and start searching for different ways or truer answers.
>
> *M. Scott Peck, M.D.*

One Student's Story

SARAH RICHMOND
Missouri University of Science and Technology, Missouri

I was in the emergency room when it hit me how far off course I was. My friend Matt had driven me to the emergency room because the Student Health Center couldn't supply the antibiotics I needed for a bad sore throat. As we sat in the waiting room talking, I told Matt that I was failing math, and I broke down and cried. I told him I was doing things in college that I had never done at home. When I was in high school, my parents were very strict. They didn't let me go out late during the week, and they'd wake me up in the morning to make sure I went to school. But in college, no one cares if you stay out all night or even if you get up and go to class. I had adopted "Why not?" as my motto, and I started doing things I knew I shouldn't be doing. My weekends had become a blur of boys and parties, and I had even started partying during the week. The parties I went to in high school were mostly small girls' nights, nothing like the drunken fraternity parties I was going to on campus. In high school I

was one of the smart kids, and even though I hardly ever studied, I was an honor student. But college was different. I was doing terrible in math and not much better in biology. It was a shock to not do as well as I had in high school.

I started getting a bleak outlook on life, and I didn't really want to be at the university. I had no idea what I wanted to major in. I thought of myself as lazy and irresponsible. I remember telling one of my friends that I should just get married, have kids, and then I'd probably be divorced by 40. After that I'd spend the rest of my life in a lousy job, struggling to survive. I felt like I couldn't do anything right. I don't know why I let everything bother me so much, but I felt awful.

Talking with Matt in the emergency room, I started realizing how lonely I felt in college. I missed my family, especially my sister. I wasn't getting along with my roommate, and we competed about everything: going out, boys, drinking, staying up late, playing video games, you name

it. A lot of the students at my university are really into playing *Halo*. I tried to fit in, but I'm no good at video games. At my school, if you're not in engineering, they tease you non-stop. One time a guy picked up my *On Course* book and starting teasing me about the class. "So what do you do in that class," he asked, "sit around and talk about your *feelings*?" I didn't bother saying that the course helped me think things out, things I wouldn't have thought about, like all of the mistakes I was making.

That day in the emergency room was my wake up call. Sitting there talking with Matt, I not only realized that I was way off course, I also realized that deep down I didn't believe in myself, and therefore I couldn't take actions today to improve my tomorrow. After that, I realized I had to make some dramatic changes. I got a new roommate, stopped partying, buckled down, and passed my math class. That was two years ago. Today I'm a junior and my life is very different. I've found a major that I love, I just finished an internship that was great, and my GPA is 3.4. Making positive changes isn't always easy. But my life started to get better that day in the emergency room when I took a good look at myself and realized just how far off course I was.

Photo: Courtesy of Sarah Richmond

Identifying Your Scripts

Focus Questions   What habit patterns in your life get you off course? How did these habit patterns develop?

Once you realize you're off course, you need to figure out how to get back on course. This can be tricky. The forces pulling us off course are often just as invisible to us as the planet Neptune was to Leverrier and his fellow observers of outer space.

As observers of inner space, psychologists seek to identify what they can't actually see: the internal forces that divert human potential into disappointment. In various psychological theories, these unconscious inner forces have been called names such as ego defenses, conditioned responses, programs, mental tapes, blind spots, schemas, and life-traps.

The term I like best to describe our unconscious internal forces was coined by psychologist Eric Berne: **scripts**. In the world of theater, a script tells an actor what words, actions, and emotions to perform onstage. When the actor gets a cue from others in the play, he doesn't make a choice about his response. He responds automatically as his script directs. Performance after performance, he reacts the same way to the same cues.

Responding automatically from a dramatic script is one sure way to succeed as an actor. However, responding automatically from a *life* script is one sure way to struggle as a human being.

ANATOMY OF A SCRIPT

Everyone has scripts. I do, your instructors do, your classmates do, you do. Some scripts have helped us achieve our present success. Other scripts may be getting us off course from our goals and dreams. Becoming aware of our unique personal scripts helps us make wise choices at each fork in the road, choices that help us create the life we want.

Scripts are composed of two parts. Closest to the surface of our awareness reside the directions for how we are to think, feel, and behave. **Thought patterns** include habitual self-talk such as *I'm too busy, I'm good at math, People different from me are a threat, I always screw up, The way we do things around here is the right way so all other ways must be wrong, I can't write.* **Emotional patterns** include habitual feelings such as anger, excitement, anxiety, sadness, and joy. **Behavior patterns** include habitual actions such as smoking cigarettes, criticizing others, arriving on time, never asking for help, and exercising regularly. When people know us well, they can often predict what we will say, feel, or do in a given situation. This ability reveals their recognition of our patterns.

Deeper in our unconscious mind lies the second, and more elusive, part of our scripts, our **core beliefs**. Early in life, we form core beliefs about the world (e.g., *The world is safe* or *The world is dangerous*), about other people (e.g., *People can be trusted* or *People can't be trusted*), and about ourselves (e.g., *I'm worthy* or *I'm unworthy*). Though we're seldom aware of our core beliefs, these unconscious judgments dictate what we consistently think, feel, and do. These beliefs become the lenses through which we see the world. Whether accurate or distorted, our beliefs dictate the choices we make at each fork in the road. What do you believe that

> A psychological script is a person's ongoing program for his life drama which dictates where he is going with his life and how he is to get there. It is a drama he compulsively acts out, though his awareness of it may be vague.
>
> *Muriel James &*
> *Dorothy Jongeward*

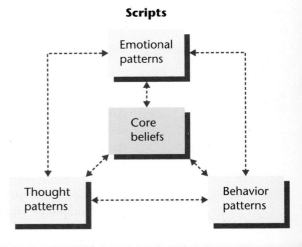

Scripts

causes you to make choices that other people think are strange? More important, what do you believe that keeps you from creating the outcomes and experiences you want?

HOW WE WROTE OUR SCRIPTS

Though no one knows exactly how we wrote our life scripts as children, reasonable explanations exist. One factor seems to be **how others responded to us.** Imagine this scene: You're two years old. You're feeling lonely and hungry, and you begin to cry. Your mother hurries in to pick you up. "There, there," she croons. "It's all right." She hugs you, feeds you, sings to you. You fall asleep full and content. If this happens often enough, what do you suppose you'd decide about the world, about other people, about yourself? Probably you'd believe *The world is kind; People will help me; I am lovable.* In turn, these beliefs would dictate your thoughts, emotions, and behaviors. With positive beliefs such as these at the core of your scripts, very likely you'd develop optimistic thought patterns (e.g., *If I ask, I'll get help*), positive emotional patterns (e.g., joy and enthusiasm), and empowering behavior patterns (e.g., asking for what you want).

Now imagine the same childhood scene with a different response. You cry but no one comes. You scream louder, but still no one comes. Finally you abandon hope that anyone will respond. You cry yourself to sleep, alone and hungry. Imagine also that being ignored happens often. You'd probably develop core beliefs such as *The world doesn't care about me; People won't help me; I'm not important.* You could very well develop pessimistic thought patterns (e.g., *I'm alone*), negative emotional patterns (e.g., anxiety and anger), and passive behavior patterns (e.g., not asking for what you want).

Now, imagine this scene one more time. As you're crying for attention and food, an adult storms into your room, screams "Shut up!" and slaps your face. After a few wounding experiences like this, you may decide *The world is a dangerous and painful place; People will hurt me; I'm unlovable!* These beliefs may lead to defensive thought patterns (e.g., *People are out to get me*), defensive emotional patterns (e.g., fear and rage), and defensive behavior patterns (e.g., immediately fighting or fleeing at the first sign of danger). Imagine how easily these patterns could get you off course later in life.

A second factor that seems to shape our scripts is **what significant adults said to us.** What did they say about the world: Is it safe or dangerous? What did they say about other people, especially those who are different from us: Can they be trusted or not? And, perhaps most important, what did important adults say about us? Psychologists have a term for qualities that tell us how we "are" or "should be": **attributions.** Common attributions tell us to be *good, quiet, rebellious, devoted, helpful, athletic, sexy, tough, independent, dependent, invisible, macho, dominant, competitive, smart, shy,* or *confident.*

Psychologists also have a term for the qualities that tell us what we "are not" or "should not be": **injunctions.** Common injunctions include *don't be yourself,*

Parents, deliberately or unaware, teach their children from birth how to behave, think, feel, and perceive. Liberation from these influences is no easy matter.

Eric Berne

The hearts of small children are delicate organs. A cruel beginning in this world can twist them into curious shapes. The heart of a hurt child can shrink so that forever afterward it is hard and pitted as the seed of a peach.

Carson McCullers

don't talk back, don't feel, don't think, don't be intimate, don't say no, don't say yes, don't get angry, don't trust people who are different from you, don't show your feelings, don't love yourself, don't be happy, don't be weak, don't believe in yourself, don't exist.

A third way we seem to write our scripts is by **observing the behavior of significant adults.** Children notice, *What did important adults do? If it's right for them, it's right for me.* When children play, we see them trying on adult behaviors, conversations, and emotions. It doesn't take a detective to figure out where they learned them. From significant adults we learn not only our unique personal scripts but our cultural programs as well. For example, some cultures believe we shape our future through our choices, whereas other cultures believe our future is determined by forces beyond our control. Some cultures place emphasis on future accomplishments, whereas others focus on the present or past. Some cultures are very time conscious, whereas others are more casual about time. Some cultures encourage individuality, whereas others place family and community above all other concerns. Each belief is deeply imbedded in the culture and becomes the lens through which its members see the world, influencing their choices, whether they are aware of the beliefs or not.

In these ways we each develop our personal scripts and cultural programs. Each is comprised of core beliefs and their resulting patterns of thoughts, feelings, and behaviors. At critical choice points, especially when we are under stress, we unconsciously default to our personal scripts and cultural programs for guidance.

The good news about our unconscious scripts and programs is that their intention is always positive—always to minimize our pain, always to maximize our pleasure. They help us adapt to the family and society in which we are born. Many of us made it through the mental, emotional, and physical challenges of growing up with the help of our childhood scripts and programs. Some of us would not have survived without them.

But, as you might guess, there is bad news as well: When we make unconscious choices as adults, we often get off course. That's because the scripts and programs we developed in childhood often do not apply to the situations of our present lives. Imagine an adult who can't stop playing a role he or she learned years ago for a grade school play! Many of us do the equivalent of this in our daily lives.

To others, a choice I make may seem strange. To me, it makes perfect sense. The important issue, though, is: Do my habitual choices help or hinder me in the pursuit of the life I want to create? To answer this question, I need to take three steps. First, I need to become aware of my Neptunes, that is, my unconscious beliefs, attitudes, biases, norms, prejudices, and values. Second, I need to assess which of my mindsets help and which hinder me in the pursuit of my goals and dreams. And finally, I need to keep and strengthen the habits that help me while revising or replacing the ones that hinder me. And it all starts with self-awareness.

> By the time we are adults, we have learned many cultural rules of behavior and have practiced those rules so much that they are second nature to us. Much of our behavior as adults is influenced by these learned patterns and rules, and we are so well practiced at them that we engage in these behaviors automatically and unconsciously.
>
> *David Matsumoto and Linda Juang*

> The more you are keenly aware of your misery-creating thoughts, feelings, and behaviors, the greater your chances are of ridding yourself of them.
>
> *Albert Ellis*

SELF-DEFEATING HABIT PATTERNS

Though our unconscious scripts are as invisible to us as the planet Neptune was to early astronomers, we can often see their influence in our lives. Put a check next to any of the following patterns of thought, emotion, and behavior that are often true of you. These habits may reveal the presence of personal scripts or cultural programs that get you off course. In particular, see if you can identify any habits that may have gotten you off course in the area you wrote about in Journal Entry 21.

> The grooves of mindlessness run deep. We know our scripts by heart.
>
> *Ellen J. Langer*

☐ **1.** I waste a lot of time doing unimportant things (e.g., television, video games).

☐ **2.** I wonder if I'm "college material."

☐ **3.** I easily get upset (e.g., angry, sad, anxious, depressed, guilty, frustrated).

☐ **4.** I hang out with people who don't support my academic goals.

☐ **5.** I believe that most people don't like me.

☐ **6.** I often turn in college assignments late.

☐ **7.** I worry that people stereotype me because of a cultural group (race, religion, sex, economic class, age, etc.) to which I belong rather than seeing me for who I really am.

☐ **8.** I worry excessively about doing things perfectly.

☐ **9.** I think most of my classmates are smarter than I am.

☐ **10.** I quit on things that are important to me.

☐ **11.** I allow a person in my life to treat me badly.

☐ **12.** I don't believe I deserve success as much as other people do.

☐ **13.** I miss more college classes than I should.

☐ **14.** I'm very critical of myself.

☐ **15.** I wait until the last minute to do important college assignments.

☐ **16.** I don't ask questions in class or participate in class discussions.

> What lies behind us and what lies before us are tiny matters compared to what lies within us.
>
> *Oliver Wendell Holmes*

☐ **17.** I often break promises I have made to myself or others.

☐ **18.** I am addicted to something (e.g., caffeine, alcohol, cigarettes, soft drinks, video games, social networking Internet sites, drugs).

☐ **19.** I experience severe test anxiety.

☐ **20.** I feel uncomfortable about asking for help.

☐ **21.** I have strong negative feelings about a particular group of people who are different from me.

☐ **22.** I often side-talk or daydream in my college classes.

☐ **23.** I seldom do my best work on college assignments.

☐ **24.** I am very critical of other people.

☐ **25.** I get extremely nervous when I speak to a group.

☐ **26.** I keep promising to study more in college, but I don't.

☐ **27.** I get my feelings hurt easily.

☐ **28.** I am a loner.

☐ **29.** I am uncomfortable being around people who are different from me.

☐ **30.** I get defensive when someone gives me feedback that I did something wrong.

☐ **31.** I . . . _____

☐ **32.** I . . . _____

Are you aware of any other of your patterns—mental, emotional, or behavioral? If so, add them to the list.

Journal Entry 22

In this activity, you will explore self-defeating patterns in your life that may reveal unconscious scripts. You're about to embark on an exciting journey into your inner world! There you can discover—and later revise—the invisible forces that have gotten you off course from your goals and dreams.

1. **Write about one of your self-defeating *behavior* patterns.** Choose a behavior pattern that you checked on the list or identify a self-defeating behavior that isn't on the list but that you do often. Remember, a behavior is something someone else can see you do. Develop your journal paragraphs by anticipating questions that someone reading it might have about this behavior pattern. (Even you might have questions when you read your journal 10 years from now.) For example,

- What exactly is your self-defeating behavior pattern?
- What are some specific examples of when you did this behavior?
- What may have caused this habit?
- What undesirable effects has it had on your life?
- How would your life be improved if you changed it?

One student began by writing, One of my self-defeating behavior patterns is that I seldom do my best work on college assignments. For example, in my biology lab. . . .

2. **Repeat Step 1 for one of your self-defeating *thought* patterns or for one of your self-defeating *emotional* patterns.** Once again, choose a pattern that you checked on the list or identify a habit that isn't on the list but that you often think or feel. You might begin, *One of my self-defeating thought patterns is that I often wonder if I am smart enough to be successful in college. I especially think this during exams. For example, last Thursday I . . . Or . . . One of my self-defeating emotional patterns is that I often feel frustrated. For example. . . .*

It is not true that life is one damn thing after another—it's one damn thing over and over.

*Edna St. Vincent Millay,
American poet*

All serious daring starts from within.

Eudora Welty

One Student's Story

JAMES FLORIOLLI
Foothill College, California

At different points in my life I've given up when I ran into a challenge. As a child, I loved baseball, but when I got hit in the face with a ball, I stopped playing. In school, I started having problems with my writing skills, and I was diagnosed with a learning disability. I got all kinds of accommodations, even more than I deserved, and I started goofing off. I convinced myself that success was getting the best grades possible with the least amount of work. After high school, college didn't seem like a viable option, so I joined the Marine Corps Reserve. Boot camp was even harder than I thought it would be. Once again, I used the minimum amount of effort necessary to complete each task, and I failed to achieve the level of success in the Marines that I could have. When I left the Marines to get a civilian job, I defined success as getting maximum compensation for minimum effort.

I got a job at the phone company and at first it seemed perfect. I'm very well paid for very little effort.

However, this situation isn't as rewarding as I thought it would be. After a few years I began to want a greater challenge. I knew I needed an education to advance in the workplace, so I started taking college courses part-time. For the first year I avoided classes that involved a lot of writing, as I was still intimidated by past failures in this area. But when poor writing began to affect my grades in other courses, I decided to take a composition class. In that class we read *On Course*, and in the chapter about self-awareness, I began to see how negative scripts could cause problems. I started wondering if there was a script contributing to the frustration I was feeling in my life. An idea kept coming up that at first I was unwilling to accept. I had always thought of myself as a hard worker, but looking back on my life I could not deny there were challenges I had run away from. When baseball had required extra work to get past my fear of the ball, I quit. When school stopped coming easily to me, I quit. When I realized how

hard I'd have to work to be a success in the Marines, I quit. Seeing this pattern was powerful for me. Finally, I felt like I understood how I ended up in the situation I am in. I realized that I'll do anything to avoid feeling bad. If I feel down in any way, I'm willing to throw everything out the window to feel better. In the past, I have doubted myself and been afraid to take risks. I overvalued security and undervalued me. I need to believe I am capable of accomplishing anything I want to.

Soon I have to pick my college major. One option is to get a computer science degree and continue working at the phone company. This would probably lead to the greatest profit and security. Or, I could choose a major that would prepare me for my dream job working in the front office of a professional baseball team. Obviously, going for my dream would be very difficult and call for a large initial pay cut. Knowing I have an issue with not following through on my most challenging commitments, I need to set my goals very carefully. No matter what I choose, I hope that when everything is said and done I will be proud of what I have accomplished. This will mean I have successfully revised my negative script of running from important challenges in my life.

Rewriting Your Outdated Scripts

 Focus Question How can you revise the self-defeating scripts that keep you from achieving your full potential?

Once in a writing class, I was explaining how to organize an essay when a student named Diana told me she didn't understand. She asked if I'd write an explanation on the board.

Earlier in the class, we'd been talking about the differences between left-brain and right-brain thinking. We'd discussed how the left side of the brain deals with logical, organized information, while the right side deals with more creative, intuitive concepts. "No problem," I said to Diana, "I hear your left brain crying out for some order. Let's see if I can help."

As I turned to write on the blackboard, she screamed, "You have no right to talk to me that way!"

I was stunned. Talk about a strange response! I took a deep breath to compose myself. "Maybe we could talk about this after class," I said.

THE IMPACT OF OUTDATED BELIEFS

Diana and I did talk, and I learned that she was in her late 30s, a single mother of an 8-year-old daughter. Our conversation wandered for a while; then Diana mentioned that she had always disliked school. In elementary school, she had consistently gotten low grades, while her sister consistently earned A's. One day, when Diana was about 12, she overheard her father and mother talking about her poor report card. "I don't know what we're going to do with Diana," her father said. "She's the *half-brain* of the family." [Do you see it yet . . . what got Diana upset with me?]

Diana accepted as a fact other people's belief that she couldn't think or learn. She developed patterns of thoughts, emotions, and behaviors that supported this belief. She decided that school was a waste of time (thought), she exploded when anyone questioned her about schoolwork (emotion), and she was often absent (behavior). Diana barely graduated from high school, then got a menial job that bored her.

For nearly 20 years, Diana heard her Inner Critic (sounding much like her father) telling her that something was wrong with her brain. Finally, another inner voice began to whisper, *Maybe—just maybe.* . . . Then one day she took a big risk and enrolled in college.

"So what happens?" she said, getting angry again. "I get a teacher who calls me a *half-brain*! I knew this would happen. I ought to just quit."

I used my best active listening skills: I listened to understand. I reflected both her thoughts and her anger. I asked her to clarify and expand. I allowed long periods of silence.

Finally, her emotional storm subsided. She took a deep breath and sat back.

I waited a few moments. "Diana, I know you think I called you a 'half-brain.' But what I actually said was *left* brain. Remember we had been talking in class about the difference between left-brain and right-brain thinking? Two different approaches to planning your essay? I was talking about that."

"But I *heard* you!"

"I know that's what you *heard*. But that isn't what I *said*. I've read two of your essays, and I know your brain works just fine. What really matters, though, is what *you* think! You need to believe in your own intelligence. Otherwise, you'll always be ready to hear people call you a 'half-brain' no matter what they really said. Worse, you'll always believe it yourself."

> We don't see things as they are,
> we see them as we are.
>
> *Anais Nin*

> We are what we think.
> All that we are arises
> With our thoughts.
> With our thoughts,
> We make the world.
>
> *The Buddha*

Diana had come within an inch of dropping out of college, of abandoning her dreams of a college degree. And all because of her childhood script.

DOING THE REWRITE

Until we revise our limiting scripts, we're less likely to achieve some of our most cherished goals and dreams. That's why realizing we're off course can be a blessing in disguise. By identifying the self-defeating patterns of thought, emotion, and behavior that got us off course, we may be able to discover and revise the underlying core beliefs that are sabotaging our success.

Diana stuck it out and passed English 101. She persevered and graduated with an Associate of Arts degree in early childhood education. When I spoke to her last, she was working at a nursery school and talking about returning to college to finish her bachelor's degree. Like most of us, she'll probably be in a tug of war with her scripts for the rest of her life. But now, at least, she knows that she, and not her scripts, can be in charge of making her choices.

One of the great discoveries about the human condition is this: We are not stuck with our personal scripts or cultural programming. We can re-create ourselves. We can keep what works and change what doesn't. By revising outdated scripts, we can get back on course and dramatically improve the outcomes and experiences of our lives.

> In developing our own self-awareness many of us discover ineffective scripts, deeply embedded habits that are totally unworthy of us, totally incongruent with the things we really value in life.
>
> *Stephen Covey*

 Journal Entry 23

In this activity, you'll practice revising your scripts, thus taking greater control of your life. As in Journal Entry 18, you'll once again be writing a conversation with your Inner Guide, a critical thinking skill that empowers you to become your own best coach, counselor, mentor, and guide through challenging times. This practical application of critical thinking greatly enhances your self-awareness, helping you take greater responsibility for making the wise choices necessary to create your desired outcomes and experiences.

1. Write a dialogue with your Inner Guide that will help you revise your self-sabotaging scripts.

Have your Inner Guide ask you the following 10 questions. After answering each question, let your Inner Guide use one or more of the active listening skills to help you dive deeper:

1. **Silence** (demonstrating that you are paying close attention to the speaker)
2. **Reflection** (expressing in your own words what you think the speaker is saying and feeling)

3. **Expansion** (requesting examples, evidence, and experiences)
4. **Clarification** (asking for an explanation)

Ten questions from Your Inner Guide:

1. In what area of your life are you off course?
2. What self-defeating **thought patterns** of yours may have contributed to this situation?
3. What different thoughts could you choose to get back on course?
4. What self-defeating **emotional patterns** of yours may have contributed to this situation?
5. What different emotions could you choose to get back on course?
6. What self-defeating **behavior patterns** of yours may have contributed to this situation?
7. What different behaviors could you choose to get back on course?
8. What limiting **core beliefs** of yours (about the world, other people, or yourself) may have led you to adopt the self-defeating patterns that we've been discussing?
9. What different beliefs could you choose to get back on course?
10. As a result of what you've learned here, what new behaviors, thoughts, emotions, or core beliefs will you adopt?

A sample dialogue follows.

Sample Dialogue with Your Inner Guide

IG: In what area of your life are you off course? (Question 1)

ME: My grades are terrible this semester.

IG: Would you say more about that? **(Expansion)**

ME: In high school I got mostly A's and B's even though I played three sports. My goal this semester is to have at least a 3.5 grade point average, but the way things are going, I'll be lucky if I even get a 2.0.

IG: What self-defeating **thought patterns** of yours may have contributed to this situation? (Question 2)

ME: I guess I tell myself I shouldn't have to work hard to get good grades in college.

IG: Why do you think that? Is there a deeper meaning? **(Clarification)**

ME: If I have to study hard, then I must not be very smart.

IG: That's a good awareness! What different thoughts could you choose to get back on course to your goal of getting at least a 3.5 average? (Question 3)

ME: I could remind myself that going to college is like moving from the minor leagues to the major leagues. The challenge is a lot greater,

It is a marvelous faculty of the human mind that we are also able to stop old programming from holding us back, anytime we choose to. That gift is called conscious choice.

Shad Helmstetter

Journal Entry 23 *continued*

and I better start studying like a major league student or I'm not going to succeed.

IG: What self-defeating **emotional patterns** of yours may have contributed to this situation? (Question 4)

ME: I get really frustrated when I don't understand something right away.

IG: So you want to understand it immediately. **(Reflection)**

ME: Absolutely. When I don't get it right away, I switch to something else.

IG: That's understandable since everything came so easy to you in high school. What different emotion could you choose to get you back on course to your goal of a 3.5 GPA? (Question 5)

ME: I could do the same thing I do in basketball when the coach asks me to shut down the other team's top scorer. I can psych myself up and push myself to study harder. My college degree is worth a lot more to me than winning a basketball game.

IG: What self-defeating **behavior patterns** of yours may have contributed to this situation? (Question 6)

ME: Like I said before, I get frustrated when I don't understand something right away, and then I put it aside. I always plan to come back to it later, but usually I don't.

IG: Are there any other self-defeating behaviors you can think of? **(Expansion)**

ME: I don't ask my teachers for help or go to the tutoring center either. I guess I hate asking for help. It's like admitting that I'm not very smart.

IG: There's that concern again about not being smart enough. **(Reflection)**

ME: I hadn't realized my Inner Critic is so loud!

IG: Now you can prove your Inner Critic wrong. What different behaviors could you choose to get back on course to your goal? (Question 7)

ME: I could ask my teachers for more help and go to the tutoring center. Also, when I set homework aside, I could write on my calendar when I'm going to work on it again. I'm really good about doing things that I write down.

IG: I like it! What limiting **core beliefs** of yours (about the world, other people, or yourself) may have led you to adopt the self-defeating patterns that we've been discussing? (Question 8)

ME: This conversation has made me realize I have some doubts about whether I'm as smart as I think I am. Maybe I don't believe I can really succeed in college unless studying comes easy for me. Maybe I got a little spoiled and lazy in high school.

IG: What different core belief could you choose to get back on course to your goal? (Question 9)

ME: I can succeed in college if I'm willing to do the work . . . and give it my best.

> Until you make the unconscious conscious, it will direct your life and you will call it fate.
>
> *Carl Jung*

> Whatever we believe about ourselves and our ability comes true for us.
>
> *Susan L. Taylor, editor-in-chief, Essence Magazine*

IG: That's great! Do the work and do your best! As a result of what you've learned here, what new behaviors, thoughts, emotions, or core beliefs will you commit to? (Question 10)

ME: When I feel like putting an assignment aside, I'll work on it for at least 15 more minutes. Then, if I stop before I'm finished, I'll write on my calendar when I'm going to work on it again and I'll go back and finish it later. If I'm still having trouble with the assignment, I'll ask my professor for help. And I'll keep reminding myself, "Do the work and do my best." If that doesn't help, I'll be back to talk to you some more. I *will* get a 3.5 average! Thanks for listening.

One Student's Story

ANNETTE VALLE
The Victoria College, Texas

Mrs. Turner, my seventh-grade math teacher, lives in my head. I haven't seen her in more than 30 years, but I can still picture her on the day I went up to her desk at the front of the room. She had fair skin, long brown hair, and hazel eyes. I can see her elbows on her big wooden desk, her eyes staring off into the distance, clicking the nail of a finger against the nail on her thumb. When I asked her to help explain the math, she turned and waved my paper at me and told me I was too stupid to learn math. All these years later, I can still hear her words. *I have no idea why you even come to this class, Annette. You're never going to pass math. You're just stupid.* Then she dismissed me with a wave of her hand.

I grew up in Houston, Texas, in the 1970s. College was something that rich, smart people did. It wasn't an option for poor Hispanic children living in the barrio. In our neighborhood, no one talked about going to college. Conversations were about drug dealers, drive-bys, and the latest girl who'd been beaten up by her husband. Our biggest goal in life was to survive. Like many of my friends, I dropped out of school. I got married at 15 and had two children by the time I was 17. After my brother got his GED in the military in 1980, he talked me into getting a GED, too. That diploma qualified me

for higher-paying jobs, like working security in a chemical plant or loading ATM machines. But they were all boring jobs that required physical labor, and I wasn't very happy.

Now fast forward to 2005. That's when I was diagnosed with rheumatoid arthritis. The doctor said I couldn't work at physical jobs any more, and I became eligible for a rehabilitation program that offered an opportunity for me to attend college. When I started my first semester at the age of 46, I was overwhelmed and scared. The campus seemed huge. I was intimidated by all of the young students and the academic requirements that I didn't understand. The teachers said, "Here's your syllabus," but I had no idea what a "syllabus" was. My English teacher told us to do our research paper in MLA format, but I had no idea what that meant either. I didn't want to ask because I figured everyone else knew. So I pretended I knew, too. I walked around campus with my head down and watched the cement. If I had a problem and someone didn't say, *Can I help you?* I would just try to figure it out on my own.

One of my courses was called Strategic Learning, where we read *On Course*. In this class I learned to overcome my fears and accept every challenge placed before me. It helped me become armed with the belief that the choices I make

and the strategies I use are what will determine what happens to me. I learned to combat the scripts in my head that were saying *You're not smart enough; You can't do this; You'll never be a good college student.* I replaced those negative thoughts with *I can do this; I will do whatever it takes to get the work done; Only I can change my path.* It's a good thing I had this class, because I was also taking math. Mrs. Turner was still in my head telling me I was stupid and would never pass math. Instead of giving in like I had when I was in her class, I tried my newly learned strategies with determination. One thing I did was take inspirational quotations from *On Course* and write them on my workspace wall at home. When I feel like giving up, I read them out loud. Then I remind myself that I am just as smart as my younger classmates and I can accomplish my dreams just as well as they can. I'm willing to do whatever it takes, even if that means spending 40 hours a week in tutoring. Maybe I'll never be a great math student, but I did pass the course.

I'm now in my fourth semester in college, and I walk across campus with my head up. When I see another student who's confused, I offer to help. I've even used some of the *On Course* techniques to encourage other students who have the same obstacles I had. The course made me a stronger person and helped me change my life. Still, I get sad when I realize that I believed Mrs. Turner for so long. I wasted a lot of years listening to her criticisms in my mind, and for a long time let her steal my thunder of achievement.

Photo: Courtesy of Annette Valle

Looking inward is the first place we need to look to find our own direction, not the last.

Clarke G. Carney & Cinda Field Wells in Career Planning

Many people spend more time choosing a movie than choosing their career. As a result, the unlucky ones later dread going to work, perhaps for the rest of their lives! Creators, by contrast, devote time and effort to one of life's most important Quadrant II activities: conscious career planning. As a result, many of them actually enjoy going to work.

Conscious career planning requires self-awareness. How else can you find a match between you and the thousands of career possibilities open to you? A place to start your planning is taking an inventory of your **hard skills.** Hard skills are the special-knowledge skills that you've learned to do throughout your life. They include such abilities as swimming, writing, programming computers, playing racquetball, solving mathematics problems, building a house, creating a budget, giving a speech, drawing blood, writing a business plan, designing a garden, cooking lasagna, backpacking, playing chess, and reading. You probably learned many of your hard skills from a teacher, coach, mentor, or book. These skills can typically be video recorded, and they tend to be applicable only in limited and specific situations; for example, writing a business plan isn't a skill of much value when you're programming computers. To begin your inventory of hard skills, ask yourself, "What talents have gotten me compliments, recognition, or awards? In which school courses have I received good grades? When did I feel fully alive, extremely capable, or very smart, and what skills was I using at the time?" Finding a match between your hard skills and the requirements of a career is essential for success.

Continue your self-assessment with an inventory of your **soft skills** (sometimes referred to as "necessary skills"). Soft skills are the ones you have developed to cope with life. They include the ones you're exploring in this book: making responsible choices, motivating yourself, being industrious, developing mutually supportive relationships, demonstrating self-awareness, finding lessons in every experience, managing your emotions, and believing in yourself. Many of these soft skills you learned unconsciously as you faced life's challenges. Usually, they are attitudes and beliefs, so they can't be videoed for playback. They are as invisible as oxygen but just as important to the quality of your life. Unlike hard skills, soft skills tend to be helpful in any career; for example, feeling confident is valuable whether you are an accountant, computer programmer, or nurse. To create an inventory of your soft skills, ask yourself, "What personal qualities have earned me compliments? What accomplishments am I proud of, and what inner qualities helped me achieve them?" Finding a match between your soft skills and the demands of a career further increases your chances of rising to the top of your profession.

To create a third component of your self-assessment, identify your **personal preferences**. To do so, go to your college's career center and ask to take one of the well-known interest inventories: the *Strong Interest Inventories* (SII), the *Self-Directed Search* (SDS), or the *Myers-Briggs Type Indicator®* (MBTI®) instrument. These tools help you discover personal preferences and suggest possible college majors and career choices that will match your interests. An additional tool, the *Holland Code,* places you in one of six personality types and suggests possible careers for each. Which of the following personality types sounds most like you?

Realistic personalities prefer activities involving objects, tools, and machines. Possible careers: mechanic, electrician, computer repair, civil engineer, forester, industrial arts teacher, dental technician, farmer, carpenter.

Investigative personalities prefer activities involving abstract problem solving and the exploration of physical, biological, and cultural phenomena for the purpose of understanding and controlling them. Possible careers: chemist, economist, detective, computer analyst, doctor, astronomer, mathematician.

Artistic personalities prefer activities involving self-expression, using words, ideas, or materials to create art forms or new concepts. Possible careers: writer, advertising manager, public relations specialist, artist, musician, graphic designer, interior decorator, inventor.

Social personalities prefer activities involving interaction with other people to inform, train, develop, help, or enlighten them. Possible careers: nurse, massage therapist, teacher, counselor, social worker, day-care provider, physical therapist.

Enterprising personalities prefer activities involving the persuasion and management of others to attain organizational goals or economic gain. Possible careers: salesperson, television newscaster, bank manager, lawyer, travel agent, personnel manager, entrepreneur.

Conventional personalities prefer activities involving the application of data to bring order out of confusion and develop a prescribed plan. Possible careers: accountant, computer operator, secretary, credit manager, financial planner.

The research of Dr. John Holland, creator of the Holland Code, shows that people tend to be satisfied in careers that are compatible with their personality type, and people are less satisfied when the match isn't there. Becoming aware of your interest preferences and personality type improves your chances of finding a satisfying career match.

Creators Wanted!

Candidates must demonstrate self-awareness, self-confidence, and positive work and life habits.

Another important area of self-knowledge is your scripts, those that support your success and especially those that don't. For example, what beliefs do you hold that might keep you from pursuing or succeeding in your chosen career? If one of your scripts is to distrust other people, then it will be difficult for you to develop the support systems that will enhance your success. This awareness allows you to make a conscious choice about revising the script. Remember, since you wrote your script originally, you can rewrite it in the service of a successful career.

Self-awareness in the workplace will also help you notice when your self-sabotaging habits get you off course. For example, you'll stop arriving at meetings late; instead, you'll arrive a few minutes early. You'll stop interrupting when others are talking; instead, you'll listen actively. You'll stop acting as if you know all the answers; instead, you'll ask others for their opinions. In short, you'll become conscious of converting destructive behaviors into constructive behaviors. If you've ever had bosses or coworkers who demonstrate any of these negative behaviors, you'll know how you wished they would become aware of what they were doing and change.

To summarize, cultivating the soft skill of self-awareness will help you choose a career that you will enjoy and bring out the behaviors, beliefs, and attitudes that will help you to excel in that profession.

BELIEVING IN YOURSELF

Write Your Own Rules

 Focus Questions   What personal rules do you have that dictate the choices you make daily? Which of these rules help you create high self-esteem?

Few things affect self-esteem more than our sense of personal power. When we feel like mere passengers in life, with no apparent choice in where we're going, self-esteem shrivels. When we feel like the pilots of our lives, with the power to choose wisely and reach our goals and dream, self-esteem grows.

Unconscious personal scripts and cultural programs can steal our sense of personal power and drag down our self-esteem. When these unconscious forces take over, we essentially give up control of our lives. Then we make those strange choices that can push us far off course and leave us wondering, "How the heck did I get over here?" Consider, for example, the cultural tradition of *marianism* in which Latinas are expected to follow rules such as these: *Place the needs of your husband and family above your own, Never criticize your husband, Remain faithful to your marriage regardless of the cost, Never share personal problems with others.* If a Latina has consciously accepted these rules as her own, she will gladly make the personal sacrifices needed, and she will achieve the outcomes and experiences of her choosing. In fact, her sense of cultural pride may very well give her self-esteem a powerful boost. However, if she unconsciously lets these rules dictate her choices, she may feel helpless and angry at the life she is living. Imagine, for example, trying to earn a college degree if you are forever setting aside your dreams to help others achieve what they want. Only when you consciously accept, revise, or replace some cultural rules are you likely to feel completely at peace with yourself. The same, of course, is true of the rules embedded in your personal scripts.

As psychologist Virginia Satir pointed out, we are all living by rules, but the important issue is *Have we chosen our own rules*? To answer that question, you'll want to identify and preserve any empowering rules that are keeping you on course. Then you'll want to become conscious of and revise any rules that are holding you back. Finally, you'll want to write new rules that will support you in achieving even greater victories. That's what former first lady Eleanor Roosevelt did. Here are some of the life rules she created to guide her choices: *Do whatever comes your way as well as you can. Think as little as possible about yourself; think as much as possible about other people. Since you get more joy out of giving joy to others, you should put a good deal of thought in the happiness that you are able to give.*

I think you're going to be very surprised to discover that you may be living by rules of which you're not even aware.

Virginia Satir

As a member of the Sikh faith, I was constantly keeping track of so many rules: what to wear, what to eat, forbidden behaviors, and my duties to my family. When I added it all up, there wasn't much left for me to decide—so many of my decision had been made for me.

Sheena Iyengar

THREE SUCCESS RULES

I have polled thousands of college instructors, and they consistently identify three behaviors that their most successful students do consistently. As you'll see, these rules apply just as well to creating great outcomes in other life roles such as your career and relationships. Consider, then, these three rules as the foundation of your personal code of conduct.

Rule 1: I Show Up

Commit to attending every class from beginning to end. Someone once said that 90 percent of success is simply showing up. Makes sense, doesn't it? How can you be successful at something if you're not there? Studies show a direct correlation between attendance and grades (as one measure of success). At Baltimore City Community College, a study found that, on average, as absences went up, grades went down, especially in introductory courses. A study by a business professor at Arizona State University showed that, on average, his students' grades went down one full grade for every two classes they missed. If you can't get motivated to show up, maybe you need new goals and dreams.

Rule 2: I Do My Best Work

Commit to doing your best work on all assignments, including turning them in on time. You'd be amazed at how many sloppy assignments instructors see. But it isn't just students who are guilty. A friend in business has shown me hundreds of job applications so sloppily prepared that they begged to be tossed in the trash. Doing your best work on assignments is a rule that will propel you to success in all you do.

Rule 3: I Participate Actively

Commit to getting involved. College, like life, isn't a spectator sport. Come to class prepared. Listen attentively. Take notes. Think deeply about what's being said. Ask yourself how you can apply your course work to achieve your goals and dreams. Read ahead. Start a study group. Ask questions. Answer questions. If you participate at this high level, you couldn't keep yourself from learning even if you wanted to.

Some students resist adopting these three basic rules of success. They say, "But what if I get sick? What if my car breaks down on the way to class? What if . . .?" I trust that by now you recognize the voice of the Inner Defender, the internal excuse maker.

Of course something may happen to keep you from following your rules. Each rule is simply your strong *intention*. Each rule identifies an action you believe will help you achieve your desired outcomes and experiences. So you *intend* to be at every class from beginning to end. You *intend* to do your very best work and turn assignments in on time. You *intend* to participate actively. Your promise *to yourself* is never to break your own rules for a frivolous reason. However, you'll always break your own rules if something of a higher value (like

The most important thing is to have a code of life, to know how to live.

Hans Selye, M.D.

People who lead a satisfying life, who are in tune with their past and with their future—in short, people whom we would call "happy"—are generally individuals who have lived their lives according to rules they themselves created.

Mihaly Csikszentmihalyi

your health) demands it. At each fork in the road, the key to your success is being aware of which choice leads to the future you want. When you are a Creator, you make each choice uncontaminated by the past (your scripts), informed by your own rules of conduct, and ultimately determined by which option, in that moment, will best support the achievement of your goals and dreams.

Changing Your Habits

Exceptional students not only follow these three basic rules of success, they also create their own rules for college and life. By choosing personal rules, they commit to replacing their limiting scripts and cultural constraints with consciously chosen habits. Here are a few of my own life rules:

- I keep promises to myself and others.
- I seek feedback and make appropriate course corrections.
- I respect others by arriving on time.
- I do my very best work on all projects important to me.
- I play and create joy.
- I care for my body with exercise, healthy food, and good medical care.
- I am kind.

Do I follow these rules every day of my life? Unfortunately, no. And when I don't, I soon see myself getting off course. Then I can reelect to follow my self-chosen rules and avoid sabotaging the life I want to create.

Once we follow our own rules long enough, they're no longer simply rules. They become habits. And once our positive actions, thoughts, and feelings become habits, few obstacles can block the path to our success.

> What is hateful to you do not to your fellowman. That is the entire Law; all the rest is commentary.
>
> *The Talmud*

Journal Entry 24

In this activity, you will write your own rules for success in college and in life. By following your own code of conduct, you will more likely stay on course toward your greatest dreams.

To focus your mind, ask yourself, "What do successful people do consistently? What are their thoughts, attitudes, behaviors, and beliefs?"

1. Title a clean journal page "MY PERSONAL RULES FOR SUCCESS IN COLLEGE AND IN LIFE." Below that, write a list of your own rules for achieving your goals in college. List only those actions to which you're willing to commit to do consistently. You might want to print your rules on certificate paper and post them where you can see them daily (perhaps right next to your affirmation). Consider adopting the following as your first three rules:

> I'll give you the Four Rules of Success:
>
> 1. Decide what you want.
> 2. Decide what you want to give up in order to get what you want.
> 3. Associate with successful people.
> 4. Plan your work and work your plan.
>
> **Blair Underwood, actor**

1. I show up.
2. I do my very best work.
3. I participate actively.

2. Write your thoughts and feelings about which of your personal rules is the most important to your success in college and in life, and why.

What if one of your rules was: I dive deep! How much would that rule improve your results in college and in life?

One Student's Story

BRANDEÉ HUIGENS
Northeast Iowa Community College, Iowa

I was never a drinker in high school, but when I turned 21, I started going out to bars with my friends. I found that "liquor courage" made me feel better about myself. When I was drinking, I was funny, had a great time, and I was happy. Then I started having blackouts. One time I woke up in my truck, surrounded by policemen, and I had no idea how I had gotten there or where I had been. Another time, I woke up in my bed and there were traffic citations all over the place. I found out later that I had spent the night in jail and the police had sent me home in a cab, but what made it worse was that I didn't remember a second of it. I had always gotten good grades before, but now I started missing my college classes. I wasn't doing as well as I wanted, especially in my nursing classes, like microbiology. I felt crappy and started putting even more pressure on myself. Then I would drink and it made me feel better, almost like a good friend. Trouble was, I'd wake up the next day and my life was falling apart. People were telling me that I could get a medical withdrawal, and I started thinking about dropping out of college.

Looking back on it now, I realize that I had completely lost control of my inner core. I've never been a quitter, though, and I started using my journal entries for this course to figure out my challenges and how to fix them. My entries would run on for five or six pages as I poured myself emotionally into my writing. I was excited because it was a way to express myself positively. About halfway through the semester, I made a new rule for myself and told my class about it: *I will abstain from drinking alcohol.* From day one, it was a rule that took over my life, and I decided to track it with a 32-Day Commitment. To support my change, I started going to AA meetings and I got a counselor at the Substance Abuse Services Center. I reread my journals for inspiration, and every day in this class we'd share how we were doing on our commitments. Of course there were times I was tempted to drink, but I successfully completed my 32 days, and then I just kept going. In the last six months, I have abstained from drinking every day but one.

Today, I think about how powerful it was to write that little sentence and make a new rule for myself. It set so many other things in motion. Some are obvious, like I got sober and stopped having blackouts. My final grades were awesome, and I even got a B in micro, the hardest course I ever took. I also got a new perspective on grades. I always wanted to be perfect so I could get approval from my family, but now I see a B as a success instead of a failure. Perhaps most of all, I learned that in trying to please everyone else but me, I had lost focus on what is important to me and all I want to accomplish. Now I've created an assertiveness rule. I've starting speaking up for myself and saying "no," and I can feel my confidence and self-esteem getting stronger. From this class and from the people I shared it with, I have learned how to stand up for myself. My inner core is not fully complete, but the seed has been planted and it is definitely starting to grow.

Wise Choices in College

TAKING TESTS

A test is a game . . . an important game, but a game nonetheless.

First, let's review why tests in college are important (as if you didn't know). Tests contribute to your course grade, and that grade becomes a part of your permanent record. If your grades are consistently low, you will be put on probation or even expelled. Low grades may cause you to lose financial aid. If you're an athlete, low grades can cost you eligibility for intercollegiate sports. However, if your grades are consistently high enough, you'll eventually earn a degree. Then your grades will be of interest to future employers, graduate schools, and car insurance companies, to name a few. One of my students told me that even the parents of his fiancé asked to see a copy of his transcript. Perhaps they thought his grades would reveal what kind of husband he would make for their daughter.

So tests are important. But they *are* just a game, and you win the test game by scoring the maximum number of points possible. Three factors determine how well you score on tests:

- **Factor one: How well have you prepared?** If you have diligently completed each step of the CORE Learning System, you are extremely well prepared! Look around the room at the other students taking the test. Remind yourself that you are as well prepared as all of them and more prepared than most of them. You have worked hard, used a powerful learning system, and the result is deep and lasting learning. You have every reason to be confident!

- **Factor two: How well do you take tests?** Most people assume that tests reveal how much you know and maybe even how intelligent you are. In an ideal world, perhaps this would be true. Here

on planet Earth, however, another critical factor influences your grades: Your skill at taking tests. Without this skill, your grades may only vaguely represent how much you know or how intelligent you are. Every game requires special skills for scoring points. In this chapter, you'll learn some of the very best skills for maximizing the number of points you earn on every test. Get ready to learn how to be "test smart."

- **Factor three: How much have you learned from previous tests?** Every test provides feedback. As you know, self-aware Creators pay attention to feedback and use it to their advantage. If a test score reveals that you're on course, you can confidently keep doing whatever you've been doing. However, if a test score reveals that you are off course, it's time to change tactics.

TAKING TESTS: THE BIG PICTURE

In previous chapters you discovered how to be a good learner. In this chapter you'll learn how to be a good "test taker." The good news is there are only so many ways an instructor can ask you to demonstrate your knowledge and skills. Your challenge is to determine the most likely ways and prepare accordingly. So, experiment with the many following strategies and, as you do, keep in mind the big picture of test taking: **Your goal for each test is to score the maximum number of points possible. Just as there is an art to learning, so is there an art to taking tests. It's called being *test smart*.**

BEFORE TAKING TESTS

1. Actively use the CORE Learning System. This means when you walk into the test room, you have already. . . .

A. **Collected** complete and accurate information from all reading assignments and class sessions,

B. **Organized** many different kinds of effective study materials,

C. **Rehearsed** these study materials with a distributed study schedule, and

D. **Evaluated** to confirm your understanding of all study materials.

2. Visualize success. Create a mental movie of yourself taking the exam with great success. In your mind, picture yourself understanding every question, answering each one quickly and correctly, finishing on time, and, later, getting your test back with the grade you want (or even higher). Playing this positive movie in your mind often will build your confidence and prepare you to think, feel, and act positively during the real test. (Review Journal Entry 11 for a refresher on how to create a visualization.)

3. Prepare yourself physically and emotionally. Be sure to get a good night's sleep and eat well before a test. You don't want to be distracted by tiredness or hunger. As your instructor hands out the test, breathe deeply and relax. Your studying is done. Now it's game time and your goal is simple: Earn the most points possible. You're ready. Repeat your affirmation. Visualize your success. Take another deep breath and get ready to score! You can do this!

WHILE TAKING TESTS

4. Preview the test. Just as previewing a reading assignment is valuable, so is previewing a test. Note the kinds of questions. Note the point value of various questions. Read the directions carefully so you understand the rules of the game. For example, on a multiple-choice test, if the directions ask you to mark *two or more* answers and you mark only one, you'll lose points. Also, be alert for directions that change the rules. In one part of the test a wrong answer may be penalized whereas in another part of the test it may not be.

This knowledge will determine whether or not you guess at an answer. Be sure you understand exactly what you are being asked to do. If unsure, ask the instructor to clarify.

5. Make a test-smart plan. Remember, your goal is to earn as many points as possible. The first rule of a test-smart plan is *Answer easy questions first*. Skim the test and answer any questions you can answer quickly and correctly. Answering easy questions first has three advantages: It makes sure you pocket these points. It builds confidence that calms test anxiety. And, while answering the easy questions, you may come across answers to other questions on the test.

The second rule of a test-smart plan is *Spend time in proportion to points available*. Having answered the easy questions, now answer the remaining questions that are worth the most points. Suppose you're taking a fifty-minute test with fifty true/false questions worth two points each. Your plan is obvious. Assign one minute to answer each question. If you spend five minutes answering one question and five minutes answering another, now you have only forty minutes to answer the remaining forty-eight questions. Or consider a different situation: You're taking a fifty-minute test with ten true/false questions worth two points each and two short-answer essay questions worth forty points each. You want to make sure you get as many of those eighty essay points as possible. Since each essay is worth 40 percent of the total points available, you assign 40 percent of the time available (twenty minutes) to each . . . which leaves ten minutes to answer the true/false questions. Without this plan, you might spend twenty minutes answering the true/false questions, leaving yourself less time to gobble up all those essay points.

6. Answer true/false questions. Obviously, the best situation is when you know whether the statement is true or false. However, all is not lost if you are unsure. Even by guessing, you'll likely get half of them correct, and here are six test-smart strategies for improving those odds:

A. If any part of a statement is false, the answer is false.

B. If the question contains an **unconditional** word (100% with no exception), such as *all, every, only, never,* or *always,* the answer is probably false.

C. If the question contains a **conditional** word (less than 100% with some exceptions), such as *generally, some, a few, occasionally, seldom, usually, sometimes,* or *often,* the answer is probably true.

D. If the statement has two negatives, cross them both out and see if the statement is true or false.

E. If the sentence contains words you've never heard of, guess false. (This suggestion assumes you've studied thoroughly and will recognize key terms in the course.)

F. If you are reduced to taking a pure guess, choose "True." It is easier for instructors to write a true statement; plus, most would prefer that you think about the correct answer.

7. Answer multiple-choice questions. Multiple-choice questions offer a statement or question, and then present alternative ways to complete the statement or answer the question. A multiple-choice question is actually a group of true/false questions. Your task, then, is to read each statement and choose the correct (true) answer. When you are stumped, here are ways to be test smart. The following options won't always get you the correct answer, but when you are reduced to making pure guesses, they can improve your odds of choosing the correct answer.

A. Note in the directions whether you can choose only one answer or more than one answer for each question.

B. Be sure to read all answers before making a choice. Answer A may be partly accurate and

tempting, but Answer D may be more accurate and therefore is the answer you should choose.

C. Cross out all obviously incorrect answers, such as those that are intended to be humorous.

D. Cross out answers with unconditional (100%) words like *all, always, never, must,* or *every.*

E. Look for grammatical clues to cross out an answer (e.g., the subject in the question doesn't agree with the verb in a possible answer).

F. When the answers are numbers, cross out the highest and lowest.

G. If two answers are similar (e.g., such as *independent* and *interdependent*), choose one of them as the correct answer.

H. If you know two or more answers are correct, choose "All of the above" as the correct answer.

I. If one answer has a more thorough answer than the others, choose that answer as correct.

J. If the question is based on a reading passage, read the question and possible answers *before* reading the passage. Then read the passage with the specific purpose of finding the answer.

8. Answer fill-in-the-blank questions. Fill-in-the-blank questions present a sentence with one or more words (or phrases) left out. Your task is to insert the correct word or phrase. Despite the increased level of challenge, being test smart can improve your chances of earning points on fill-in-the-blank questions.

A. Unless the directions say you will be penalized for a wrong answer, always write something in the blank.

B. Make sure your answer fits grammatically into the sentence (e.g., don't insert a noun if the space in the sentence requires a verb).

C. Use the length of the blank to indicate whether the correct answer is one or more words.

D. If you see two or more blanks, realize you need to have a different word or phrase in each blank.

E. Since fill-in-the-blank questions usually ask about key concepts, these concepts are often mentioned elsewhere in the test. Keep alert for them as you do other parts of the test.

F. After inserting the answer, read the sentence to make sure it makes sense.

9. Answer short-answer questions. Short-answer questions are mini-essays, usually one paragraph in length. The best approach, then, is to state a main idea. Then offer specific supporting details to demonstrate your thorough understanding of the idea. It's difficult to fake knowledge on a short-answer question, but there are some test-smart strategies that can maximize the number of points you earn.

A. Always write something. Your instructor can't give you points for a blank space.

B. Circle the *guide word* in the writing prompt. (e.g., Describe the advantages of using a tracking form.) Guide words reveal the way in which the instructor expects you to develop the topic. See Figure 6.1 for a description of twelve common guide words.

C. Underline the topic in the writing prompt. (e.g., Describe the advantages of using a tracking form.) Referring to the underlined words helps you stay focused on the topic.

D. On a blank sheet of paper or the back of a test page, jot down any related ideas and supporting details you can think of. If you have time, write a rough draft of your answer and copy it onto the test.

E. Begin writing your answer by turning the question or writing prompt into your main idea.

Again, imagine that the prompt is "Describe the advantages of using a tracking form." Begin your answer, "Using a tracking form has a number of advantages." This beginning helps you stay focused on the topic as you write your paragraph.

F. Flesh out your paragraph with supporting details such as examples, evidence, explanations, and experiences. If you're at a loss for supporting details, see if you can find some in other questions on the test.

G. The space provided usually indicates how much writing your instructor expects, so plan your answer to fit in that space (unless there's a note such as "Continue your answer on the back of this page").

H. End your paragraph with a wrap-up sentence (e.g., "There are other advantages to using a tracking form, but these are three of the most valuable").

I. Proofread your paragraph. Even if instructors don't consciously take off points for errors, such distractions can undermine an otherwise positive impression of your answer.

10. Answer essay questions. Essay questions require an in-depth discussion of a topic. In Chapter 7, you will learn many writing skills that will help you excel in answering essay questions. Here we will address two writing challenges that are unique to taking an essay test. First, you usually need to write your essay from information stored in your memory (not in your notes). Second, you have a time limit in which to write (unless it is a take-home exam). Thus, essay questions not only test your knowledge of the course content, they also test your writing ability. Here are some test-smart strategies for answering essay questions:

A. Read the directions carefully. As with short-answer questions, circle guide words in the essay prompt. Words such as *define, compare, contrast, describe, evaluate, summarize,* and

Guide Words	What to Do	Example Questions
1. Analyze	Identify the parts of something and explain how those parts contribute to the whole.	*Analyze* the skills of a test-smart student. *Analyze* the symbolism of the white whale in Herman Melville's *Moby Dick*.
2. Compare	Show similarities of two or more things. (Note: some instructors also want you to show differences as well.)	*Compare* linear and graphic organizers. *Compare* democracy and socialism.
3. Contrast	Show differences between two or more things.	*Contrast* Creators and Victims. *Contrast* Flemish and Italian painters during the Renaissance.
4. Define	State the meaning of something.	*Define* a self-sabotaging script. *Define* standard deviation.
5. Describe	Tell about in some detail.	*Describe* an effective self-management system. *Describe* the efforts of England's King Henry VII to consolidate royal power.
6. Discuss (or Explain) Why	Provide a detailed account showing cause.	*Discuss why* it is important to be an active learner. *Explain why* Chebyshev's theorem is important.
7. Discuss (or Explain) Effect	Give the results of something.	*Discuss* the long-term *effects* of stress on physical health. *Explain* the *effect* of global warming.
8. Discuss (or Explain) How	Provide the details of a process.	*Discuss how* students can maintain or increase their academic motivation. *Explain how* hydrogen and oxygen combine to make water.
9. Evaluate	Assess strengths and weaknesses, providing reasons.	*Evaluate* the quality of writing in your first *On Course* journal entry. *Evaluate* a vegetarian diet.
10. Explain	Make clear or comprehensible.	*Explain* the three components of a logical argument. *Explain* the health risks of binge drinking.
11. Illustrate	Offer an example.	*Illustrate* the use of the Wise Choice Process. *Illustrate* the benefits of using cascading style sheets in the creation of a website.
12. Summarize	Provide a condensed version, highlighting main points only.	*Summarize* the reasons that interdependence is important in the workplace. *Summarize* the plot of *Huckleberry Finn* by Mark Twain.

Figure 6.1 One Dozen Common Guide Words

For Better or For Worse®

by Lynn Johnston

explain the cause require different sorts of responses. Be sure you understand what you are being asked to write. (See Figure 6.1: One Dozen Common Guide Words.)

B. Underline all key terms in the writing prompt. Suppose the topic says "Describe the following economic theories: Classical, Marxist, and Keynesian." If you do a great job on Classical and Keynesian theories but don't mention Marxist theory, you'll lose many possible points.

C. If the question gives you a choice of topics to write about, be sure to write the correct number of essays. If you write more than asked for, you're wasting precious time on questions you didn't need to answer (and probably won't get points for). And if you answer fewer, you'll certainly lose points.

D. Don't start writing immediately. Instead, brainstorm by jotting down ideas related to the topic. If you need more ideas, glance over the rest of the test to see if other questions or answers suggest additional ideas or supporting details to add to your brainstorm.

E. Revise the question or topic and use it as the first sentence of your essay. (See Strategy 9E for how to do this.)

F. Organize your ideas with your preferred method (e.g., outline or concept map). Creating a clear organization helps you maximize points earned. If you have more main ideas in your plan than you have time to write about, cross out the ones for which you have the fewest supporting details. You're likely to earn more points for four to six well developed paragraphs than you will for seven to ten poorly developed paragraphs.

G. Develop each main idea in a separate paragraph, offering specific support such as examples, evidence, explanations, and experiences. Don't leave information out of your essay because you think the instructor already knows it. Remember, this is not a test to see if your *instructor* can answer the question; the test is to determine if *you* can. You'll be wise to write to a general audience: a group of intelligent, interested readers who know very little about your topic. This approach will assure that you include all relevant information that could earn you points. (Strategy 15 in Chapter 7 offers more information on how to develop a paragraph effectively.)

H. Write a satisfying conclusion, perhaps summarizing the main points you have made. (Strategy 17 in Chapter 7 provides suggestions for concluding your essay.)

I. Save time for revising. As you read over what you have written, identify and answer questions your reader may have about your ideas. For example, readers often want to know "Why?" and "How do you know?" Add additional supporting details (examples, evidence, explanations, experiences) to undeveloped paragraphs.

J. Proofread carefully for grammar, spelling, and punctuation errors.

K. If your handwriting is difficult to read, recopy for legibility. For further neatness, consider printing, writing on every other line, and writing on one side of the paper only.

Here are some final tips for maximizing essay points:

- Always write something. Your instructor can't give you points for a blank page.

- Leave three or four blank lines after each answer in case you think of something later that you can add at the end.

- If you can't finish, provide an outline or concept map for what you would have written with more time. You may get partial points for your plan.

- If you can type, consider asking if you can bring a laptop to the test. You'll be able to write faster and make corrections more easily. Of course, you'll need some way to print your test before handing it in.

11. Solve math problems. Mathematics tests usually ask you to solve problems of the type you have been studying. If you have been solving practice problems successfully throughout the course, you are well prepared. Here are some test-smart strategies to apply during a math test:

A. As soon as you get the test, write notes and formulas on the test. If you freeze up later, you'll have access to this essential information.

B. Do a first pass through the test and solve all of the problems you can do easily. You never want to lose points by leaving a problem undone that you could have solved, but ran out of time.

C. Make a second pass through the test to work on the more challenging problems. Begin to solve each problem by estimating the answer.

D. As you do a problem, write out every step of your solution. Even if you get the answer wrong, the instructor may give you some points.

E. When finished with each problem, compare your answer with your estimate. If the two answers are very different, recheck your computations.

F. As time allows, revisit each problem and double-check all calculations.

12. If you get stuck, move on. Don't sit there wasting time on a question you can't answer. Not only will you lose time that you need for earning points, you'll also undermine your confidence by focusing on what you *don't* know instead of what you *do* know. If you doubt an answer that you've given or you've given no answer at all, put a light check mark next to the question. If time allows, return later and review your answer with fresh eyes.

13. Review your answers. Start with the sections that offer the most points. Then, check answers in other parts of the test in descending order of points available. For math problems, look for possible errors in each line of your solution.

14. Provide an answer for every question. When you have reviewed all of your answered questions, revisit unanswered questions. Run your finger along the words and read the question aloud (whisper). Highlight key words. Close your eyes and see if you can picture the answer in your study materials.

Glance through the test to see if the answer may be included in another question. As a final resort, guess. You might just get some points if your guess is close.

AFTER TAKING TESTS

15. Reward yourself. No matter how you think you did on the test, give yourself a treat for your efforts before and during the test—go out to dinner, call an old friend, take a bubble bath, rent a movie.

16. Study the instructor's feedback. When you get the test back, don't just look at the grade. Read the instructor's comments. For recognition questions (e.g., true/false, multiple-choice, or matching), all you may see are X's to indicate errors. For recall questions (e.g., essay or math problems), your instructor may provide commentary to explain why you earned or lost points. Whatever feedback the instructor provides, its purpose is to get you on course. Gobble it up. If there's an error or comment you don't understand, make an appointment with your instructor to discuss your confusion.

17. Analyze your errors. By analyzing your errors, you can determine how to score more points on the next test. There are seven problems that typically cost students points on a test. For example, you might have lost points because you studied the wrong material or because you didn't have a test-smart plan. Use the Test Debrief (Figure 6.2 on page 214) to identify where you lost points, and make a plan for earning more points on your next test.

18. Get help. Before the next test, seek help from your instructor, tutors, or classmates. Go to the learning center on your campus. If you haven't already created a study group, start one. If offered, attend workshops on test preparation and test anxiety. By seeking help, you can learn the information you got wrong on the previous test and improve your preparation for the next one.

TEST-TAKING EXERCISE

Create a twenty-five-question test for a course you are now taking; write out your answers to each question. Include five questions each of the following kinds: (1) true/false, (2) matching, (3) fill in the blank, (4) multiple choice, and (5) short answer or essay. Or, for a mathematics or science course, prepare problems similar to the ones you have been studying. Design your questions so that a student who answers correctly will be demonstrating the essential knowledge/skills covered in this course. Have a meeting with your instructor and ask for feedback on the quality of your questions and answers. Revise them based on what you discover in the conversation with your instructor. BONUS: Exchange tests with a partner and each of you create a test-smart plan for taking the other's test.

TEST DEBRIEF

Directions: Consider the seven test-taking problems below, and estimate the number of points you lost on the test for each problem. Circle the problem(s) that cost you the most points, and implement the solution(s) as you prepare for the next test.

Problem 1: I didn't study some of the information or skills covered on the test.
Points lost: _____
Solution: Be more assertive about discovering what content will be covered on the test. Check the course syllabus; ask classmates, tutors, and especially the instructor. Add this material to your CORE Learning System.

Problem 2: I did study the information or skills covered on the test, but I got questions wrong anyway.
Points lost: _____
Solution: Experiment with **Organizing** new kinds of study materials. Try different ways of **Rehearsing** your study materials. Distribute your studying over longer periods of time and increase your time on task. Implement more **Evaluations** to assess your understanding (e.g., have study team members and/or tutors test your knowledge).

Problem 3: I wasn't good at answering the kind of questions the instructor asked.
Points lost: _____
Solution: Do all you can to determine what kind of questions will be on the test. Construct and take practice tests that use those kinds of questions. Have study team members also construct questions of this kind. Show the questions you create and your answers to a tutor or your instructor for feedback. Keep creating and answering these kinds of questions until you become skilled at answering them.

Problem 4: I didn't follow the directions.
Points lost: _____
Solution: Take time to read all of the directions carefully, circle guide words, and underline key terms. When you proofread, confirm that you have done what was asked.

Problem 5: I lost points for questions I could have answered but didn't get to.
Points lost: _____
Solution: Make a test-smart plan that focuses on accumulating the greatest number of points possible. Determine where the easy, point-rich questions are and make a plan to answer those questions first. Set time limits for each section so you don't get stuck and lose points by not answering questions in other parts of the test.

Problem 6: I knew the answers but made careless mistakes.
Points lost: _____
Solution: Move steadily through the test, but don't rush. Think carefully about what each question is asking and about the best way to answer it. Allow time at the end to check all answers and proofread carefully before handing in the test.

Problem 7: I panicked and was too stressed to answer questions, even those for which I knew the answer.
Points lost: _____
Solution: Overlearn the content and take numerous practice tests under "game" conditions to build test-taking skills and confidence. Visualize your success and create a positive affirmation about your test-taking ability. Make and follow a test-smart plan. If you get stuck during the test, don't waste time on a tough question; move on. If you feel anxious, refocus. Keep reminding yourself that taking tests is a game and that your job is simply to earn the most points possible. If test anxiety continues to plague you, consider seeing a counselor for further suggestions and help.

Points lost for the Seven Problems should total the number of points you lost on the test.

Figure 6.2 | Test Debrief

Adopting Lifelong Learning

7

As a Creator, I take personal responsibility for learning all of the information, skills, and life lessons necessary to achieve my goals and dreams.

I learn valuable lessons from every experience I have.

SUCCESSFUL STUDENTS ...	STRUGGLING STUDENTS ...
develop a learning orientation to life, seeking new learning experiences that offer valuable lessons and strengthen their learning "muscles" for future challenges.	avoid new learning experiences, believing they have a fixed amount of intelligence that may not be up to the challenge.
discover their preferred ways of learning, utilizing strategies that allow them to maximize their learning of valuable new information and skills.	often experience frustration, boredom, or resistance when their instructors don't teach the way they prefer to learn.
employ critical thinking, using probing questions and higher-order reasoning skills to evaluate complex situations, make wise choices, and solve important problems.	use poor thinking skills that result in confusion, unsound judgment, enduring problems, and even exploitation by others.

Case Study in Critical Thinking

A FISH STORY

One September morning, on their first day of college, two dozen first-year students made their way into the biology laboratory. They sat down six at a lab table and glanced about for the professor. Because this was their first college class, most of the students were a bit nervous. A few introduced themselves. Others kept checking their watches.

At exactly nine o'clock, the professor, wearing a crisply pressed white lab coat, entered the room. "Good morning," he said. He set a white plate in the middle of each table. On each plate lay a small fish.

"Please observe the fish," the professor said. "Then write down your observations." He turned and left the room.

The students looked at each other, puzzled. This was *bizarre!* Oh, well. They took out scrap paper and wrote notes such as, *I see a small fish.* One student added, *It's on a white plate.*

Satisfied, they set their pens down and waited. And waited. For the entire class period, they waited. A couple of students whispered that it was a trick. They said the professor was probably testing them to see if they'd do something wrong. Time crawled by. Still they waited, trying to do nothing that would get them in trouble. Finally, one student mumbled that she was going to be late for her next class. She picked up her books and stood. She paused. Others rose as well and began filing out of the room. Some looked cautiously over their shoulders as they left.

When the students entered the biology lab for their second class, they found the same white plates with the same small fish already waiting on their laboratory tables. At exactly nine o'clock, the professor entered the room. "Good morning. Please take out your observations of the fish," he said.

Students dug into their notebooks or book bags. Many could not find their notes. Those few who could held them up for the professor to see as he walked from table to table.

After visiting each student, the professor said, "Please observe the fish. Write down all of your observations."

"Will there be a test on this?" one student asked. But the professor had already left the room, closing the door behind him. Frustrated, the student blurted, "Why doesn't he just tell us what he wants to know?"

The students looked at one another, more puzzled. They peered at the fish. Those few who had found their notes glanced from the fish to their notes and back again. Was the professor crazy? What else were they supposed to notice? It was only a stupid fish.

About then, one student spied a book on the professor's desk. It was a book for identifying fish, and she snatched it up. Using the book, she quickly discovered what kind of fish was lying on her plate. She read eagerly, recording in her notes all of the facts she found about her fish. Others saw her and asked to use the book, too. She passed the book to other tables, and her classmates soon found descriptions of their fish. After about 15 minutes the students sat back, very pleased with themselves. Chatter died down. They waited. But the professor didn't return. As the period ended, all of the students carefully put their notes away.

The same fish on the same white plate greeted each student in the third class. The professor entered at nine o'clock. "Good morning," he said. "Please hold up your observations." All of the students held up their notes immediately. They looked at each other, smiling, as the professor walked from table to table, looking at their work. Once again, he walked toward the door. "Please . . . *observe* the fish. Write down *all* of your observations," he said. And then he left.

The students couldn't believe it. They grumbled and complained. *This guy is nuts. When is he going to teach us something? What are we paying tuition for, anyway?* Students at one table, however, began observing their fish more closely. Other tables followed their example.

The first thing all of the students noticed was the biting odor of aging fish. A few students recorded details about the fish's color that they had failed to observe in the previous two classes. They wondered if the colors had been there originally or if the colors had appeared as the fish aged. Each group measured its fish. They poked it and described its texture. One student looked in its mouth and found that he could see light through its gills. Another student found a small balance beam, and each group weighed its fish. They passed around someone's pocket knife. With it, they sliced open the fish and examined its insides. In the stomach of one fish they found a smaller fish. They wrote quickly, and their notes soon overflowed onto three and four sheets of paper. Finally someone shouted, "Hey, class was over 10 minutes ago." They carefully placed their notes in three-ring binders. They said good-bye to their fish, wondering if their finny friends would be there on Monday.

They were, and a vile smell filled the laboratory. The professor strode into the room at exactly nine o'clock. The students immediately thrust their notes in the air. "Good morning," the professor said cheerfully, making his way from student to student. He took longer than ever to examine their notes. The students shifted anxiously in their chairs as the professor edged ever closer to the door. How could they endure the smell for

another class period? At the door, the professor turned to the students.

"All right," he said. "Now we can begin."

*—Inspired by Samuel H. Scudder,
"Take This Fish and Look at It" (1874)*

Based on what you observed in this biology class, rate the professor on the scale below. Be prepared to explain your rating.

Terrible ← 1 2 3 4 5 6 7 8 9 10 → Excellent

▶ **DIVING DEEPER** If you had been in this biology lab class, what lessons about college and life would you have learned from the experience? When you think you have discovered one life lesson, dive deeper and find another, even more powerful lesson. And then another and another.

Developing a Learning Orientation to Life

 Focus Question How can you maximize your learning in college and in life?

"Uh-oh," I thought. "I am in big trouble!"

I was 18 years old at the time, but I recall that scary moment as if it were yesterday. I was about to start my first semester in college. Our entire class was on campus for orientation, and one task was to choose our first-semester classes. I was sitting with one of my new roommates exploring course descriptions. John was going down the reading list for a literature course we were considering. "I've read this book," he said, ticking the title with the tip of his pen, "and this one . . . and this one. . . . and this one . . . and this one." Like many of my classmates, John had gone to a private high school. I had gone to a public high school. John had read every book on the list. I had never even *heard* of the books on the list. That's when I thought: "Uh-oh . . . I am in big trouble!"

In that moment, I made an unconscious and unfortunate choice. I went into survival mode: *I just want to survive the next four years and graduate.* As a result, I filled my schedule with courses I thought would be easy. One course turned out to be more difficult than I thought, so I dropped it. During classes, I seldom spoke, afraid I would say something stupid. At the end of my first semester, I breathed a sigh of relief. I had passed all of my courses. My grades were much lower than they had been in high school, but I had survived. For the next seven semesters, I avoided taking classes with a professor who had a reputation of being "hard." When it came time to pick a major, I chose the one a friend told me was the easiest. My grades crept steadily upward as I got better and better at playing the grade game. After four years, I achieved my goal. I graduated. By most standards I was a success in college. But was I?

GROWTH MINDSETS AND FIXED MINDSETS

It turns out that psychologist Carol Dweck and others have studied the way I approached learning as an undergraduate. Apparently my approach is fairly common. Psychologists call it a "fixed mindset." The opposite is a "growth mindset." As I describe these mindsets, see if they sound familiar.

Learners with a **fixed mindset** believe people are born with a fixed amount of ability and talent. When it comes to intelligence, they've either got it or they don't. If they do well in school, it's because they're smart. If they don't do well in school, it's because they aren't. Dweck found that students with a fixed mindset prefer tasks they can already do well. New challenges are threatening because they fear their intelligence may not be up to the task. Thus, when they encounter a challenge, they tend to avoid it or quit as a method of self-protection. Mistakes and failures scare them because, in their mindset, such outcomes reflect poorly on their fixed level of intelligence. I've seen students complete all of the courses they need to graduate except one. That course is inevitably in the subject they fear: perhaps math, writing, or a foreign language. When students with a fixed mindset experience a challenge, setback, or failure, their inner chatter judges them (*I'm just not smart enough*) and they may give up. Does this sound like Victim behavior to you?

By contrast, learners with a **growth mindset** believe that intelligence is like a muscle—it gets stronger the more it's used. Interestingly, this mindset is consistent with what we know about how the brain learns. As mentioned in Chapter 1, the more we exercise our brains, the more neural networks are created and the "smarter" we become. A growth mindset encourages us to accept challenges, to work hard, to learn from mistakes, to change course if needed, and to keep going despite setbacks and failures. Learners in this mindset believe their hard work and persistence can overcome initial difficulties in mastering a subject or a skill. If what they are doing isn't working, their Inner Guide explains,

---

Too many students are hung up on grades and on proving their worth through grades. Grades are important, but learning is more important.

Carol Dweck

. . . a miracle is just a shift in perception.

Marianne Williamson

"I didn't work hard enough" or "There's a better way to do it," or both. They accept responsibility and they make a new plan. I trust that by now you recognize the response of a Creator.

Dweck has tested her theory about fixed and growth mindsets on students from preschool through college. One was an experiment with pre-med students at an Ivy League university. These students were taking a very challenging course in organic chemistry. The stakes were high because their grade in the course would play a big role in whether or not they got into medical school. Students with a growth mindset distinguished themselves from students with a fixed mindset in three important ways: (1) they enjoyed the course more, (2) they more effectively bounced back from setbacks such as poor test scores, and (3) their final grades were higher.

Psychologist Joshua Aronson and colleagues also tested Dweck's theory. They asked Stanford University students to be pen pals with local middle school students and help the younger students stay in school. The experimenters asked the Stanford students to tell their young pen pals things such as "Humans are capable of learning and mastering new things at any time in their lives." In other words, the Stanford students were encouraging their young pen pals to adopt a growth mindset. What the experimenters actually wanted to see was what impact expressing a growth mindset might have on the Stanford students. When later compared to a control group, the Stanford students in the experiment earned higher grades and reported more often that they enjoyed their academic work.

Dweck and others have explored what causes some people to adopt a fixed mindset while others take on the more empowering growth mindset. One explanation is that fixed mindsets result when important adults (e.g., parents or teachers) praise us for our intelligence: *You did so well in math. You're obviously very smart!* The message here is that success is the result of being smart. The problem is, now we're nervous about trying something new. After all, if we fail that means we're not smart enough . . . and we believe there's no way to get more "smarts." By contrast, a growth mindset is more likely to develop when important adults praise us for our effort (rather than our intelligence): *You did so well in math. You're obviously a hard worker!* The message here is that success is the result of effort. Armed with this belief, we're more likely to respond positively to future challenges because we're confident we can work harder if the outcome or experience is worth it.

Like other mindsets, fixed and growth mindsets seem to be shaped by deep-culture beliefs. For example, Japanese and Chinese parents are more likely to attribute success to a strong effort (growth mindset). They believe that all students can learn if they work hard enough. By contrast, North American parents are more likely to attribute success to inborn intelligence or ability (fixed mindset). This cultural belief shows up in the American educational system where "gifted" students are given enriched academic programs.

If you've developed a growth mindset, you have a core belief that will help you achieve success in college and beyond. However, if you realize you've developed a fixed mindset, you aren't stuck with it. You can revise your mindset.

> The purpose of learning is growth, and our minds, unlike our bodies, can continue growing as we continue to live.
>
> *Mortimer Adler*

> If there is no dark and dogged will, there will be no shining accomplishment; if there is no dull and determined effort, there will be no brilliant achievement.
>
> *Chinese proverb*

HOW TO DEVELOP A GROWTH MINDSET

Here are four ways to develop or strengthen a growth mindset.

Think of your brain as a muscle: Like a muscle, the more you use your brain, the "smarter" and more capable it becomes. The technical term is neuroplasticity. *Neuroplasticity* is the ability of your brain to use new experiences to revise old neural networks and create new ones. This is how learning happens. Once you understand this concept, you'll realize that—with mental effort—your brain is designed to grow and change. The idea that each human brain has a fixed capacity belongs on the scrapheap of faulty beliefs along with "the world is flat." Just because you may be challenged to learn something today doesn't mean that you can't learn it. Because of your brain's neuroplasticity, effort and persistence combined with effective study strategies are the keys to effective learning. For more information about this concept, revisit "Becoming an Active Learner" in Chapter 1.

> It's never too late to change your mindset. Mindsets are beliefs—powerful ones and ones that shape our motivation—but beliefs can be changed.
>
> *Carol Dweck*

Set learning goals . . . as well as performance goals: When I was an undergraduate, I set performance goals. My main goal was to see my grade point average improve every semester. I achieved that goal every semester, but I paid a price. To assure success, I played it safe, wasting many learning opportunities. I avoided courses that might have introduced me to a whole new world. I steered clear of "hard" professors who might have become mentors or guides. By studying only to get grades, I learned just enough to pass tests. Sure, I got a degree and, with it, a ticket into the world of employment . . . but at what cost? Don't misunderstand, there's nothing wrong with setting a goal to get good grades. Obviously, good grades are the means to many future goals, such as a job or graduate school. But there is something wrong if our *only* goal is to earn a grade. Such a goal limits our potential. It keeps us from developing knowledge, skills, and wisdom that could help us create a richer, more personally fulfilling life. The solution is to combine both kinds of goals. *Performance goals* provide you with measurable accomplishments (like grades), whereas *learning goals* offer knowledge and skills you can use for the rest of your life.

> We now accept the fact that learning is a lifelong process of keeping abreast of change. And the most pressing task is to teach people how to learn.
>
> *Peter Drucker*

So, what would a learning goal look like? Suppose you're taking a writing class. A performance goal would be to earn an A in the course. A *learning* goal would be to master three ways to write an effective introductory paragraph. Suppose you want to lose weight. A performance goal would be to weigh 150 pounds by June 30. A learning goal would be to learn three important principles of good nutrition. Suppose you're taking an organic chemistry course. A *performance* goal would be to finish reading your text book by December 1. A *learning* goal would be to learn the discipline to read challenging content for at least 20 minutes without losing focus. Notice that performance goals usually give us a defined (often measurable) outcome. By contrast, learning goals help us grow, giving us skills and abilities we can use to achieve future performance goals. Whereas my *performance* goal might be to achieve x, my *learning goal* might be to learn five strategies to help me do x. Those same five strategies may also help me to achieve other goals for the rest of my life. Take a look back to the goals you set in Journal Entry 10 and see what kind of goals you created there. If they are mostly performance goals, consider adding a couple of learning goals.

Seek feedback: Feedback is essential to learning. Luckily, life offers us helpful feedback every day. Sadly, many ignore it . . . especially those with a fixed mindset. At first, feedback taps us politely on the shoulder. If we pay no attention, feedback shakes us vigorously. If we continue to ignore it, feedback may knock us to our knees, creating havoc in our lives. This havoc might be failing out of school or getting fired from a job. There's usually plenty of feedback long before the failure or firing if we will only heed its message. Your Inner Defender may see feedback as a threat, but your Inner Guide knows it is vital for success.

> Once you embrace unpleasant news, not as a negative but as evidence of a need for change, you aren't defeated by it. You're learning from it.
>
> *Bill Gates*

In college, think of yourself as an airplane pilot and your instructors as your personal air traffic controllers. When they correct you in class or write a comment on an assignment or give you a grade on a test, what they are really saying is, *You're on course, on course . . . whoops, now you're off course, off course . . . okay, that's right, now you're back on course.* Airplane pilots appreciate such feedback. Without it they might not get to their destination. They might even crash. Likewise, effective learners welcome their instructors' feedback and use it to stay on course. They heed every suggestion that instructors offer on assignments; they understand the message in their test scores; they request clarification of any feedback they don't understand; and they ask for additional feedback. Maybe the idea of paying attention to feedback sounds obvious to you, but I can't tell you how many students I've known who made the same mistakes over and over, ignoring both my feedback and the reality that when you keep doing what you've been doing, you'll keep getting what you've been getting.

Everywhere in life, heeding feedback is vital to creating the life you want. The feedback may be something said by friends, lovers, spouses, parents, children, neighbors, bosses, coworkers, and even strangers. Or it may be more subtle, coming in the form of an unsatisfying relationship, a boring job, blackouts from drinking too much, or runaway credit card debt. Any areas of discomfort or distress are red flags of warning: *Hey, wake up! You're headed away from your desired outcomes and experiences. You're off course!* And that awareness leads to a fourth way for developing a growth mindset.

> All human beings are periodically tested by the power of the universe . . . how one performs under pressure is the true measure of one's spirit, heart, and desire.
>
> *Spike Lee*

Change course when needed: It's one thing to realize you are off course. It's quite another to do something about it. Course correction takes courage. You need to admit that what you are doing isn't working, seek alternatives, abandon the familiar, and to walk into the unknown. Victims stay stuck. Creators learn, change, and grow.

One of my off-course students was feeling overwhelmed by all she had to do, and then she made a course correction, changing the way she tackled large projects. In her journal she wrote, "When I break a huge task into chunks and do a little bit every day, I can accomplish great things."

Another off-course student discovered he was an expert at blaming his failures in college on other people: his boss, his teachers, his parents, his girlfriend. He decided to change and hold himself more responsible. He learned, "In the past I have spent more energy on getting people to feel sorry for me than I have on accomplishing something worthwhile."

A third off-course student was filled with hate for her father, who she felt had abandoned her, and then she decided to change. She forgave him and moved on with her life. She wrote, "Spending all of my time hating someone leaves me little time to love myself."

A fourth off-course student realized how little effort and care he put into everything he did, including his college assignments. He discovered, "I'm always looking for ways to cut corners, to get out of doing what's necessary. It doesn't work. I have to do my best in order to be successful."

And one more off-course student realized that the only goal he'd ever set in school was to get good grades. As a graduate student, he discovered, "When I focus on learning, my grades take care of themselves. Better yet, I learn things I can use to improve the quality of my life!" He regretted all of the learning he had missed out on, but he got excited by all there still is to learn. He started taking courses that excited him. He found new ways to apply what he was learning and created a whole new life for himself. He was grateful that he had given himself the gift of a major course correction, one that changed his outcomes and experiences. In case you haven't guessed, I was this off-course student.

We seldom move toward our goals and dreams in a straight line. With constant course corrections, however, we improve our chances of getting there eventually. And along the way, the University of Life offers us exactly the lessons we need to develop our full potential. We only have to listen, learn, change, and grow.

> The capacity to correct course is the capacity to reduce the differences between the path you are on now and the optimal path to your objective. . . .
>
> *Charles Garfield*

> To me, earth is a school. I view life as my classroom. My approach to the experiences I have every day is that I am a student, and that all my experiences have something they can teach me. I am always asking myself, "What learning is available for me now?"
>
> *Mary Hulnick, vice-president,*
> *University of Santa Monica*

 Journal Entry 25

In this activity, you will explore course corrections you have made or you need to make to improve your outcomes and experiences.

Make a choice: Write about one of the following:

A. **Describe an important course correction you have made in the past.** Explain how you became aware that you were off course, what you did to change course, and how your efforts turned out. Most important, what did you learn from this experience?

B. **Identify where you are presently off course and offer a plan for making a course correction.** Explain an aspect of your life (e.g., college, social life, finances, spirituality) that is off course. Describe the feedback you received—from inside or outside of you—informing you that you're off course. What will you do differently to get on course? Most important, what lesson do you think the University of Life wants you to learn from this situation?

If we don't change direction soon, we'll end up where we're going.

Professor Irwin Corey

One Student's Story

JESSIE MAGGARD
Urbana University, Ohio

The first friends I made in college were my teammates on the soccer team. After practice we started riding around, shopping, and going to parties. We almost never talked about school or personal problems. To them, play time was more important. I wasn't getting much sleep and I was exhausted all the time. I didn't feel like studying and when I went to class, I wasn't learning much. Then a couple of things happened that shook me up. First, my English teacher handed back a paper and told me it wasn't very good. I thought all day about what she said and it really bothered me. I'm the first person in my family to go to college, and I started worrying about whether I was going to make it. If I was doing poorly in a class that I thought was easy, what would happen in more difficult classes? Second, I learned that my parents were getting divorced.

I tried talking about my feelings with some of my teammates, but they just listened and didn't say anything. I might as well have been talking to a wall, and I realized they weren't really interested in my problems.

The *On Course* book talks about how easy it is to get off course even when you want to be successful. That is so true. By the time soccer season ended, I was *way* off course and I knew I had to make some serious changes. At first I spent more time by myself. I wrote out a schedule and started to get more organized. Then I slowly began spending more time with people in my dorm, and over time I developed friendships with six amazing people who have really touched me. Doing well in school is important to them, too. We started studying together, and my grades began to improve. I even got comments from my teachers

about how I had changed. Still, I felt weighed down by my parents' divorce and it was a huge distraction from my schoolwork. One of my new friends had gone through her parents' divorce, and she gave me tips on how she had gotten through it. She encouraged me to sit down with my parents and talk about my feelings. I did, and it helped so much to talk with them and understand why they had fallen out of love with each other.

Through all of this, I've learned that when you get off course, you have to do something different. My soccer friends had different goals. I'm not trying to put them down. Their goals weren't bad, they just weren't my goals. My goal is to get my degree and teach kindergarten, and when I was hanging out with my soccer friends, I was headed in the wrong direction. I totally changed my peer group, and now I am back on course. I know I'm the only person who can change my life. I just need the courage to stand up for myself. At the time, changing seemed so difficult, but now in the big picture, it seems so easy.

Photo: Courtesy of Jessie Maggard

Discovering Your Preferred Ways of Learning

FOCUS QUESTIONS   What is your preferred way of learning? What can you do when your instructor doesn't teach the way you prefer to learn?

Today, we're well into the information age. That means staying on course to our goals and dreams requires learning vast amounts of information, facts, theories, and skills. Once you master the CORE Learning System introduced in Chapter 1, all that learning should be easy, right? Not quite.

You see, in addition to learning approaches that are common to us all, each of us has our own preferred learning experiences. Each of us has our own favored ways of taking in and deeply processing our learning experiences. Each of us has our own preferred ways of creating meaning from the rush and jumble of information we encounter in college, at work, at home, and everywhere else in life. Knowing how *you* prefer to learn gives you a great advantage everywhere in life, but especially in college when you get an instructor who doesn't teach the way you prefer to learn.

> It is very natural to teach in the same way we learn. It may be difficult for us to believe that others could learn in a way that is foreign and difficult for us.
>
> *Carolyn Mamchur*

SELF-ASSESSMENT: HOW I PREFER TO LEARN

Before reading on, take the following self-assessment inventory. It will give you insights about how you prefer to gather and process information.

LEARNING PREFERENCE INVENTORY

In each group below, rank all four answers (A, B, C, D) from the least true of you to the most true of you. Give each possible answer a different score. There are no right or wrong answers; your opinion is all that matters. Remember, items that are MOST TRUE OF YOU get a 4. You can also take this self-assessment online by accessing the CourseMate for *On Course* at www.cengagebrain.com.

Least true of you   ← 1 2 3 4 →   **Most true of you**

1. I would prefer to take a college course
   _____ A. in science.
   _____ B. in business management.
   _____ C. in group dynamics.
   _____ D. as an independent study that I design.

2. I solve problems by
   _____ A. standing back, thinking, and analyzing what is wrong.
   _____ B. doing something practical and seeing how it works.
   _____ C. leaping in and doing what feels right at the time.
   _____ D. trusting my intuition.

3. Career groups that appeal to me are
   _____ A. engineer, researcher, financial planner.
   _____ B. administrator, city manager, military officer.
   _____ C. teacher, social worker, physical therapist.
   _____ D. entrepreneur, artist, inventor.

4. Before I make a decision, I need to be sure that
   _____ A. I understand all of the relevant ideas and facts.
   _____ B. I'm confident my solution will work.
   _____ C. I know how my decision will affect others.
   _____ D. I haven't overlooked a more creative solution.

5. I believe that
   _____ A. life today needs more logical thinking and less emotion.
   _____ B. life rewards the practical, hard-working, down-to-earth person.
   _____ C. life must be lived with enthusiasm and passion.
   _____ D. life, like music, is best composed by creative inspiration, not by rules.

6. I would enjoy reading a book titled
   _____ A. *Great Theories and Ideas of the Twentieth Century.*
   _____ B. *How to Organize Your Life and Accomplish More.*
   _____ C. *The Keys to Developing Better Relationships.*
   _____ D. *Tapping into Your Creative Genius.*

7. I believe the most valuable information for making decisions comes from
   _____ A. logical analysis of facts.
   _____ B. what has worked in the past.
   _____ C. gut feelings.
   _____ D. my imagination.

8. I am persuaded by an argument that
   _____ A. offers statistical or factual proof.
   _____ B. presents the findings of recognized experts.
   _____ C. is passionately presented by someone I admire.
   _____ D. explores innovative possibilities for future change.

9. I prefer a teacher who
   _____ A. lectures knowledgeably about the important facts and theories of the subject.
   _____ B. provides practical, step-by-step, hands-on activities with clear learning objectives.
   _____ C. stimulates exciting class discussions and group projects.
   _____ D. challenges me to think for myself and explore the subject in my own way.

10. People who know me would describe me as

_____ A. logical.

_____ B. practical.

_____ C. emotional.

_____ D. creative.

Total your 10 scores for each letter and record them below:

_____ A. THINKING   _____ C. FEELING

_____ B. DOING   _____ D. INNOVATING

Your scores suggest the following:

30–40   **You have a strong preference to learn this way.**

20–29   **You are capable of learning this way when necessary.**

10–19   **You avoid this way of learning.**

Each of us develops preferred ways of learning. These preferred ways of learning are more pleasurable, require less effort, and usually produce more successful learning than a less preferred learning experience. For a quick understanding of learning preferences, recall the last time you learned a new video game or assembled something with a number of parts. Some people prefer to start playing or assembling immediately. They dive right in. Other people prefer to read the directions first. Only after they digest the written information do they start playing or assembling. Notice that you could approach these learning tasks either way, but you *prefer* one learning experience over the other.

Although there is no preferred way for everyone to learn, there is a preferred way or ways for *you* to learn. Your scores on the self-assessment indicate your order of preference for four different learning approaches: THINKING, DOING, FEELING, and INNOVATING. More specifically, your scores suggest what types of questions motivate you, how you prefer to gather relevant information, and how you prefer to process information to discover meaningful answers.

Traditional college teaching is characterized by lectures and textbook assignments. These learning experiences typically favor the learning preference of Thinkers, and, to a somewhat lesser degree, Doers. However, as more instructors discover the importance of learning preferences, many are adapting their teaching methods to help all learners maximize their academic potential.

> Knowledge of our brain dominance empowers us as individuals and groups to achieve more of our full potential.
>
> *Ned Herrmann*

As you might guess, you're bound to get instructors whose teaching methods don't match your learning preference(s). When you do, experiment with some of the suggestions that follow. Perhaps most important of all, develop flexibility in how you learn. The more choices you have, the richer your learning experience will be and the greater your success.

In the table on pages 228–229, you'll discover how Thinkers, Doers, Feelers, and Innovators prefer to learn. You may want to start by reading the section about your own learning preference(s), based on your self-assessment score. There you'll find options to use when your instructors don't teach as you prefer to learn. By looking at the other learning preferences as well, you'll see additional ways to expand your menu of effective learning strategies. Your goal here is to find deep-processing strategies that are compatible with and supportive of your preferred way(s) of learning as well as to expand your ability to learn in many ways.

Highly effective learners realize that not all instructors will create the kind of learning experiences they prefer. They take responsibility for not only *what* they learn but also *how* they learn it. They are confident that, with smart studying and persistence, their brains are up to the task. They discover deep-processing methods that maximize their learning, regardless of the subject or the way the instructor teaches.

Education is our passport to the future, for tomorrow belongs to the people who prepare for it today. . . . Give your brain as much attention as you do your hair and you'll be a thousand times better off.

Malcolm X

	Thinking Learners	Doing Learners	Feeling Learners	Inn...
Motivating questions that energize	**"What?" questions** *What theory supports that claim?* *What does a statistical analysis show?* *What is the logic here?* *What facts do you have?* *What experts have written about this?*	**"How?" questions** *How does this work?* *How can I use this?* *How will this help me or others?* *How did this work in the past?* *How can I do this more efficiently?* *How do experts do this?*	**"Why?" or "Who?" questions** *Why do I want or need to know this subject?* *Who is going to teach me?* *Who is going to learn this with me?* *Why do they want to know this information?* *Who here cares about me?* *Whom here do I care about?*	
Preferred ways of gathering information	• enjoy pondering facts and theories • learn well from instructors who present information with lectures, visual aids, PowerPoint slides, instructor-modeled problem solving, textbook readings, independent library research, and activities that call upon logical skills, such as debates • benefit from time to reflect on what they are learning	• enjoy taking action • learn well from instructors who present factual information in a step-by-step, logical manner; who present models or examples from experts in the field; and who allow students to do hands-on work in guided labs or practice applications • benefit from the opportunity to dive right in and do the work	• enjoy personal connections and an emotionally supportive environment • learn well from instructors who are warm and caring; who value feelings as well as thoughts; and who create a safe, accepting classroom atmosphere with activities such as group work, role-playing, and sharing of individual experiences • benefit from an opportunity to relate personally with both their instructors and classmates	• enjoy imagining possibilities and making unexpected connections • learn well from instructors who encourage students to discover new and innovative applications; who allow students to use their intuition to create something new; and who use approaches such as independent projects, flexible rules and deadlines, a menu of optional assignments, metaphors, art projects, and visual aids • benefit from the freedom to work independently and let their imaginations run free
Preferred ways of processing information	• respect logical argument supported by documented facts and data • are uncomfortable with answers that depend on tradition, emotion, personal considerations, or intuition • excel at analyzing, dissecting, figuring out, and using logic to arrive at reasoned answers • like well-organized and well-documented information • benefit from deep-processing strategies that bring order to complex information, such as creating outlines or comparison charts	• honor objective testing of an idea or theory, whether their own or an expert's • are uncomfortable with answers based on abstract theories, emotion, personal considerations, or intuition • excel at being unbiased, taking action and observing outcomes, following procedures, and using confirmed facts to arrive at reasoned answers • appreciate well-organized and well-documented information • benefit from deep-processing strategies that bring order to complex information, such as creating flow charts or a model of the concepts to be learned	• honor their emotions and seek answers that are personally meaningful • are uncomfortable with answers based on abstract theories or dispassionate facts and data • excel at responding to emotional currents in groups, empathizing with others, considering others' feelings in making decisions, and using empathy and gut feelings to arrive at personally relevant answers	• honor personal imagination and intuition • are uncomfortable with answers based on abstract theories, cold facts, hard data, emotion, or personal considerations • excel at trusting their inner vision, their intuitive sense of novel and exciting possibilities, and their imaginations

	Thinking Learners	Doing Learners	Feeling Learners	Innovating Learners
When your instructor doesn't teach to your preferred style *What you can do:*	• Construct important "What?" questions and search for their answers in class sessions and homework assignments. • Construct and answer other types of questions your instructor might ask: What? Who? Why? What if? • Read all of your textbook assignments carefully, creating well-organized notes that identify the key points. • Resist getting upset if your instructor asks you to work in groups or has students do some of the teaching. • Organize your lecture and reading notes in a logical fashion, using outlines and comparison charts wherever appropriate. • Study with classmates who have different preferred ways of learning from your own, as they may provide insights about how to learn best from your instructor's teaching style.	• Construct important "How?" questions and search for their answers. • Construct and answer other types of questions your instructor might ask: What? Who? Why? What if? • Practice using the course information or skills outside of class. • Find someone who uses the course information or skills in his or her work and shadow that person for a day or more. • Resist getting upset if your instructor seems more interested in theories than in application. • Organize your lecture and reading notes in a step-by-step fashion, using outlines and comparison charts wherever appropriate. • Study with classmates who have preferred ways of learning different from your own, as they may provide insights into how to learn best from your instructor's teaching style.	• Construct important "Who?" and "Why?" questions and search for their answers. • Construct and answer other types of questions your instructor might ask: What? How? What if? • Discover the value of this subject for you personally. • Organize your notes and study materials using concept maps. • Resist feeling upset if your instructor seems distant or aloof. • Practice using the course information or skill with people in your life. • Make friends with classmates and discuss the subject with them outside of class. • Record class sessions (with permission) and listen to the recordings during free time. • Study with classmates who have different preferred ways of learning from your own, as they may provide insights into how to learn best from your instructor's teaching style. • Teach what you are learning to someone else.	• Construct important "What if?" and "What else?" questions and search for their answers. • Construct and answer other types of questions your instructor might ask: What? How? Who? Why? • Resist feeling upset when your instructor or classmates don't immediately see something as you do. • Organize your notes and study materials using concept maps and personally meaningful symbols or pictures. • Think about the content creatively (how could I adapt this?) and metaphorically (what is this like?). • Study with classmates who have different preferred ways of learning from your own, as they may provide insights into how to learn best from your instructor's teaching style.
Ask your instructor to do the following:	• Answer your important "What?" questions in class or in a conference. • List important points on the board or on handouts. • Provide handouts of PowerPoint presentations. • Allow students time to answer discussion questions in writing before answering them aloud. • Suggest additional readings, especially those written by recognized authorities in the subject. • Provide examples of past test questions. • Demonstrate the step-by-step solution of a math or science problem. • Provide data or other objective evidence that supports theories presented.	• Answer your important "How?" questions in class or in a conference. • Explain practical applications for theories taught in the course. • Provide a visual model of the concept (such as the Scripts Model in Chapter 6). • List important steps on the board or on handouts. • Demonstrate the information or skill in a step-by-step manner. • Invite guest speakers who can explain real-world application of the course information or skill in their daily work. • Observe and give corrective feedback as you demonstrate your hands-on understanding of the subject.	• Answer your important "Who?" and "Why?" questions in class or in a conference. • Explain how you might make a personal application of the course information. • Meet with your instructor outside of class, perhaps for tutoring, so you can get to know one another better and feel more comfortable in the class. • Provide occasional opportunities for small-group activities within the classroom. • Tell stories about how he or she (or someone else) has personally used the information or skills taught in the course. • Let you do some of the course assignments with a partner or in a group. • Allow students time to talk in pairs about discussion questions before answering them in front of the whole class.	• Answer your important "What if?" and "What else?" questions in class or in a conference. • Allow you to design some of your own assignments for the course. • Use visual aids to explain concepts in class. • Recommend a book for you to read by the most innovative or rebellious thinker in the field. • Evaluate your learning with essays and independent projects rather than with objective tests.

Journal Entry 26

In this activity, you'll apply what you have learned about your preferred ways of learning to improve your results in a challenging course.

1. **Write about the most challenging course you are taking this semester.** Using what you just learned about how you prefer to learn, explain why the course may be difficult for you: Consider the subject matter, the teaching methods of the instructor, the textbook, and any other factors that may contribute to making this course difficult for someone with your preferred ways of learning. (If you are not taking a challenging course this semester, write about the most challenging course you have taken at any time in your education.)

2. **Using what you now know about the way you prefer to learn, write about choices you can make that will help you learn this challenging subject more easily.** Refer to pages 228–229 for possible choices.

By choosing different ways of learning in a challenging course, you can avoid the excusing, blaming, and complaining of a Victim and apply the solution-oriented approach of a Creator.

Young cat, if you keep your eyes open enough, oh, the stuff you would learn! The most wonderful stuff!

Dr. Seuss

One Student's Story

MELISSA THOMPSON
Madison Area Technical College, Wisconsin

The challenge for me was chemistry. In lecture, the words were coming at me but the material wasn't sticking. The teacher was dry, standoffish, and intimidating, and he never joked around. I could read the book, reread it, and still wonder what I had just read. I was so frustrated because I needed to pass chemistry to get into my major. Realizing this, I was spending 10 to 12 hours a week studying, and I even started a study group and got a tutor. With all this help, I was doing fine on the assignments, but the tests were killing me. I would

take one look at them and my mind would go blank. I was stressed and so tempted to drop the course.

About that time I took the self-assessment in *On Course* about how I prefer to learn. I scored highest as a *feeling* learner, with *doing* learner second. I learned it's important for me to relate well personally with my instructors and classmates. Also, I want to see and touch what I'm learning, and I'm not comfortable with abstract theories and dispassionate facts. BINGO! The light went on. My favorite subjects in high school were classes like art and English where I

could be creative and hands-on. My favorite teacher was my art teacher, a kind, caring person who told lots of stories that related art to lessons in life. Now I'm in chemistry, which is exactly the type of subject I'm uncomfortable with, and I have a professor who is distant and intimidating. I knew what I had to do, and I probably wouldn't have done it before taking my College Success class.

I asked my chemistry instructor if I could stay after class to talk with him. I explained what I had discovered about my learning preference and why I was so challenged by chemistry. He agreed to meet with me after every class. During lecture, I'd write questions in the margins of my notes or leave a space wherever I got lost. I'd also highlight things in my book that I didn't understand. Going over my questions with him after class was helpful because everything was fresh in my mind. He would take my questions and answer them in different ways than he had in class. Then I would tell him what I thought he was saying and he would coach me until I had it right. Once I got to know him, I realized he was actually very friendly and helpful. He's a quiet person, but I could tell how much he loves chemistry. Before, when I walked into class, I felt intimidated, but before long I felt more comfortable.

Soon after these meetings started, my grades began to come up. I was retaining the information and it showed. I worked hard, and in the end I did pass chemistry. If I hadn't found out about my learning preference and done something different, I don't think I would have passed. My professor is definitely a "thinker," and he handles things so differently than I do. Once I understood the situation, though, I knew I had to step up and be in control of my life, and I did.

Employing Critical Thinking

 Focus Questions   How can you determine the truth in this complex and confusing world? How can you present your truths in a way that is logical and persuasive to others?

Imagine this: While deciding what classes to take next semester, you decide to register for Psychology 101. After checking the various times it will be offered, you're delighted to discover that one section of the course fits perfectly into your schedule. The instructor is Professor Skinner. Because two of your friends are taking the course with Professor Skinner this semester, you wisely ask for their opinions.

One friend says, "Dr. Skinner is terrible. Don't even think about taking his course!" But your second friend says, "Dr. Skinner is the best instructor I've ever had! You should definitely take his class." Darn. Now what do you do?

Before deciding, you'd be smart to apply some critical thinking. The term "critical" derives from the Greek word *kritikos,* which means having the ability to understand or decide by using sound judgment. Critical thinking helps us better understand our complex world, make wise choices, and create more of our desired outcomes and experiences. Because they know the importance of critical thinking in many realms of life, most college educators place it high on the list of skills they want their students to master.

Here's good news. You've already been using a powerful critical thinking skill—the Wise Choice Process. As you've experienced, thoughtfully answering the six questions of the Wise Choice Process guides you through the steps of identifying options, looking at likely outcomes, and choosing the best option(s) available at the time. Making wise choices, then, is a key use of critical thinking.

In addition, critical thinking helps in another important realm: constructing and analyzing persuasive arguments. Think of the countless times others have tried to persuade you to think or do something: *Mathematics is a fascinating subject* (think this), *Let me copy your chemistry notes* (do that), *Global warming*

> Higher-order thinking, critical thinking abilities, are increasingly crucial to success in every domain of personal and professional life.
>
> *Richard Paul*

is a huge threat (think this), *Major in accounting* (do that), *My roommate is so inconsiderate* (think this), *Go to graduate school* (do that). And, of course, you're doing the same to them. Think this . . . do that.

Thus, much of life is a mental tug-of-war. Efforts to influence others' thoughts and actions lie at the heart of most human interaction, from conversations to wars. Think this . . . do that. It's no wonder the quality of your life is so greatly affected by your ability to construct and analyze persuasive arguments. You can even use these skills to decide whether or not to register for Professor Skinner's Psychology 101 class.

CONSTRUCTING LOGICAL ARGUMENTS

At many colleges, entire courses, even majors, are devoted to the study of argumentation. Here, we'll focus on two skills that are essential to the construction and analysis of persuasive arguments. The first skill is the ability to **construct a *logical argument***. Three components of a logical argument are (1) reasons, (2) evidence, and (3) conclusions. As the building blocks of a logical argument, these ingredients may be offered in any order. Suppose, for example, someone wants to convince you to participate in your college's Sophomore Year Abroad Program. Here's how she might present her argument: *You should apply for our college's Sophomore Year Abroad Program. It'll change your life. I read an article in our college newspaper about the Sophomore Year Abroad Program. The author surveyed students who have completed the program, and 80 percent rated their experience as "life changing."*

Here's what this argument looks like when organized by its components:

1. REASONS (also called *premises, claims,* or *assumptions*) answer the question "Why?" Reasons explain why the audience should think or do something. Reasons are presented as true, but they may not be.	**WHY?** *The Sophomore Year Abroad Program will change your life.*
2. EVIDENCE (also called *support*) answers the question "How do you know?" Evidence provides support to explain how the persuader knows the reason(s) to be true. Evidence should be verifiable as true. Three common kinds of evidence are facts, data, and stories.	**HOW DO I KNOW?** *I read an article in our college newspaper about the Sophomore Year Abroad Program. The author surveyed students who have completed the program, and 80 percent rated their experience as "life changing."*
3. CONCLUSIONS (also called *opinions, beliefs,* or *positions*) answer the question "What?" Conclusions state what the persuader wants the audience to think or do.	**WHAT SHOULD YOU THINK OR DO?** *You should apply for our college's Sophomore Year Abroad Program.*

ASKING PROBING QUESTIONS

Essential to analyzing a logical argument is a second critical thinking skill: **asking probing questions**. A probing question exposes conclusions built on unsound reasons, flawed evidence, and faulty logic. Probing questions are the kind that a good lawyer, doctor, educator, parent, detective, lover, shopper, or

---

Intelligence is something we are born with. Thinking is a skill that must be learned.

Edward de Bono

The problem with many youngsters today is not that they don't have opinions but that they don't have the facts on which to base their opinions.

Albert Shanker

friend asks to expose a hidden truth. The following chart lists some of the questions that critical thinkers might ask of any persuasive argument. Asking and answering these questions (and others) can help you both construct powerful arguments of your own and analyze the arguments of others.

Questions About Reasons	Sample Probing Questions
• What reasons have been offered to support the conclusion?	• When your brother studied for a year in Australia, was the experience life changing for him?
• Based on your experience and knowledge, do the reasons make sense?	• What did the students mentioned in the newspaper article mean by "life changing"?
• Did the reasons derive from careful reflection and logical thinking, or are they misguided beliefs or prejudices?	• Does it seem likely that such a program would change my life?
• Are there important exceptions to the reason?	• Do I even want to change my life?
• Are the definitions of all key terms clear?	
• Are strong emotions being substituted for reasons?	

Questions About Evidence	Sample Probing Questions
• Is the source of the evidence reliable?	• Could the group of students polled have been specially selected to support the author's point of view about the Sophomore Year Abroad Program?
• Is the evidence true?	
• Is the evidence objective and unbiased?	• Does the person persuading me stand to gain if I choose to participate in the program?
• Is the evidence relevant?	
• Is the evidence current?	• Were enough students polled to make their results significant?
• Is there enough evidence?	
• Does contradictory evidence exist?	• What percent of students from all previous Sophomore Year Abroad groups rated the experience as "life changing"?
• Is the evidence complete?	

Questions About Conclusions	Sample Probing Questions
• Why?	• Could there be another cause for the students' life-changing experiences besides the Sophomore Year Abroad Program?
• Is the conclusion logical, or are there errors in the reasoning?	
• Could a different conclusion be drawn from the same reasons and/or evidence?	• Did the students who rated their experience as "life changing" have anything else in common that might have been the cause of their life-changing outcome instead of the program?
	• Is the program today the same program that changed the lives of students in the survey?

> Always the beautiful answer who asks a more beautiful question.
>
> *e.e. cummings*

> The real value of learning lies in answering questions and questioning answers.
>
> *Marty Grothe*

APPLYING CRITICAL THINKING

Let's observe these critical thinking skills in action. Listen in as two students debate their conclusions about the biology professor described in "A Fish Story" (the case study that opens this chapter). Note how they explain the reasons and evidence that lead them to their conclusions. And watch as each uses probing questions to challenge the argument of the other.

> **Emiko:** I rated the biology professor as "terrible." I'd hate to have him as my instructor. **[Conclusion]**
>
> **Frank:** Why? **[Probing question]**
>
> **Emiko:** Are you kidding? College instructors are called "professors" for a reason. They're paid to "profess," and to profess means to *tell*. Professors are supposed to be the experts, so their job is to *tell* students what they need to know. **[Reason]**
>
> **Frank:** Of course college instructors need to be experts in their subject. But is it really their job to tell students what they need to know? **[Probing question]** I think an instructor's job is to help students learn to think for themselves, not just memorize facts. **[Reason]** I'd love to have an instructor like that. I rated him as "excellent." **[Conclusion]**
>
> **Emiko:** In the whole first week of the class, all he did was give his students a fish and then leave the room. **[Evidence]** Don't you think an instructor has a responsibility to at least be in the room? **[Probing question]**
>
> **Frank:** The issue isn't whether the instructor was in the room. The issue is whether he was helping students learn. **[Reason]** The biology instructor did a lot more than give his students a fish and leave the room. He asked students to observe the fish and write down everything they observed. That request got them actively engaged in thinking like biologists on the first day of the course. **[Evidence]** In my opinion, that makes him an excellent instructor. **[Conclusion]**
>
> **Emiko:** If a professor wants to get students actively engaged in their education, that's fine. But an instructor shouldn't frustrate and make students anxious on their very first day in college. Good instructors make their students feel comfortable. **[Reason]** Look at how anxious they were while waiting for the professor to return. They had no clue what was going on. **[Evidence]** That's why I think this instructor is terrible. **[Conclusion]**
>
> **Frank:** Maybe the students were a bit anxious, but isn't that a good thing? **[Probing question]** Sometimes we need to be a little uncomfortable to learn something. **[Reason]** The best teacher I ever had in high school made everyone in the class uncomfortable by firing questions at us as fast as she could, especially at people who weren't paying attention or hadn't done the homework. I learned more in that

The abilities you develop as a critical thinker are designed to help you think your way through all of life's situations.

John Chaffee

class than in all my other high school classes combined. **[Evidence]** I would rather get a C from a professor who makes me think than get an A from a professor who simply feeds me answers to put on a test. **[Reason]**

Emiko: You wouldn't think that way if you wanted to be a doctor like I do. If I get a couple of C's, I can pretty much forget about getting into a good medical school. **[Reason]** That's why I would avoid this professor like the plague. He's terrible! **[Conclusion]**

Although their arguments aren't air tight, these students deserve credit for using critical thinking skills. They are clearly making an effort to provide reasons and evidence to support their conclusions. Additionally, they're asking probing questions about each other's reasons, evidence, and conclusions. Like all critical thinkers, they are respectful skeptics.

To some, it may appear that the purpose of critical thinking is to win arguments. Although critical thinking can certainly do that, it actually has a loftier goal. Critical thinking helps us find the truth. That's why, to be an effective critical thinker, you must be willing to abandon your position whenever you find another view that is a better explanation of reality. The ultimate goal of a critical thinker is not victory, then, but learning.

> I had learned at twenty-one that you couldn't just say a thing is so because it might not be so, and somebody brighter, smarter, and more thoughtful would come out and tell you it wasn't so. Then if you still thought it was, you had to prove it. Well, that was a new thing for me. I cannot, I really cannot describe what that did to my insides and to my head. I thought: I'm being educated finally.
>
> *Barbara Jordan*

Journal Entry 27

1. **Return to the beginning of this section where you were asked to imagine getting contradictory opinions about Dr. Skinner, the Psychology 101 instructor. Make a list of at least 10 probing questions you could ask your two friends to help you find the "truth" and make a wise choice about whether or not to take Dr. Skinner's class.** Your questions should probe their reasons, their evidence, and their conclusions. Among others, consider asking questions that use your knowledge of learning preferences.

2. **Write a logical argument that explains which character you think is most responsible for the group's grade of D in the case study "Professor Roger's Trial"** (found at the beginning of Chapter 5). Be sure to state clearly your conclusion (who is most responsible), your reasons for this conclusion, and evidence from the case study to support your reasons. For example, your journal might begin, *I think the person most responsible for the group's grade of D is . . . The first reason I think this is . . . The evidence in the case study shows that . . . A second reason I think this person is most responsible is . . .* and so on.

> Education's purpose is to replace an empty mind with an open one.
>
> *Malcolm S. Forbes*

Lifelong Learning
AT WORK

The intellectual equipment needed for the job of the future is an ability to define problems, quickly assimilate relevant data, conceptualize and reorganize the information, make deductive and inductive leaps with it, ask hard questions about it, discuss findings with colleagues, work collaboratively to find solutions and then convince others.

Robert B. Reich,
former U.S. Secretary
of Labor

Some students believe that once they graduate from college they'll finally be finished with studying and learning. In fact, a college diploma is merely a ticket into the huge University of Work. In one year recently, U.S. employers spent more than 55 billion dollars for employee training, according to the American Society for Training and Development.

Continuing education in the workplace includes instruction in hard skills, such as mastering a new product line, a computer system, or government regulations. Companies also offer their employees instruction in many of the same soft skills that you're learning in *On Course,* skills such as listening, setting goals, and managing your time and work projects. In fact, soft skills are in such demand in the workplace today that top training consultants charge many thousands of dollars *per day* to teach these skills to employees of American businesses.

Smart workers take full advantage of the formal classes provided by their employers. They also take full advantage of the informal classes provided by the University of Life. In this university, you have the opportunity to learn from every experience you have, especially those on the job. Lifelong learners aren't devastated by a setback, such as having a project crumble or even losing their job. They learn from their experiences and come back stronger and wiser than ever. A report by the Center for Creative Leadership compared executives whose careers got off course with those who did well. Although both groups had weaknesses, the critical difference was this: Executives who did *not* learn from their mistakes and shortcomings tended to fail at work. By contrast, those executives who *did* learn the valuable lessons taught by their mistakes and failures tended to rebound and resume successful careers.

Your work-world learning begins as soon as you get serious about finding your ideal job. Unless you're sure about your career path, you'll have much research to do. Even if you do feel sure about your career choice, further research might lead to something even better. More than 20,000 occupations and 40,000 job titles exist today, and you'll want to identify careers that match the personal talents and interests you identified in your self-assessment.

Your college's library or career center probably has a number of great resources to learn about careers. For example, computerized programs such as DISCOVER, SIGI PLUS, CHOICES, and CIS may be available to explore thousands of career possibilities. Helpful books include the *Dictionary of Occupational Titles* (DOT), which offers brief descriptions of several thousand occupations; *The Guide for Occupational Exploration*

(GOE), another source of occupational options; and the latest edition of the *Occupational Outlook Handbook* (OOH), which provides information about the demand for various occupations. With these resources, you can learn important facts about careers you may never have heard of, including the nature of the work, places of employment, training and qualifications required, earnings, working conditions, and employment outlook. Keep in mind that in today's fast-paced world, occupations will be available when you graduate that don't even exist today.

Ned Herrmann, creator of the Brain Dominance Inventory, wrote, "Experience has shown that alignment of a person's mental preferences with his or her work is predictive of success and satisfaction while nonalignment usually results in poor performance and dissatisfaction." So use your discoveries in this chapter about your preferred thinking styles to help you choose a compatible career. See Figure 7.1 for some examples.

When you have narrowed your career choices, you may want to learn even more before committing yourself. To get the inside scoop on how a career may fit you, get some hands-on experience. Find part-time or temporary work in the field, apply for an internship, or even do volunteer work. At one time I thought I wanted to be a veterinarian, but one summer of working in a veterinary hospital quickly taught me that it was a poor career match for me. I'm sure glad I found out *before* I went through many years of veterinary school!

Now it's time for your job interviews. Keep in mind that most employers are looking for someone who can learn the new position and keep learning new skills for years to come. In fact, a recent U.S. Department of Labor study found that employers of entry-level workers considered specific technical skills less important than the ability to learn on the job. So, how can you present yourself in the interview as a lifelong learner? First, of course, have a transcript with good grades to demonstrate your ability to learn in college. Be ready for questions such as, "How do you keep up with advancements in your field? What workshops or seminars have you attended?

Creators Wanted!

Candidates must demonstrate a commitment to lifelong learning, strong critical thinking skills, and the ability to adapt to new challenges.

A. Thinking Learner: biologist, stock broker, engineer, city manager, science teacher, computer designer/programmer, computer technician, detective, educational administrator, radiologist, electrical engineer, financial planner, lawyer, chemist, mathematician, medical researcher, physician, statistician, veterinarian

B. Doing Learner: reporter, accountant, librarian, bookkeeper, clinical psychologist, credit advisor, historian, environmental scientist, farmer, hotel/motel manager, marketing director, military personnel, police officer, realtor, school principal, technical writer

C. Feeling Learner: actor, social worker, clergy, sociologist, counseling psychologist, human resource manager, public relations specialist, journalist, musician, teacher, nurse, occupational therapist, organizational development consultant, recreational therapist, sales, writer

D. Innovating Learner: dancer, poet, advertising designer, florist, psychiatrist, artist, creative writer, entrepreneur, fashion artist, playwright, filmmaker, graphic designer, humorist, inventor, landscape architect, nutritionist, photographer, editor, program developer

Figure 7.1 | Learning Preferences and Compatible Careers

Lifelong Learning AT WORK *continued*

"*Even though you're exceptionally well qualified, Kate, I'd say that 'victim' is not a good career choice.*"

What kind of reading do you do?" Go to the interview prepared to ask good questions of your own. And demonstrate that one of the things you're looking for in a particular job is its ability to help you keep learning your profession.

Today's work world is marked by downsizing and rightsizing. Companies are operating with leaner staffs, and this means that every employee is critical to the success of the business. It also means that someone who can't keep up with inevitable changes is expendable. One powerful way to give yourself a competitive advantage is to continually learn new skills and knowledge, even before you need them on your job. When your supervisor says, "Does anyone here know how to use a desktop publishing program?" you'll be able to say, "Sure, I can do that." Another way to keep learning on the job is to seek out feedback. Superior performers want to hear what others think of their work, realizing that this is a great way to learn to do it even better.

According to Anthony J. D'Angelo, author of the *College Blue Book,* world knowledge doubles every 14 months. Suppose he's way off, and knowledge actually doubles only every five years as others claim. That still means we'll have to keep learning a little every day just to keep pace and a lot every day to get ahead. Educator Marshall McLuhan once said, "The future of work consists of *learning* a living (rather than *earning* a living)." His observation becomes truer with each passing day. Future success at work belongs to lifelong learners.

BELIEVING IN YOURSELF

Develop Self-Respect

 Focus Questions   What is your present level of self-respect? How can you raise your self-respect, and therefore your self-esteem, even higher?

Self-respect is the core belief that I AM AN ADMIRABLE PERSON. If self-confidence is the result of **what** I do, then self-respect is the result of **how** I do it.

Two crucial choices that build up or tear down my self-respect are whether or not I live with integrity and whether or not I keep my commitments.

LIVE WITH INTEGRITY

The foundation of integrity is my personal value system. What is important to me? What experiences do I want to have? What experiences do I want others to have? Do I prize outer rewards such as cars, clothes, compliments, travel, fame, or money? Do I cherish inner experiences such as love, respect, excellence, security, honesty, wisdom, or compassion?

Integrity derives from the root word *integer,* meaning "one" or "whole." Thus we create integrity by choosing words and deeds that are one with our values. Many students say they value their education, but their actions indicate otherwise. They leave assignments undone; they do less than their best work; they miss classes; they come late. In short, their choices contradict what they say they value. Choices that lack integrity tear at an aware person's self-respect.

One of my greatest integrity tests occurred during my first year in college. First, a little background. In the public high school I'd attended, cheating was widespread. You could say it was part of the student culture. As for me, I prided myself that I never cheated . . . except in Latin. (Yes, at that time my high school actually offered three levels of Latin.) I knew cheating was wrong, but my Inner Defender was ever ready with excuses: *Everyone cheats. No one uses Latin anymore, so it's a huge waste of time. And if I don't cheat, everyone else will . . . and then my grade will suffer.* I became masterful at writing vocabulary words and verb conjugations on the tiniest pieces of paper imaginable.

Now fast forward to the middle of my first semester in college. All of us were preparing for midterm exams. My Inner Critic, you may recall, had convinced me that I was in serious danger of failing out of college. Every one of my classmates, I believed, was smarter and better prepared than I was. They had read books I hadn't even *heard* of. They had completed courses my high school didn't even *offer*. They

Always aim at complete harmony of thought and word and deed.

Mohandas K. Gandhi

I would prefer even to fail with honor than to win by cheating.

Sophocles

could probably talk intelligently about ancient Rome with Julius Caesar . . . in *Latin*. If I was going to survive in college, I would have to cheat. As I studied for midterms, I created some of the finest crib notes on planet Earth.

However, I was in for a jolt. When I arrived at my first college exam, the professor told us to write and sign the following statement on the front of our exam booklets: "I pledge my honor that I have neither given nor received assistance on this examination." And then he left the room!

Talk about a fork in the road! There I was with all of my cleverly miniaturized crib notes and (A) I had just signed a promise that I would not use them and (B) there was no instructor present to catch me if I did. Drat. What to do?

Academic integrity is another aspect of the deep culture of higher education. Chances are your college has a written policy or honor code that upholds the value of academic honesty and condemns cheating. You'll find it in your college's catalog or on its website. Here's part of one from Amherst College: . . . *the College considers it a violation of the requirements of intellectual responsibility to submit work that is not one's own or otherwise to subvert the conditions under which academic work is performed by oneself or by others.*

Academic dishonesty, the Amherst policy explains, *refers to any act that is intended to produce an academic assessment that is not commensurate with an individual's performance, or any act that is intended to unfairly assist or hinder an individual's academic efforts.* Because one of the purposes of higher education is to seek truth, stamping out cheating seems like a good idea.

So, you might wonder, how's the "stamping out" going? If you do an Internet search for "academic integrity," you'll get more that 4,500,000 results. Clearly a hot topic. Donald McCabe, a professor at Rutgers University, has studied this topic for years. He surveyed 1,800 students from nine universities. Seventy percent of them admitted to cheating on exams, while 84 percent said they cheated on assignments. According to the Educational Testing Service (ETS), a website that sells term papers averages about 80,000 hits per day. Ironically, I found one such website that offers a choice of 60 term papers on the topic of academic integrity. In other words, you can cheat by buying a paper that condemns cheating.

So, it would appear that many students cheat. Why not join them? Here are three, among many, reasons.

First, let's be practical. You might get caught. Because cheating is so widespread, educators are combating it in many ways. For example, just as there are websites for students to buy term papers, there are websites where instructors can check to see if a term paper has ever been turned in before. How about consequences? Better check your college's penalties for cheating. They can range from failing the test or assignment, to failing the course, or even to being expelled. Some colleges note the infraction on a student's transcript, a chilling message to all future employers.

Second, you'll learn more. If you're in college only to get a degree and what you learn doesn't matter, you might not care—that is until you're in a job and need some of the skills you were supposed to learn in that course you cheated

> If you want to be respected by others, the great thing is to respect yourself. Only by that, only by self-respect will you compel others to respect you.
>
> *Fyodor Dostoyevsky*

> The willingness to accept responsibility for one's own life is the source from which self-respect springs.
>
> *Joan Didion*

your way through. If you're a nursing student, I sure hope I never come under your care. If you're an engineering student, I sure hope I never drive over one of your bridges.

Finally, your self-respect will increase. At least that's what I experienced. You see, at my first college midterm exam many years ago, I decided not to cheat. My first thought was, *With the professor gone, it's too easy.* My second thought was, *If I cheat, I'll never know what I'm capable of . . . maybe it's a lot more than I think.* And then I thought, *It would be wrong. Even if no one else ever finds out, I'll know I cheated.* In that moment, at the ripe old age of 18, I decided that the cost of cheating is too high. And that's a choice I've never regretted.

Here's what I learned. Each time we contradict our personal values, we make a withdrawal from our self-respect account. Each time we are true to our personal values, we make a deposit. When you find that your choices are out of alignment with your values, you need to make a change . . . for your own sake. You can't abandon what you hold sacred and still retain your self-respect.

KEEP COMMITMENTS

Now let's consider another choice that influences your self-respect. Imagine that someone has made a promise to you but doesn't keep it. Then he makes and breaks a second promise. And then another and another. Wouldn't you lose respect for this person? What do you suppose happens when the person making and breaking all of these promises is YOU?

True, your Inner Defender would quickly send out a smoke screen of excuses. But the truth would not be lost on your Inner Guide. The fact remains: You made commitments and broke them. This violation of your word makes a major withdrawal from your self-respect account.

To make a deposit in your self-respect account, keep commitments, especially to yourself. Here's how:

- **Make your agreements consciously.** Understand exactly what you're committing to. Say "no" to requests that will get you off course; don't commit to more than you can handle just to placate others.

- **Use Creator language.** Don't say, *I'll try to do it.* Say, **I will** *do it.*

- **Make your agreements important.** Write them down. Tell others about them.

- **Create a plan; then do everything in your power to carry out your plan.** Use your self-management tools to track your promises to yourself and others.

- **If a problem arises or you change your mind, renegotiate** (don't just abandon your promise).

The person we break commitments with the most is, ironically, ourselves. How are you doing in this regard? Here's some evidence: How are you doing

> This above all; to thine own self be true
> And it must follow, as the night the day
> Thou canst not then be false to any man.
>
> *Polonius, in Shakespeare's Hamlet*

> Whenever I break an agreement, I pay the price first. It breaks down my self-esteem, my credibility with myself, my self-trust, my self-confidence. It causes me not to be able to trust myself. If I cannot trust myself, whom can I trust?
>
> *Patricia J. Munson*

with the commitment you made to your goals and dream in Journal Entry 10? How are you doing with your 32-Day Commitment from Journal Entry 15?

If you haven't kept these commitments (or others), ask your Inner Guide, *What did I make more important than keeping my commitment to myself?* A part of you wanted to keep your agreement. But another, stronger part of you obviously resisted. Pursue your exploration of this inner conflict with total honesty and you may uncover a self-defeating pattern or limiting core belief that is crying out for a change. After all, our choices reveal what we *really* value.

Keeping commitments often requires overcoming enormous obstacles. That was the case with one of my students. Rosalie had postponed her dream of becoming a nurse for 18 years while raising her two children alone. Shortly after enrolling in college, her new husband asked her to drop out to take care of his two sons from a former marriage. Rosalie agreed, postponing her dream once more. Now back in college 10 years later, she made what she called a "sacred vow" to attend every class on time, to do her very best on all work, and to participate actively. This time she was committed to getting her nursing degree. Finally her time had come.

Then, one night she got a call from one of her sons who was now married and had a two-year-old baby girl. He had a serious problem: His wife was on drugs. Worse, that day she had bought $200 worth of drugs on credit, and the drug dealers were holding Rosalie's granddaughter until they got paid. Rosalie spent the early evening gathering cash from every source she could, finally delivering the money to her son. Then, all night she lay awake, waiting to hear if her grandchild would be returned safely.

At six in the morning, Rosalie got good news when her son brought the baby to her house. He asked Rosalie to watch the child while he and his wife had a serious talk. Hours passed, and still Rosalie cared for the baby. Closer and closer crept the hour when her college classes would begin. She started to get angrier and angrier as she realized that once again she was allowing others to pull her off course. And then she remembered that she had a choice. She could stay home and feel sorry for herself, or she could do something to get back on course.

At about nine o'clock, Rosalie called her sister who lived on the other side of town. She asked her sister to take a cab to Rosalie's house, promised to pay the cab fare, and even offered to pay her sister a bonus to watch the baby.

"I didn't get to class on time," Rosalie said. "But I got there. And when I did, I just wanted to walk into the middle of the room and yell, 'YEEAAH! I MADE IT!'"

If you could have seen her face when she told the class about her ordeal and her victory, you would have seen a woman who had just learned one of life's great lessons: When we break a commitment to ourselves, something inside of us dies. When we keep a commitment to ourselves, something inside of us thrives. That something is self-respect.

To me integrity is the bottom line in self-esteem. It begins with the keeping of one's word or doing what you say you will do, when you say you will do it, whether you feel like it or not.

Betty Hatch, president, National Council for Self-Esteem

You will always be in fashion if you are true to yourself, and only if you are true to yourself.

Maya Angelou

Journal Entry 28

In this activity, you will explore strengthening your self-respect. People with self-respect honor and admire themselves not just for *what* they do but for *how* they do it.

Make a choice. Write about one of the following:

1. **Write about a time when you passed a personal integrity test.** Tell about an experience when you were greatly tempted to abandon one of your important values. Describe how you decided to "do the right thing" instead of giving in to the temptation.

2. **Write about a time when you kept a commitment that was difficult to keep.** Fully explain the commitment you made to yourself or to someone else, and discuss the challenges—both inner and outer—that made it difficult for you to keep this promise. Explain how you were able to keep the commitment despite these challenges.

Asking probing questions leads to meaningful answers. Anticipate questions a curious reader might ask you about your stories . . . and answer them.

Character, simply stated, is doing what you say you're going to do. A more formal definition is: Character is the ability to carry out a worthy decision after the emotion of making that decision has passed.

Hyrum W. Smith

Wise Choices in College

WRITING

Along with reading, few academic skills support your success in college more than effective writing. In most college courses, you'll be asked to do at least some—and perhaps much—writing. You'll write compositions, lab reports, term papers, journal entries, and research papers. Additionally, you'll take many tests and exams that contain essay questions. Obviously, then, writing well increases your ability to earn good grades in college. But this is only one of writing's many benefits.

After you graduate, writing well can help you acquire and advance in the career of your choice. In fact, you'll likely write more in your career than you ever expected. With the growth of the Internet and a global economy, more and more business is transacted through e-mail and websites. The popularity of social networking sites and the explosion of blogging create additional needs for good writing. In both your professional and personal life, writing gives you a means to inform, persuade, or even entertain people. And writing helps you maintain relationships, especially with people who are far away. While these benefits may be evident, here is one that may be less obvious: **Writing well enhances learning.**

Consider what experienced writers say:

- *We do not write in order to be understood; we write in order to understand.*
  –Robert Cecil Day-Lewis

- *Writing became such a process of discovery that I couldn't wait to get to work in the morning. . . .*
  –Sharon O'Brien

- *The best way to become acquainted with a subject is to write a book about it.*
  –Benjamin Disraeli

- *Writing is making sense of life.*
  –Nadine Gordimer

- *Learn as much by writing as by reading.*
  –Lord Acton

Among other reasons, writing enhances learning because the process raises questions that require answers. For instance, if you were writing an essay about self-awareness, you might anticipate a question your reader will want answered: *What childhood experience caused the author to adopt a negative script about her math skills?* Or, more academically, you might find yourself wondering, *How does the activity of neurons contribute to self-awareness?* Your effort to **Collect**, **Organize**, and write answers to these questions (and others) expands your understanding of yourself, other people, and the world. And that is the essence of learning!

Here's another reason why writing enhances learning: Like learning, writing is a process. Most experts recognize four components in the writing process: prewriting, writing, revising, and editing. As you'll see, these four have much in common with the four components of the CORE Learning System. In fact, knowing the CORE Learning System gives you a real advantage when it comes to writing.

- **Prewriting** (also called *invention*) includes any preparation you do before actually writing. Guiding this process is an awareness of your audience and your purpose for writing. Prewriting activities include **Collecting** ideas and supporting details, then **Organizing** these raw materials into a possible structure. Prewriting is a step that many novice writers unwisely skip.

- **Writing** (also called *drafting*) is the act of creation—turning your raw materials into a document that achieves your defined purpose. As you write, your mind both **Rehearses** the ideas you want to express and **Evaluates** your understanding of them. Thus, while writing you may realize that you need to **Collect** more information, re-**Organize** the information you already have, or both. When the first draft is complete, novice writers often pat themselves on the back and declare themselves done. Experienced writers know they have only just begun.

- **Revising** (also called *rewriting*) means "seeing again." When revising, you "re-see" in order to **Evaluate** your present draft. Does it say what you mean? Will it achieve your purpose for writing? If you have a poor understanding of your subject, your writing will likely be muddy and unclear. Revising, which is a kind of **Rehearsing**, helps identify what you don't understand and encourages you to think more critically about the subject. With this effort come both a deeper understanding and the ability to express that understanding more effectively in writing. That's why experienced writers often spend as much (or even more) time revising as they took planning and writing the first draft.

- **Editing** (also called *proofreading*) eliminates surface problems (e.g., errors in grammar, sentence structure, and spelling). When writing is littered with errors, your readers may wonder if your thinking is as careless as your proofreading. Worse, they may not understand what you mean. Either way, surface errors undermine the achievement of your purpose. Editing is your final **Evaluation** of how well you think your writing will achieve its purpose.

Perhaps now you understand why so many instructors require writing. To write well requires you to be the most active of learners, developing deep and lasting learning. And that, after all, is the goal of all good teaching.

WRITING: THE BIG PICTURE

So, experiment with the many writing strategies that follow and, as you do, keep in mind the big picture of writing: **The goal of the four steps of the writing process is to inform, persuade, or entertain your intended audience. Thus, writing requires that you anticipate and answer the questions that engaged readers will have about your subject. In the act of asking and answering these questions, you will implement all of the steps of the CORE Learning System. That's why good writing is not only an important means of communication; it is also one of the most powerful ways to create deep and lasting learning.**

BEFORE WRITING

1. Create a positive affirmation about writing. Create an affirming statement such as, *I use all steps of the writing process to express my ideas clearly and effectively.* Use this affirmation to develop a "growth mind-set" about writing. Remember, a "growth mind-set" is a core belief that you can improve your academic outcomes by employing effective strategies and hard work. (The opposite belief is that there is nothing you can do to improve your academic results, which is a Victim stance.)

2. If you get to choose the topic, select one that truly interests you. You'll enjoy researching and writing about something meaningful to you, and your grades will probably improve as well. Even if your instructor assigns the topic, look for an approach to the topic that appeals to you.

3. Carry index cards for Collecting ideas. Once you begin thinking about a subject, ideas will pop into your mind at the strangest times. You might be ordering French fries in the cafeteria when a great idea hits you. Don't think you'll remember the idea later. Pull out an index card and write yourself a note. Keep the cards rubber-banded together for **Organizing** later.

4. Create focus questions. Make a list of questions to guide your **Collection** of information. Choose questions that arouse your curiosity. If you want to know the answers yourself, you'll be more motivated to find answers that you can shape into a successful writing assignment. For example, suppose you're going to write about financial aid. You might be very interested to know:

- What are the secrets for getting the most scholarship money?

- What mistakes keep students from getting all of the financial aid available to them?

- Is there a legal way to avoid repaying student loans?

Write each question on a separate index card or type a list of questions into your computer file.

5. Discuss your topic with others. Engage as many people as possible in a conversation about your topic. Start by asking your focus questions and follow where they lead. If possible, interview experts. For example, think how much you could learn about financial aid by talking with the head of your college's financial aid office. Having a conversation about your topic will get your neurons firing and your creative juices flowing. **Collect** the best ideas and supporting details by writing them on index cards.

6. Group your notes. Once you've **Collected** a stack of note cards on your topic, it's almost time to write . . . but not quite yet. First, group your notes by sorting them into piles, with one pile for each main idea or focus question. Better yet, type your notes into a computer; then, cut and paste them into clusters of related ideas. In our example about financial aid, three of these clusters would contain ideas related to your focus questions:

- Secrets of getting the most in scholarship money

- Mistakes that keep students from getting all of the financial aid available to them

- Legal ways to avoid repaying student loans

It's likely that you'll have gathered additional information as well. Find logical categories for these extra ideas as well. For example, you might group ideas together related to:

- The differences between grants, scholarships, and loans

- Government sources of financial aid

- Private sources of financial aid

- Ways to qualify for low-interest loans

- The consequences of not paying back student loans

7. Identify your audience. Every piece of writing has one or more intended readers. After all, there's no point in writing to no one. In most college writing, you will be informing your instructors about what you have learned. Perhaps you see the challenge: You'll be telling instructors about subjects that they know more about than you do. Usually the best approach is to write to a general audience. Picture a *general audience* as a group of interested, well-educated readers who know little or nothing about the topic. In this way, you will be more likely to provide all of the ideas and supporting details needed to show your instructors that you have mastered their course content. Sometimes instructors will specify your audience (e.g., readers of your college newspaper). If so, use this information to make choices as you write such as: *What tone (formal or informal) to adopt? What information to include or exclude? How much evidence is needed to overcome resistance?*

8. Define your thesis. A thesis states the most important idea you want to convey to your audience. Everything else you write merely supports this idea by answering questions that an engaged reader might have about your thesis. A thesis is made up of two elements: (1) the *topic* you're writing about and (2) the *claim* you make about the topic. Thus, a thesis statement is usually one sentence and has the following structure:

[Topic] + [Claim].

The two most common kinds of writing in college are informative and persuasive. The thesis of **informative** writing tells your readers something they presumably don't already know. For example:

[*Subprime mortgage loans*] + [*are those made to borrowers with questionable ability to pay back the money they borrow*].

The thesis of **persuasive** writing asks your readers to think or do something that presumably they are not inclined to think or do:

Think: [*Franklin Pierce*] + [*was one of the finest American presidents*].

Do: [*The student government*] + [*is an organization you should join*].

Sometimes you'll know immediately what your thesis is. Other times you may need to think and write for a while before a thesis emerges. Even after you've settled on your thesis, be prepared to change it as the process of writing causes you to learn more about your topic. Eventually, though, you'll need to settle on a clearly stated thesis, because an essay without a thesis is like a body without a spine—nothing holds it together.

9. Organize your ideas and supporting details. In Chapter 3, we looked at linear and graphic ways to **Organize** information. These methods also work well for **Organizing** information during prewriting. Let's revisit two of these strategies and introduce a third. The one you favor is probably explained by your preferred way of learning, as shown on the self-assessment you took at the beginning of this chapter.

Outline. (For a review of how to create an outline, along with an example, see pages 106–107.) When creating an outline for a writing assignment, place your thesis statement at the top of a page (realizing that it may change as you write). Below it and flush to the left margin, add the subject of each of the groups you determined in Strategy 6. These are now your main ideas (Level 1). Next, indent a few spaces and add secondary ideas (Level 2) beneath each main idea. Finally, indent a few more spaces and add supporting ideas (Levels 3 and 4). Most word processing programs have a feature to help you create an outline. In Microsoft Word, for example, you'll find it in the View menu.

Concept Map. (For a review of how to create a concept map, along with an example, see pages 106 and 108.) To create a concept map for a writing assignment, write your thesis statement at the top of a page. Then write the key concept in the middle of the page and either underline or circle it. Now draw lines out from the key concept and write the topic of each of the groups you determined in Strategy 6; these will be your main ideas (Level 1). Next, draw lines out from your main ideas, and write secondary ideas (Level 2). Farther out from the center of the concept map, write your supporting details (Levels 3 and 4). If you like organizing with concept maps, you may want to experiment with computer software designed for creating them. To find such software, search for "concept map software" using an Internet search engine.

Question Outline. Here's a variation of an outline that's easy, quick, and effective. After determining your thesis, choose the most interesting questions from the list you created in Strategy 4. Make sure you have enough information to answer each question thoroughly . . . or **Collect** more. Use one question as the topic of each body paragraph. Thus, if you choose four questions, you'll probably be writing a six-paragraph essay (after adding your introduction and conclusion). It is possible, of course, that you could write two or more paragraphs to answer a question, making your essay longer than six paragraphs. Here's what a Question Outline about scripts might look like:

– Introduction (including the thesis)

– What are scripts?

– How do we write our scripts?

– Why do some scripts sabotage our success?

– How can we revise self-sabotaging scripts?

– Conclusion

WHILE WRITING

10. Use an essay blueprint. When you want to assemble something with many parts, a picture can help. For beginning writers, a blueprint showing a good way to assemble the parts of an essay is also a big help. Just as there are many blueprints for building a house, so are there many blueprints for writing an essay. But the one in Figure 7.2 is both effective and easy to understand. When one of my students saw this essay blueprint, she exclaimed, "So *that's* what the structure of an essay looks like? I can do *that*!" Each part in the blueprint is explained in the strategies that follow. As you add these parts to the essay blueprint, realize that the structure is flexible and can be modified. For example, the essay blueprint shows a six-paragraph essay; if you have a different number of main ideas, simply add or delete body paragraphs. Also, Paragraph 5 in the essay blueprint presents a feature (refutation) that is useful in a persuasive essay but usually unnecessary in an informative essay. As you become a more skilled writer, you will begin to take more and more liberties with this blueprint. Ultimately you'll be creating your own original ways to organize your main ideas and supporting details.

Paragraph 1: Introduction
   Hook
   Thesis
   Agenda

Paragraph 2: Body Paragraph #1
   Transition (presenting Main Idea #1)
   Secondary Ideas and Supporting Details (4E's)

Paragraph 3: Body Paragraph #2
   Transition (presenting Main Idea #2)
   Secondary Ideas and Supporting Details (4E's)

Paragraph 4: Body Paragraph #3
   Transition (presenting Main Idea #3)
   Secondary Ideas and Supporting Details (4E's)

Paragraph 5: Refutation (included in a persuasive essay)
   Transition (presenting opponents' argument)
   Refutation (presenting reasons and evidence to weaken opponent's argument)

Paragraph 6: Conclusion
   Summary or Echo
   Restatement of Thesis

Figure 7.2 | Essay Blueprint

11. Write a hook. The beginning of your essay should hook your readers' interest. To do so, start with an engaging strategy such as a question, quotation, humor, surprising data, shocking statement, or fascinating story. Even though a *hook* is the first thing your audience reads, you don't have to write it first. In fact, you may think of a good hook only after writing the entire first draft of your essay. If you read the beginning of any essay in this book, you will see my efforts to "hook" your interest. For example, I began the section on "Rewriting Your Outdated Scripts" in Chapter 6 with the story of my student Diana screaming at me in class. My hope was that Diana's dramatic and unexpected outburst would hook your attention and motivate you to read on to find out more.

12. Add your thesis statement. After hooking your reader's attention, present your thesis—the key concept about which you are writing. Your thesis statement may be exactly as you wrote it in Strategy 8, or you may now decide that it needs revision. In fact, it's possible (even probable) that you will revise your thesis statement a number of times as the writing process helps you learn even more deeply about your topic.

13. Write an agenda. An agenda for a meeting lists the main ideas that will be discussed. Similarly, an agenda for an essay states the main ideas that readers can expect to encounter. Although agendas appear more commonly in long essays, articles, or even books, they can be a great help to keep both your readers and you (the author) focused even in a short essay. For example, suppose your thesis is *Students should get involved in campus activities.* Your agenda might give a list of the reasons: *First, getting involved in campus activities will increase your chances of earning a degree. Second, you'll meet people who may become lifelong friends. And finally, involvement in campus activities offers valuable learning experiences that are unavailable in an academic classroom.* This three-part agenda lets your readers know exactly the points you intend to present. Even if you choose not to include an agenda in your essay, having one in your mind helps keep your essay organized.

14. Use transitions. A transition is a bridge between ideas. Transitional words, phrases, or sentences help your readers follow the flow of your ideas. One important place to use a transition is at the beginning of a paragraph. You want to make sure you don't lose your readers as you shift to a new thought (or to answer a new question, if using a Question Outline). A good transition connects the idea just discussed with a new idea . . . and maybe even includes a reminder of the thesis. For example, suppose your thesis intends to persuade your readers to get involved with campus activities. Further, suppose that you have just completed a paragraph about how involvement in campus activities increases a student's chances of earning a degree. The first sentence of your next paragraph might be: *Not only will getting involved with campus activities increase your chances of earning a degree, you'll also meet people who may very well become lifelong friends.* Notice how the transition does three things:

- It reminds readers of the thesis: *Get involved with campus activities.*

- It reminds readers about the main idea made in the previous paragraph: *Getting involved in campus activities increases your chances of earning a degree.*

- It makes a bridge to the main point of the new paragraph: *By getting involved in campus activities, you'll meet people who may very well become lifelong friends.*

The beginning of paragraphs is only one place in your essay where transitions are helpful. When you offer concrete support for main ideas, you can signal with transitional words such as *for example, as an illustration,* or *for instance.* When you point out similarities, signal with *likewise* or *similarly*. When you point out differences, signal with *by contrast, but, however,* or *on the contrary*. When you summarize or conclude, signal with *in other words, in summary, in conclusion,* or *finally*. Treat your readers like tourists in a strange land. As their guide, you don't want to lose or confuse them.

15. Add support. To generate specific and sufficient support, expand each body paragraph with secondary ideas and supporting details. This is easy to do when you remember to use the 4E's. The 4E's represent four questions that almost always need answering as you develop a paragraph:

- Can you give an EXAMPLE of that?
- Can you give an EXPERIENCE to illustrate that?
- Can you EXPLAIN that further?
- Can you give EVIDENCE to support that?

Answering one or more of the 4E's causes you to dive deeper and makes your writing more complete and fully developed.

16. Offer a refutation in a persuasive essay. When you write to persuade, assume your readers are resistant to what you want them to think or do. (After all, if they already agree with you, there's no need to persuade them.) Put yourself in their place and see if you can empathize with their reasons for resisting. Then dispute those reasons. For example, why might fellow students resist your efforts to persuade them to get involved in campus activities? Maybe they think they are too busy with their classes, assignments, and possibly a job. How could you refute their belief that they are too busy? As another example, in Chapter 1 ("A Few Words of Encouragement" on page 10), I used refutation in my efforts to persuade you to give the strategies

in *On Course* a fair chance. Take a look back and see if . . .

A) I empathized with a reason that you may have resisted this course (if you did) and

B) I offered a refutation that reduced or even eliminated your resistance.

17. Write a satisfying conclusion. One easy way to conclude is to summarize the main points you have made (e.g., *So, if you want to become better at self-management, learn to use a calendar, next actions list, tracking form, and thirty-two-day commitment.*). For a more sophisticated conclusion, end with an **echo**. An echo restates all or part of an idea presented early in your essay, perhaps in your hook. For example, suppose your hook said, *Do you realize that college graduates earn nearly a million dollars more in their lives than non-grads?* You might echo this thought in your conclusion by ending with this sentence: *So, if you want to raise your lifetime earnings by nearly a million dollars, make getting your college degree a high priority.*

AFTER WRITING

18. Incubate. Set your writing aside and do something else . . . in fact, anything else. That's right—don't even think about what you wrote for at least a couple of hours. Better yet, for a couple of days. When you return to your writing later, you'll see your writing with new eyes. You'll notice problems and possibilities that earlier were invisible to you.

19. Revise. As mentioned earlier, "re-vision" means to "see again." After incubation, you'll be ready to see your writing with new eyes. Look for major changes to improve the quality of your communication. Consider a revised thesis statement, better organization, additional support (4E's: examples, experience, explanation, evidence), improved transitions, a catchier hook, a stronger conclusion. Perhaps most important, make sure that you have answered all important reader questions. Remember, good writing anticipates and answers questions that interested readers might ask. Even if you created questions before writing and answered them as you wrote, be alert for new questions that emerge as you revise. Two questions that almost always need answering are "*Why?*" and "*How do you know?*" Other important questions begin with *What? When? Who? Where? How?* and *What if?*

20. Edit carefully. Writing filled with errors is distracting to readers. At best, errors will cause them to think less of what you have to say (especially college instructors). At worst, your readers may misunderstand. The challenge with proofreading your own writing is that you know what is *supposed* to be there . . . and that is what you will often see instead of what is *actually* there. Here's a proofreading trick that can help: Start proofreading with the last sentence. Then proofread the second-to-last sentence. And continue proofreading from the bottom of your writing to the top. In this way, you can focus on the surface details of grammar, spelling, and punctuation without being distracted by the flow of ideas. If writing on a computer, remember that a computer's spell check will not pick up words used incorrectly but spelled correctly (such as using *there* for *their*). Your computer may also help you identify possible grammar errors that need to be corrected. But be careful, because sometimes it will point out "errors" that aren't errors at all.

21. Keep an Error Log. Some instructors, especially for a writing class, will point out your grammar and punctuation errors. When you get a writing assignment back with errors noted, enter them in an Error Log. An Error Log is a record of every sentence in which you had a grammar or punctuation problem. Below the error sentence, rewrite

the sentence correctly. Then, write the relevant grammar or punctuation rule(s) so you can learn to correct all errors of the same kind. You'll find this information in the grammar section of a writing handbook, or you can ask a writing tutor to help you identify the rule. Everyone makes errors, but Creators seldom make the same mistake twice. Here's an example:

> **Error Sentence:** I went to the tutoring center, the tutor I was supposed to see wasn't there.

> **Corrected Sentence:** I went to the tutoring center, but the tutor I was supposed to see wasn't there.

> **Rule:** When two complete sentences are joined with only a comma, this error is called a comma splice. There are three ways to correct a comma splice: (1) Replace the comma with a period, thus creating two complete sentences. (2) Replace the comma with a semi-colon. (3) Add a coordinating conjunction (i.e., *and, but, or, nor, for, so,* or *yet*) after the comma.

Keeping an error log is time-consuming at first, but seeing your errors disappear from future papers is a great reward.

22. Rewrite graded papers. Most instructors provide feedback on substantive problems with your writing (e.g., unclear purpose, poor organization, lack of support). Use this feedback to rewrite and improve your assignment. Such a revision is the ultimate **Rehearsal** of your writing skills, and can help you immensely. Impressed with your initiative, most instructors will be glad to meet with you to discuss your revision. Some will even raise your grade if your revision shows improvement. Regardless of how your instructor responds to your rewrites, realize that there is as much, if not more, learning available to you in revising as there was in writing the original.

WRITING EXERCISE

Compare the quality of your writing in Journal Entries 1 and 2 with the quality of your writing in Journal Entries 27 and 28. Be prepared to answer the following questions:

- Has the quality of your writing improved? If so, how? Offer specific examples.

- If your writing has not improved, why do you suppose it hasn't?

- Which of your journal entries do you think is the most well-written?

- What could you do to improve the writing in your remaining journal entries?

- How did you feel about writing when you began this course?

- Have your feelings about writing changed while keeping your journal? If so, how? And why?

Developing Emotional Intelligence

8

Creating worldly success is meaningless if I am unhappy. That means I must accept responsibility for creating the quality of not only my outcomes but also my inner experiences.

I create my own happiness and peace of mind.

SUCCESSFUL STUDENTS ...	STRUGGLING STUDENTS ...
demonstrate emotional intelligence, using feelings as a compass for staying on course to their goals and dreams.	**allow themselves to be hijacked by emotions,** making unwise choices that get them off course.
effectively reduce stress, managing and soothing emotions of upset such as anger, fear, and sadness.	**take no responsibility for managing their emotions,** instead acting irrationally on impulses of the moment.
create flow, feeling fully and positively engaged in college and the rest of their lives.	**frequently experience boredom or anxiety in their lives.**

Case Study in Critical Thinking

AFTER MATH

When **Professor Bishop** returned midterm exams, he said, "In 20 years of teaching math, I've never seen such low scores. Can anyone tell me what the problem is?" He ran a hand through his graying hair and waited. No one spoke. "Don't you people even care how you do?" Students fiddled with their test papers. They looked out of the window. No one spoke.

Finally, Professor Bishop said, "Okay, Scott, we'll start with you. What's going on? You got a 35 on the test. Did you even *study?*"

Scott, age 18, mumbled, "Yeah, I studied. But I just don't understand math."

Other students in the class nodded their heads. One student muttered, "Amen, brother."

Professor Bishop looked around the classroom. "How about you, Elena? You didn't even show up for the test."

Elena, age 31, sighed. "I'm sorry, but I have a lot of other things besides this class to worry about. My job keeps changing my schedule, I broke a tooth last week, my roommate won't pay me the money she owes me, my car broke down, and I haven't been able to find my math book for three weeks. I think my boyfriend hid it. If one more thing goes wrong in my life, I'm going to scream!"

Professor Bishop shook his head slowly back and forth. "Well, that's quite a story. What about the rest of you?" Silence reigned for a full minute.

Suddenly **Michael**, age 23, stood up and snarled, "You're a damn joke, man. You can't teach, and you want to blame the problem on us. Well, I've had it. I'm dropping this stupid course. Then I'm filing a grievance. You better start looking for a new job!" He stormed out of the room, slamming the door behind him.

"Okay, I can see this isn't going anywhere productive," Professor Bishop said. "I want you all to go home and think about why you're doing so poorly. And don't come back until you're prepared to answer that question honestly." He picked up his books and left the room. Elena checked her watch and then dashed out of

the room. She still had time to catch her favorite soap opera in the student lounge.

An hour later, Michael was sitting alone in the cafeteria when his classmates Scott and **Kia**, age 20, joined him. Scott said, "Geez, Michael, you really went off on Bishop! You're not really going to drop his class, are you?"

"Already did!" Michael snapped as his classmates sat down. "I went right from class to the registrar's office. I'm outta there!"

I might as well drop the class myself, Kia thought. Ever since she was denied entrance to the nursing program, she'd been too depressed to do her homework. Familiar tears blurred her vision.

Scott said, "I don't know what it is about math. I study for hours, but when I get to the test, I get so freaked it's like I never studied at all. My mind just goes blank." Thinking about math, Scott started craving something to eat.

"Where do you file a grievance against a professor around here, anyway?" Michael asked.

"I have no idea," Scott said.

"What?" Kia answered.

Michael stood and stomped off to file a grievance. Scott went to buy some French fries. Kia put her head down on the cafeteria table and tried to swallow the burning sensation in her throat.

Listed below are the five characters in this story. Rank them in order of their emotional intelligence. Give a different score to each character. Be prepared to explain your choices.

| Most emotionally intelligent | ← 1 2 3 4 5 → | Least emotionally intelligent |

___ **Professor Bishop**   ___ **Elena**   ___ **Kia**

___ **Scott**   ___ **Michael**

▶ **DIVING DEEPER** Imagine that you have been asked to mentor the person whom you ranked number 5 (least emotionally intelligent). Other than recommending a counselor, how would you suggest that this person handle his or her upset in a more emotionally intelligent manner?

Understanding Emotional Intelligence

Focus Questions   What is emotional intelligence? How can you experience the full range of natural human emotions and still stay on course to a rich, fulfilling life?

During final exam period one semester, I heard a shriek from the nursing education office. Seconds later, a student charged out of the office, screaming, scattering papers in the air, and stumbling down the hall. A cluster of concerned classmates caught up to her and desperately tried to offer comfort. "It's all right. You can take the exam again next semester. It's okay. Really." She leaned against the wall, eyes closed. She slid down the wall until she sat in a limp heap, surrounded by sympathetic voices. Later, I heard that she dropped out of school.

At the end of another semester, I had the unpleasant task of telling one of my hardest-working students that she had failed the writing proficiency exams. Her mother had died during the semester, so I was particularly worried about how she would handle more bad news. We had a conference, and upon telling her the news, I began consoling her. For about a minute, she listened quietly and then said, "You're taking my failure pretty hard. Do you need a hug?" Before I could respond, she plucked me out of my chair and gave me a hug. "Don't worry," she said, patting my back "I'll pass next semester," and sure enough, she did.

For most of us, life presents a rough road now and then. We fail a college course. The job we want goes to someone else. The person we love doesn't return our affections. Our health gives way to sickness. How we handle these distressing experiences is critical to the outcomes and experiences of our lives.

Success depends on much more than a high IQ and academic success. Karen Arnold and Terry Denny at the University of Illinois studied 81 valedictorians and salutatorians. They found that 10 years after graduation, only 25 percent of these academic stars were at the highest level of their professions when compared with others their age. Actually, many were doing poorly. What seems to be missing for them is **emotional intelligence**.

An experiment during the 1960s shows just how important emotional control is to success. Four-year-old children at a preschool were told they could have one marshmallow immediately. Or if they could wait for about 20 minutes, they could have two. More than a dozen years later, experimenters examined the differences in the lives of the one-marshmallow (emotionally impulsive) children and the two-marshmallow (emotionally intelligent) children. The adolescents who as children were able to delay gratification scored an average of 210 points higher on their SATs (Scholastic Aptitude Tests). Additionally, the two-marshmallow teenagers had borne fewer children while unmarried and had experienced fewer problems with the law. Clearly, the ability to endure

> I know it is hard to accept, but an upset in your life is beneficial, in that it tells you that you are off course in some way and you need to find your way back to your particular path of clarity once again.
>
> *Susan Jeffers*

> In the realm of emotions, many people are functioning at a kindergarten level. There is no need for self-blame. After all, in your formal education, how many courses did you take in dealing with feelings?
>
> *Gay & Kathlyn Hendricks*

some emotional discomfort in the present in exchange for greater rewards in the future is a key to success.

FOUR COMPONENTS OF EMOTIONAL INTELLIGENCE

As a relatively new field of study, emotional intelligence is still being defined. However, Daniel Goleman, author of the book *Emotional Intelligence,*[*] identifies four components that contribute to emotional effectiveness. The first two qualities are personal and have to do with recognizing and effectively managing one's own emotions. The second two are social and have to do with recognizing and effectively managing emotions in others.

1. **EMOTIONAL SELF-AWARENESS: Knowing your feelings in the moment**. Self-awareness of one's own feelings as they occur is the foundation of emotional intelligence and is fundamental to effective decision making. Thus, people who are keenly aware of their changing moods are better pilots of their lives. For example, emotional self-awareness helps you deal effectively with feeling overwhelmed instead of using television (or some other distraction) as a temporary escape.

2. **EMOTIONAL SELF-MANAGEMENT: Managing strong feelings**. Emotional self-management enables people to make wise choices despite the pull of powerful emotions. People who excel at this skill avoid making critical decisions during times of high drama. Instead they wait until their inner storm has calmed and then make considered choices that contribute to their desired outcomes and experiences. For example, emotional self-management helps you resist dropping an important class simply because you got angry at the teacher. It also helps you make a choice that offers delayed benefits (e.g., writing a term paper) in place of a choice that promises instant gratification (e.g., attending a party).

3. **SOCIAL AWARENESS: Empathizing accurately with other people's emotions**. Empathy is the fundamental "people skill." Those with empathy and compassion are more attuned to the subtle social signals that reveal what others need or want. For example, social awareness helps you notice and offer comfort when someone is consumed by anxiety or sadness.

4. **RELATIONSHIP MANAGEMENT: Handling emotions in relationships with skill and harmony**. The art of relationships depends, in large part, upon the skill of managing emotions in others. People who excel at skills such as listening, resolving conflicts, cooperating, and articulating the pulse of a group do well at anything that relies on interacting smoothly with others. For example, relationship management helps a person resist saying something that might publicly embarrass someone else.

> Every great, successful person I know shares the capacity to remain centered, clear and powerful in the midst of emotional "storms."
>
> *Anthony Robbins*

> Academic intelligence has little to do with emotional life. The brightest among us can founder on the shoals of unbridled passions and unruly impulses; people with high IQ's can be stunningly poor pilots of their private lives.
>
> *Daniel Goleman*

KNOWING YOUR OWN EMOTIONS

The foundation of emotional intelligence is a keen awareness of our own emotions as they rise and fall. None of the other abilities can exist without this one. Here are some steps toward becoming more attuned to your own emotions.

Build a Vocabulary of Feelings

Learn the names of emotions you might experience. There are hundreds. How many can you name beyond anger, fear, sadness, and happiness?

Be Mindful of Emotions as They Are Happening

Learn to identify and express emotions in the moment. Be aware of the subtleties of emotion, learning to make fine distinctions between feelings that are similar, such as sadness and depression.

Understand What Is Causing Your Emotion

Look behind the emotion. See when anger is caused by hurt feelings. Notice when anxiety is caused by irrational thoughts. Realize when sadness is caused by disappointments. Identify when happiness is caused by immediate gratification that gets you off course from your long-term goals.

Recognize the Difference Between a Feeling and Resulting Actions

Feeling an emotion is one thing; acting on the emotion is quite another. Emotions and behaviors are separate experiences—one internal, one external. Note when you tend to confuse the two, as a student did who said, "My teacher made me so angry I had to drop the class." You can be angry with a teacher and still remain enrolled in a class that is important to your goals and dreams. A fundamental principle of emotional intelligence is, ***Never make an important decision while experiencing strong emotions.***

You will never reach your full potential without emotional intelligence. No matter how academically bright you may be, emotional illiteracy will limit your achievements. Developing emotional wisdom will fuel your motivation, help you successfully negotiate emotional storms (yours and others') and enhance your chances of creating your greatest goals and dreams.

A common confusion generated by the English language is our use of the word "feel" without actually expressing a feeling. For example in the sentence, "I feel I didn't get a fair deal," the words "I feel" could be more accurately replaced with "I think."

Marshall B. Rosenberg

In the midst of great joy do not promise to give a man anything; in the midst of great anger do not answer a man's letter.

Chinese proverb

Journal Entry 29

In this activity, you will explore your ability to understand your own emotions and recognize them as they are occurring. This ability is the foundation for all other emotional intelligence skills.

It made me feel better sometimes to get something down on paper just like I felt it. It brought a kind of relief to be able to describe my pain. It was like, if I could describe it, it lost some of its power over me. I jotted down innermost thoughts I couldn't verbalize to anyone else, recorded what I saw around me, and expressed feelings inspired by things I read.

Nathan McCall

1. Write about an experience when you felt one of the following emotions: **FRUSTRATION or ANGER, FEAR or ANXIETY, SADNESS or DEPRESSION.** Describe fully the cause (what happened) and your emotional reaction. Because emotions are difficult to describe, you may want to try a comparison like this: *Anger spread through me like fire in a pile of dry hay. . . .* or *I trembled in fear as though I was the next person to stand before a firing squad,* or *For weeks, depression wrapped me in a profound darkness.* Of course, create your own comparison. Your journal entry might begin, *Last week was one of the most frustrating times of my entire life. It all began when . . .* Most important, be aware of any emotions that you may feel *as* you are writing.

2. Write about an experience when you felt **HAPPINESS or JOY.** Once again, describe fully the cause (what happened) and your emotional reaction. A possible comparison: *Joy bubbled like champagne, and I laughed uncontrollably.* Most important, be aware of any emotions that you may feel *as* you are writing.

3. Write about any emotional changes you experienced *as you described* each of these two emotions. What did you learn or relearn about how you can affect your emotions? If you weren't aware of any changes in your present emotions as you described past emotions, see if you can explain why. Were you not experiencing any emotions at all? Or could you have been unaware of the emotions you were feeling?

One Student's Story

LINDSEY BECK
Three Rivers Community College, Connecticut

When I started college, I had been in an abusive relationship for almost three years. I was terrified to leave this man (I'll call him Henry) because we have a child together and he had convinced me that I had no worth as a human being without him. At 6'4", Henry is a foot taller and weighs twice as much as I do. He would punch or kick me until I was in so much pain I couldn't go to my classes. When I did go, I'd often leave early because he became convinced I was cheating on him and I didn't want to give him another reason to beat me. I have a fair amount of academic ability and I did well in high school, but I started allowing my emotions to overrun my intelligence. It was like I had a bunch of emotions in a bowl and I'd just pull one out at random when something happened. One day when my mother expressed concern about my bruises, I got furious at her. But instead of getting angry at Henry for beating me, I'd feel afraid, confused, and depressed. Rather than stepping back and thinking logically about what was going on, I allowed my emotions to control me.

Studying became my escape. In my freshman-year experience course, I loved expressing myself in my journals. In Chapter 8, I started writing about my emotions, and for the first time in years, I wasn't ashamed of my feelings. I decided to be totally honest, and I wrote down exactly what was going on and how I *really* felt about it (not how Henry told me I felt about it). Writing the journals really made me look at

myself and ask, *What am I doing in this relationship?* When I read about all of the positive ways I could manage my emotions, I started looking at things as though I wasn't going to take it any more. I got stronger every day, and then one day I made the decision to leave Henry.

I've always done well at writing papers, studying, and taking tests, but I've never really taken responsibility for my emotions before. I learned that I need to get my emotional life under control if I want the rest of my life to work. I now realize that how I feel at one moment isn't necessarily how I'll feel 10 minutes later. Emotions change. Why let

things control me that are so temporary? By growing emotionally, I'm able to control my emotions instead of letting them control me. I am finally starting to picture a positive life for myself without Henry, and I am growing more confident every day. My dream is to earn a degree in microbiology and make a difference by working for the World Health Organization. Enrolling in this course was the best life decision I will probably ever make. If I hadn't, 10 years from now, I might not have wanted to change my life. However, I have been able to do that, and now I have my whole life ahead of me.

Photo: Courtesy of Lindsey Beck

Reducing Stress

Focus Question   How can you soothe stressful feelings that make life unpleasant and threaten to get you off course?

Changes and challenges are inevitable in our lives; thus, so is the potential for stress. Maybe you waited until the last minute to print your essay for English class and the printer wouldn't work. Stress. Or you bounced a $6 check and the bank charged you a $25 penalty. Stress! Or you've got a test coming up in history and you're two chapters behind in your reading. STRESS!

Even life's pleasant events, like a new relationship or a weekend trip, can bring on a positive form of stress called *eustress*. If we're not careful, stress of one kind or another can bump us off course.

> The process of living is the process of reacting to stress.
>
> *Stanley J. Sarnoff, M.D.*

WHAT IS STRESS?

The American Medical Association defines stress as any interference that disturbs a person's mental or physical well-being. However, most of us know stress simply as the "wear and tear" that our minds and bodies experience as we attempt to cope with the challenges of life. The body's response to a stressor is much the same today as it was for our ancestors thousands of years ago. As soon as we perceive a threat, our brains release the stress hormones cortisol and epinephrine (also known as adrenaline), and instantly our bodies respond with an increase in heart rate, metabolism, breathing, muscle tension, and blood pressure. We're ready for "fight or flight."

To our ancestors, this stress response literally meant the difference between life and death. After they'd survived a threat (a saber-toothed tiger, perhaps), the stress hormones were gone from their bodies within minutes. In modern life, however, much of our stress comes from worrying about past events, agonizing about present challenges, and fretting about future changes. Instead of stress hormones being active in our bodies for only minutes, they may persist for months or even years. For many of us, then, stress is a constant and toxic companion.

> Every stress leaves an indelible scar, and the organism pays for its survival after a stressful situation by becoming a little older.
>
> *Hans Selye, M.D.*

WHAT HAPPENS WHEN STRESS PERSISTS?

Ongoing stress is bad news for our health, damaging almost every bodily system. It inhibits digestion, reproduction, growth, tissue repair, and the responses of our immune system. As just one example of the impact of long-term stress on our health, Carnegie Mellon University researchers exposed 400 volunteers to cold viruses and found that people with high stress in their lives were twice as likely to develop colds as those with low stress.

In fact, the National Institute for Mental Health estimates that 70 to 80 percent of all doctor visits are for stress-related illnesses. Physical symptoms of stress can be as varied as high blood pressure, muscle tension, headaches, backaches, indigestion, irritable bowel, ulcers, chronic constipation or diarrhea, muscle spasms, tics, tremors, sexual dysfunction, fatigue, insomnia, physical weakness, and emotional upsets.

Important to college students is the discovery that stress has a negative impact on memory. It also hinders other mental skills such as creativity, concentration, and attention to details. When you're feeling stressed, you can't do your best academic work, let alone enjoy doing it. So, when you feel stressed, what are your choices?

> Of all the drugs and the compulsive behaviors that I have seen in the past twenty-five years, be it cocaine, heroin, alcohol, nicotine, gambling, sexual addiction, food addiction, all have one common thread. That is the covering up, or the masking, or the unwillingness on the part of the human being to confront and be with his or her human feelings.
>
> *Richard Miller, M.D.*

UNHEALTHY STRESS REDUCTION

When stressed, people in a Victim mindset seek to escape the discomfort as fast as possible. To do so, they often make unwise choices: drinking alcohol to excess, going numb for hours in front of a television or computer, working obsessively, fighting, taking anesthetizing drugs, going on shopping binges, eating too much or too little, smoking excessively, gulping caffeine, or gambling more than they can afford to lose. When confronted with the damage of their self-sabotaging behavior, they typically blame, complain, and make excuses. *Stress made me do it!*

Like the impulsive children of the marshmallow experiment, Victims seek instant gratification. They give little thought to the impact of these choices on their futures. By making one impulsive and ill-considered choice after another, Victims move further and further off course.

HEALTHY STRESS REDUCTION

People in a Creator mindset find a better way to reduce stress. They realize that managing emotions intelligently means making wise choices that release the grip of stress, not just mask it. Effective at identifying their distressing feelings early, Creators take positive actions to avoid being hijacked by emotional upset. Here's a menu of healthy and effective strategies for managing four of the most common symptoms of stress.

A special note to the highly stressed: Your Inner Defender may take one look at the list of strategies that follows and say something like, "I can't deal with this right now. It's just going to make me even *more* stressed out!" If that's really the case, consider making an appointment at your campus counseling office to get some caring, professional help for your stress.

Victim   Creator

To reduce your stress on your own, here's a simple, two-step plan. First, read the following section that addresses your most pressing symptoms of stress: feeling overwhelmed, angry, anxious, or sad. In that section, pick one stress reduction strategy and make a 32-Day Commitment (page 133) to do it. In little more than a month, you'll likely feel less stressed. Better yet, you'll have proven that *you,* and not stress, are in charge of your life.

Overwhelm

Feeling overwhelmed is probably the most common stressor for college students. Its message, if heeded, is valuable: Your life has gotten too complicated, your commitments too many. Feeling overwhelmed warns us that we've lost control of our lives. Creators may notice a tightness or pain in their jaws, shoulders, or lower backs. Or lack of sleep. Or they may notice themselves thinking, "If one more thing goes wrong, I'm going to scream!" Or, maybe they *do* scream! With this awareness, Creators understand it's time to take action. Many positive strategies exist for rescuing your life from the distress of feeling overwhelmed.

Choose new behaviors: Here are some actions you can take when you feel that your life is stretched a mile wide and an inch thin. As you'll see, many of them are variations of self-management strategies you learned in Chapter 4:

- *Separate from an external stressor.* Perhaps the external stressor is a neighbor's loud music or a demanding job. You can choose to study in the library where it's quiet or find a new job with fewer demands.

- *List and prioritize everything you need to do.* Using a next actions list (page 125), record all of your incomplete tasks according to life roles.

> When you take full responsibility here and now for all of your feelings and for everything that happens to you, you never again blame the people and situations in the world outside of you for any unhappy feelings that you have.
>
> *Ken Keyes*

Assign priorities to each task: A = Important & Urgent actions. B = Important & Not Urgent actions. C = All Unimportant actions.

- *Delete C's.* Identify where you are wasting time and cross them off your list.
- *Delegate A's and B's.* Where possible, get another person to complete some of your important tasks. Ask a friend to pick up your dry cleaning. Pay someone to clean your apartment. This choice frees up time to do the tasks that only you can do, like your math homework.
- *Complete remaining A's and B's yourself.* Start with your A priorities, such as a looming term paper or a broken refrigerator. Handle them immediately: Visit the library and take out three books to begin researching your term paper topic. Call an appliance repair shop and schedule a service call. Spend time doing only A and B priorities and watch your overwhelm subside.

- *Discover time-savers.* Consciously make better use of your time. For example, keep an errand list so you can do them all in one trip. Or study flashcards during the hour between classes.
- *Eliminate time-wasters.* Identify and eliminate Quadrants III and IV activities. For example, reduce the time you spend on Facebook. Cut down on watching television. Stop playing video games.
- *Say "no."* Admit that your plate is full, and politely refuse requests that add to your commitments. If you do agree to take on something new, say "no" to something already on your plate. If saying "no" is difficult for you, do role-plays with a friend to practice. Or put it in writing.
- *Keep your finances organized.* A survey of 11,000 adults by *Prevention* magazine revealed that their number one source of stress is worry over personal finances. So curtail unnecessary spending, pay bills when due, balance your checkbook. Use the money-management strategies later in this chapter for stress relief as well as debt relief.
- *Exercise.* Aerobic exercise increases the blood levels of endorphins, and these hormones block pain, create a feeling of euphoria (the exercise high), and reduce stress. One caution: Consult your doctor before dramatically changing your level of exercise.
- *Get enough sleep.* If sleep is a problem, don't eat after 7 o' clock and go to bed by 10. If thoughts keep running through your mind, write them down. Breathe deeply and relax. Clear your mind. If sleep eludes you, consider seeing a doctor. You can't learn effectively when deprived of sleep.

Choose new thoughts: Because we create the inner experience of feeling overwhelmed in our mind, we can un-create it. Here's how:

- *Elevate.* See each problem in the bigger picture of your whole life. Notice how little importance it really has. From this new perspective, ask, "Will this problem really matter one year from now?" Often the answer is "no."

Much of the stress that people feel doesn't come from having too much to do. It comes from not finishing what they've started.

David Allen

I like what exercise does for my mind. If I've had a bad day, if I'm feeling stressed out, if I'm feeling overwhelmed — it takes it all away.

Kelly Ripa

- *Trust a positive outcome.* How many times have you been upset by something that later turned out to be a blessing in disguise? Because it's possible, expect the blessing.
- *Take a mental vacation.* Picture a place you love (e.g., a white-sand beach, mountain retreat, or forest path) and spend a few minutes visiting it in your mind. Enjoy the peace and rejuvenation of this mini-vacation.

Anger

Healthy anger declares a threat or injustice against us or someone or something we care about. Perceiving this violation, the brain signals the body to release catecholamines (hormones) that fuel both our strength and our will to fight. Creators become conscious of oncoming anger through changes such as flushed skin, tensed muscles, and increased pulse rates.

With this awareness, Creators can pause and wisely choose what to do next, rather than lashing out impulsively. Emotions don't ask rational questions, so we must. For example, Creators ask, *Will I benefit from releasing my anger, or will it cost me dearly?*

When you perceive a true injustice, use the energy produced by your anger to right the wrong. However, to avoid being hijacked by anger and doing something you will regret later, here are some effective strategies:

Choose new behaviors: Allow the tidal wave of anger-producing hormones about 20 minutes to recede. Here's how:

- *Separate.* Go off by yourself, allowing enough time to regain your ability to make rational, positive choices.
- *Exercise.* Moving vigorously assists in reducing anger-fueling hormones in your body.
- *Relax.* Slowing down also aids in calming your body, returning control of your decisions to you (as long as you don't spend this time obsessively thinking about the event that angered you).
- *Journal.* Write about your feelings in detail. Rant and rave to your journal. Explore the cause and effect of your anger. Take responsibility for any part you play in creating the anger. Honest expression of emotions can help the dark storm pass and rational thoughts return.
- *Channel your anger into positive actions.* That's what Candy Lightner did when a drunk driver—a repeat offender—killed her 13-year-old daughter, Cari, as she walked through their neighborhood. Lightner turned her anger into action and created Mothers Against Drunk Driving (MADD). Now a nationwide organization, MADD strives to end drunk driving and provide support for its victims. After your anger has subsided, the Wise Choice Process can help you decide on positive actions that you might take.

The sign of intelligent people is their ability to control emotions by the application of reason.

Marya Mannes

I promised myself on the day of Cari's death that I would fight to make this needless homicide count for something positive in the years ahead.

Candy Lightner

Choose new thoughts: Because thoughts stir emotional responses, revising our anger-producing thoughts can calm us. Here's how:

- *Reframe.* Look at the problem from a different perspective. Search for a benign explanation for the anger-causing event. If you realize you were wronged unknowingly, unintentionally, or even necessarily, you can often see the other person's behavior in a less hostile way.

- *Distract yourself.* Consciously shift your attention to something pleasant, stopping the avalanche of angry thoughts. Involve yourself with uplifting conversations, movies, books, music, video games, puzzles, or similar diversions.

- *Forgive.* Take offending people off the hook for whatever they did, no matter how offensive. Don't concern yourself with whether *they* deserve forgiveness; the question is whether *you* deserve the emotional relief of forgiveness. The reason for forgiveness is primarily to improve *your* life, not theirs. We close the case to free ourselves of the daily self-infliction of poisonous judgments. Of course, forgiveness doesn't mean we forget and allow them to misuse us again.

- *Identify the hurt.* Anger is often built upon hurt: Someone doesn't meet me when she said she would. Below my anger I'm hurt that she seems to care about me so little. Shift attention from anger to the deeper hurt. Consider expressing the hurt in writing.

> Living life as an art requires a readiness to forgive.
>
> *Maya Angelou*

Anxiety

Healthy anxiety delivers a message that we may be in danger. Our brain then releases hormones that fuel our energy to flee. Many Victims, though, exaggerate dangers, and their healthy concern is replaced by paralyzing anxiety or even terror about what could go wrong.

Creators become conscious of oncoming anxiety through their bodies' clear signals, including shallow breathing, increased pulse rate, and "butterflies" in the stomach. With this awareness, Creators can pause and wisely choose what to do next rather than fleeing impulsively from or worrying constantly about a nonthreatening person or situation.

One of the areas where emotions hinder academic performance is test anxiety. Unless you minimize this distress, you will be unable to demonstrate effectively what you know. Many colleges offer workshops or courses that offer instruction in anxiety-reducing strategies. Here are some wise choices to avoid being hijacked by anxiety especially anxiety generated by a test.

> Anxiety ... sabotages academic performance of all kinds: 126 different studies of more than 36,000 people found that the more prone to worries a person is, the poorer their academic performance, no matter how measured—grades on tests, grade-point average, or achievement tests.
>
> *Daniel Goleman*

Choose new behaviors: As with anger, help the anxiety-producing chemicals to recede. Here's how:

- *Prepare thoroughly.* If your anxiety relates to an upcoming performance (e.g., test or job interview), prepare thoroughly and then prepare some more. Confidence gained through extensive preparation diminishes anxiety. Using your CORE Learning System is a great way to increase your realistic expectations for success on any test.

- *Relax.* Slowing down helps you reclaim mastery of your thoughts and emotions (but don't spend this time obsessing about the cause of your anxiety).
- *Breathe deeply.* Anxiety and fear constrict. Keep oxygen flowing through your body to reverse their physiological impact.
- *Bring a piece of home to tests.* For example, bring a picture of your family.
- *Request accommodations.* Visit your college's disability services to see about making special arrangements, such as a longer time to take tests.

Choose new thoughts: Changing our thoughts can soothe irrational anxieties. Here's how:

- *Detach.* Once you have prepared fully for an upcoming challenge (such as a test), there's no more you can do. Worrying won't help. So do everything you can to ready yourself for the challenge; then trust the outcome to take care of itself.
- *Reframe.* Ask yourself, "If the worst happens, can I live with it?" If you fail a test, for example, you won't like it, but could you live with it? Of course you could! (If not, consider seeking help to regain a healthy perspective.)
- *Visualize success.* Create a mental movie of yourself achieving your ideal outcomes. Play the movie over and over until the picture of success becomes stronger than your fear.
- *Assume the best.* Victims often create anxiety through negative assumptions. Suppose your professor says, "I want to talk to you in my office." Resist assuming the conversation concerns something bad. In fact, if you're going to assume, why not assume it's something wonderful?
- *Face the fear.* Do what you fear, in spite of the fear. Most often you will learn that your fear was just a False Expectation Appearing Real.
- *Say your affirmation.* When anxiety-producing thoughts creep into your mind, replace them with the positive words of your affirmation.

> If your images are positive, they will support you and cheer you on when you get discouraged. Negative pictures rattle around inside of you, affecting you without your knowing it.
>
> *Virginia Satir*

Sadness

Sadness is the natural response to the loss of someone or something dear. Fully grieving our loss is essential, for only in this way do we both honor and resolve our loss. Sadness and feeling "down" are also understandable reactions to the academic and social pressures that college students may experience, especially in their first year. Unhealthy sadness, however, becomes a lingering depression, a dark, helpless feeling that anesthetizes us, keeping us from moving on to create a positive experience of life. If you feel gripped by such a depression, see a counselor at your college. Help is available!

For bouts with short-term sadness, however, there are numerous ways to bounce back on your own. First, recognize your body's clear signals: low energy, constant fatigue, and lack of a positive will to perform meaningful tasks. With this awareness, take steps to regain a positive experience of college and life. Here are some healthy options for doing so:

Choose new behaviors: Help your body produce natural, mood-elevating hormones. Here's how:

- *Do something (anything!) toward your goals.* Get moving and produce a result, no matter how small. Accomplishment combats the blues.
- *Exercise.* Moving vigorously helps your body produce endorphins, causing a natural high that brightens your mood.
- *Listen to uplifting music.* Put on a song that picks up your spirits. Avoid sad songs about lost love and misery.
- *Laugh.* Like exercise, laughter is physiologically incompatible with melancholy. So rent a funny movie, go to a comedy club, read joke books or cartoons, or visit your funniest friend.
- *Breathe deeply.* Like fear, sadness constricts. Keep breathing deeply to offset the physiological impact of sadness.
- *Help others in need.* Assisting people less fortunate is uplifting. You experience both the joy of lightening their burden and the reminder that, despite your situation, you still have much to be grateful for.
- *Journal.* Writing about your feelings can help you come to terms with them more quickly and effectively. Often our emotions on paper seem much less distressing than those roaming unexamined in our minds and hearts.
- *Socialize with friends and loved ones.* Isolation usually intensifies gloominess. Socializing re-engages you with people who matter and helps you gain a healthier perspective on your situation.

Choose new thoughts: As with other distressing emotions, changing our thoughts soothes sadness. Here's how:

- *Dispute pessimistic beliefs.* Dark thoughts thrive on pessimism. So challenge negative beliefs that make your present situation seem permanent, pervasive, or personal. Think, instead, how life will improve over time, how the problem is limited to only one part of your life, and how the cause is not a personal flaw in you, but something you can remedy with an action.
- *Distract yourself.* As with anger, consciously replacing gloomy thoughts with pleasant ones will help stop the distress. So involve yourself with engaging activities that will take your thoughts on a pleasant diversion.

> Bad things do happen; how I respond to them defines my character and the quality of my life. I can choose to sit in perpetual sadness, immobilized by the gravity of my loss, or I can choose to rise from the pain and treasure the most precious gift I have - life itself.
>
> *Walter Anderson*

> The greatest weapon against stress is our ability to choose one thought over another.
>
> *William James*

- *Focus on the positive.* Identify your blessings and successes. Think of all the things for which you are grateful, perhaps even making a list. Appreciate what you *do* have instead of regretting what you don't.

- *Find the opportunity in the problem.* At the very least, learn the lesson life has brought you and move on. At best, turn your loss into a gain.

- *Remind yourself, "This, too, shall pass."* A year from now, you'll be in an entirely different place in your life, and this emotional upset will be only a memory.

- *Identify others who have much more to be sad or depressed about.* Realize by this comparison how fortunate you actually are, changing your focus from your loss to all that you still have.

> The greater part of our happiness or misery depends on our dispositions and not our circumstances.
>
> *Martha Washington*

CHOOSE YOUR ATTITUDE

When dealing with stress, the critical issue is, *Do you manage your emotions or do they manage you?* If you have made an honest effort to manage your emotions and they have defied you still, you may want to seek the help of a counselor or therapist. In some cases, persistent emotional distress is the result of a chemical imbalance that can be treated with prescription drugs. But if it's inspiration you seek, consider Viktor E. Frankl, a psychiatrist imprisoned in the Nazi concentration camps during World War II. In his book *Man's Search for Meaning,* Frankl relates how he and other prisoners rose above their stressful conditions to create a positive inner experience.

In one example, Frankl tells of a particularly bleak day when he was falling into a deep despair. With terrible sores on his feet, he was forced to march many miles in bitter cold weather to a work site, and there, freezing and weak from starvation, he endured constant brutality from the guards. Frankl describes how he "forced" his thoughts to turn to another subject. In his mind he imagined himself "standing on the platform of a well-lit, warm and pleasant lecture room." Before him sat an audience enthralled to hear him lecture on the psychology of the concentration camp. "By this method," Frankl says, "I succeeded somehow in rising above the situation, above the sufferings of the moment, and I observed them as if they were already of the past."

> The greatest discovery of my generation is that human beings, by changing the inner attitudes of their minds, can change the outer aspects of their lives.
>
> *William James*

From his experiences and his observations, Frankl concluded that everything can be taken from us but one thing: "the last of the human freedoms—to choose one's attitude in any given set of circumstances, to choose one's own way."

Creators claim the power to choose their outcomes whenever possible and to choose their inner experiences always. If Victor Frankl could overcome the stress of his inhumane imprisonment in a concentration camp, surely we can find the strength to overcome the stresses of our ordinary lives.

Journal Entry 30

In this activity you will practice identifying positive methods for reducing the stress in your life.

1. **Write about a recent time when you felt overwhelmed, angry, sad, or anxious.** Choose an experience different from the one you described in Journal Entry 29. Fully describe the situation that caused your emotional response; then describe the feelings you experienced; finally, explain what you did (if anything) to manage your emotions in a positive way.

2. **Identify two or more strategies that you could use in the future when you experience this emotion.** Explain each strategy in a separate paragraph, and remember the power of the 4Es—examples, experiences, explanation, and evidence—to improve the quality of your writing. When you're done, notice if simply writing about your stressors and ways to manage them may have reduced your level of stress. It did for students in a study at Southern Methodist University.

Emotion comes directly from what we think: Think "I am in danger" and you feel anxiety. Think "I am being trespassed against" and you feel anger. Think "Loss" and you feel sadness.

Martin Seligman

One Student's Story

JAIME SANMIGUEL
Miami Dade College, Florida

I don't consider myself someone who lives in fear, and very few things in life intimidate me. However, the one fear that I could never overcome was my dread of public speaking. When I had to give a speech or read an essay aloud in junior high or high school, I would develop a shaky voice, get sweaty palms, and turn completely red. When I got to college, I took a fundamentals of speech class in which much of our grade depended on two speeches that we had to give using a PowerPoint presentation. My first speech didn't go very well. I hadn't really learned to use PowerPoint, and the slides didn't seem to fit what I was talking about. I began to feel insecure, and I started going all over the place. My teacher said the speech was okay, but I wasn't happy with it, especially because my goal is to work in public relations, where I'll need to be able to speak to groups with confidence.

I was taking SLS 1125, Student Support Seminar, at the same time, and I discovered many helpful hints in *On Course* to overcome my fears. The first thing I did for my next speech was to make sure I was thoroughly prepared. This time I wrote out my whole speech first and then put my key points on index cards. I learned how to work PowerPoint and made sure all of the slides went with what I was talking about. I practiced giving my speech a number of times, with my dog as my audience. Another student in my class gave a great speech on the history of watches, and I visualized myself doing some of the things she had done, like using my hands effectively, looking relaxed, smiling, and being more natural and friendly. I also did some relaxing and deep breathing, and that helped take my mind off my concerns. I used to worry that people would think I didn't know what I was talking about, but I changed these worries by picturing my audience as friends who want to know what I have to say. When I actually gave my speech, I picked out individual students and talked to each of them one at a time. These techniques helped me believe in myself more and not be so self-conscious in front of an audience, and in the end I passed the course with a B.

But just as important, in *On Course* I learned, "If you keep doing what you've been doing, you'll keep getting what you've been getting." I took ownership of the fact that if

I want to be successful in a public relations career, I have to face and overcome my fears of giving presentations. I think I'm well on my way to achieving this goal.

Creating Flow

Focus Questions   What are you doing when you feel most happy to be alive—when you become so absorbed that time seems to disappear? How can you create more of these peak experiences in college and beyond?

Happiness has been called the goal of all goals, the true destination of all journeys. After all, why do we pursue any goal or dream? Isn't it for the positive inner experience our success will create?

For centuries, explorers of human nature have pondered how we can consciously and naturally create happiness. Psychologist Mihaly Csikszentmihalyi has called highly enjoyable periods of time **flow states**. Flow is characterized by a total absorption in what one is doing, by a loss of thoughts or concerns about oneself, and by a distorted sense of time (often passing very quickly). His studies offer insights into how we can purposely create such positive inner experiences in college and beyond.

Csikszentmihalyi believes that the key to creating flow lies in the interaction of two factors: the **challenge** a person perceives himself to be facing and the related **skills** he perceives himself to possess. Let's consider examples of three possible relationships of skill level and challenge. First, when a person's perceived skill level is higher than a perceived challenge, the result is *boredom:* Think how bored you'd feel if you took an introductory course in a subject in which you were already an expert.

Second, when a person's perceived skill level is lower than that needed to meet a perceived challenge, the result is *anxiety:* Think how anxious you'd feel if you took an advanced mathematics course before you could add and subtract.

Third, when an individual's perceived skill level is equal to or slightly below the challenge level, the result is often *flow:* Recall one of those extraordinary moments when you lost yourself in the flow—maybe while conversing with a challenging thinker or playing a sport you love with a well-matched opponent. In flow, participation in the activity is its own reward; the outcome doesn't matter. Flow generates the ultimate in intrinsic motivation: We do the activity merely for the positive experience it provides.

Creating Flow

Skill level HIGH and challenge level LOW = Boredom

Skill level LOW and challenge level HIGH = Anxiety

Skill level EQUAL TO or SLIGHTLY BELOW challenge level = Flow

---

Nadja Salerno-Sonnenberg, one of the world's great concert violinists, describes her own experience of flow this way: "Playing in the zone is a phrase that I use to describe a certain feeling on stage, a heightened feeling where everything is right. By that I mean everything comes together. Everything is one . . . you, yourself, are not battling yourself. All the technical work and what you want to say with the piece comes together. It's very, very rare but it's what I have worked for all my life. It's just right. It just makes everything right. Nothing can go wrong with this wonderful feeling."

> Being able to enter flow is emotional intelligence at its best; flow represents perhaps the ultimate in harnessing the emotions in the service of performance and learning.
>
> *Daniel Goleman*

COLLEGE AND FLOW

What if you could have this kind of experience in your college courses? Creators do all they can to maximize that possibility, and how you choose your courses and your instructors is a good first step. Victims typically create their course schedule based on convenience: *Give me a class at noon because I don't like to get up early.*

Creators have a very different approach. They realize that it's worth a sacrifice to get a course with an outstanding instructor, one who creates flow in the classroom. As you plan your schedule for next semester, ask other students to recommend instructors who . . .

> We tend to experience flow when we become absorbed in something challenging.
>
> *Jere Brophy*

1. demonstrate a deep knowledge of their subject,
2. show great enthusiasm for the value of their subject,
3. set challenging but reasonable learning objectives for their students,
4. offer engaging learning experiences that appeal to diverse learning preferences, and
5. provide a combination of academic and emotional support that gives their students high expectations of success.

Imagine taking courses with instructors who are knowledgeable, enthusiastic, challenging, engaging, and supportive! These are the instructors who are going to create flow in their classrooms, help you achieve academic success, and inspire you to be a lifelong learner.

WORK AND FLOW

It is also important to consider flow when choosing your academic major and your career. You may be surprised by what psychologist Csikszentmihalyi found in his research: Typical working adults report experiencing flow on their jobs three times more often than during free time. When it comes to creating flow, work trumps evenings, weekends, and even vacations. The lesson is clear: If you want to create a positive experience of life, engage in work that appeals to your natural inclinations. When will you have time for boredom if you wake up every morning excited about your day's work?

Carolyn, a 20-year-old student of mine, was studying to be a nurse, which was the career her mother wanted for her. Carolyn's dream was to dance, but she made keeping the peace at home more important. "If I even mention dancing, my mother goes ballistic," Carolyn confided. "It's not worth the hassle to fight her."

I saw Carolyn some years after our first conversation and asked what she was doing.

"I'm a nurse now," she said.

"Any dancing in your life?"

"I've sort of stopped thinking about that."

As best I could tell, Carolyn had abandoned her dreams.

Have you? Are you headed for a career that represents your passion? Is it the work you would choose if you had absolutely no restrictions, either from outside you or inside you?

For the next couple of decades at least, you'll probably spend many of your waking hours at work. You don't have to settle for just a paycheck. Some people do what they love. Why shouldn't you?

I spent more than a year of my life doing work that wasn't me, and I know how quickly my joy shriveled. I woke up many mornings with a stomachache. I lived for weekends, but by Sunday afternoon I began to dread Monday morning. Finally, I heeded the feedback from my emotional distress and sought work where I was happy. I urge you to follow your bliss. This choice may require self-discipline to get you through the education or training necessary to qualify for your desired career, but it's worth all of the discomfort in the present for all of the rewards in the future.

One more point remains to be made about the benefits of creating flow in college, at work, and everywhere else in your life. Not only does flow improve your inner experience, but it also promotes your professional and personal growth. Each time you create flow by testing your present skills against a new challenge, your skills improve. To create flow the next time, you have to increase the difficulty of the challenge, which in turn offers an opportunity to improve your skills once again. Over time, by creating flow again and again, your skills improve greatly, and this growth adds even more to the success and happiness in your life.

The best career advice to give the young is "Find out what you like doing best and get someone to pay you for doing it."

Katherine Whitehorn

When you study people who are successful as I have over the years, it is abundantly clear that their achievements are directly related to the enjoyment they derived from their work.

Marsha Sinetar

Journal Entry 31

In this activity, you will explore ways to create flow in your life. The more flow you create day to day, the more positive will be your inner experience of life. Make a choice; write about one of the following:

1. **Write about a specific past event when you experienced flow in any part of your life.** Remember, flow is characterized by total absorption in what you're doing, an altered awareness of time, and a sense of performing at your very best. Fully describe the experience so that a reader will be able to experience it with you.

2. **Write about your perfect work of the future, the kind that you believe will create the most flow in your life.** Think about any past or present work experiences. Identify the feelings these jobs generated in you (particularly boredom, anxiety, or flow). Then let your imagination run free. Design your perfect job, its challenges, rewards, fellow workers, hours, location, and environment. Consider everything that will make this work something you would love to do *even if you didn't get paid.* Indulge in some no-limit thinking!

Consider illustrating this journal entry with drawings, stickers, pictures cut from magazines, or clip art.

Think back to a time in your childhood when you were doing what you loved to do, and how each day flew by. Hours seemed like minutes. When you love your work, when you love your life, then every day is like that.

Bernie Siegel, M.D.

Emotional Intelligence

AT WORK

During nearly twenty years working as a consulting psychologist to dozens of companies and public agencies, I have seen how the lack of emotional intelligence undermines both an individual's and a company's growth and success, and conversely how the use of emotional intelligence leads to productive outcomes at both the individual and the organizational levels.

Hende Weisnger,
Emotional
Intelligence at Work

Imagine this: The local store manager of a large retail chain sends a one-line email to her department heads: "Quarterly sales figures on my desk by 9:00 a.m. tomorrow!" The head of the menswear department reads the email, feels insulted by the demanding tone, and fires back an angry email response: "I've been working here a hell of a lot longer than you have, and I don't need your nasty reminders about when sales reports are due. You might try treating people more like colleagues and less like servants awaiting your every command." On an impulse, he copies his response to the company president and the five vice-presidents at the store's national headquarters.

How much lost time and productivity do you think will result from this exchange of two emails? How much damage will be done to the employees' professional relationship and their ability to work well together in the future? How might their reputations and careers suffer when others hear rumors of this incident?

Now consider how different this event might have been if the head of the menswear department had followed a fundamental principle of emotional intelligence: ***Never make an important decision while in the grip of strong emotions***. Suppose he'd read the store manager's email, taken a deep breath, and read it again. Feeling angry at what appeared to be the manager's dictatorial tone, what if he had waited about 30 minutes before responding? During that time, maybe he would have done some deep breathing. Maybe he would have recalled that the store manager has been very respectful of him since she took over the store six months before. Having calmed his initial upset, suppose he now went to the store manager's office and asked for a brief meeting. "You know," he says to her in this revised scene, "I just read your email about turning in the third-quarter sales figures, and I got that you're angry or upset. Is there something we need to talk about?" "What? Oh no," she responds, "there's no problem. I meant to send you a reminder last week, but I'm so far behind in my paperwork that I forgot. When I remembered this morning, I wrote the email while I was doing five other things. Sorry if it sounded like I was upset with you. On the contrary, I think you're doing a terrific job!"

Another name for emotional intelligence in the workplace is "professionalism." Professionals are aware of their own emotions, and they've developed methods for managing them. They're also good at perceiving emotions in others, and they know how to communicate effectively, building alliances rather than destroying them. Notice that in the revised scene just described, the department head doesn't reply to his manager with another email. He communicates with her in person. And he does so only after getting his emotions under control. Choices like these make all the difference when it comes to building a reputation as a business professional. And that reputation can be destroyed with one careless tantrum—or, in the digital age, with one reckless email. ▶

Emotional Intelligence AT WORK *continued*

Your emotional intelligence begins to impact your work life as soon as you consider a career path. If you choose work for which you have no passion or emotional commitment, you're starting your career with a huge handicap. Unmotivated by the outcomes or experiences of your work, you'll likely cut corners, doing less than is necessary to propel your career to success. By contrast, when you match your interests and talents to your career choice, you'll find work stimulating and success more likely. As Shoshana Zuboff, a psychiatrist and professor at Harvard Business School put it, "We only will know what to do by realizing what feels right to us."

Emotional intelligence continues to support your success during your job search. Chances are, every applicant invited for an interview has the training to do the job. So, what will distinguish you from the crowd? One answer lies in what employers are looking for beyond job skills. A 1997 survey of major corporations, done by the American Society for Training and Development, discovered that four out of five companies seek emotional intelligence as one of the qualities they look for in new employees. Realizing this, you'll know to communicate not only your academic and job-related skills, but your emotional intelligence competencies as well.

Employers have good reason to seek employees with emotional intelligence. In his book *Working with Emotional Intelligence,* Daniel Goleman writes, "We now have twenty-five years' worth of empirical studies that tell us with a previously unknown precision just how much emotional intelligence matters for success." Goleman presents his analysis of what 121 companies reported as the necessary competencies for success in 181 different career positions. He found that two out of three of the abilities considered essential for effective job performance are emotional competencies. Put another way, according to employers themselves, emotional competence matters *twice* as much as other factors in job effectiveness.

You might think that the soft skills associated with emotional intelligence would be less important for those employed in highly technical and intellectual fields such as engineering, computer science, law, or medicine. Paradoxically, the exact opposite is true. Because academic success and high intelligence are required of all who enter these careers, virtually everyone in these careers is "book smart." However, not everyone is emotionally intelligent. In these professions, there is more variation in the "soft" domain than there is in education and IQ. Therefore, if you're at the top end of the emotional intelligence scale, you have a great advantage over your emotionally illiterate colleagues. As Goleman puts it, "'Soft' skills matter even more for success in 'hard' fields."

Although emotional intelligence is important in entry-level positions, as one moves up the ladder into leadership positions, it becomes essential. According to Goleman, employers report emotional intelligence as making up 80 to 100 percent of the skills necessary to be an outstanding leader. As just one example of its importance, leaders need to be able to spot and resolve conflicts that happen in their workforce. Otherwise such upsets can get an individual, group, division, or even the whole company off course.

Doug Lennick, executive vice-president at American Express Financial Advisors, sums up the case for emotional intelligence in the workplace: "The aptitudes you need to succeed start with intellectual horsepower—but people need emotional competence, too, to get the full potential of their talents. The reason we don't get people's full potential is emotional incompetence."

► BELIEVING IN YOURSELF

Develop Self-Love

Focus Questions   How much do you love yourself? What can you do to love yourself even more?

Self-love is the core belief that **I AM LOVABLE.** It's the unwavering trust that, no matter what, I will always love myself and other people will love me as well.

Self-love is vital to success. It empowers us to make wise, self-supporting choices instead of impulsive, self-destructive ones. These wise choices create a rich, full life of outer achievement and inner happiness.

Adults who have difficulty loving themselves typically felt neglected or abandoned as children. Many grew up in families in which they felt unappreciated and unloved. What meager love they did experience was often little more than a short-lived reward for giving in to their parents' expectations and demands. For children who felt unloved, each new day meant a desperate search for something they could say or do to earn approval from others.

A student in my English class once wrote an essay about the outrageous stunts she'd done to become "head rabbit" for her fifth grade's spring festival. As she read her story, everyone laughed loudly. Afterward, someone asked, "Why did you go to all that trouble just to be the head rabbit?"

The student paused. "Simple. The head rabbit got to wear the best costume." Then a serious look came over her face. "The truth is, I thought people would like me more if I was the head rabbit." She paused again. "And, I guess I hoped that *I* would like me more, too."

Like my student, we may believe that self-love depends upon our outer accomplishments and what others think of them. This kind of self-love is conditional: *I'll love myself after I earn my degree, after I get a great job, after I marry the perfect person, after I buy my dream house. . . .*

If the belief that accomplishment creates self-love were accurate, then why do so many people who appear successful on the outside feel so empty on the inside? Worldly success will not fill all the empty places in our souls. But love for ourselves will.

> Ultimately, for most of us, the journey comes down to the same issue: learning to love freely. First ourselves, then other people.
>
> *Melody Beattie*

> Self-esteem is the capacity to experience maximal self-love and joy whether or not you are successful at any point in your life.
>
> *David Burns, M.D.*

DESIGN A SELF-CARE PLAN

If we felt unloved as children, we may need to learn how to love ourselves as adults and do so without confusing self-love with egotism, arrogance, or self-righteousness.

First, we might ask, *How do we know when other people truly love us?* Isn't it when they treat us well, when they consider our welfare along with their own, concern themselves with our success and happiness, treat us with respect even when our behavior seems least deserving, give us honest feedback, and make sacrifices for the betterment of our lives? Don't we feel loved when others nurture the very best in us with the very best in them?

Our parents' job was to love and nurture us when we were children. Some parents did a great job; some did a terrible job. Most parents probably fell somewhere in between. Now that we are adults, we are responsible for continuing (or beginning) our own nurturing. The more we care for ourselves, the more we feel lovable. And the more we feel lovable, the more overflow of compassion and love we have for others.

Nurturing yourself can begin today with a conscious self-care plan. As you consider the following options for nurturing yourself, look for choices you could adopt to increase your self-love.

Nurture Yourself Physically

People who love themselves make wise choices to nurture their bodies for a long, healthy life. How's your diet? The next time you're about to eat or drink something, ask yourself: *Would I be proud to serve this to someone I love?* This question will raise your awareness, encouraging you to make wiser choices about eating and drinking. Visit your college's health office or library for valuable information on improving your diet.

Do you exercise regularly? Even moderate exercise done routinely helps most people stay stronger and healthier. Regular exercise strengthens the immune system and produces hormones that give us a natural sense of well-being. Your physical education department can help you begin a safe, effective, and lifelong exercise program.

Do you have habits that harm your body? Do you drink too much coffee, smoke cigarettes, drink alcohol to excess, take dangerous drugs? If so, consider giving up the immediate pleasure of such substances for the improved health you'll gain. Substance abuse is misnamed. You're not abusing the substance—you're abusing yourself. Would you abuse someone you love? Your college's health office can provide you with information on how to stop these self-destructive habits. Additional community resources include Alcoholics Anonymous (AA), Narcotics Anonymous (NA), Overeaters Anonymous (OA), and other 12-step programs.

Here are additional ways to nurture your body: Get enough rest. Swing on a swing. Have regular medical checkups. Hug someone dear to you. Laugh until your sides ache. Take a bubble bath. Go dancing. Get a massage. Do nothing for an hour. Stretch like a cat. Breathe deeply. Relax.

The extent to which we love ourselves determines whether we eat right, get enough sleep, smoke, wear seat belts, exercise, and so on. Each of these choices is a statement of how much we care about living.

Bernie Siegel, M.D.

If I knew I'd live this long, I would have taken better care of myself.

Eubie Blake, American pianist and composer who lived to be 100 years old

Nurture Yourself Mentally

How you talk to yourself, especially when you're off course, will greatly influence your sense of self-love. Whenever your Inner Critic begins to condemn you, stop. Replace these negative judgments with positive, supportive comments.

You may find it difficult at first to choose self-loving thoughts rather than self-criticism. To help, try separating the doer from the deed. If you fail a test, your Inner Critic may label you a failure. But your Inner Guide knows you're not. You're a person who, with many other successes in life, got one F on one test. Keep your self-talk focused on facts, not judgments. When you create an undesirable outcome, learn from the experience, forgive yourself for judging your shortcomings, and move on.

Here are additional ways to nurture yourself mentally. Say your affirmation(s) often, read uplifting books (many are listed in the bibliography on pages 299–301), ask a motivating question and seek the answer, learn new words, visualize your success, balance your checkbook, sing or listen to a song with positive lyrics, analyze a difficult situation and make a decision, teach someone something you know how to do.

Nurture Yourself Emotionally

The times you need self-love the most are often the times you feel self-love the least. You may be feeling shame instead of self-acceptance, helplessness instead of confidence, timidity instead of assertiveness, self-contempt instead of self-respect, self-loathing instead of self-love.

An emotional antidote for toxic self-judgments is *compassion*. Treat yourself with the same kindness you'd offer a loved one who's struggling to make sense of this huge, confusing, and sometimes painful world. Realize that how you treat yourself as you go through difficult times—with judgment or compassion—is what will continue to affect your self-love long after the difficult times have passed.

Here are more ways to nurture yourself emotionally: Feel your feelings, share your feelings with a friend, write about your feelings in your journal, see an uplifting and inspiring movie, spend time with loved ones, listen to inspiring music, do something special for yourself, remind yourself that strong feelings, like storms, will pass.

Deep self-love is the ongoing inner approval of who you are, regardless of your accomplishments. You are not your results. When you learn to love yourself even when you're off course and struggling, your belief in yourself will soar.

I believe that the black revolution certainly forced me and the majority of black people to begin taking a second look at ourselves. It wasn't that we were all that ashamed of ourselves, we merely started appreciating our natural selves . . . sort of, you know, falling in love with ourselves just as we are.

Aretha Franklin

The First Best-Kept Secret of Total Success is that we must feel love inside ourselves before we can give it to others.

Denis Waitley

One of the ways I nurture my own soul is by waking every morning around four-thirty and spending two hours by myself—for myself—doing yoga, visualization, meditation, or working on dreams. . . . Another way I nurture my soul is by keeping a daily journal. . . . This is what my two solitary hours in the morning are about—experiencing the core of my soul and discovering the truth that I have to live.

Marion Woodman

Journal Entry 32

In this activity, you will explore ways to develop greater self-love. Typically, people who love themselves achieve many of their goals and dreams and, regardless of the outer circumstances of their lives, often experience positive feelings.

1. **On a blank journal page, draw a circle. Within the circle, create a symbolic representation of your most LOVABLE INNER SELF.** If people could get a glimpse of you without your protective scripts, patterns, and habits, this is what they'd see. Such a picture is a kind of "mandala." Roughly translated from the classical Indian language of Sanskrit, mandala means "circle." As a circle represents wholeness, let your mandala symbolize your own personal wholeness. Let it represent your greatest potential as a human being, your ideal self. This picture needs to make sense only to you. Use colors, words, or shapes as appropriate. To create your mandala, feel free to draw, add personal photographs, or clip and paste pictures cut from magazines. The image here is an example of a mandala.

Mandala Illustration created by Marcia Backos

2. **Outside of the mandala circle, write different ways that you could take care of yourself PHYSICALLY, MENTALLY, and EMOTIONALLY.** In this way you are creating a self-care plan for the LOVABLE INNER SELF depicted in your mandala. Look back at the text for examples of ways to nurture yourself physically, mentally, and emotionally. If appropriate for you, add ways to nurture yourself spiritually as well.

3. **On the next page in your journal, write an explanation of your mandala and the self-care plan that you have created.** Think of questions an inquisitive reader would ask you, and let your Inner Guide answer them. For example, what is the significance of the shapes, pictures, words, lines, and colors that you have chosen to represent your full potential as a human being? What personal characteristics have you depicted as representing your best self? Why are these qualities important to you? In what ways have you decided to take care of yourself? And why have you chosen these particular ways to nurture yourself?

One Student's Story

WYNDA ALLISON PAULETTE
National Park Community College, Arkansas

When I started back to college, I **was 41 years old**. I was on a "wing and a prayer." I didn't know if I had it in me to be successful in school, with all the responsibilities I had in my life. I didn't know if I was smart enough or even had the abilities to work on a college level after so many years. But what I did know was that I wanted to succeed. I would do my best. I had managed well in every other facet of my life, and I wanted to prove to myself that I could get a good education and set a good example for my children.

So, there I was in Success Seminar class, reading *On Course*. I read the "One Student's Stories" and began taking a personal inventory of my own life. Some of the journal entries I wrote left me mentally exhausted, because our instructor was always asking us to "dig deeper," and deeper I would go. I would write about subjects that I had left firmly in my past, re-open them, and give myself the opportunity to see them in a whole new light. Eventually, I was able to look at the "horrible" mistakes I had made in my life as lessons instead of failures. I could lay down negative thoughts that I harbored about myself, and begin to see the ways I had grown as a human being. I began taking steps unknowingly to practice self-love and acceptance. I learned so much about myself and

got so much out of the class that when the end of the semester came, and we were required to turn in our notebooks, I wrote this poem/story to include for my instructor. It only took a few minutes to write, but summed up my journey quite well.

The Friend

I once had a person in my life who I pro-
fessed to care about; but the truth is,
I didn't like Her much at all.

My friends would say how pretty and
smart She was; I would silently
disagree.

I made decisions that would hurt Her . . .
choices that would inconvenience Her
and take Her off track.

I never worried about Her wellbeing. In my
eyes, She didn't deserve my love.

I single handedly set that poor girl back
20 years, with all the unnecessary
problems I put in Her path.

I silently watched Her go through bad relationships, unproductive friendships,
and unnecessary hardships without
bothering to intercede.

I saw Her sink farther and farther from Her
dreams, and thought She got what
She deserved.

I judged Her so harshly, disrespected Her,
and felt no remorse. . . .

UNTIL-

One day I looked at that person, REALLY
took the time to see Her and started to
see the good in Her. . . .

I began to respect Her for the grace with
which She handled even the hardest
of times . . . and for the optimistic way
She viewed the world.

I began to see Her worth shine from within
brighter than a whole vault full of
gold.

I saw a beauty within Her so great that it
made me weep.

I began to encourage Her every day, and
assure Her that Her dreams could be
realized and that She could accomplish anything She set Her brilliant
mind to do.

I fell in love with Her for the first time. I
began to admire and respect Her.

I regretted the horrible times I had put Her
through: the setbacks, the wrongs. . . .

But now, looking back, I realize that
woman I now love would not be the
person She is

If She had not traveled the dark paths I led
Her through. . . .

. . . Nor would She appreciate the sunshine
nearly as much.

For within Her is a well-seasoned, understanding, empathetic, responsible,
caring human being.

That woman is ME.

My story is still ongoing. There will always be struggles; nothing will ever be "laid at my feet." But I also learned through all the hard work I put into Success Seminar, and all of the valuable lessons and infor-mation that I was able to reap from the text and the exercises, that life is full of possibility. There are no dead-end roads, only new routes to forge through and lessons to learn. Most of all, we have to learn to love and believe in ourselves.

Photo: Courtesy of Wynda Allison Paulette

Wise Choices in College

MANAGING MONEY

When asked why they enrolled in college, many students say, "To get a better-paying job." Quite understandably, they want what money can buy: a nice house, quality medical care, good food, reliable transportation, nice clothing, and time for recreation, to name just a few. They also want the peace of mind that financial security can offer. In a nutshell, they want the good life for themselves and for those they love.

These students are correct that a college degree correlates with greater abundance. Check out Figure 8.1 to see how level of education affects the earnings and unemployment rate of people aged 25 and older.

Clearly, earning a degree increases the likelihood of abundance. Sadly, however, many students' inability to manage money keeps them from completing the very degree that would help them

earn the income they want. Managing money is a skill as important and challenging as reading and writing. And, just as poor reading or writing skills are barriers to college success, so, too, are poor money management skills. To earn money, many students work so many hours that their learning and grades suffer. Still others drop out of college because they decide they just can't afford the cost. Creators, however, treat a money problem as they would any other. They identify their goal, analyze their options, make a plan, carry it out, and, finally, assess its level of success. They will not be denied.

In this section, you will learn some of the basics of money management. There is, of course, much more to know. But if you apply these basic skills effectively, you can look forward to building a bank account that

Level of Education	Median Earnings	Unemployment Rate
Less than a high school diploma	$23,088	14.9%
High school diploma, no college	$32,552	10.3%
Some college, no degree	$37,024	9.2%
Associate degree	$39,884	7.0%
Bachelor's degree	$53,976	5.4%
Master's degree	$66,144	4.0%
Doctoral degree	$80,600	1.9%
Professional degree	$83,720	2.4%

Figure 8.1 | Yearly Salaries and Unemployment Rates by Levels of Education
Source: U.S. Bureau of Labor Statistics, Current Population Survey, 2010.

will provide you with many of the things that money can provide, including a college education.

MANAGING MONEY: THE BIG PICTURE

When I was a young college instructor, a colleague and I were complaining one day about how little money we were making. Both of us had young families, and our salaries barely got us from paycheck to paycheck. One day we decided to stop complaining and do something about it. We decided to award ourselves a raise. To do so, we brainstormed how we could save or earn more money. Our first discovery was that we were both paying about $6 a month for our checking accounts. We switched to free checking and gave ourselves an instant raise of $72 a year. By itself, no big thing. But we also thought of 21 other ways to make or save money. All told, our self-awarded raises amounted to more than $1,000 a year. And that was just the beginning of our realization that we had more control over our money than we had thought.

So, be a Creator when it comes to money. As you examine the following strategies, keep in mind the big picture of managing money. **Do everything legal to increase the flow of money *into* your personal treasury and decrease the flow of money leaking *out*. The better you become at these two complementary skills, the more abundance you will create to enhance your life and the lives of the people you love**.

INCREASE MONEY FLOWING IN

1. Create a positive affirmation about money. Many people hold negative beliefs about money and their ability to accumulate it. These doubts keep them from making wise choices that would cause more money to flow in their direction, or reduce the amount of money flowing away from them. Create an affirming statement about money, such as, *I am creating unlimited abundance in my life*. Along with your personal affirmation, repeat this financial affirmation to revise your choices about money. There is great abundance on our planet, and there is no reason why you shouldn't enjoy your share of it.

2. Create a financial plan. Like a life plan, a financial plan helps you define and achieve your goals. It helps you make important decisions about the dollars flowing in and out of your bank account. Beginning your financial plan is as simple as filling out the form on the next page of this section. As a guideline, some financial experts suggest that expenditures in a healthy financial plan should be close to the following percentages of your net income (i.e., the money remaining after all required federal, state, and local tax deductions):

31% Housing	7% Entertainment
20% Transportation	7% Savings
16% Food	6% Clothing
8% Miscellaneous	5% Health

Obviously, after subtracting all of your expenses from your income, your goal is to have a positive and growing balance. If you have a negative balance, with each passing month you'll slide deeper into debt. To avoid debt, you need to increase your income, decrease your expenses, or both.

3. Find a bank or credit union. A bank or credit union helps you manage your money with services such as checking accounts, savings accounts, and easy access to cash through automated teller machines (ATMs). Your ideal financial institution offers a free checking account that requires no minimum balance and pays interest. Further, it offers a savings account with competitive interest rates. And, finally, your ideal financial institution offers free use of its ATMs and those belonging to other banks or credit unions as well. If you need to pay for any of these services, seek to minimize the yearly cost. Credit unions typically offer lower rates on these services than banks do. If you don't know of a credit union for which you qualify, contact the Credit Union National Association (800-358-5710) to get the phone number of your state's credit union league, where you'll get help in finding one you may be able to join. Whether your checking

My Financial Plan		
STEP A: MONTHLY INCOME	**AMOUNT**	**BALANCE**
Support from parents or others		
Scholarships		
Loans		
Investments		
Earned income		
Total Monthly Income (A)		
STEP B: NECESSARY FIXED MONTHLY EXPENSES		
Housing (mortgage or rent)		
Transportation (car payments, insurance, bus pass, car pool)		
Taxes (federal and state income, Social Security, Medicare)		
Insurance (house, health, and life)		
Child care		
Tuition		
Bank fees		
Debt payment		
Savings and investments		
Total Necessary Fixed Monthly Expenses (B)		
STEP C: NECESSARY VARIABLE MONTHLY EXPENSES		
Food and personal care items		
Clothing		
Telephone		
Gas and electric		
Water		
Transportation (car repairs, maintenance, gasoline)		
Laundry and dry cleaning		
Doctor and medicine		
Child care		
Books and software		
Computer/Internet access		
Total Necessary Variable Monthly Expenses (C)		
STEP D: OPTIONAL FIXED AND VARIABLE MONTHLY EXPENSES		
Eating out (including coffee, snacks, lunches)		
Entertainment (movies, theater, night life)		
Travel		
Hobbies		
Gifts		
Charitable contributions		
Miscellaneous (CDs, magazines, newspapers, etc.)		
Total Optional Variable Monthly Expenses (D)		
Money Remaining or Owed at End of Month (A − B − C − D = ?)		

account is with a bank or a credit union, be sure to balance your account regularly. This will save you the embarrassment and expense of bounced (rejected) checks because of insufficient funds.

4. Apply for grants and scholarships. A great place to get an overview of financial aid sources is provided on the Internet by the U.S. government at http://www.ed.gov/fund/grants-college.html. The process of applying for financial aid dollars begins with the FAFSA: Free Application for Federal Student Aid. Using information you report on this form, the government decides what you or your family can afford to pay toward your education and what you may need in the way of financial assistance. Get copies of the form from your college's financial aid office or online at http://www.fafsa .ed.gov/. There is also a "forecaster" at this site that will help you estimate the amount of financial aid you can expect to receive. The deadline for completing the FAFSA form is early July; however, some colleges use the information from the FAFSA form to determine their own financial aid, so be sure to check your school's deadline or you could be out of luck (and money) for that year. The benefit of qualifying for grants and scholarships is that, unlike loans, you don't need to pay them back. Federal Pell Grants provide financial support to students with family incomes up to $60,000; however, most Pell awards go to students with family incomes below $30,000. In 2011–12, the grants ranged from $555 to $5,500, with an average grant in 2009–10 of approximately $3,600. You can get comprehensive information from the Federal Student Aid Information Center in Washington at 800-433-3243 (http:// www.studentaid.ed.gov). Here you can order a free copy of *The Student Guide*, and learn about programs that make up nearly three-fourths of all financial aid awarded to students. You can also search without cost for scholarships at Internet sites such as http://apps.collegeboard.com/cbsearch_ss/ welcome.jsp, http://collegeanswer.com, and http:// www.fastweb.com (so, don't waste money paying a private service to find you scholarships). Perhaps most important, spend time with a counselor in

your college's financial aid office and let him or her help you get your share of the financial support available for a college education. Ron Smith, former head of financial aid at Baltimore City Community College, offers this advice: "Students should apply early, provide accurate information, and follow up until an award has been received."

5. Apply for low-cost loans. Stafford loans are guaranteed by the federal government, so they generally offer the lowest interest rates. For dependent students, subsidized Stafford loans of up to $5,500 per year for first-year students, $6,500 for sophomores, and $7,500 for juniors and seniors are awarded on the basis of financial need. The U.S. government pays interest until repayment begins, usually after graduation. For independent students, loan maximums are approximately $4000 per year higher. Unsubsidized Stafford loans do not depend on financial need, but the interest accumulates while you are in college. You can apply for them through the Federal Direct Loan Program at 800-848-0979 (http://www.ed.gov/offices/OSFAP/ DirectLoan/index.html) or through a private lender such as a bank. Other federally guaranteed student loans include PLUS loans (made to students' parents) and Perkins loans (for lower-income students). You may be approved for more loan money than you actually need and be tempted to borrow it all; just remember that what you take now, you'll need to repay later. You don't want to finish your education with the burden of an unnecessarily large debt. The standard repayment plan for student loans is equal monthly payments for 10 years. That's a long time to pay for an earlier bad choice.

6. Work. Even with grants, scholarships, and low-cost loans, many college students need employment to make ends meet. If this is your situation, figure out how much money you need each month beyond any financial aid, and set a goal to earn that amount while also adding work experience in your future field of employment. In other words, your purpose for working is both to make money *and* to accumulate valuable employment experience and recommendations. In this way, you make it easier to find employment after college and perhaps even negotiate a higher starting salary. One place that may help you achieve this double goal is your campus job center. Additionally, on some campuses, instructors are able to hire student assistants to help them with their research. If you try but can't find employment that provides valuable work experience (or you're not sure what your future employment plans are), then seek work that allows you to earn your needed income in the fewest hours (saving you time to excel in your studies). Because many jobs you'll encounter in the newspaper pay little more than minimum wage, you may do better to create a high-paying job for yourself by using skills you already possess (or could easily learn). For example, one student noticed that each autumn the rain gutters of houses near his college became clogged with falling leaves. With a gasoline-powered leaf blower and a ladder in hand, he knocked on doors and offered to clean gutters for only $20. Few homeowners could resist such a bargain, and averaging two houses per hour, he earned nearly $700 each fall weekend.

7. Save and invest. If you haven't done so already, open a savings account and begin making regular deposits, even if it's only $20 per month (about what you'd pay for a pizza and a movie). Set a goal to accumulate a financial reserve for emergencies equal to three months' living expenses. After that, begin regular deposits in higher-income investments such as stocks, bonds, and mutual funds, topics beyond the scope of this book, but well worth your effort to research. (For a brief overview, visit http://www.fool.com/60second/indexfund .htm?ref=prmpgid.) To gain practical experience and guidance, consider joining (or starting) an investment club on your campus. You don't have to be an economics major to realize that by investing money regularly and benefiting from compound interest (earning interest on interest), even people with modest incomes can accumulate significant wealth. A way to make your savings grow even faster is to invest in a tax-deferred retirement

account in which the money you deposit is not taxed until you withdraw it many years later, increasing the amount you can potentially save by many thousands of dollars. You can open such an account through your employer (who may even make additional contributions) or by opening an IRA (Individual Retirement Account) on your own. Some experts even suggest that you invest in such a tax-deferred retirement account before making deposits in a savings account. Your safety net in this approach is your credit cards, which you use only in an emergency (as you would use your savings account, if you had one). Of course, this latter approach depends on your responsible use of credit cards and isn't for everyone, but it is another choice to consider.

DECREASE MONEY FLOWING OUT

8. Lower transportation expenses. Cars are expensive. Beyond car payments, there's also the cost for insurance, registration, regular maintenance, gasoline, repairs, tolls, and parking. And if you're under 25, you'll pay more for insurance than someone over 25 (especially young men, whose rates are double or triple those of older men). So, if money is tight, consider whether you can get along without a car for now. If you live on campus, this option should be fairly easy; if you commute, you could use public transportation or offer gas money to a classmate for rides to school. If you decide that you do need to buy a car, one expert suggests the following strategy for getting a good purchase price: After determining the model and options you want, call or email a number of dealers (preferably on the last day of the month when they are more likely to be anxious to make sales quotas), saying, "I'm going to buy this car today from the dealer who gives me the best price, so what's your lowest offer?" After receiving responses from at least six to eight dealers, contact the one with the second-to-lowest bid, reveal your lowest bid, and ask if they'll beat it. If so, buy the car. If not, purchase the one with the lowest bid. You can confirm that you're getting a fair price on a new or used car by visiting Kelley Blue Book (http://www.kbb.com) or Edmund's (http://www.edmunds.com).

9. Shop for car loans and insurance. *Before* you shop for your car, check interest rates for car loans with at least two banks and a credit union, and check insurance rates with at least three insurance companies. Knowing available interest rates will protect you from being pressured into signing a high-interest loan contract with the car dealer. On a car purchase, a lower interest rate can mean hundreds (even thousands) of dollars in savings over the life of the loan. You can also check for low interest rates on the Internet at http://www.Bankrate.com or http://www.Lendingtree.com. Likewise, automobile insurance rates for the same coverage can vary significantly from company to company. If you have good grades, tell the agent. A high GPA can reduce your premium by up to 25 percent with some companies! Oh, and think twice before allowing friends to drive your car; if they get in an accident, it's *your* insurance record and premiums that suffer, not your friend's.

10. Use credit cards wisely. You'll very likely be swamped with invitations to open credit card accounts. You're not alone. From 1990 to 2000, the average credit card debt of college students jumped 305 percent, from $900 to $2,748, and nearly 10 percent of college students owe greater than $7,000 on their credit cards, according to a 2000 survey by Sallie Mae, a major national handler of student loans. "These credit card issuers circle the campus like sharks circling a fish," says Elizabeth Warren, a Harvard Law School professor. So, first, consider whether you should even *have* a credit card. Visa, Master Card, and other credit cards provide you with short-term loans to purchase anything you want up to your credit limit. These companies are counting on you to postpone paying off the loan beyond the grace period (the time during which the loan is free), and thus to accumulate interest at their high rates. The consequences to your finances can be staggering. Suppose you're 20 years old and owe $3,500 on a credit card that charges 17 percent interest and you regularly pay the minimum charge. You won't pay off that debt until you're 53 years old, and the amount you will ultimately pay is nearly $11,000! And if you ever miss a payment, you'll incur a triple penalty. First, you'll be charged a late fee that can be as much as $35 for being even one day overdue. Next, some banks punish late payers by raising their interest rates to "penalty rates" of 20 percent or more. Finally, late payments can show up on your credit report, making it difficult for you to get loans later for a house or car. Additional penalties will be assessed if you go over your credit limit. How serious is the problem of credit card misuse by college students? One widely quoted statement attributed to an administrator at the University of Indiana noted, "We lose more students to credit card debt than to academic failure." So, use a credit card only if you can discipline yourself to pay off most, and preferably all, of your balance every month. If you can't, a wiser choice would be to cut up your credit cards (or not even apply for one in the first place). To understand the true cost of buying with credit cards, try the exercise "The Cost of Credit" on the CourseMate website for *On Course* at www.cengagebrain.com.

11. Choose credit cards wisely. If you decide that you do have the discipline to use a credit card wisely, realize that all credit cards are not created equal. Compare your options and choose the one with the lowest interest rates, the longest grace period (time you get to use the money before paying interest), and the lowest annual fee (preferably free). Some cards offer a reward for using them, such as rebates for purchases or frequent flyer miles that can be exchanged for airline tickets. To find the best deals on credit cards, visit Internet sites such as http://www.bankrate.com or http://www.cardratings.com/.

12. Use debit cards wisely. A debit card is similar to a credit card, except that the funds come not as a loan from the credit card company but as a withdrawal from your own checking account. The danger is that you may not record and track every purchase made on your debit card, as you more likely would if you wrote a check. Consequently, you can easily overdraw your checking account and incur financial penalties for bounced checks (not to mention annoying your creditors). Use a debit card only if you have the discipline to track its every use and keep your checking account balance current.

13. Use ATM cards wisely. An ATM card, like a debit card, draws from your personal account, but here the withdrawal is in cash. ATM cards are so easy to use that some financial experts refer to them as "death cards." Say you withdraw $100 in cash on Monday, and by Thursday the money has dribbled away, so you take out another $100 that disappears by the weekend. After a couple of weeks like this, your money runs out before the month does, and you're slipping ever deeper into debt. Use an ATM card only if you have the self-discipline to record every withdrawal and track what you do with your cash.

14. Pay off high-rate debt. When you pay off a loan (such as a credit card balance) that charges 17 percent, that's the same as investing your money at a guaranteed 17 percent rate of return. Better yet, the 17 percent return is tax free, so you're actually earning a return of more than 20 percent. Compare that to the puny interest rate you'd be earning in a savings account. If you don't have extra money in savings to pay off money you owe, a variation is to transfer debt from high-interest-rate loans to lower-interest-rate loans (but watch carefully for hidden transfer costs on some accounts).

15. Dispute inaccurate charges. Don't assume all of your bills are correct. Inspect your credit card bill, your bank statement, and all of your bills carefully for suspicious charges, such as a purchase you didn't make or an inaccurate late fee. Call the number on your statement and explain pleasantly but assertively why you believe the charge is an error. Usually the person you talk to is empowered to correct such errors. In fact, if you have a good credit history, it may even pay to question legitimate charges. I once forgot to pay my credit card bill on time and got charged more than $100 in late fees and interest; I called the credit card company, asked the representative to look at my excellent record of paying on time, and requested that the penalties be waived this once. She agreed, making my five-minute phone call well worth the effort!

16. Avoid credit blunders. There are serious consequences for being financially irresponsible. Every time you create a debt, national credit agencies are keeping detailed records. When you later apply for credit, potential lenders will have access to how much you owe, to whom you owe, and how well you pay your debts. In fact, they'll learn your credit history for at least the past seven years, including late payments, underpayments, and lack of payments. This financial record tells lenders whether you are a good or bad risk, and, if you're seen as a bad risk, your application for a house or car loan may be turned down or only offered to you with extremely high interest rates. Your credit report might even wind up in the hands of a potential landlord or employer, affecting your ability to rent an apartment or even get your dream job. So, unwise financial choices in the present will follow you for years into the future, possibly affecting the quality of your life and the life of your family. To see your present credit report and verify its accuracy, order a copy from Equifax at 800-685-1111 (http://www.equifax.com), Experian at 888-397-3742 (http://www.experian .com), or Trans Union at 800-888-4213 (http://www.tuc.com). Depending on where you live, the report will range in cost from free to about $8. If you make a credit blunder, immediately contact the company you owe and work out a payment schedule. The sooner you clean up your credit report, the sooner your past mistakes will stop sabotaging your future success. If you need help with debt, contact the National Foundation for Credit Counseling (NFCC) for low- or no-cost credit assistance at 800-388-2227 (http://www.nfcc.org).

17. Use tax credits. Tax credits are expenses you can subtract directly from your federal income tax. If you're paying for college yourself, you may be eligible for a Hope Credit of up to $3,000 in your first two years. For details on the Hope Credit (as well as the Lifetime Learning Credit), get a copy of IRS (Internal Revenue Service) Publication 970, *Tax Benefits for Higher Education,* or go to http://www .irs.gov/publications/p970/ch02 .html#en_US_publink100020759.

18. Avoid the "Let's Go Out" trap. You or a friend says, "Let's go out." You go for food or drinks and spend $20 . . . or more. Do this a couple times a week and you'll wind up dropping hundreds of dollars a month into a deep, dark hole. One student reported that even after she ran out of money for the month, friends would say, "Oh, c'mon out with us. I'll loan you the money." That meant she was already spending next month's income. By all means, put entertainment money into your monthly financial plan, but, when it's gone, have the self-discipline to stop going out. Instead, invite friends over and make it BYO—Bring Your Own. Or, you could make a great financial choice by staying home and studying. Studying costs you nothing now and makes a great investment in your future income.

19. Track your expenditures. To plug a leak, you have to know where it is. So, carry a note pad with you and record every penny you spend for at least a week, preferably longer. (Of course your Inner Defender will probably say, "This is stupid and boring." Okay, it is boring, but the benefit is worth it!) Examine your recorded expenses and look for financial leaks that don't show up in your financial plan. One student was shocked to discover that he was spending an average of $21 per week ($1,144 per year!) on fast-food lunches; he started packing his lunch and saved a bundle.

20. Examine each expense line in your financial plan for possible reductions. Here are some of the money-saving options my students have come up with: Find a roommate to reduce housing costs. Exchange babysitting with fellow students to minimize child-care expenses. Car pool to share commuting costs. Cut up credit cards. Change banks to lower or eliminate monthly checking fees. Exchange music CDs with friends instead of buying new ones. Shop at discount clubs and buy nonperishables (such as toilet paper and laundry detergent) in bulk. Read magazines and newspapers at the library, instead of buying them. Pay creditors on time to avoid penalty charges. Delay purchases until the item goes on sale (such as right after Christmas). Find other money saving ideas on the Internet at http://www.lowermybills.com.

MONEY MANAGEMENT EXERCISE

To help *increase* your flow of money in, make a list of skills you have that you could possibly turn into a high-hourly-wage self-employment opportunity. To help *decrease* your flow of money out, make a list of choices you could make that would each save you $25 or more per year. If you need help, try an Internet search for "saving money" or "budget tips." Compare your two lists with those of classmates to see if you can find additional choices you didn't think of. Add up all of the items on your list (income and outflow) and see how much you could improve your financial picture in one year by making these choices.

Staying On Course to Your Success

9

SUCCESSFUL STUDENTS...	STRUGGLING STUDENTS...
gain self-awareness, consciously employing behaviors, beliefs, and attitudes that keep them on course.	**make important choices unconsciously**, being directed by self-sabotaging habits and outdated life scripts.
adopt lifelong learning, finding valuable lessons and wisdom in nearly every experience they have.	**resist learning new ideas and skills**, viewing learning as fearful or boring rather than as mental play.
develop emotional intelligence, effectively managing their emotions in support of their goals and dreams.	**live at the mercy of strong emotions** such as anger, depression, anxiety, or a need for instant gratification.
believe in themselves, seeing themselves as capable, lovable, and unconditionally worthy human beings.	**doubt their competence and personal value**, feeling inadequate to create their desired outcomes and experiences.

Planning Your Next Steps

Focus Questions How have you changed while writing your journal entries? What changes do you still want to make?

Although our travels together are coming to an end, your journey has really just begun. Look out there to your future. What do you want to have, do, or be? What actions do you need to take to achieve your desired outcomes and experiences? Make a plan and go for it!

Sure, you'll get off course at times. But now you have the strategies—both outer and inner—to get back on course. Before heading out toward your goals and dreams, take a moment to review those strategies. Anytime you want, you can look over the table of contents of this book for an overview of what you've learned. Scan the chapter-opening charts to review the choices of successful and struggling people. Reread a strategy as a reminder. Review the study skills you chose to create your CORE Learning System. Perhaps most important of all, reread your journal. At any time you can return to *On Course* and to your journal to remind yourself of anything you forget. And, believe me, you *will* forget. But you have the power to remember . . . and to make wise choices . . . and to achieve the life of your dreams.

ASSESS YOURSELF, AGAIN

On the next page is a duplicate of the self-assessment you took in Chapter 1. Take it again. (Don't look back at your previous answers yet.) In Journal Entry 33, you will compare your first scores with your scores today, and you'll consider the changes you have made. Acknowledge yourself for your courage to grow. Look, also, at the changes you still need to make to become your best self.

You now have much of what you need to stay on course to the life of your dreams. The rest you can learn on your journey. Be bold! Begin today!

Onward!

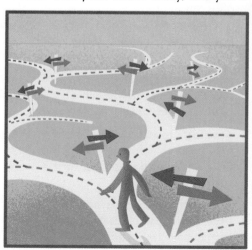

> Destiny is not a matter of chance; it is a matter of choice. It is not a thing to be waited for; it is a thing to be achieved.
>
> *William Jennings Bryant*

> It isn't where you came from; it's where you're going that counts.
>
> *Ella Fitzgerald*

SELF-ASSESSMENT

Visit www.cengagebrain.com to access this *On Course* self-assessment online through CourseMate for *On Course*.

You're about to retake the self-assessment you took in Chapter 1. For now, it's important that you **do not look back at your scores from Chapter 1**. You'll be able to do that in just a little while.

First, read the following 64 statements. Decide how true you believe each statement was about you at the *beginning* of this course. Write that score in the column labeled "THEN."

Next, decide how true you believe that same statement is about you at the *end* of this course. Write the score in the column labeled "NOW."

To get an accurate picture of yourself, consider what you remember **WAS** honestly true about you at the beginning of the course and what you believe **IS** honestly true about you now. Remember, there are no right or wrong answers. Assign each statement two scores (THEN and NOW) from 0 to 10, as follows:

Totally False	←	0	1	2	3	4	5	6	7	8	9	10	→	Totally True

	THEN	NOW	
1.	_____	_____	I control how successful I will be.
2.	_____	_____	I'm not sure why I'm in college.
3.	_____	_____	I spend most of my time doing important things.
4.	_____	_____	When I encounter a challenging problem, I try to solve it by myself.
5.	_____	_____	When I get off course from my goals and dreams, I realize it right away.
6.	_____	_____	I'm not sure how I prefer to learn.
7.	_____	_____	Whether I'm happy or not depends mostly on me.
8.	_____	_____	I'll truly accept myself only after I eliminate my faults and weaknesses.
9.	_____	_____	Forces out of my control (such as poor teaching) are the cause of low grades I receive in school.
10.	_____	_____	I place great value on getting my college degree.
11.	_____	_____	I don't need to write things down because I can remember what I need to do.
12.	_____	_____	I have a network of people in my life that I can count on for help.
13.	_____	_____	If I have habits that hinder my success, I'm not sure what they are.
14.	_____	_____	When I don't like the way an instructor teaches, I know how to learn the subject anyway.
15.	_____	_____	When I get very angry, sad, or afraid, I do or say things that create a problem for me.
16.	_____	_____	When I think about performing an upcoming challenge (such as taking a test), I usually see myself doing well.
17.	_____	_____	When I have a problem, I take positive actions to find a solution.
18.	_____	_____	I don't know how to set effective short-term and long-term goals.
19.	_____	_____	I am organized.

20. _____ _____ When I take a difficult course in school, I study alone.
21. _____ _____ I'm aware of beliefs I have that hinder my success.
22. _____ _____ I'm not sure how to think critically and analytically about complex topics.
23. _____ _____ When choosing between doing an important school assignment or something really fun, I do the school assignment.
24. _____ _____ I break promises that I make to myself or to others.
25. _____ _____ I make poor choices that keep me from getting what I really want in life.
26. _____ _____ I expect to do well in my college classes.
27. _____ _____ I lack self-discipline.
28. _____ _____ I listen carefully when other people are talking.
29. _____ _____ I'm stuck with any habits of mine that hinder my success.
30. _____ _____ My intelligence is something about myself that I can improve.
31. _____ _____ I often feel bored, anxious, or depressed.
32. _____ _____ I feel just as worthwhile as any other person.
33. _____ _____ Forces outside of me (such as luck or other people) control how successful I will be.
34. _____ _____ College is an important step on the way to accomplishing my goals and dreams.
35. _____ _____ I spend most of my time doing unimportant things.
36. _____ _____ I am aware of how to show respect to people who are different from me (race, religion, sexual orientation, age, etc.).
37. _____ _____ I can be off course from my goals and dreams for quite a while without realizing it.
38. _____ _____ I know how I prefer to learn.
39. _____ _____ My happiness depends mostly on what's happened to me lately.
40. _____ _____ I accept myself just as I am, even with my faults and weaknesses.
41. _____ _____ I am the cause of low grades I receive in school.
42. _____ _____ If I lose my motivation in college, I don't know how I'll get it back.
43. _____ _____ I have a written self-management system that helps me get important things done on time.
44. _____ _____ I seldom interact with people who are different from me.
45. _____ _____ I'm aware of the habits I have that hinder my success.
46. _____ _____ If I don't like the way an instructor teaches, I'll probably do poorly in the course.
47. _____ _____ When I'm very angry, sad, or afraid, I know how to manage my emotions so I don't do anything I'll regret later.
48. _____ _____ When I think about performing an upcoming challenge (such as taking a test), I usually see myself doing poorly.
49. _____ _____ When I have a problem, I complain, blame others, or make excuses.
50. _____ _____ I know how to set effective short-term and long-term goals.
51. _____ _____ I am disorganized.
52. _____ _____ When I take a difficult course in school, I find a study partner or join a study group.

53. _____	_____	I'm unaware of beliefs I have that hinder my success.
54. _____	_____	I know how to think critically and analytically about complex topics.
55. _____	_____	I often feel happy and fully alive.
56. _____	_____	I keep promises that I make to myself or to others.
57. _____	_____	When I have an important choice to make, I use a decision-making process that analyzes possible options and their likely outcomes.
58. _____	_____	I don't expect to do well in my college classes.
59. _____	_____	I am a self-disciplined person.
60. _____	_____	I get distracted easily when other people are talking.
61. _____	_____	I know how to change habits of mine that hinder my success.
62. _____	_____	Everyone is born with a certain amount of intelligence, and there's not really much you can do to change that.
63. _____	_____	When choosing between doing an important school assignment or something really fun, I usually do something fun.
64. _____	_____	I feel less worthy than other people.

Transfer your scores to the scoring sheets on the next two pages. For each of the eight areas, total your scores in columns A and B. Then total your final scores as shown in the sample.

SELF-ASSESSMENT SCORING SHEET FOR "THEN" (BEGINNING OF COURSE)

	SAMPLE		**SCORE #1: ACCEPTING PERSONAL RESPONSIBILITY**		**SCORE #2: DISCOVERING SELF-MOTIVATION**

A	B	A	B	A	B
6. _8_	29. _3_	1. ___	9. ___	10. ___	2. ___
14. _5_	35. _3_	17. ___	25. ___	26. ___	18. ___
21. _6_	50. _6_	41. ___	33. ___	34. ___	42. ___
73. _9_	56. _2_	57. ___	49. ___	50. ___	58. ___
_28_ + 40 − _14_ = _54_		___ + 40 − ___ = ___		___ + 40 − ___ = ___	

SCORE #3: MASTERING SELF-MANAGEMENT		**SCORE #4: EMPLOYING INTERDEPENDENCE**		**SCORE #5: GAINING SELF-AWARENESS**	
A	B	A	B	A	3
3. ___	11. ___	12. ___	4. ___	5. ___	13. ___
19. ___	27. ___	28. ___	20. ___	21. ___	29. ___
43. ___	35. ___	36. ___	44. ___	45. ___	37. ___
59. ___	51. ___	52. ___	60. ___	61. ___	53. ___
___ + 40 − ___ = ___		___ + 40 − ___ = ___		___ + 40 − ___ = ___	

SCORE #6: ADOPTING LIFELONG LEARNING		**SCORE #7: DEVELOPING EMOTIONAL INTELLIGENCE**		**SCORE #8: BELIEVING IN MYSELF**	
A	B	A	B	A	3
14. ___	6. ___	7. ___	15. ___	16. ___	8. ___
30. ___	22. ___	23. ___	31. ___	32. ___	24. ___
38. ___	46. ___	47. ___	39. ___	40. ___	48. ___
54. ___	62. ___	55. ___	63. ___	56. ___	64. ___
___ + 40 − ___ = ___		___ + 40 − ___ = ___		___ + 40 − ___ = ___	

INTERPRETING YOUR SCORES

A score of . . .

0–39   Indicates an area where your choices will **seldom** keep you on course.

40–63   Indicates an area where your choices will **sometimes** keep you on course.

64–80   Indicates an area where your choices will **usually** keep you on course.

SELF-ASSESSMENT SCORING SHEET FOR "NOW" (END OF COURSE)

SAMPLE

A	B
6. _8_	29. _3_
14. _5_	35. _3_
21. _6_	50. _6_
73. _9_	56. _2_

_28_ + 40 − _14_ = _54_

SCORE #1: ACCEPTING PERSONAL RESPONSIBILITY

A	B
1. ___	9. ___
17. ___	25. ___
41. ___	33. ___
57. ___	49. ___

___ + 40 − ___ = ___

SCORE #2: DISCOVERING SELF-MOTIVATION

A	B
10. ___	2. ___
26. ___	18. ___
34. ___	42. ___
50. ___	58. ___

___ + 40 − ___ = ___

SCORE #3: MASTERING SELF-MANAGEMENT

A	B
3. ___	11. ___
19. ___	27. ___
43. ___	35. ___
59. ___	51. ___

___ + 40 − ___ = ___

SCORE #4: EMPLOYING INTERDEPENDENCE

A	B
12. ___	4. ___
28. ___	20. ___
36. ___	44. ___
52. ___	60. ___

___ + 40 − ___ = ___

SCORE #5: GAINING SELF-AWARENESS

A	B
5. ___	13. ___
21. ___	29. ___
45. ___	37. ___
61. ___	53. ___

___ + 40 − ___ = ___

SCORE #6: ADOPTING LIFELONG LEARNING

A	B
14. ___	6. ___
30. ___	22. ___
38. ___	46. ___
54. ___	62. ___

___ + 40 − ___ = ___

SCORE #7: DEVELOPING EMOTIONAL INTELLIGENCE

A	B
7. ___	15. ___
23. ___	31. ___
47. ___	39. ___
55. ___	63. ___

___ + 40 − ___ = ___

SCORE #8: BELIEVING IN MYSELF

A	B
16. ___	8. ___
32. ___	24. ___
40. ___	48. ___
56. ___	64. ___

___ + 40 − ___ = ___

INTERPRETING YOUR SCORES

A score of . . .

0–39   Indicates an area where your choices will **seldom** keep you on course.

40–63   Indicates an area where your choices will **sometimes** keep you on course.

64–80   Indicates an area where your choices will **usually** keep you on course.

CHOICES OF SUCCESSFUL STUDENTS

SUCCESSFUL STUDENTS...	STRUGGLING STUDENTS...
accept personal responsibility, seeing themselves as the primary cause of their outcomes and experiences	**see themselves as victims,** believing that what happens to them is determined primarily by external forces such as fate, luck, and powerful others.
discover self-motivation, finding purpose in their lives by discovering personally meaningful goals and dreams.	**have difficulty sustaining motivation**, often feeling depressed, frustrated, and/or resentful about a lack of direction in their lives.
master self-management, consistently planning and taking purposeful actions in pursuit of their goals and dreams.	**seldom identify specific actions needed to accomplish a desired outcome,** and when they do, they tend to procrastinate.
employ interdependence, building mutually supportive relationships that help them achieve their goals and dreams (while helping others do the same).	**are solitary,** seldom requesting, even rejecting, offers of assistance from those who could help.
gain self-awareness, consciously employing behaviors, beliefs, and attitudes that keep them on course.	**make important choices unconsciously,** being directed by self-sabotaging habits and outdated life scripts.
adopt lifelong learning, finding valuable lessons and wisdom in nearly every experience they have.	**resist learning new ideas and skills,** viewing learning as fearful or boring rather than as mental play.
develop emotional intelligence, effectively managing their emotions in support of their goals and dreams.	**live at the mercy of strong emotions,** such as anger, depression, anxiety, or a need for instant gratification.
believe in themselves, seeing themselves as capable, lovable, and unconditionally worthy human beings.	**doubt their competence and personal value,** feeling inadequate to create their desired outcomes and experiences.

Journal Entry 33

In this activity, you will examine the changes you have made since the beginning of this course, and you'll plan your next steps toward success in college and in life.

1. Copy the chart below into your journal. In Column 1, put your scores from the scoring chart on page 8 (FIRST scores). In Column 2 put your scores from the scoring chart on page 294 (THEN scores). In Column 3 put your scores from the scoring chart on page 295 (NOW scores).

	Column 1 FIRST Scores (from page 8)	Column 2 THEN Score (from page 294)	Column 3 NOW scores (from page 295)
1. Accepting personal responsibility	_____	_____	_____
2. Discovering self-motivation	_____	_____	_____
3. Mastering self-management	_____	_____	_____
4. Employing interdependence	_____	_____	_____
5. Gaining self-awareness	_____	_____	_____
6. Adopting lifelong learning	_____	_____	_____
7. Developing emotional intelligence	_____	_____	_____
8. Believing in myself	_____	_____	_____

> And the end of all our exploring
> Will be to arrive where we started
> And know the place for the first time.
>
> *T. S. Eliot*

2. **Compare your scores in Column 1 (FIRST Scores) with your scores in Column 2 (THEN Scores).** Since both scores are supposed to represent how you were at the beginning of the course, you might expect them to be the same . . . but often they are different. In what areas are your FIRST scores and THEN scores different? Why do you suppose there is a difference? For example, if one of your eight scores went down, consider that this result may not indicate that you became less effective; rather, it may indicate that you are now more honest with yourself or more aware of what is necessary to excel in this area.

3. **Compare your FIRST and THEN (Columns 1 & 2) scores with your NOW (Column 3) scores. Write about the area(s) in which you have raised your scores the most.** Remember to answer questions that a thoughtful reader would have about what you are writing. Dive deep by using the 4E's (examples, explanations, experiences, and evidence)!

4. **Write about the area(s) in which you most want to continue improving.** Remember the saying "If you keep doing what you've been doing, you'll keep getting what you've been getting." With this idea in mind, identify the specific changes you'd like to make in your behaviors, thoughts, emotions, and beliefs in the months and years to come. Dive deep.

5. **Write one last entry in which you sum up the most important discoveries you have made about yourself while keeping your journal. Dive deep!**

One Student's Story

STEPHAN J. MONTGOMERY
Washtenaw Community College, Michigan

In 2002, I hit rock bottom when I moved into a homeless shelter. For the next four years, I cycled in and out of one shelter after another. There, I saw how people can become passive and numb, with no life or hope left in their eyes. They smell bad, walk with their heads down, and are filled with negativity. Their only goal in life is getting a handout. I knew I couldn't allow a sheltered life to become my life.

I was a Detroit police officer from 1985 to 1998. In 1996 I lost my mother and not long after that my 17-year-old son died of an asthma attack. In my mind, crying on someone's shoulder was a sign of weakness, so I kept it all inside. I had been drinking before, but now I started drinking even more. I left the police force in 1998 and started a limo service. Four years later, I was arrested for drunk driving and lost my license. When I couldn't pay rent, the woman I was living with put me out, and I lived in my car for two months. That's when I turned to a homeless shelter for help.

My first concern was to become self-supporting, but I wasn't sure where to start. I went to a state employment service and told a counselor, "I want a college degree; not one of those low-paying jobs listed in the job bank." She told me about scholarships at the local community college, and with her help, I registered for classes in 2007. I hadn't been a student for 30-plus years, and the thought of attending college scared me. But I had a goal.

I wanted to become a computer systems security analyst, a career that starts at about $48,000. The money sure sounded good.

In my English Fundamentals class I encountered *On Course*. The book gave me insights into my past failures and successes and provided specific strategies for achieving success in college and in my life. I realized that many of my past problems were rooted in Victim language. When I was on the police force, I felt that some of the supervisors picked on me. I'd say they didn't like me because I wasn't in the right group. The truth was, I was missing a lot of work, but I always shifted the blame. After reading about Victim/Creator, I told myself, *You have to rebuild yourself. No one else is going to do it for you.* I even started telling people back at the shelter about what I was learning in this class.

My greatest concern about attending college was how to organize my time. The newly discovered Creator in me used the Four-Quadrant Chart to prioritize my daily tasks. As I used the self-management tools in the book, I developed self-confidence that I would do well in college. I showed the next actions list to others and told them how important it is to have a list to keep you focused. If someone tells you they have tickets to the Detroit Pistons game, you have to say no and do what is important for your goals.

Along with how to organize my time, I discovered the beauty of interdependence. Two of my English

classmates and I decided to meet in the writing center after each class and work on our assignments together. We encouraged each other and became teachers as well as students. Our newfound interdependence made us feel valuable and gave us increased confidence and feelings of self-worth. This confidence translated into academic success as well. I earned a 3.88 GPA, high honors, for my first semester.

In the next semester I got a part-time job in the writing center. I love to see a twinkle in students' eyes when I help them do well on a paper. I also started volunteering at the Washtenaw Literacy program. I continue to use *On Course* principles in my daily life, and I share them at the tutoring center, in my volunteer work, and at the shelter. These principles provide the best hope for people to lead successful, happy, and unsheltered lives. Two of the men from the shelter are now enrolled at the college, and they come to me when they have a problem. One guy still has a Victim mentality. I tell him, "Why do you blame your woe-is-me on everyone else and not look in the mirror and see yourself as the cause? If I can help you, I will. But you have to help yourself first."

People have to learn to stand on their own two feet, and I now have the skills to help others do that. I've even changed my career goal. I plan to teach elementary school. For me it's no longer about the money. It's about sharing myself. After experiencing the lessons in *On Course*, I feel I have something to share. My fear of failure is gone. Being a Creator, I believe in myself and feel confident that I can solve any problems I face. Now I want to share that feeling with others.

Photo: Courtesy of Stephan J. Montgomery

Bibliography

Adams, Kathleen. *Journal to the Self: Twenty-Two Paths to Personal Growth.* Warner Books, 1990.

Allen, David. *Getting Things Done.* Viking, 2001.

———. *Making It All Work.* Viking. 2009.

Brandon, Nathaniel. *The Psychology of Self-Esteem.* Jossey-Bass, 2001.

Bucher, Richard D. *Building Cultural Intelligence: Nine Megaskills.* Pearson, 2008.

Burka, Jane B., and Lenora M. Yuen. *Procrastination.* DeCapo, 2008.

Burns, David, M.D. *Feeling Good.* William Morrow & Company, 1980.

Buzan, Tony. *Make the Most of Your Mind.* Simon and Schuster, 1977.

Cappacchione, Lucia. *The Creative Journal.* Newcastle, 1989.

Ciarrochi, Joseph. *Emotional Intelligence in Everyday Life.* Psychology Press, 2001.

Covey, Stephen R. *7 Habits of Highly Effective People.* Simon and Schuster, 1989.

Csikszentmihalyi, Mihaly. *Flow: The Psychology of Optimal Experience.* Harper & Row, 1990.

Davis, Martha, Elizabeth Robbins Eshelman, and Matthew McKay. *The Relaxation and Stress Reduction Workbook.* New Harbinger, 2000.

deBono, Edward. *deBono's Thinking Course.* Facts on File, 1982.

Doidge, Norman. *The Brain That Changes Itself.* Penguin, 2007.

Dweck, Carol. *Mindset: The New Psychology of Success.* Random House, 2006.

Fieori, Neil. *The Now Habit.* Tarcher, 2007.

Firestone, Robert W., Lisa Firestone, Joyce Catlett, and Pat Love. *Conquer Your Critical Inner Voice.* New Harbinger, 2002.

Frankl, Viktor E., M.D. *Man's Search for Meaning.* Washington Square Press, 1959.

Garfield, Charles. *Peak Performers.* Avon Books, 1986.

Gladwell, Malcolm. *Outliers: The Story of Success.* Back Bay Books, 2011.

Glasser, William. *Reality Therapy.* Harper & Row, 1978.

Goleman, Daniel. *Emotional Intelligence.* Bantam Books, 1995.

———. *Working with Emotional Intelligence.* Bantam Books, 2000.

Griessman, B. Eugene. *The Achievement Factors.* Dodd, Mead, 1987.

Harmon, Willis, and Howard Rheingold. *Higher Creativity.* J. P. Tarcher, 1984.

Harris, Thomas. *I'm OK, You're OK.* Harper & Row, 1967.

Helmstetter, Shad. *Choices*. Simon and Schuster, 1989.

Herrmann, Ned. *The Creative Brain*. Brain Books, 1989.

Holden, Robert. *Success Intelligence*. Hay House, 2009.

Howard, Pierce J. *The Owner's Manual for the Brain*. Bard Press, 2006.

Iyengar, Sheena. *The Art of Choosing*. Twelve Publishers, 2010.

James, Muriel, and Dorothy Jongeward. *Born to Win*. Addison-Wesley, 1978.

Jensen, Eric. *Enriching the Brain*. Jossey-Bass, 2008.

Keirsey, D., and M. Bates. *Please Understand Me*. Prometheus Nemesis Books, 1978.

Kernis, Michael. *Self-Esteem: Issues and Answers*. Psychology Press, 2006.

Lehrer, Jonah. *How We Decide*. Houghton Mifflin Harcourt, 2009.

Leyden-Rubenstein, Lori. *The Stress Management Handbook*. Keats Publishing, 1998.

Mandino, Og. *A Better Way to Live*. Bantam Books, 1990.

Matsumoto, David and Linda Juang. *Culture & Psychology*. Wadsworth, 2008.

Mazlow, Abraham H. *Toward a Psychology of Being*. Van Nostrand Reinhold, 1968.

McKay, Matthew, Patrick Fanning, Carole Honeychurch, and Catherine Sutker. *The Self-Esteem Companion*. MJF Books, 2001.

Merlevede, Patrick E., Denis Bridoux, and Rudy Vandamme. *7 Steps to Emotional Intelligence*. Crown House, 2001.

Merrill, A. Roger. *Connections: Quadrant II Time Management*. Publishers Press, 1987.

Moule, Jean. *Cultural Competence: A Primer for Educators*. Wadsworth/Cengage, 2012.

Myers, David G. *The Pursuit of Happiness*. Avon Books, 1992.

Myers, Isabelle. *The Myers-Briggs Type Indicator*. Consulting Psychological Press, 1962.

Ostrander, Sheila, and Lynn Schroeder. *Super-learning*. Dell, 1979.

Peck, M. Scott, M.D. *The Road Less Traveled*. Simon and Schuster, 1978.

Peterson, Brooks. *Cultural Intelligence: A Guide to Working with People from Other Cultures*. Intercultural Press, 2004.

Progroff, Ira. *At a Journal Workshop*. Dialogue House Library, 1975.

Restak, Richard, M.D. *The Mind*. Bantam Books, 1988.

Rosenberg, Marshall B. *Nonviolent Communication*. PuddleDancer Press, 2005.

Satir, Virginia. *The New People-making*. Science and Behavior Books, 1988.

Schiraldi, Glen R., Patrick Fanning, and Matthew McKay. *The Self-Esteem Workbook*. New Harbinger, 2001.

Segal, Jeanne. *Raising Your Emotional Intelligence*. Henry Holt, 1997.

Seligman, Martin. *Learned Optimism*. Alfred A. Knopf, 1991.

Smith, Hyrum W. *The 10 Natural Laws of Successful Time and Life Management*. Warner Books, 1994.

Sousa, David A. *How the Brain Learns*. Corwin Press, 2006.

Steiner, Claude M. *Scripts People Live*. Bantam Books, 1974.

Stone, Hal, and Sidra Stone. *Embracing Your Inner Critic*. HarperCollins, 1993.

Tobias, Sheila. *Overcoming Math Anxiety*. W. W. Norton & Co., 1993.

vonOech, Roger. *A Whack on the Side of the Head*. Warner Books, 1983.

Ward, Francine. *Esteemable Acts: 10 Actions for Building Real Self-Esteem*. Broadway Books, 2003.

Index

Book titles are listed in italics; f following page numbers refers to figures

Numbers
The 7 Habits of Highly Effective People, 113
32-day commitment form, 130, 133f

Abbreviations, in notes, 109
Absences, from class, 35
Achievable quality, 86
Acrostics, 179
Action, purposeful, 113–117
Active learning, 21–30
Active listening, 157–161
Active reading, 69
Acton, Amy, 174
Acton, Lord, 244
Adler, Mortimer, 219
Adults, influencing children, 188–189
Advisor, college, 34
Affirmation, personal, 98–102, 104
Agenda, for essay, 249–250
Ali, Muhammad, 99
Allen, David, 120, 122, 262
Amygdala, 184
Anderson, Walter, 266
Angelou, Maya, 49, 156, 242, 264
Anger, 263–264
Annan, Kofi, 162
Annotating text, 72
Anxiety, 264–265
APA (American Psychological
        Association) format, 16
Arguments, logical, 232
Arnold, Karen, 255
Aronson, Joshua, 219
Artistic personalities, 200
Assertiveness, 169–173
Assistance, for reading, 74
Association, and memorization, 179
Attributions, 188
Audience, for writing, 246

Beal, Louise, 154
Beattie, Melody, 275
Beck, Lindsey, 258–259
Behavior patterns, 187–188
Behaviors, choosing, 3–4
Beliefs, choosing, 3–4
Bell, Terrell, 77
Bembenutty, Hefer, 19
Berne, Eric, 187, 188

Bissonette, Robert, 43
Blake, Eubie, 276
Blaming, 169–170
Blige, Mary J., 166
Blueprint, essay, 248
Boggs, Holt, 132
Bolles, Richard, 95
Books, for college courses, 35
Bradshaw, John, 98
Brain, human, 21–22
Brainstorming, 56–57
Branden, Nathaniel, 31, 50, 52, 56, 167
Brophy, Jere, 81, 270
Brown, Les, 84
Bryant, William Jennings, 57, 290
Bucher, Richard, 15
Buddha, 193
Building Cultural Intelligence, 15
Burke, Edmund, 166
Burns, David, 275
Burns, Thomas, 63

Caldwell, Taylor, 27
Calendars, 119–120, 124f, 134
Campbell, Joseph, 88
Campus life, 36
Camus, Albert, 18
Career search, 236–237
Carney, Clarke G., 199
Carroll, Lewis, 86
Catalogue, college, 34
Chaffee, John, 234
Chapman, Joyce, 41, 57, 99
Chapter information, 71
Character, 243
Cheating, 239–241
Chee Meng Vang, 83–84
Choa, Ruth K., 78
Choices
        of behaviors, beliefs, 3–4
        at forks in the road, 10
        and personal responsibility, 44–46
        of successful students, 1, 9
        wise process for, 55–59, 70
Claiming, of desired qualities, 98–100
Classmates, 35
Clinton, Bill, 151
Cochise, 170
Cole, Johnetta B., 115

Collect, as part of CORE
        defined, 25
        in note-taking, 103–104, 110
        in study system, 141, 142,
                146–147
        using in college, 69–74
        in writing, 244–247
College
        active listening in, 159
        and CORE system, 69–74
        deep culture of, 16–17
        dropping out, 77
        and flow, 270
        vs. high school, 18–21
        importance, in different cultures,
                78–79
        and inner motivation, 77–84
        journaling on, 18–20
        learning available at, 2
        learning customs of, 34–38
        and money management, 280–288
        organizing study materials, 141–148
        rehearsing, memorizing study
                materials, 175–180
        as support system, 152–153
        taking notes for, 103–110
        test-taking, 205–214
        understanding culture of, 13–20
        writing in, 244–252
College Blue Book, 238
Commitment
        32-day form for, 130, 133f
        creating method, 91
        journaling on, 131–132
        keeping, 93, 241–243
        making, 92, 261
Concept map, 106, 108f, 144
Conclusions, in argument, 232,
                234–235, 250
Conventional personalities, 200
Core beliefs, 187
Core curriculum, 34
CORE learning system
        diminishing anxiety, 265
        elements of, 25–30
        in studying, 141
        in test-taking, 205–206
        using in college, 69–74
        and writing, 244–245

Cormier, Kase, 28
Cornell study sheets, 145–146, 147f,
    148, 177
Course corrections, 221–223
Course load, 35
Covey, Stephen, 113, 133, 159, 194
Creator language, 47–51, 51–52
Creator mindset
    and anger, 263
    and anxiety, sadness, 264, 267
    and choice, 44–46, 58–59
    defined, 39
    and flow, 270
    and leveling, 169–171
    and life plans, 88–89
    making requests, 171
    and money management, 281
    Parks example of, 42–43
    and personal responsibility, 41–43
    and personal rules, 203
    and purposeful action, 113
    and Quadrant II Time Management,
        114–115
    responsibility and control for, 43–44
    saying "No," 171–172
    and stress, 261
    success identity for, 136
    as support system, 154
    and teacher expectation, 79
    using, 298
    vs. victim mindset, 51–52
    visualization by, 138–139
    at work, 61–62
Credit, debit, ATM cards, 285–286
Critical thinking
    case study in, 76
    for emotional intelligence, 254
    employing, 231–235
    for interdependence, 150
    on lifelong learning, 216–217
    on personal responsibility, 40
    on procrastinating, 112
    for self-awareness, 182
    for self-management, 112
    on self-motivation, 76–77
Cross, K. Patricia, 78
Crystal, David, 73
Csikszemtmihaly, Mihaly, 82, 202,
    269, 271
Cultural Competence, 16
Cultural Intelligence, 14
Culture
    and choices, 17–18
    clash and shock, 15
    defined, 13–14
    differences in, 161–162
    of higher education, 15–17, 20–21
    individualistic vs. collectivistic,
        151–152
    influence on college education, 78–79
    journaling on, 18–20
    learning from adults, 189

programming, 14
    rules of, 201
    showing respect, 162–166
    time in, 118–119
    visible and invisible, 14
    See also Deep culture
cummings, e.e., 233

D'Angelo, Anthony J., 238
DAPPS qualities, 86–87, 171, 173
Dated quality, 86
Davila, Freddie, 60
Day-Lewis, Robert Cecil, 244
de Bono, Edward, 232
Deci, Edward, 172
Decision-making, 55–59
Deep culture
    defined, 14
    and integrity, 240
    as intellectual curiosity, 16–17
    of North American college
        education, 44
    and value seen in college, 78–79
Deep processing, 23–24
Definitions, 73
Delaney, Bessie, 139
Denny, Terry, 255
Dewey, John, 24
Dictionary of Occupational Titles
    (DOT), 236
Didion, Joan, 240
Diller, Jerry V., 163
Discussing, after reading, 74
Disraeli, Benjamin, 244
Distributed practice, 24
Documents, college, 37
"Doing diligence," 134
Doing learner, 226–229, 237
Dominitz, Ben, 91
Dorothy Gale (character), 16
Dostoyevsky, Fyodor, 240
Douglas, Clair, 65
Dreams, discovering, 87–88
Drucker, Peter, 220
Dunham, Katherine, 52
Dweck, Carol, 141, 218–219, 220

Earning power, 80–81
Edelman, Marian Wright, 131
Edison, Thonas, 113
Editing (proofreading), 245, 251
Educational Testing Service (ETS), 240
Elaborative rehearsal, 175–176
Electronic calendars, 119
Eliot, Charles W., 160
Eliot, T.S., 297
Ellis, Albert, 41, 63–64, 65–66, 189
Emerson, Ralph Waldo, 121
Emotional intelligence
    awareness of, 257
    creating flow, 269–272
    and self-love, 275–279

and stress reduction, 259–269
    for successful students, 253
    understanding, 255–259
    at work, 273–274
Emotional patterns, 187–188
*Employability Skills Profile: The Critical
    Skills Required of the Canadian
    Work Force*, 30
Empowerment, and choices, 17
Encouragement, for students, 10–11
Enterprising personalities, 200
Error log, for writing, 251
Essay blueprint, 248
Essay questions, 208, 210–211
Ethnocentrism, 164–165
Eustress, 259
Evaluate, as part of CORE, 26, 148,
    177, 245
Evidence, in argument, 232, 234–235
Expectation, and motivation, 78, 79
Expenses, and money management,
    284–287

FAFSA (Free Application for Federal
    Student Aid), 283
Fanning, Patrick, 32, 48, 64
Federal Student Air Information
    Center, 283
Feedback, 147, 221
Feeling learner, 226–229, 237
"Fight or flight," 260
Fill-in-the-blank questions, 207–208
Fitzgerald, Ella, 290
Fixation, in reading, 72
Fixed mindset, 218–219
Flash cards, 143–144, 178
Floriolli, James, 192
Flow, flow states, 269–272
Focus, 128
Focus questions, 245–246
Foer, Joshua, 23
Forbes, Malcolm S., 235
Forces, unconscious, 184–185
Ford, Henry, 160
Formatting, 71
Frankl, Viktor E., 267
Franklin, Aretha, 277
Free Application for Federal Student Aid
    (FAFSA), 283
Free writing, 4–5
Freeman, Ashley, 140
Fritz, Robert, 45, 113

Gabler, June E., 154
Gandhi, Mohandas K., 239
Garfield, Charles, 93, 100, 137, 222
Garvey, Marcus, 139
Gates, Bill, 221
Gawain, Shakti, 101
General education requirements, 34
Gesturing, 163
Givens, Charles J., 92, 114, 128

Glasow, Arnold H., 83
Glasser, William, 56
Goals
    committing to, 90–95
    DAPPS qualities of, 86–87
    learning vs. performance, 220–221
    and life roles, 85–86
    qualities needed for, 98
    short- and long-term, 84–85, 96
Goleman, Daniel, 256, 264, 270, 274
Gordimer, Nadine, 244
Grade point average (GPA), 36–37
Grasseth, Dominic, 68
Grothe, Marty, 233
Growth mindset, 141, 218–222
The Guide for Occupational Exploration
    (GOE), 236–237
Guide words, common, 209f

Habits, changing, 203
Hard skills, 199
Harman, Willis, 184
Haskins, Joseph, 12
Hatch, Betty, 242
Hayes, Dennis, 120
Heam, Lefcadio, 121
Helmstetter, Shad, 55, 195
Hemingway, Ernest, 157
Hendricks, Gay and Kathlyn, 53, 169, 255
Henley, William E., 44
Hermann, Ned, 226, 237
Higher education. *See* College
Hill, Napoleon, 86
Hoffer, Eric, 22
Hofstede, Geert, 13, 151
Holland, John, 200
Holland Code, 199
Holmes, Oliver Wendell, 190
Hook, in writing, 249
How the Brain Learns, 21
Hubbard, Elbert, 89
Huigens, Brandeé, 204
Hulnick, Mary, 222
Huxley, Thomas Henry, 129

Importance, in self-management,
    113–115, 120
Index cards, for writing, 245
Information-gathering interview, 62
Injunctions, 188–189
Inner conversation, 63–67
Inner critic
    about, 48–49
    on failure, 239–240
    in personal affirmation, 98–100
    placating, 169
    and scripts, 193
    in self-defeatism, 64–68
    visualization by, 138
Inner defender
    about, 49–50
    blaming, 169

on cheating, 239
excuses to quit, 128
in personal affirmation, 98
in self-defeatism, 64–68
and stress, 261
Inner guide
    about, 50–51
    and active listening, 160–161
    consulting, 183
    conversing with, 194–197
    in personal affirmation, 99
    regaining focus, 128–129
    in self-defeatism, 67
Inner motivation
    formula for, 77–80
    journaling on, 83
    lack of, 77
    student's story of, 83–84
    and value of college experiences,
        81–82
    and value of college outcomes, 80–81
Innovating learner, 226–229, 237
Instructors, communicating with, 35–36
Integrity, living with, 239–241
Intellectual curiosity, 16
Interdependence
    and active listening, 157–161
    assertiveness, 169–173
    insights into, 298
    respecting cultural difference,
        161–168
    for successful students, 149
    support system for, 151–157
    at work, 167–168
Interview, 62
Investigative personalities, 200
Irrational beliefs, disputing, 65–66
Iyengar, Sheena, 10, 151, 164–165, 201

Jacobs, Robert, 22
James, Henry, 160
James, Muriel, 26, 89, 158, 187
James, William, 266, 267
Jeffers, Susan, 53, 101, 255
Jensen, Eric, 21–22
Job interview, 237–238
Johns, Michael, 66–67
Johnson, Earvin (Magic), 154
Jongeward, Dorothy, 26, 89, 158, 187
Jordan, Barbara, 235
Journaling
    about guided, 4–5
    on active listening, 160–161
    on assertiveness, 172–173
    on course corrections, 222–223
    on Creator mindset, 46
    on critical thinking, 235
    on desired outcomes, experiences, 83
    disputing inner critics, defenders,
        67–68
    on emotional intelligence, 258
    exploring active learning, 27

exploring self-esteem, 33
on flow, 272
on getting off-course, 185
inventory of strengths, weaknesses, 12
on life plans, 89–90
on personal affirmations, 101
on preferred ways of learning, 230
on Quadrant II Time Management, 116
on respect, 166
on script revision, 194–197
on self-assessment, 297
on self-confidence, 139
on self-defeating patterns, 191
on self-discipline, 131–132
on self-love, 278
on self-management systems, 123
on self-respect, 243
and stress reduction, 268
on support systems, 156
on surface and deep culture, 18–20
using Creator language, 53
on visualization, 93–94
on wise choice process, 59
on writing own rules, 203–204
Juang, Linda, 163, 189
Judgment, in self-talk, 50
Jung, Carl, 17, 33, 196

Kafka, Franz, 44
Kanevskiy, Alexsandr, 54
Katz, Lillian Vernon, 136
Keller, Helen, 153
Key concept, 69, 106–107
Keyes, Ken, 51, 170, 261
Kiam, Victor, 29
Kiewra, Kenneth, 103
King, Martin Luther Jr., 113
Kübler-Ross, Elisabeth, 43

Langer, Ellen J., 190
Lansing, Sherry, 130
Lazarus, Arnold A., 65
Learning. *See* Active learning;
    Lifelong learning
Learning goals, 220–221
Learning preference inventory, 224–227
LeDoux, Joseph, 184
Lee, Spike, 221
Lennick, Doug, 274
Lepage, Allysa, 127
Lerner, Harriet Goldhor, 88
Leveling, 169–171
Life plans, roles, 84–90
Lifelong learning
    and critical thinking, 231–235
    discovering preferred ways of,
        224–231
    inventory of preferences for, 224–227
    orienting toward, 217–223
    and self-respect, 239–243
    for successful students, 215
    at work, 236–238

Lightner, Candy, 87, 263
Lincoln, Abraham, 90
Loans, for students, 283
Loci technique, 179
Locus of control, 43–44
Loden, Jason Matthew, 157
Logan, Richard, 41
Ludwick, Donna, 102

Maggard, Jessie, 223
Main idea (thesis), 69
Major, college, 34–35
Maltz, Maxwell, 138
Mamchur, Carolyn, 224
Mankiller, Wilma, 153
Mannes, Marya, 263
Man's Search for Meaning, 267
Marianism, 201
Marinelli, Bobby, 90
Marking text, 72
Martens, Andy, 66–67
Math charts, three-column, 177–178
Math problems, solving, 211
Matsumoto, David, 163, 189
Maxwell, Elaine, 56
McCabe, Donald, 240
McCall, Nathan, 136–137, 258
McCullers, Carson, 188
McKay, Matthew, 32, 48, 64
McLuhan, Marshall, 238
Memorization, 178–179
Mentoring, 168
Microaggression, 165
Millay, Edna St. Vincent, 191
Miller, Richard, 260
Mindless reading, 69
Mindset, 42
Mindsets, fixed and growth, 218–222
MLA (Modern Language Association)
        format, 16, 198
Money management
        banking, 281, 283
        exercise for, 288
        financial plan for, 281
        form for, 282f
        grants, scholarships, loans, 283
        and level of education, 280f
        savings, investments, 284
        tracking expenses, 284–287
        and work, 283–284
Montagu, Ashley, 3
Montgomery, Stephan J., 298
Montgomery bus boycott, 42–43
Moodle, 16
Moore, Brian, 47
Morely, Christopher, 3
Mothers Against Drunk Driving (MADD),
        87, 263
Motivation, 1
        See also Inner motivation;
        Self-motivation
Moule, Jean, 16, 44, 164, 165

Multiple-choice questions, 207
Munson, Patricia J., 241
Murray, William Hutchison, 94
Myers, Rochelle, 158, 183
Myers-Briggs Type Indicator (MTBI), 199

NASA Systems Engineering Handbook, 56
National Foundation for Credit Counseling
        (NFCC), 286–287
Negative messages, 99–100
Nehru, Jawaharlal, 46
Neptune analogy, 184–185, 186, 189
Neural network, 21–22
Neuroplasticity, 220
Next actions list, 120–121, 125f, 134,
        261–262
Niebuhr, Reinhold, 32
Nietzsche, Friedrich, 82
Nin, Anais, 193
"No," saying, 171–172
Nolen, William A., 2
Nonverbal behaviors, 163–164
Notetaking, 103–110

O'Brien, Sharon, 244
Occupational Outlook Handbook
        (OOH), 237
Office Depot, mission statement of, 96–97
Ogbu, John, 78
Onaga, Jalayna, 13
Organize, as part of CORE
        defined, 25–26
        in note-taking, 104
        and Quadrant II Time
                Management, 115
        in study system, 141, 142–143,
                144, 148
        in writing, 244–247
Origin-like students, 43
Ormstein, Robert, 26
Outcomes, of college, 80–81
Outlining, 106–107, 143, 247
Owens, Jesse, 11

Parks, Rosa, 42–43
Patterns, of awareness, 187–188, 190–192
Pauk, Walter, 145
Paul, Benjamin, 14
Paul, Richard, 231
Paulette, Wynda Allison, 279
Pawn-like students, 43
Peck, M. Scott, 127, 185
Pell Grants, 283
Penfield, Wilder, 184
Performance goals, 220–221
Persistence, 129–130
Personal affirmation, 98–102, 104
Personal preferences, 199
Personal quality, 86–87
Personal responsibility
        and choice, 44–46
        and Creator mindset, 41–44

inner guide for, 50
language for, 51–52
model of, 45f
and success, 1
at work, 61–62
Personality types, 200
Peterson, Brooks, 14, 42
Placating, 169–170
Polonius (character), 241
Portman, Natalie, 27
Positive quality, 87
Postman, Neil, 25
Powell, Colin, 130
Pozsgay, Jason, 117
Prerequisites, 34
Prewriting (invention), 244
Price, Luther D., 33
Prior learning, 23, 24b
Processing, quality, quantity of, 23–24, 141
Procrastination, 1, 112, 114
Professionalism, workplace, 273–274
Progoff, Ira, 183
Project folder, 121–122, 134
Purposeful action, 113–117

Quadrant II Time Management System®,
        113–117
Quality, of processing, 23–24, 141
Quantity, of processing, 24–25, 141
Question outline, 247
Questions, asking, 36
Questions, probing, 232–234

Ray, Michael, 158, 183
Reading
        activities after, 73–74
        activities during, 71–73
        mindful, 69–70
        mindless vs. active, 69
        preparing for, 70–71
Realistic personalities, 200
Reality Therapy, 56
Reasons, in argument, 232, 234–235
Recitation, 176
Reciting, 72
Recording, 109
Refutation, in essay, 250
Rehearse, as part of CORE
        defined, 26
        in study system, 141, 142, 148,
                175–180
        in writing, 245, 251
Reich, Robert B., 236
Requests, making, 171
Rereading, 73
Respect, advocating for, 165–166
Respect, in college, 38
Responsibility. See Personal responsibility
Restak, Richard, 184
Revising (rewriting), 245, 250–251
Richmond, Sarah, 186
Riley, Pat, 42, 153, 154

Ripa, Kelly, 262
Robbins, Anthony, 256
Rockefeller, David, 134
Rogers, Carl, 78
Roosevelt, Eleanor, 59, 87, 201
Roosevelt, Theodore, 161
Rosenberg, Marshall B., 257
Rote rehearsal, 175–176
Rotter, Julian, 43
Rules, personal, 201–203

Sadness, 265–267
Salaries, and level of education, 280f
Salerno-Sonnenberg, Nadja, 270
Sandberg, Carl, 118
Sanmiguel, Jaime, 268–269
Sarnoff, Stanley J., 259
Satir, Virginia, 31, 119, 169, 201, 265
Satoro, Ryunosuke, 156
Saying "No," 171–172
Schmader, Toni, 66–67
Schutz, Will, 58
Scripts
    anatomy of, 187–188
    describing, 186–187
    outdated beliefs in, 193–194
    rewriting, 192–198
    as self-knowledge, 200
    writing, 188–189
Scudder, Samuel H., 217
Secondary idea, 69–70
Secretary's Commission on Achieving
    Necessary Skills (SCANS),
    29–30
Self-assessment
    learning preference inventory for,
    224–227
    scoring sheets for, 294–296
    test for, 6–8, 290–293
Self-awareness
    emotional, 256
    getting off course, 183–186
    identifying scripts, 186–192
    for successful students, 181
    through journaling, 4–5
    at work, 199–200
    writing own rules, 201–205
Self-care plan, 275–277
Self-confidence
    celebrating successes, talents, 137
    as core belief, 136
    success identity for, 136–137
    visualization for, 137–139
Self-defeating patterns, 190–192
Self-Directed Search (SDS), 199
Self-discipline, 127–130
Self-esteem
    and core beliefs, 31–32
    and inner conversation, 63–65
    knowing, accepting self, 32–33
    lack of, 31
Self-love, 275–279

Self-management
    defined, 1
    emotional, 256
    leak-proof system for, 118–127
    monthly calendar, 119–120, 124f, 134
    next actions list, 120–121, 125f, 134
    project folder, 121–122, 134
    and Quadrant II Time Management,
    113–117
    rewards of effective, 122
    and self-discipline, 127–133
    for success, 111
    time and culture, 118–119
    tracking form, 121, 126f, 134
    waiting-for list, 121, 134
    at work, 134–135
Self-motivation
    belief in oneself, 98–102
    critical thinking in, 76
    defined, 1
    and goal commitment, 90–95
    and life plan design, 84–90
    student's story of, 83–84, 94–95
    by successful students, 75
    at work, 95–97
    See also Inner motivation
Self-respect, 239–243
Self-sabotage, 183–185, 200
Self-talk, 47–51
Selye, Hans, 202, 260
Sergiovanni, Thomas, 18
Shanker, Albert, 232
Sher, Barbara, 171
Short-answer questions, 208
Siebert, Al, 122
Siegel, Bernie, 93, 173, 272, 276
Simmons, John, 123
Sinetar, Marsha, 5, 137, 271
Skill level, and challenge, 269–270
Smart phones, 119
Smith, Francie Larrieu, 85
Smith, Hyrum W., 243
Smith, Ron, 283
Social awareness, 256
Social personalities, 200
Soft skills, 29–30, 199
Solitariness, 1
Sophocles, 239
Sousa, David, 21, 23
Space, personal, 163
Specific quality, 87
Speedreading, 71–72
Spencer, Edmund, 63
Spradlin, Lynn Kell, 118
Staples, vision statement of, 96
Steele, Claude M., 66
Stereotype threat, 66–67
Stereotyping, 164
Stine, Jean Marie, 159
Stinkin' thinkin', 63–65
Stone, Hal, 47, 64
Stone, Sidra, 47, 64

Stress
    and anger, 263–264
    and anxiety, 264–265
    being overwhelmed by, 261–263
    choosing attitude for, 267
    consequences of, 260
    defined, 259–260
    healthy reduction of, 261–267
    and sadness, 265–267
    unhealthy reduction of, 260
Strong Interest Inventories (SSI), 199
The Student Guide, 283
Students' stories
    on course corrections, 223
    on emotional intelligence,
    258–259
    failing at college, 13
    on getting off-course, 186
    on inner scripts, 198
    on interdependence, 174
    on personal affirmations, 102
    on preferred ways of learning,
    230–231
    on Quadrant II Time Management, 117
    on self-assessment, 298
    on self-confidence, 140
    on self-defeatism, 192
    on self-discipline, 132
    on self-love, 279
    on self-management systems, 127
    on self-motivation, 83–84, 84–85
    on self-motivation, 94–95
    on stinkin' thinkin', 68
    on stress reduction, 268–269
    on support systems, 157
    using active learning principles, 28
    using Creator language, 54–55
    using Creator mindset, 47
    on wise choice process, 60
    on writing own rules, 204
Study chart, three-column, 144–145
Study group, 176, 177
Study schedule, 142
Study sheets, Cornell, 145–146, 147f,
    148, 177
Success, 2–4, 289
Sue, Derald Wing, 165
Suinn, Richard, 138
Summaries, chapter, 71
Support, for writing, 250
Support system
    college resources as, 152–153
    developing, 151–152
    instructors as, 152
    project team as, 153
    study group as, 153–155
Supporting details, 70
Syllabus, 35

"Take This Fish and Look at It," 217
Talmud, 203
Tax credits, 287

Taylor, Susan L., 196
Teachers, 76, 79
Team covenant, 154
Tecumseh, 46
Terrell, James, 94
Test questions, 143
Test-taking
  actions after, 212
  actions during, 206–208, 210–212
  debriefing, 214
  exercise for, 213
  factors in scoring, 205
  importance of, 205
  preparing for, 205–206
Thesis (main idea), 69, 246–247
Thesis statement, 249
Thinking learners, 226–229, 237
Thomas, Debi, 131
Thompson, Melissa, 230–231
Thoreau, Henry David, 114
Thought patterns, 187–188
Three-column notes, 109, 177–178
Time, in culture, 118–119
Time on task, sufficient, 24
Tomlin, Lily, 87
Topic, for writing, 245–246
Tracking form, 121, 126f, 134
Tracy, Brian, 85
Transcripts, 36
Transitions, in writing, 249
Transportation expenses, 284–285
Triesman, Uri, 153–154
True-false questions, 206–207
Tuberville, Gus, 80
Turner, Cathy, 92

Underwood, Blair, 203
Urgency, in self-management,
  113–115, 120

Valle, Annette, 198
Vallerand, Robert, 43
Value
  of college experiences, 81–82
  of college outcomes, 80–81
  and motivation, 78, 79
VanDerveer, Tara, 135
Victim mindset
  about, 42
  and choice, 45, 58
  communicating, 170
  vs. creator mindset, 51–52
  defined, 39
  insights into, 298
  making requests, 171
  and outside, inside forces, 42
  and stress, 260
  and teacher expectation, 79
  at work, 61–62
Victimization, 1
Visual elements, in reading, 71
Visualization, for success, 137–139
Visualization, of future, 92–93
Von Oech, Roger, 82
Vonnegut, Kurt Jr., 98
VxE=M formula, 78, 79, 83

Waiting-for list, 121, 134
Waitley, Denis, 4, 278
Walter, Tim, 122
Ware, Eugene F., 12

Warren, Elizabeth, 285
Washington, Harold, 92
Washington, Martha, 267
Weingartner, Charles, 25
Wells, Cinda Field, 199
Welty, Eudora, 191
Whistling Elk, Agnes, 51
Whitehorn, Katherine, 271
Williamson, Marianne, 218
Winfrey, Oprah, 45, 152, 185
Wise choice process, 55–59, 70
Withdrawal, from class, 37
Woodman, Marion, 278
Work, and flow, 271
Work, for students, 283–284
*Working with Emotional
  Intelligence*, 274
Writing
  audience for, 246
  as drafting, 245
  enhancing learning, 244
  exercises after, 250–252
  notes for, 245–246
  outlines for, 247
  parts of essay, 248–250
  and positive affirmation, 245
  prewriting, revising, editing,
    244–245
  thesis for, 246–247
  topics for, 245–246

X, Malcolm, 227

Zilbergeld, Bernie, 65
Zuboff, Shoshana, 274

Chapter One: Choosing a Framework

Student Learning Outcome: Incorporating Learning Theories & Meta-Cognitions

As you read the chapters, do the following:

1. <u>Put on a pair of Glasses,</u> from one of the theories below, to understand the chapter from that framework.

2. Decide, what parts of this chapter can help you in the below areas of your life:
   a. Academics   b. Career   c. Personal life

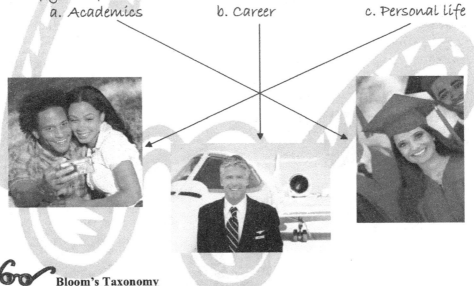

Bloom's Taxonomy

Knowledge, Comprehension, Applications Analysis, Synthesis, Evaluation

Stage Theory

To acknowledge one's thinking through systematic assessment, monitoring, and transformation. The elements of thinking consist of **Inquiry** that seeks **Knowledge**, which in turn we make **Inferences** based on the knowledge. Our inferences come from our own **Assumptions** that come from and elicit **Concepts** that lead to **Conclusions, Implications** and **Consequences.**

<u>Other</u>

<u>Chapter Two: Choosing a Framework</u>

Student Learning Outcome: Autonomous Learner, Behavior Management & Critical Thinking

As you read the chapters, do the following:

1. <u>**Put on a pair of Glasses,**</u> from one of the theories below, to understand the chapter from that framework.
2. Decide, what parts of this chapter can help you in the below areas of your life:

    a. Academics   b. Career   c. Personal Life

<u>Bloom's Taxonomy</u>   <u>Stage Theory</u>   <u>Other</u>

<u>Mottos</u>: A statement created by you, based on your own values and beliefs, which guides your decision making.

Chapter Three: Choosing a Framework

Student Learning Outcome: Critical Thinking & Behavior Management

As you read the chapters, do the following:

1. **Put on a pair of Glasses,** from one of the theories below, to understand the chapter from that framework.

2. Decide, what parts of this chapter can help you in the below areas of your life:

    a. Academics   b. Career   c. Personal life

Bloom's Taxonomy   **Stage Theory**

ABC Theory: The idea that what people think drives our emotions and behaviors. This is the "go to" theory that provides the systematic assessment, monitoring, and transformation that you need to think and function within the higher stages of stage theory.

Other

Chapter Four: Choosing a Framework

Student Learning Outcome: Behavior Management & Critical Thinking

As you read the chapters, do the following:

1. <u>Put on a pair of Glasses,</u> from one of the theories below, to understand the chapter from that framework.
2. Decide, what parts of this chapter can help you in the below areas of your life:
   a. Academics   b. Career   c. Personal life

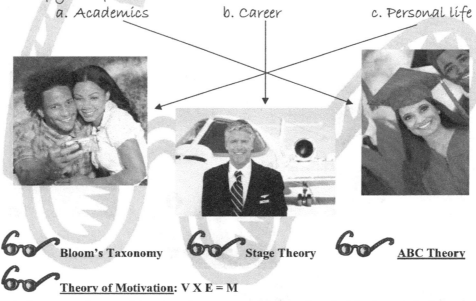

Bloom's Taxonomy   **Stage Theory**   **ABC Theory**

Theory of Motivation: V X E = M

This theory says that people's values times expectation gives them insight about their chances of success. When "support" is added as an important factor this gives people further insight.

The Four Quadrants of Self-Management:

This theory says that people have better time management by prioritizing according to our goals and values.

Chapter Five: Choosing a Framework

As you read the chapters, do the following:

1. **Put on a pair of Glasses,** from one of the theories below, to understand the chapter from that framework.
2. Decide, what parts of this chapter can help you in the below areas of your life:
   - a. Academics
   - b. Career
   - c. Personal life

Bloom's Taxonomy   <u>Stage Theory</u>   <u>Mottos</u>

Theory of Motivation   <u>ABC Theory</u>   <u>Other</u>

Chapter Six: Choosing a Framework

Student Learning Outcomes: Critical Thinking & Meta-Cognitions

As you read the chapters, do the following:

1. <u>Put on a pair of Glasses,</u> from one of the theories below, to understand the chapter from that framework.
2. Decide, what parts of this chapter can help you in the below areas of your life:
   a. Academics   b. Career   c. Personal life

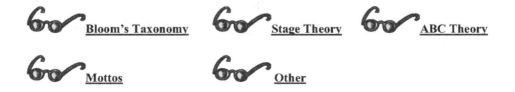

Bloom's Taxonomy   **Stage Theory**   **ABC Theory**

Mottos   **Other**

Chapter Seven: Choosing a Framework

Student Learning Outcomes: Incorporating Learning Theories, Information Literacy-Research Debate Issues, & Ethical Reasoning

As you read the chapters, do the following:

1. **Put on a pair of Glasses,** from one of the theories below, to understand the chapter from that framework.

2. Decide, what parts of this chapter can help you in the below areas of your life:
   a. Academics   b. Career   c. Personal life

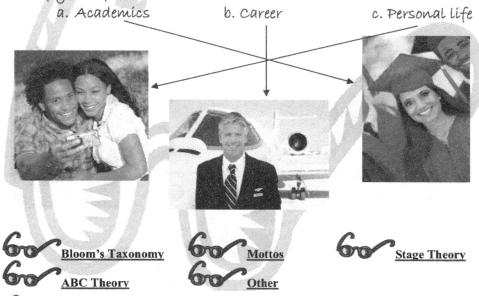

Bloom's Taxonomy   **Mottos**   **Stage Theory**

ABC Theory   **Other**

Kolhberg's Theory of Moral Development: States that people develop morally through developmental stages. These stages are distinguished by age groups and influenced by life experiences.

Bronfenbrenner's Ecololgical Development: States that people represent and impact more than just themselves (i.e. local, microsystem, mesosystem, exosystem, macrosystem, and chronosystem).

Chapter Eight: Choosing a Framework

Student Learning Outcomes: Behavior Management

As you read the chapters, do the following:

1. <u>Put on a pair of Glasses,</u> from one of the theories below, to understand the chapter from that framework.
2. Decide, what parts of this chapter can help you in the below areas of your life:
     a. Academics   b. Career   c. Personal life

<u>Bloom's Taxonomy</u>   <u>Stage Theory</u>   <u>ABC Theory</u>

<u>Other</u>

Chapter Nine: Choosing a Framework

Student Learning Outcomes: Evidence Based Learning—ePortfolio assignment

As you read the chapters, do the following:

1. <u>**Put on a pair of Glasses,**</u> from one of the theories below, to understand the chapter from that framework.
2. **Decide,** what parts of this chapter can help you in the below areas of your life:
   a. Academics   b. Career   c. Personal life

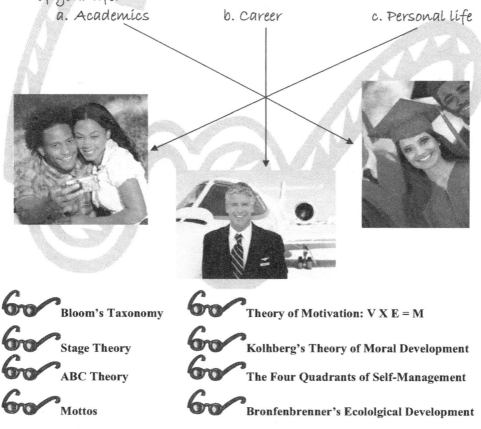

Bloom's Taxonomy   Theory of Motivation: V X E = M

Stage Theory   Kolhberg's Theory of Moral Development

ABC Theory   The Four Quadrants of Self-Management

Mottos   Bronfenbrenner's Ecololgical Development